The U.S. Supreme Court and New Federalism

The U.S. Supreme Court and New Federalism

From the Rehnquist to the Roberts Court

Christopher P. Banks and John C. Blakeman

ROWMAN & LITTLEFIELD PUBLISHERS, INC.
Lanham • Boulder • New York • Toronto • Plymouth, UK

Published by Rowman & Littlefield Publishers, Inc.
A wholly owned subsidiary of The Rowman & Littlefield Publishing Group, Inc.
4501 Forbes Boulevard, Suite 200, Lanham, Maryland 20706
www.rowman.com

10 Thornbury Road, Plymouth PL6 7PP, United Kingdom

British Library Cataloguing in Publication Information Available

Library of Congress Cataloging-in-Publication Data
Banks, Christopher P.
The U.S. Supreme Court and new federalism : from the Rehnquist to the Roberts court / Christopher P. Banks and John C. Blakeman.
p. cm.
Includes index.
ISBN 978-0-7425-3504-6 (cloth : alk. paper) — ISBN 978-1-4422-1858-1 (electronic)
1. Federal government—United States. 2. Federal government—United States—Philosophy. 3. Constitutional law—United States—Interpretation and construction. 4. Conservatism—United States. 5. United States. Supreme Court. I. Blakeman, John C., 1966– II. Title.
KF4600.B36 2012
320.473'049—dc23

ISBN 978-0-8108-9553-9 (pbk : alk. paper) 2012014424

∞™ The paper used in this publication meets the minimum requirements of American National Standard for Information Sciences—Permanence of Paper for Printed Library Materials, ANSI/NISO Z39.48-1992.

Printed in the United States of America

For our mentors,
Professors Henry J. Abraham and
David M. O'Brien

Contents

Figures and Tables

FIGURES

TABLES

Acknowledgments

We thank many different scholars for their insights, comments, and help in bringing this project to fruition. We'd like to thank the many panelists and commentators on several panels at the American Political Science Association annual meetings and the Midwest, Southwestern and Western Political Science annual meetings where we presented parts of our research. Those conference panels over the course of a few years help us to clarify our thinking about federalism and the Supreme Court. It was during one of those panels that Chris met John Domino, who graciously invited Chris to join in on his research about the Rehnquist Court and its federalism decisions—although our professional collaboration was destined to remain brief, it serves as the cornerstone of what emerged in the pages that follow, and Chris is most grateful.

Second, we thank our respective institutions, Kent State University and the University of Wisconsin–Stevens Point, for providing much-needed travel funds and other support to attend the many conferences that we did. Without that institutional support, this project would not have been completed. Chris extends his appreciation for the time and interest that his colleagues in the political science department, too numerous to mention at the exclusion of others, have given and shown as Chris made the transition to Kent State—and who performed the critical roles of being listeners and constructive critics about many of the ideas presented in this book, especially at the department brown bags in which Chris outlined his research on the Supreme Court. Similar appreciation is extended to Chris's former colleagues at the University of Akron Law School—former dean Richard Aynes and his colleagues were very kind in permitting Chris to present his work on the Rehnquist Court and the Section 5 enforcement clause at law school conferences on the historical and legal significance of the Fourteenth Amendment. John would like to thank Deans Lance Grahn and Chris Cirmo of the UWSP College of Letters and Science for supporting this project over the course of a few years.

Third, we thank John Dinan and the editorial board at *Publius: The Journal of Federalism*, as well as several anonymous reviewers whose comments and suggestions helped us address certain problems and clarify various aspects of our research. Some of that important feedback allowed us to keep the momentum going as we moved to the final stages of completing the manuscript, and we are most grateful.

Fourth, our colleagues in the political science departments at Kent State University (for Chris) and the University of Wisconsin–Stevens Point (for John) provided a lot of helpful feedback on parts of our analysis, as did our students. John would especially like to acknowledge his students from his courses on religion and law, and civil liberties, who helped (and required) him to explain his thinking on federalism and religious liberty. Chris would like to thank the efforts of his own constitutional law and judicial process students, but especially those of Kevin White, a doctoral student studying the courts at Kent State, for his research assistance and copyediting feedback, especially as the book went to press.

Fifth, our mentors from the University of Virginia, Professors Henry J. Abraham and David M. O'Brien, had much to do with the formation of our thinking on how to study the new federalism and the Supreme Court, and it's fair to say that what we learned in our seminars on constitutional law with Henry and the Supreme Court and judicial policymaking (with David) several years ago still affects our fundamental approach to studying and understanding federalism and the Court today. Their lessons to us have extended well beyond the classroom, and we are humbled to be in a position to dedicate this book to both of them.

Sixth, we thank the editorial and publication staff at Rowman & Littlefield, who have been an absolute pleasure to work with. We are especially grateful for Jon Sisk's belief in the project from its inception, and for his patience in receiving the manuscript, and we also thank Patricia, Jennifer, Darcy, and many others, for their copyediting, cover art, and overall general shepherding of the book to print.

Finally, we would like to thank our respective families for their ongoing support in our scholarly endeavors. For Chris, his love and appreciation is extended to his wife, Diane, who played an instrumental behind-the-scenes role in discussing many of the ideas in this book (even though she has no interest in them whatsoever), and to his son, Zach, and his daughter, Sammie, who each contributed to this book in their own special way. John would like to thank his family—Kathryn, Margaret, Angus, and Caroline—for making home such a nice place to work. Janet, Judith, David, and the extended clan—Rachel, Jeff, Ryan and Henry, Michael, Rak, Max, and Ben—all deserve special mention too for their support.

1

"A Notably Conservative Court?"

The 2011–2012 term of the U.S. Supreme Court, the seventh under the leadership of Chief Justice John Roberts and the one before the politically divisive 2012 presidential election, promised to be "one that's really for the ages."[1] Even Justice Anthony Kennedy said in front of the media covering a judicial conference right before the new session began that the Court's docket seemed to be changing. Whereas early terms dealt with a fair share of mundane actions litigating the rights of big corporations and finding ways to limit class actions in civil lawsuits, the new term featured several high-profile cases, many of which involved civil rights and liberties and the scope of government's power. The Court, for example, was scheduled to review key First Amendment cases, such as those fixing the scope of government's capacity to regulate nudity and offensive language on television shows, and criminal prosecutions that revisited virtually every aspect of the criminal justice system, including whether the police could attach a GPS tracking device on a suspect's car without a warrant for weeks at a time or if defendants have basic rights to receive competent counsel, and whether they can be protected from arbitrary strip searches when they are put in jail for minor offenses. Also within the Court's sights were petitions involving the constitutionality of affirmative action programs, the rights of same-sex couples to marry, the ability of state governments to control illegal immigration, and, in an lawsuit that "promises to be a once-in-a-generation blockbuster," the right of the government to force individuals to buy health insurance under President Barack Obama's Patient Protection and Affordable Care Act.[2]

While many Supreme Court cases touch citizen's lives in the states in which they live, the federal government's power to control legally what is happening in Ohio, Wisconsin, New York, or California is an ever-present issue as well. The judiciary's role in deciding federalism cases, or issues litigating the proper boundaries of concurrent power between the federal and state governments, is a closely watched and controversial topic of political science and legal scholarship. The way federalism affects ordinary citizens is less obvious but no less powerful. Consider what happened to Diana Levine, in Vermont, when she sought medical treatment for migraine headaches and nausea. Levine, a professional musician, went to a Vermont clinic for help. At the clinic a physician assistant gave her an intramuscular injection of Demerol and Phenergan (promethazinehydrochloride), an anti-nausea drug manufactured by Wyeth, a global pharmaceutical company. After little improvement, she was directly injected with Phenergan through an "IV-push," a riskier method of vein drug delivery than having an "IV-drip." IV-drips are safer because the drug is filtered through a saline solution and an intravenous bag. The option and availability to use either method is significant: since the mid-1950s Phenergan's label has warned that using IV-pushes is more dangerous because of the likelihood that the drug could enter an artery and cause irreversible gangrene, which it did in Levine's case. The onset of gangrene led to amputation and the loss of Levine's arm, a devastating outcome for an accomplished cellist.

Although the way the drug was labeled generally alerted patients and doctors to IV-push risks, Wyeth provided no specific warnings as to the dangers, even though it allegedly had known of the problems it caused, dating back to the 1960s. Moreover, the drug maker did not take advantage of using existing Federal Drug Administration (FDA) rules that clearly allowed manufacturers to change or strengthen their labeling without getting prior FDA approval. As a result, Levine sued Wyeth in state court under Vermont common law negligence and product liability theories, specifically asserting Wyeth's labeling of Phenergan was defective due to its failure to warn patients of the risks connected to using IV-pushes. Wyeth answered that her right to sue in state courts was lost because of federal preemption: FDA's federal regulations eliminated Levine's right to use state tort law because federal rules conflicted with state law. Under "conflict preemption" principles, Wyeth argued that federal labeling rules made it impossible for drug manufacturers to obey any state common law duty to change its labeling and to warn patients of the risks of injecting patients with Phenergan through IV-pushes. Wyeth's interpretation meant that it could only change Phenergan's label in response to new information the FDA had not considered, and in this case, the absence of new data ended its legal duty to warn anyone of the risks of IV-pushes (which allegedly made it pointless for Wyeth to strengthen its warnings without violating federal labeling guidelines). Regardless, the Vermont trial and appellate courts sided with Levine by upholding a jury's verdict to award her several million dollars for her injuries.

As a last resort, and because the lawsuit raised issues of federal law, Wyeth sought relief in the U.S. Supreme Court, posing this question: Did federal law preempt Levine's failure-to-warn tort claim in state court? In a stunning verdict against the pharmaceutical industry, in *Wyeth v. Levine* the politically conservative Roberts Court did not think so. Writing for the Court in a 6–3 decision, Justice John Paul Stevens, the leader of the liberal bloc typically consisting of Justices David Souter, Ruth Bader Ginsburg, and Stephen Breyer, explained that Congress did not *expressly* preempt (by its plain language in the law) state tort remedies in the Federal Food, Drug, and Cosmetic Act (FDCA). As a result, there was no conflict between the choice of complying with federal labeling requirements and recognizing failure-to-warn cases based in state law. Furthermore, invoking state law tort remedies in failure-to-warn litigation was not viewed by the six justices as an obstacle to achieving Congress's intent or purposes relating to drug labeling requirements. The Court thus reasoned there was no *implied* preemption.[3]

Levine's victory supports prevailing studies by judicial scholars, which find that courts and judges write their political preferences or attitudes into law. The 6–3 split, which had two conservatives in the majority opinion for different reasons (Justices Anthony Kennedy and Clarence Thomas), notably featured Justice Samuel Alito's dissent, which was joined by Chief Justice John Roberts and Justice Antonin Scalia, a trio from the conservative wing.[4] While the final outcome got some conservative support, the basic ideological differences centered on recurring but contentious issues of federalism and preemption. Pro-liberal justices (like Stevens) are arguably more apt to limit the federal agency power to override state tort judgments without a clear intention by Congress to do so in the text, purposes, or legislative history of regulatory statutes such as the FDCA, whereas conservative justices (like Alito) may be inclined to give federal agencies a wide berth of regulatory discretion, which, if exercised, would disallow contrary state court or jury verdicts favoring plaintiffs. In political terms, the divergence in preemption policy is readily bracketed as an issue of corporate liability and individual rights under tort law. Liberal justices often construe preemption principles to let citizens take advantage of state tort law remedies in lawsuits against big businesses and insurance underwriters. In contrast, conservative justices do the opposite to insulate corporations from tort liability and potentially large jury verdicts.[5]

Similar ideological fault lines are found outside the judiciary. In May 2009, President Barack Obama issued an executive memorandum on preemption policy to the heads of federal agencies, directing them to promulgate regulations that have statements of preemption only when there is a "sufficient legal basis" to do so, as established by Congress. The memo's purpose is to deter agencies from engaging in "regulatory preemption," a practice sanctioned by the 1999 Clinton administration Executive Order 13132 allowing it and one followed by the G. W. Bush presidency.[6] For conservative critics, Obama's memo "places a premium on express preemption and makes it unlikely that the Administration will argue that any state law claims are impliedly preempted,"[7] the liberal position reflected in Justice Stevens's *Levine* opinion. From another perspective, liberal trial bar organizations have made it a legislative priority to achieve greater corporate accountability, in part by lobbying Congress to enact the Medical Device Safety Act (H.R. 1346/S. 540), a bill to protect patients from defective medical devices by explicitly declaring that federal regulations do not preempt state tort lawsuits in product liability claims. Antiliberals thus counter that the American Association for Justice's (previously, the Association of Trial Lawyers of America) legislative agenda is to overturn *Riegel v. Medtronic,* a Supreme Court ruling immunizing medical device manufacturers from liability on preemption of state tort grounds.[8]

Apart from these developments, the Supreme Court continues to weigh in on preemption in several cases, among them *Bruesewitz v. Wyeth,* holding that federal law preempts state tort lawsuits that sue drug companies for negligently designing childhood vaccines. *Bruesewitz*'s public policy impact and the continuing political relevance of high court federalism cases are clear. With Justice Elena Kagan's recusal, the 6–2 decision to interpret the National Childhood Vaccine Injury Act to foreclose parents from claiming a right to compensation in state law shuts the courthouse door on scores of lawsuits asserting causation between negligently produced vaccines and the emergence of debilitating childhood diseases, such as autism. In making aggrieved parents sue in so-called no-fault Vaccine Courts that Congress created to handle such claims, the Court favored allowing federal agency experts, instead of juries in state courts, to make the epidemiological call to award monies to injured children—a judgment that proved to be decisive for Justice Stephen Breyer in his own decision not to join his liberal colleagues (Justices Ruth Bader Ginsburg and Sonia Sotomayor) in dissent but to side instead with the preferences of drug companies and the conservative bloc of Chief Justice John Roberts and Justices Antonin Scalia, Clarence Thomas, and Samuel Alito. Notably, a week after *Bruesewitz* was decided, another conflict preemption ruling was delivered in *Williamson v. Mazda Motor of America, Inc.,* but this time with a unanimous bench and an opposite finding allowing a state tort lawsuit claiming that a car manufacturer should have installed lap-

and-shoulder belts, not just lap belts, for the rear inner seats of minivans to proceed on the grounds that it was *not* preempted by federal law.[9]

When seen in this light, federalism rulings cannot be understood as simple conflicts of power between federal and state sovereigns—although admittedly the law books are filled with precedents from the high court that take full advantage of the type of rhetoric that makes federalism case rationales memorable, but also at times disingenuous.[10] A more complete understanding of the U.S. Supreme Court and federalism speaks to defining judicial behavior in political terms. That knowledge can be reached by achieving an appreciation for the underlying law, attitudes, and strategies of those occupying the bench[11] or, in conjunction or apart from such explanatory models, by linking the work of courts in the context of broader developments and specific factors, including history, political regimes, institutional dynamics, interest group activity, or popular support.[12] Regardless of the research methodology used, the analytical framework for expressing the Court's political views begins with federalism litigation. The precedents the judiciary creates necessarily reflect ideological struggles over the force of precedent as well as the policy parameters buried deep inside *Wyeth v. Levine*—namely, corporate liability, consumer safety, and tort reform.[13] While all judicial outcomes cannot be explained by politics, *Riegel*, *Levine*, *Bruesewitz*, and *Williamson* are potent reminders that political ideology is the touchstone for comprehending internal judicial conflict, as well as exogenously shaping interest group, congressional, and executive agendas that substantively affect agency regulatory practices and consumer safety.

While scholars, interest group advocates, and pundits have acknowledged the political importance of preemption in the U.S. Supreme Court,[14] other topics in the legal and social science federalism literature are germane and deserve further study. One concerns the constitutional scope and public policy impact of the "federalism revolution" in the Rehnquist Court (1986–2005). William H. Rehnquist, a Nixon appointee and a staunch conservative jurist, first established his reputation as the "Lone Dissenter" as an associate justice on the politically moderate Burger Court (1969–1986).[15] In time, his stature grew as a champion and consensus builder of states' rights, especially after President Ronald Reagan tapped him for chief justice in 1986, the same year Antonin Scalia, another conservative and spokesperson for originalism, was elevated to the high court.[16] By 1986, he was already the colleague of Sandra Day O'Connor, and the confirmations of Scalia, Anthony Kennedy, and Clarence Thomas positioned the Court to implement the kind of judicial restraint that characterizes Rehnquist's judicial writings. As the conservatives coalesced into a majority, the Rehnquist Court gained a reputation for boldly curtailing Congress's power under the commerce clause and the Tenth Amendment. Those decisions were accompanied by others that revitalized the Eleventh Amendment as a means to limit federal judicial power, sometimes in conjunction with a series of subsequent far-reaching Fourteenth Amendment, Section 5 cases that also had the effect of restricting federal authority.[17]

Notably, a strident bloc of liberal opposition fought the Rehnquist Court's "federalism five" and its "federalist revival."[18] The division's intensity is captured by studies showing that the Court's liberal activists were more inclined than conservatives to write their preferences into law in federalism cases, regardless of whether the challenged law came from the federal or state government.[19] Perhaps that is why the Court's drive to construct a new federalism is often perceived against a backdrop of 5–4 splits replete with "vigorous dissents." It may also explain why some critics assail Rehnquist Court federalism as an aggressive but illegitimate assault on national power, bordering on becoming judicial supremacy. Not all scholars agree, however, with many flatly asserting that the Rehnquist Court's impact on federalism is overstated and hardly revolutionary.[20]

After Chief Justice Rehnquist's death, court watchers turned their attention to the Roberts Court to see if it would be identical to the Rehnquist Court and perhaps continue its federalism revolution. While the issue is far from settled, critics observe that *Heller v. District of Columbia* and *Citizens United v. Federal Election Commission*, rulings that overturned precedents by affirming a Second Amendment right to own guns and declaring a virtually unrestricted First Amendment right of corporations to spend freely in political campaigns, only prove the Roberts Court is an activist bench favoring corporate interests.[21] Still, Robert Alt, a Heritage Foundation conservative, claimed in his testimony at Elena Kagan's 2010 confirmation hearings that it is fanciful to say the Roberts Court always sides with corporate interests or, more significantly, to deny that its liberal-leaning justices never do so. Law professor Jonathan Adler agrees, reporting that there was little business bias in a study of Roberts Court environmental cases, a finding echoed by law professor Robin H. Conrad in another review of business litigation. In contrast, other law academics discover a correlation between the participation of the Chamber of Commerce of the United States as a party or a third-party amicus and its litigation success, winning thirty of forty (nearly 70 percent) business cases in the Roberts Court's first three terms. Also, liberals counter that the Supreme Court's decision-making displays a pro-business slant that is empirically confirmed by the hard science of academic studies.[22] *New York Times* columnist Adam Liptak thus reasons that academics using "widely accepted political science data tell an unmistakable story about a notably conservative court."[23]

The attempt to discover a link between the Roberts Court's judicial ideology and its federalism jurisprudence remains an open question in light of new appointments and the change in the Supreme Court's membership since 2005. Roberts's confirmation, along with Barack Obama's 2008 presidential victory, became the impetus for the "federalism five" voting bloc, a fixture on the Rehnquist Court for several years, to change. The retirements of Justices Sandra Day O'Connor (2006; appointed by President Ronald Reagan), David Souter (2009; G. H. W. Bush), and John Paul Stevens (2010; Gerald Ford) created vacancies filled by Justice Samuel Alito, a G. W. Bush appointment, and two Obama choices, Sonia Sotomayor and Elena Kagan. The new personnel brought a decisive end to the unusually long natural court stability that defined the Rehnquist Court in its latter years. It also coincided with a rapidly changing political environment outside the judiciary.

To illustrate, the foreign affairs and post-9/11 antiterrorism focus of Republican G. W. Bush's administration was at least temporarily eclipsed by the "hope and change" political campaign that swept President Obama and a Democratic congressional majority into office, thus redirecting national attention to the domestic policy agenda. New progressive legislation, ostensibly a comprehensive federal health-care bill and financial regulatory reform, was enacted, which in turn led to the rise of the Tea Party movement and a return to conservative values as a by-product of growing disenchantment with the Obama administration. The persistent impact of the 2009 recession, sharply felt by ordinary Americans who cannot find a job, with an unemployment rate closing in on 10 percent and expressed poignantly in the Occupy Wall Street mass protests of 2011 highlighting corporate greed, has set the political agenda, perhaps foreshadowing another change in the electoral landscape after the 2012 presidential election. The new electoral mood, for instance, permitted the Republicans to take back the U.S. House of Representatives after the 2010 midterm elections and to secure overwhelming nationwide victories in governors' mansions and state houses.[24] The contentious and increasingly uncivil partisanship in Congress over the political battles to raise the debt ceiling in the federal budget threatened to shut down the government in 2011, and citizens have responded by resoundingly telling public opinion pollsters that they have lost faith in their political leaders because the country is politically dysfunctional. Additionally, apart from domestic concerns in the United States, new globalization trends and the growing disaggregation of the state[25] have captured the world stage by greatly affecting the stability of world financial markets and the exercise of foreign policy in the Middle East, ostensibly due to popular uprisings in Egypt, Libya, and elsewhere and the ongoing war against terrorism. Such issues and controversies, which provide the backdrop for this book, continue to underscore the crucial role the judiciary will play in an evolving era of federalism and multilayered governance.[26]

PLAN OF THE BOOK

The book's foundation rests on achieving an understanding of the political principle of federalism, as interpreted and shaped by the judicial decisions of the Supreme Court of the United States. At the founding, federalism was at the core of the framing debate about how to best reconcile the parochial interests of citizens and states with the need to unite the nation under a political theory of republicanism. As the country and its political institutions matured, the doctrine evolved, and it became instrumental in creating a national economy in the nation's early years, not only in trying to heal the deep scars of the North and South because of the Civil War, but also in providing a political structure for the role the federal government would play during the New Deal and aftermath of World War II. It also has served as the touchstone for comprehending the scope and impact of deregulation under the Reagan administration and subsequent political efforts to scale back on the inroads created with the onset of post–New Deal government expansion, especially during President Lyndon Johnson's administration and the Great Society. What the justices did at the Supreme Court mattered considerably during all of those great moments in political history. At a very fundamental level, the Court's policymaking determines if the federal government can exercise sovereignty over the states and its citizens. As such, Supreme Court judicial intervention helps strike the necessary balance between competing political ideologies and salient public policies, and ultimately it determines the scope of political freedom citizens enjoy in a political system defined by limited government and the rule of law. What was true at the founding remains apparent today.

The ongoing political controversies described above raise several important themes and questions of law and politics that are addressed in the following pages. One theme relates to the judicial role the U.S. Supreme Court has played in federalism litigation over time as the nation matured. Another addresses the Rehnquist Court's (1986–2005) contribution in reinvigorating the new federalism debate by allegedly casting aside old doctrinal legacies of judicial deference to congressional legislation and advancing traditional principles of federalism accentuating the need to protect sovereignty, mainly through the creation of structural limitations on the constitutional exercise of power. Similarly, the challenges facing the Roberts Court in trying to balance its own approach with the purported states' rights legacy of its predecessor Court in an era of increasing globalization are explored. Put differently, in light of the Rehnquist Court's federalism jurisprudence and the ascendency of the Roberts Court afterward, this book investigates if the Roberts Court is assuming a different kind of jurisprudence or institutional role than the Rehnquist Court did in superintending federalism litigation.

The book's research is oriented by federalism precedents, case studies, empirical data, and political science and legal scholarship suggesting that the Supreme Court's legal policy is profoundly shaped by judicial conflict from within the Court, as well as by ideological considerations and exogenous forces that ultimately strike a workable balance between the forces of centralization and state-centered conceptualizations of sovereignty. Several questions inform the research:

1. Are federalism policy outcomes and the judicial conflict on the Supreme Court (especially by Justice Clarence Thomas, arguably the Court's most provocative remaining "federalist" judge on the bench) driven by the justices' political behavior toward protecting the traditional focus of federalism studies (i.e., federal or state governments as sovereign entities), or are the Court's decisions affected by a mixture of constitutive variables, such as other social, cultural, or legal factors?[27]
2. Is the collective or individual judicial behavior of the Supreme Court an exercise of judicial supremacy or activism in federalism cases?
3. Is the collective or individual judicial behavior of the Supreme Court an affirmation or rejection of domestic or exogenous globalization trends in federalism cases?
4. What is the scope and nature of new federalism, as a source of both legal and political doctrine, and how has it influenced the judicial policymaking of the Rehnquist and Roberts Courts?

The next two chapters begin to address these questions by exploring the historical role the U.S. Supreme Court plays as an arbiter of federalism litigation from the founding to the heralded "federalism revival" initiated by the Rehnquist Court in the early 1990s. Chapter 2, "Federalism Politics and Policies: Old, New, and Progressive Trends," outlines the types of old, new, and progressive trends underlying federalism issues as they inform and accentuate the political complexity of the Supreme Court's review of its docket and its public policy lawmaking. Next, the linkages between judicial behavior and ideology are presented with specific illustrations of the Court's impact in key federalism moments spanning from the founding to the pre–Rehnquist Court. The historical and contemporary examples underscore what may be "new" about federalism jurisprudence insofar as it speaks to the ongoing efforts of courts to police the margins of intergovernmental relationships over time.

Accordingly, chapter 3, "The Rehnquist Court, New Federalism, and States' Rights," details the origins and development of new federalism doctrine as it relates to the Rehnquist Court (1986–2005). Using qualitative and empirical analyses, it asks whether its justices were successful in formulating a unique and enduring antifederalist conception of state sovereignty or autonomy that disrupted the post–New Deal presumption favoring centralization. The research initially focuses on William Rehnquist's judicial conception of constitutional structure and its relationship to the judicial philosophies of his conservative or liberal brethren on federalism issues, particularly through the Court's interpretation of the Tenth, Eleventh, and Fourteenth Amendments as limitations on federal authority. Next, the scope of prevailing descriptive and empirical studies is expanded by considering the Court's strategic use of substantive constitutional principles and process-based rules in order to enforce its vision of federalism on political institutions and the courts. As a result, the Court's judicial review of clear statement rules in statutory cases affecting federalism is analyzed, along with the judicial lines drawn to curb state power in federal preemption and dormant commerce clause cases. While the sum of its work may not be revolutionary, the Rehnquist Court's decision-making helps to frame an understanding of the Roberts Court's superintendence of federalism litigation and the scope of the states' concurrent regulatory authority in the policymaking process.[28]

Whereas chapters 2 and 3 provide the historical and contemporary context for Supreme Court new federalism, through case studies the next two chapters undertake a more detailed analysis of two topics that have not been extensively explored by scholars: religious freedom and foreign policy preemption. From different perspectives (one internal to the court and the other external), the case studies address how competing ideological conceptions influence the Court's role and its lawmaking as it struggles to create a coherent set of federalism principles that help guide the states' response to judicial policy. In chapter 4, "Federalism, Justice Clarence Thomas, and Religious Freedom in the States," the focus turns to the efforts of Justice Clarence Thomas, conservative legal scholars, and Supreme Court litigants to recast the First Amendment's establishment clause as a federalism provision that limits federal power in its regulation of state and local religious activities, thus affecting other relationships between church and state at the subnational level. After exploring the attention the Rehnquist Court brought to the issue in light of its own dissatisfaction with existing religious freedom jurisprudence, the ongoing internal judicial conflict is juxtaposed against Justice Thomas's originalist clarion call to reinterpret the establishment clause as a federalism-jurisdictional provision solely limiting federal authority, thus affording significant discretion over religion and politics to local and state governments. The salience and success of Justice Thomas's line drawing is measured against the support or opprobrium it generates among his brethren, conservative and liberal interest groups, and the states themselves in federalism litigation that continues to appear on the Roberts Court's docket. As such, the case study provides key insight into the Roberts Court's impact on the synergy and dynamics of judicial conflict, intergovernmental relations, and religious policymaking.

Chapter 5, "Federalism and Globalization," visits the understudied topic of globalization by assessing the judiciary's response to increasing state foreign policy activism amid an international order in flux. Historically the Supreme Court has respected executive or congressional prerogatives to conduct foreign affairs without judicial interference under the political questions doctrine. The corollary, dictating that states are likewise preempted from impeding U.S. foreign relations on federalism grounds, has also been consistently reaffirmed in Rehnquist Court precedents. The Court's minimalist role, as well as the unanimity of its decision-making, stands in contrast to other doctrinal areas that typically divide the justices and tend to confuse litigants and their legal expectations. Regardless, the case study infers that the usual posture of deference may be challenged or reinforced for different reasons in the Roberts Court by future developments occurring outside the court. The research asks if U.S. state and local foreign policymaking activism, which is increasingly becoming a part of the disaggregation of national sovereignty in the international system, can allow the states to pursue successfully their own foreign policy initiatives in light of contrary Supreme Court doctrine that traditionally prevents states from assuming any sort of meaningful role in foreign affairs. It underscores the fact that the Supreme Court's capacity to rein in the states remains problematic because the judiciary cannot police this area of federalism well, thus effectively committing the process to the states and federal officials instead of to the federal judiciary.

The last chapter, "The Roberts Court and New Federalism," measures the Roberts Court's federalism jurisprudence against the precedents set by the Rehnquist Court and its allegedly revolutionary effort to return sovereign power or autonomy back to the states. It examines what the Roberts Court, in its first six terms, has accomplished in its own right in managing its federalism docket; in doing so, the chapter also infers that the Court's legal outcomes share a conservative political bias, and a conceptualization of the federal constitutional structure, that is different from what scholars have observed in the Rehnquist Court. It weighs the impact that the Court's newest justices (Roberts, Alito, Sotomayor, and Kagan) have in forging their own institutional identities in constitutional law affecting concurrent regulatory authority. While the new appointments replaced key members of the conservative "States' Rights Five" voting bloc found in the Rehnquist Court, it thus remains uncertain at best whether a newly reconstituted majority will coalesce to pursue an identical pro–states' rights agenda or, consequently, erect new limits on federal authority that go beyond existing precedents. Still, the attention the Roberts Court is paying to statutory construction and preemption cases and its likely impact in adjudicating the limits of Congress's commerce power in light of the Obama administration's health-care legislation may shed important light on the ultimate contribution the Roberts Court will make to new federalism judicial policy. In light of the persistent ideological disagreements over federalism that historically divide the justices and nation, the Court's institutional role is likely to continue to evolve as it works to reconcile its own judicial conflict and negotiate the external barriers it faces in domestic and global political environments that often constrain the exercise of judicial lawmaking in federalism issues.

NOTES

1. Robert Barnes, "Supreme Court Term Will Include Cases Highlighting Extent of Federal Power," *Washington Post*, October 1, 2011, at www.washington post.com (accessed October 3, 2011).

2. Adam Liptak, "In New Term, Supreme Court Shifts Focus to Crime and First Amendment," *New York Times*, October 1, 2011, at www.nytimes.com (accessed October 3, 2011).

3. 555 U.S. 555 (2009).

4. Justice Kennedy is often considered the swing vote on the U.S. Supreme Court. Justice Thomas, of the conservative bloc, wrote only a concurrence in the result, explaining his agreement with the outcome but not the underlying rationale offered by Stevens. Helen J. Knowles, *The Tie Goes to Freedom: Justice Anthony M. Kennedy on Liberty* (Lanham, MD: Roman & Littlefield, 2009), 2. See also Jeffrey A. Segal and Harold J. Spaeth, *The Supreme Court and the Attitudinal Model Revisited* (Cambridge: Cambridge University Press, 2002).

5. See the Federalist Society, "Litigation: The Future of Federal Preemption," *New York University Journal of Law and Liberty* 6 (2011): 184.

6. Lawrence S. Ebner, "President Obama's 'Preemption Memo': Much to Do about Very Little," *Legal Backgrounder* 24, no. 21 (June 19, 2009), www.wlf.org/publishing/publication_detail.asp?id=2084 (accessed June 5, 2011). See also Barack Obama, "Memorandum for the Heads of Executive Departments and Agencies," White House, May 20, 2009, www.whitehouse.gov/the-press-office/presidential-memorandum-regarding-preemption (accessed June 5, 2011). For liberals, regulatory preemption is rote agency action having the effect of preempting state tort damage claims, thus protecting big business from liability as a matter of federal policy; David C. Vladeck, "The Emerging Threat of Regulatory Preemp-

tion," *Advance: The Journal of the ACS Issue Groups* 2, no. 1 (Spring 2008), www.acslaw.org/publications/advance/2/1-0 (accessed June 6, 2011).

7. Jack Park, "Vaccines, Preemption, and Federalism Rightly Understood: Why the Supreme Court Should Find Preemption in *Bruesewitz v. Wyeth, Inc.*," Legal Memorandum No. 59, Heritage Foundation, November 12, 2010, www.heritage.org/research/reports/2010/11/vaccines-preemption-and-federalism-rightly-understood (accessed June 5, 2011).

8. Ibid. See also *Riegel v. Medtronic*, 555 U.S. 555 (2008); "Dawning of New 'Decade of Corporate Accountability,'" American Association for Justice, January 11, 2010, www.justice.org/cps/rde/xchg/justice/hs.xsl/11430.htm (accessed January 18, 2011).

9. *Williamson v. Mazda Motor of America, Inc.*, 131 S. Ct. 1131 (2011) (8–0, with Justice Breyer writing the opinion for the Court and Justice Kagan not participating). See also *Bruesewitz v. Wyeth*, 131 S. Ct. 1068 (2011); and Matthew Scarola, "Opinion Analysis: Vaccine Manufacturers Immunized from Design-Defect Liability," SCOTUSblog, February 23, 2011, www.scotusblog.com/?p=114239 (accessed April 18, 2011).

10. Rorie Spill Solberg and Stefanie A. Lindquist, "Activism, Ideology, and Federalism: Judicial Behavior in Constitutional Challenges before the Rehnquist Court, 1986–2000," *Journal of Empirical Legal Studies* 3 (2006): 237–61; Harold J. Spaeth, "The Judicial Restraint of Mr. Justice Frankfurter—Myth or Reality," *Midwest Journal of Political Science* 8 (1964): 22–38.

11. Lawrence Baum, *Judges and Their Audiences: A Perspective on Judicial Behavior* (Princeton, NJ: Princeton University Press, 2006).

12. Mitchell J. Pickerill and Cornell W. Clayton, "The Rehnquist Court and the Political Dynamics of Federalism," *Perspectives on Politics* 2 (2004): 233–48; Keith Whittington, "Taking What They Give Us: Explaining the Court's Federalism Offensive," *Duke Law Journal* 69 (2002): 429–94.

13. Ernest A. Young, "The Rehnquist Court's Two Federalisms," *Texas Law Review* 83 (2004): 50.

14. William W. Buzbee, ed., *Preemption Choice: The Theory, Law, and Reality of Federalism's Core Question* (Cambridge: Cambridge University Press, 2009); Alan E. Untereiner, *The Preemption Defense in Tort Actions: Law, Strategy and Practice* (Washington, DC: U.S. Chamber Institute for Legal Reform, 2008); and Richard A. Epstein and Michael Greve, eds., *Federal Preemption: States' Powers, National Interests* (Washington, DC: AEI Press, 2007).

15. Nina Totenberg, "Rehnquist: From Lone Dissenter to Consensus-Builder," NPR, September 4, 2005, www.npr.org/templates/story/story.php?storyId=4832353 (accessed June 5, 2011).

16. Tinsley E. Yarbrough, *The Rehnquist Court and the Constitution* (New York: Oxford University Press, 2000): 11.

17. Christopher P. Banks, "The Constitutional Politics of Interpreting Section 5 of the Fourteenth Amendment," *University of Akron Law Review* 36 (2003): 427–73.

18. Kathleen M. Sullivan, "From States' Rights Blues to Blue States' Rights: Federalism after the Rehnquist Court," *Fordham Law Review* 75 (2006): 799. See also John Q. Barrett, "The 'Federalism Five' as Supreme Court Nominees, 1971–1991," *St. John's Journal of Legal Commentary* 21 (2007): 485–96.

19. Solberg and Lindquist, "Activism, Ideology, and Federalism," 259–60.

20. John Dinan, "The Rehnquist Court's Federalism Decisions," *Publius: The Journal of Federalism* 41 (2011): 158–67. See also Sullivan, "From States' Rights Blues to Blue States' Rights," 800–1; John T. Noonan, *Narrowing the Nation's Power: The Supreme Court Sides with the States* (Berkeley: University of California Press, 2003).

21. Adam Liptak, "Justices Offer Receptive Ear to Business Interests," *New York Times*, December 18, 2010, A1; Adam Liptak, "Court under Roberts Is Most Conservative in Decades," *New York Times*, July 24, 2010, A1. See also *Heller v. District of Columbia*, 554 U.S. 570 (2008), and *Citizens United v. Federal Election Commission*, 130 S. Ct. 876 (2010).

22. Alliance for Justice, "*New York Times* Reports on the Corporate Court (December 20, 2010)," http://afjjusticewatch.blogspot.com/2010/12/new-york-times-reports-oncorporate.html (accessed January 18, 2011); Liptak, "Justices Offer Receptive Ear to Business Interests," A1; Lee Epstein, William M. Landes, and Richard A. Posner, "Is the Roberts Court Pro-Business?," (December 17, 2010), http://epstein.law.northwestern.edu/research/RobertsBusiness.pdf (accessed June 5, 2011). See also David L. Franklin, "What Kind of Business-Friendly Court? Explaining the Chamber of Commerce's Success at the Roberts Court," *Santa Clara Law Review* 49 (2009): 1019–1057; Jonathan H. Adler, "Business, the Environment, and the Roberts Court: A Preliminary Assessment," *Santa Clara Law Review* 49 (2009): 943–76; and Robin H. Conrad, "The Roberts Court and the Myth of a Pro-Business Bias," *Santa Clara Law Review* 49 (2009): 997–1017.

23. Liptak, "Court under Roberts Is Most Conservative in Decades," A1.

24. Politico, "2010 Election Map (January 23, 2010)," www.politico.com/2010/maps (accessed June 5, 2011).

25. Pierre-Hugues Verdier, "Transnational Regulatory Networks and Their Limits," *Yale Journal of International Law* 34 (2009): 113–72.

26. Christopher E. Martin, "Sovereignty, Meet Globalization: Using Public-Private Partnerships to Promote the Rule of Law in a Complex World," *Military Law Review* 202 (2009): 91; Rolf H. Weber, "Multilayered Governance in International Financial Regulation and Supervision," *Journal of International Economic Law* 13 (2010): 683–704; George Katrougalos, "Constitutional Limitations of Privatization in the USA and Europe: A Theoretical and Comparative Perspective," *Constellations* 17 (2010): 407–25.

27. See Spaeth, "The Judicial Restraint of Mr. Justice Frankfurter—Myth or Reality," 22–38; Thomas Keck, *The Most Activist Supreme Court in History: The Road to Modern Judicial Conservatism* (Chicago: University of Chicago Press, 2004).

28. See Ernest A. Young, "The Story of *Gregory v. Ashcroft* (1991): Clear Statement Rules and the Statutory Constitution of American Federalism," in *Statutory Interpretation Stories*, ed. William N. Eskridge Jr. et al. (New York: Foundation Press, 2010), 197–225; Ernest A. Young, "Executive Preemption," *Northwestern University Law Review* 102 (2008): 869–901; and Young, "The Rehnquist Court's Two Federalisms."

2

Federalism Politics and Policies: Old, New, and Progressive Trends

Only moments after President Barack Obama put down his ceremonial signing pen on March 23, 2010, thirteen state attorneys general rushed to federal courthouses to file lawsuits challenging the administration's progressive health-care reform bill. The Patient Protection and Affordable Care Act (PPACA) remains Obama's most important first-term accomplishment and in all likelihood will define his political legacy. For the White House, the law transformed the flawed private insurance market, thus making health care more affordable for middle-class Americans while providing accountability for insurers who would thereafter be challenged to deny medical coverage due to preexisting conditions.[1] Yet, for critics, it registers a dangerous and unconstitutional encroachment by the federal government into areas of policy traditionally governed by local citizens and their elected state leaders. The litigation response was punctuated by Virginia attorney general Ken Cuccielli's highly publicized vow to obstruct the new law "as soon as the ink is dry," a promise accompanied by his decision to file a lawsuit less than five minutes after the bill was signed into law.[2]

State Attorney General Cuccielli hardly stood alone as his lawsuit was absorbed as only one of many others that were filed across the nation challenging the law in U.S. district courts. Lying beneath the dispute are core questions involving the scope and impact of state sovereignty and whether Congress is constitutionally permitted to use its commerce and implied powers to force states to erect marketplace exchanges to allow citizens and small businesses to buy private insurance with federal subsidies or to direct that citizens to buy their own health coverage. In late

January 2011, District Court Judge Roger Vinson, sitting in the Northern District of Florida and an appointee of President Ronald Reagan, erased the entire health-care bill in *State of Florida v. U.S. Department of Health and Human Services*, thus becoming the first judge to do so on the grounds that Congress had overstepped its constitutional authority. In August 2011, the Eleventh Circuit affirmed in part, striking down the individual mandate (the requirement that individuals buy health insurance or pay a penalty) but upholding the rest of the health-care law.[3]

Yet before the start of the U.S. Supreme Court's 2011–2012 term, the precise legal status of the health-care bill remained highly uncertain because a plethora of active lawsuits were challenging it, including a decision from the Sixth Circuit that upheld the individual mandate—which helped prompt the Court to accept review of the issue in light of the split of authority present in the federal appeals courts.[4] Notably, the issue of whether Congress has the commerce authority to force citizens to buy health insurance is not the only focus of the underlying litigation, as several health-care reform challenges raise other complex constitutional and procedural issues, including those touching upon the scope of Congress's spending power and whether certain plaintiffs have proper legal standing to have their full arguments heard before the courts.[5] Against this legal context scholars and pundits from both sides of the ideological spectrum have thus cast the struggle over health care as a referendum on the Obama presidency and, of course, the influence of the high court's partisanship.[6]

There is little doubt that the swift legal response to the controversial legislation is a manifestation of twenty-first-century progressive federalism politics. It underscores a long-standing political debate that emerged at the nation's founding between nationalists and antifederalists, or state's rights advocates. In light of Obama's 2008 election as a "man of the Left"[7] favoring proactive federal solutions, political opposition from the Right supporting states' interests remains grounded in two closely aligned ideological beliefs. One strain of conservative thought asserts the PPACA, along with the massive February 2008 economic stimulus package designed to ease the sting of the mortgage financial crisis that preceded it, is clear evidence of a breach of the boundaries that otherwise properly set apart national and state power. Under this view, intrusions into health care, a traditional policy domain of the states, are beyond the scope of permissible national authority and signal the onset of a Second New Deal.[8]

Other like-minded conservatives similarly agree there is overreaching but add that the libertarian principle of protecting individual rights is also violated. For conservative libertarians, Obama's progressivism is offensive to those thinking the federal government has no business making personal choices for citizens about the type of health care they want. Apart from the political rhetoric, these ideas capture a mixture of old and new values that paradoxically remain aligned with Ronald Reagan's presidency, the U.S. Chamber of Commerce, and the libertarian Cato Institute. Depending upon the nuance of conservative preference at issue, right-wing conservatism is grounded in basic convictions that fervently strive to achieve government deregulation and to respect state or individual rights.[9]

These partisanship divisions involving federalism frame differences between adversaries and even allies who seldom agree on the proper role of government in solving public policy problems. They predictably flow from the ideological repercussions of Obama's election and past political struggles. Before Obama, Presidents Richard Nixon, Ronald Reagan, and Bill Clinton expressed commitments to increasing state autonomy, typically with grant incentives and policy decisions scaling back the federal government's reach over certain entitlement programs. But events such as September 11, the Iraq and Afghanistan wars, and Hurricane Katrina allowed their successor, President George W. Bush, to centralize executive power and continue the general drift of authority to Washington, DC, that started with previous administrations. The policy implications for resolving federalism questions are clear: the rising number of federal programs and the countervailing need to attract grant dollars constrain state officials as they try to implement national policies while they try to achieve state policy change creatively. As a result, they undertake cooperative and independent efforts to deal with unfunded mandates across a broad spectrum of policy areas, including education, homeland security, welfare, election reform, gay rights, the death penalty, and greenhouse gas emissions.[10]

Identical crises and new social problems will undoubtedly shape the federalism landscape well beyond Obama's administration. The Wall Street mortgage meltdown, an intractable recession, the bailouts of the automobile industry, the burgeoning federal deficit and dramatic budget shortfalls in the states, the protracted war in Afghanistan, efforts to control illegal immigration, the need to clean up the BP oil spill in the Gulf of Mexico and fund federal disaster relief responsibly, and the ongoing political arguments over the federal budget and the proper government response to curb deficit spending as a key issue pervading the 2012 presidential election all place new obligations on national and state governments to respond in ways that match ideological interests and federalism priorities. Contemporary political dynamics coincide with the Obama administration's ready acceptance of the use of federal power to accomplish political reform. That reality has increased ideological conflict and explains other institutional developments, including the emergence of the

Tea Party movement, the persistence of ongoing federalism litigation in state and federal courts, and heightened organized group advocacy. The fluidity and increasing partisanship of the policy environment, in turn, arguably has begun to turn traditional conceptions of federalism values on their head.[11]

For different reasons the presidencies of George W. Bush and Barack Obama have reignited the passions of conservatives and liberals who have vested interests in adopting new strategies to winning federalism contests. Progressives, however, have been actuated by ideological conceptions of federalism that date back to the New Deal but that continue to press forward. Before the late 1930s the lines of authority between the federal and state governments were strictly drawn and enforced by the courts. This dual federalism model yielded to the weight of the Depression and the need to enlarge the scope of federal power, a fact that the judiciary seemed to understand. Post–New Deal cooperative federalism differed, though, from dual federalism because states had concurrent powers with the federal government. Yet the operative assumptions of cooperative federalism changed after World War II, partially in reaction to the Supreme Court's decision in *Brown v. Board of Education*,[12] a ruling that divided the country along racial lines, and other legal policy decisions from the Warren Court (1953–1969) that were deemed by critics to be highly activist.

As the federal government increased its commitment to enforce civil rights law in the states in the post-*Brown* era, federalism arguably became "understood as [a] constitutional protection for states from national meddling" or, put differently, "a convenient shield for local obstruction of federal efforts to guarantee civil rights."[13] For many liberals, this perception was associated with a resurgence of states' rights and racism. That criticism continued into the 1980s and politically became aligned with conservative efforts to limit the national government's power over traditional state functions, including education, crime, and general welfare policies. As the liberal Warren Court was replaced by the conservative Burger (1969–1986) and Rehnquist (1986–2005) Courts, any hope that the federal judiciary would give national officials the constitutional power to fix unconstitutional violations in the states was dashed, mainly because the highest court in the land was thought to be meshed with the institutionalization of political coalitions favoring states' rights and a limited national government.

Nevertheless, the old liberal lament in federalism politics has softened somewhat in light of recent developments reflecting increasing federal centralization, a phenomenon (as described earlier) that is reinforced by post-9/11 Bush and Obama administration policies. A new facet of the political debates concerns how the states and ideologues react to federal omnipotence. Some progressives and others observe that the growth in federal power has been matched by efforts in the states to legislate in social policy areas that traditionally have been ignored or scorned by federal officials, especially in times of conservative control. These initiatives, which encompass advancing gay and lesbian rights, banking regulation, health care, environmental control, and international law principles, have coalesced to form "blue state federalism," a progressive metaphor favoring the cooperative brand of federalism that defined post–New Deal politics up until the 1960s. Notably, blue state federalism stands in stark contrast to the conservative "Constitution in Exile" movement of an earlier time period, which fits more comfortably with the model of dual federalism and its assumption of strictly defined governmental powers.[14]

The old, new, and progressive trends of federalism register the significance of the judicial role, which remains at the base of comprehending the merits of political arguments and policy outcomes that comprise the American federalism heritage. The issue is germane simply because federalism stands as "both a conception of governance and a principle of constitutional law in the United States."[15] The linkages between official control and constitutionalism are at the heart of the competing political arguments resonating from the New Deal to the present, and they help to explain the centrality of U.S. Supreme Court decision-making in creating national and state public policies. As the next section details, however, the precise contours of federalism remained unclear as a practical form of governance, both at the founding and afterward, in large part because the constitutional principles defining federalism have evolved and constantly changed over time. While many federalism and constitutional scholars can agree that the framers made the assumption that the federal courts would hold a critical place in managing conflicts between the states and the central government, the manner and interpretation of the Supreme Court's federalism power remain unpredictable and in flux.

FEDERALISM AT THE FOUNDING

The United States has a federal design greatly influenced by British political traditions and philosophy. Specifically, its political system consists of a representative republic with separation of powers, checks and balances, and a respect for individual liberty at its foundation. Perhaps no less important to the founding conception of American republicanism is the division between, and the concurrent authority of, the centralized government and its relationship to a large body of sovereign states. The coexistence of dual sovereignties, essential to a federalism design, is built upon a constitutional assumption of delegated and residual powers: authority not assigned by the Constitution to the national government becomes part of the states' remaining powers. Even so, the boundaries between sovereigns have never been clearly established, and the necessity for constructing a federal blueprint became apparent at the founding, and that plan is closely aligned with a theory of constitutionalism that is substantially informed by a political theory, ideological conceptions originating from colonial imperial rule, and the practical necessities of the time.[16]

Before the Constitutional Convention, leading political statesmen realized the existing charter of government, the Articles of Confederation, was increasingly flawed because its decentralization prevented it from becoming a cornerstone of a unified nation. With the Articles, each state enjoyed sovereign rights in a loose confederation of voluntary cooperation, and state legislatures controlled what became a system of weak central government. There was no power to coerce the states into compliance on issues affecting the national interest, including congressional apportionment, the payment of Revolutionary War debts, managing conflicts with indigenous tribes, and the distribution of western lands. Local economies were dysfunctional, in part because states issued devalued paper money as legal tender to pay outstanding obligations.[17] The national assembly could not act without a majority consensus from the states, and, similarly, there was a weak executive and no national court system. The confederal structure meant that any attempt to act collectively was undercut by state independence. With a unicameral assembly and a diluted executive and nonexistent judiciary, the Articles symbolized an ineffectual league of friendship among the states that prevented states from joining together to repel domestic or foreign threats.[18]

The absence of national sovereignty put the country at risk in the aftermath of a hard-fought war for independence from Great Britain, and it led increasingly to insistent calls for political reform. Most elite statesmen, whose own economic self-interest was arguably jeopardized, agreed a more robust central government would best preserve economic stability and individual property rights, provided the people of the United States consented. Although it was imperative to reconcile national and state interests with a carefully crafted principle of political representation, arresting instability in the states, particularly in legislative assemblies, was a primary concern in trying to achieve meaningful constitutional reform. Influential statesman such as John Jay and John Marshall agreed with James Madison's view, as shaped by his years as a Virginia politician, that state legislatures could not be trusted.[19] As Madison therefore put it, a new government had to provide a check against state legislative majorities because they churned out "multiple" and "mutable" laws that combined to produce "injustice of the laws of the States."[20]

While fixing the Articles remained a possibility, enlightened political theorists such as Madison used the history of failed republics as a template for creating a different kind of republicanism. One of the most important ends of government, securing individual liberty, is safeguarded as well if the framework is built on principles restraining government and what was feared to be unchecked human passion. Madison's republicanism thus assumed constitutional structure would temper personal self-interest, and in this way it operated as a "self-balancing machine." If properly set up, the machine's design would succeed in spite of the natural tendency of human frailties, avarice, and self-interest to undermine political institutions.[21]

Analytically, the traditional preconception and definition of what a constituted a good republic had to change. In Madison's mind, the proposed Constitution had to foster a large republic. Size mattered because only expanded republics could soften the destructive influence of groups actuated by majority rule, or factions, which typically dominated the governing process and overwhelmed minority opposition. As he reiterated in Federalist No. 10, the absence of auxiliary precautions, among them separation of powers, checks and balances, and federalism, would prove fatal to the new republic, as it was for ancient and modern confederacies in Greek and Roman times. Accordingly, a key element of Madison's theory was to extend the sphere of the republic, a solution that facilitated economic diversity by reducing class and sectarian strife, as well as unequal property distribution. The idea, which captures the modern political science tenets of social and cultural pluralism, significantly departed from the conventional wisdom of the time. Other key political thinkers in the founding period, such as Montesquieu in *The Spirit of the Laws*, argued that only small confederate republics could properly strike a balance between popular sovereignty and political liberty.[22]

The new conceptual framework meant that federalism could never operate as a simple division of power between the state and central governments. Federalism in a large republic was more complex. As Madison said in Federalist No. 39, "The proposed Constitution . . . is, in strictness, neither a national nor a federal Constitution, but a composition of both." Put differently, Madison's federalism sought a "middle ground" between the "supremacy of the national authority" and the inclusion of "local authorities" so they could be "subordinately useful." The middling course tilted heavily in favor of vesting the central government with sufficient powers to compel state citizens to heed the national interest. The institutional design created a "compound republic"—a political structure dispersing governmental authority into separate national and local spheres (federalism), juxtaposed against another subdivision of three distinct national departments (separation of powers). In this way Federalist No. 51

declared that "a double security" protected the people because the "different governments will control each other" while "each [simultaneously] will be controlled by itself." In short, federalism helped offset the destructive loss of republican (civic) virtue that unchecked factional interests and state legislative misrule helped to foster in political systems.[23]

The nature and scope of the proposed 1787 constitutional compact caused ongoing political controversies lasting well beyond the founding. The wisdom of consolidation was debated by the founders in several ways. The convention's agenda was set early on by the introduction of the Virginia Plan, a proposal favoring the large states and centralization. One aspect, the Article VIII provision calling for a Council of Revision, sought to create a hybrid executive and judicial body that vested the central government with a limited veto, allowing it to prejudge the validity of national laws (including those nullifying state laws). After two weeks of review by committee, the council proposal was rejected. Thereafter a revision of the Virginia Plan was ultimately submitted to the full convention, but only after it had evaluated, and rejected, the merits of the New Jersey Plan—a set of resolutions offered in response to the large states' plan and one favoring the states, as well as the creation of a judiciary requiring state courts to adhere to laws enacted under the revised articles of union.[24]

Apart from the Virginia Plan's Council of Revision and the New Jersey Plan's response, Madison made another proposal to have the central government armed with a negative, or veto, over all states' laws, "in all cases whatsoever." Like the Council of Revision, it did little to allay the fears of anti-consolidation supporters.[25] In drawing from the British imperial practice of using a privy council (an executive and legislative entity representing the king and his counselors) to determine the validity of colonial laws, the federal negative was similarly conceived to empower Congress to review the acceptability of state legislation *ex ante*, or before enactment.[26] The nullification safeguard proactively imbued Congress with irrevocable authority to render state laws impotent at inception. Still, the negative was vital to republican theory because it supplied balance to the constitutional structure in at least two ways.

As a defensive measure, the veto discouraged state encroachments on federal authority. As such, it affirmatively insulated citizens from state violations of republican liberty through the operation of unjust laws. In this fashion the negative blunted the impact majority factions would have as they worked to destroy republican integrity. Whereas critics aligned the negative and Madison's support for it with British imperialism in the colonial era, Madison insisted it did not impose a form of hierarchical control on the states. Rather, its purpose was to act simply as a mechanism that prevented states from spinning out of their centrifugal orbits. In this sense, the federal negative was not a substantive rule of decision or policymaking that invalidated state laws running afoul of the Constitution.[27] Instead, it was designed to fix the core problem of the confederacy. State governments repeatedly transgressed against union interests by restoring estates and forgiving debts in violation of the Treaty of Paris, by interfering with private contracts and levying taxes at unreasonable rates, and by issuing unsecured paper money that wiped out public and private debts. Consequently, the veto was akin to a procedural safeguard, albeit one that supplied and institutionalized methodology for national supervision over disruptive state legislation. In Madison's words, it actually was "the mildest expedient that could be devised for preventing these mischiefs."[28]

Given its fundamental place in the nascent republic, Madison was deeply disappointed when the convention voted not to adopt the negative. He was convinced that its absence was "mortal to the ancient Confederacies, and to be the disease of the modern," and he held onto that view long after the Philadelphia meeting. The negative's defeat had lasting implications for the judicial enforcement of federalism principles as well. That ironically quickly became apparent when the convention's delegates wrestled with the difficulty of creating a union while respecting state sovereignty. In weighing the negative's merits, they strategized about the best way to strike a workable balance between levels of governments. They determined that satisfactorily reconciling the multiplicity of interests meant trusting either state or federal judges to enforce federal law against recalcitrant states. While many statesmen endorsed the checking principle at the negative's base, several feared it would operate too harshly against the states and be tantamount to a direct military order. Under this view it could be used as a weapon against the South and slavery. A less threatening alternative implicated the federal supremacy clause, a characteristic of the New Jersey Plan (the small states' proposal debated alongside the large states' Virginia Plan). The supremacy clause, it was reasoned, could be a functional substitute for Madison's legislative negative, especially since its legitimacy came from the principal set of resolutions favoring the states.[29]

With this in mind the convention jettisoned the negative and shortly thereafter crafted the supremacy clause. In doing so the framers decisively put the responsibility of federal law enforcement on the shoulders of federal judges, but given the untested nature of the new federalism they engineered, they never could anticipate how it would work in practice or what its future consequences might be. Nonetheless the combination of the supremacy clause and Article III judicial authority served notice that American federalism would be a province of the federal courts. Additionally, whereas the original promise of Madison's veto leaned toward a greater institutional place for Congress to strike a balance between multiple sovereigns, its defeat heralded an ideological shift that was oriented toward fashioning judicially centered remedies.[30]

In this light the historical evidence suggests that the power of judicial review—a court's institutional license to annul anticonstitutional legislative or executive action—emerged from a reconfiguration of constitutional and federalism principles that can be traced back to the colonial experience and extended forward to the 1787 Constitutional Convention. The revision of political ideas had the ultimate institutional effect of anointing federal courts as the de facto mediators of national and state conflicts. Yet locating the fulcrum of institutional supremacy did not answer the question of how either level of court would use judicial review in practice. "The rejection of the negative and adoption of the Supremacy Clause," law professor Alison LaCroix explains, "gave state judges the power to interpret the law of the federal polity while, in the same stroke, bringing those judges under the occasional control of that polity."[31] Also, for some historians judicial review was understood not to be a horizontal threat: few thought it would be used to negate presidential or congressional prerogatives at the federal level.[32] Consequently, the insecurity of knowing how it was going to work vertically—that is, in and against the states—was a more acute but unpredictable concern.

Although the framers may have thought that the power of judicial review over state laws would be applied and enhanced through the supremacy clause, the hostility shown against New York and Rhode Island judges who tried to claim it against state assemblies indicates a different interpretation of the framing. The impossibility of ascertaining how any judge would use judicial review at this point in the nation's history—especially since state judges would surely test the limits of their authority by using it against federal encroachments—confirms the complexity underlying what the supremacy clause and judicial review might represent in the founding mind-set. As a legal standard, the supremacy clause for state judges was probably only an aspiration and not much of an incentive or a mandate that could realistically be applied at the time. Although the supremacy clause might have constrained judicial behavior, it is implausible to think state judges would never abuse their authority when confronted with the question of what law they should apply to any given hypothetical fact situation.[33]

In the end the risk that state judges would bypass the supremacy clause to decide cases against national interests thus probably constrained the framers to rely upon the U.S. Supreme Court to act as the final arbiter of federalism disputes. In discussing the reach of national powers under the proposed Constitution, Madison implied as much in Federalist No. 39. After acknowledging the states retain "a residuary and inviolable sovereignty" over matters going beyond their enumerated constitutional powers, he nonetheless flatly stated, "It is true that in controversies relating to the boundary between the two jurisdictions, the tribunal which is ultimately to decide is to be established under the general government."[34] In sum, the convention debates over the negative over state laws, the supremacy clause and its operation, and the likely scope and application of judicial review suggests the U.S. Supreme Court was in all likelihood intended to superintend, and inevitably decide, who the ultimate victor would be in federalism struggles between national institutions and subgovernments.

THE EVOLUTION OF FEDERALISM JURISPRUDENCE

Federalism theory and what it represents over time is inherently ambiguous, imprecise, and controversial. Scholars remain at odds over its meaning or significance. For legal scholars Malcolm Feeley and Edward Rubin, federalism is nihilistic and characterized by a loss of autonomous political identity by geographical subunits and citizens in a centralized regime of managerial decentralization. Judicial enforcement of its doctrine is incoherent and inconsistent, whereas legal historian Edward Purcell asserts it is a historical amalgamation of doubly blurred, fractionated, instrumental, and contingent structures, with its operation superficially reflecting only the "social, political, and ideological commitments" of its adherents. The risk of conflating federalism theory with politics is echoed by Feeley and Rubin, and political scientist John Nugent adds that federalism scholars often speak past each other and fail to synthesize a variety of distinct interdisciplinary contributions that potentially could inform law, political science, or public administration studies.[35]

There is little disagreement that the U.S. Supreme Court's supervision of federalism principles began shortly after the Constitution's ratification. Still, the judicial lines the judiciary has drawn have fluctuated historically, predictably in response to the governing political climate and germane policy preferences. In this way "federalism's emergence and development" join with "particular moments and particular debates [that aid in] finding the appropriate balance of theory, experience, contingency, and expediency."[36] The historical ebb and flow of American political development and intergovernmental relationships may also be perceived as having connections to several distinct federalism eras. The first spans from the founding to the Civil War in the 1860s. A second, regularly linked with dual federalism, ranges from the Civil War to the onset of the New Deal in the 1930s, and a third, cooperative federalism, emerges after the New Deal and lasts until about the late 1950s. Other variations are likely to be more contemporary in scope under different headings (e.g., creative, new, and co-optive federalisms), developing from the 1960s to the present, which represent a response to, and an amalgam of, past eras.[37]

While it may advance a particular federalism theory, correlating federalism's evolution with discrete time periods is defensible. Using descriptive and temporal labels supplies historical grounding and factual context for appreciating federalism's complexity, and it helps to understand the Supreme Court's relevance in umpiring its theoretical underpinnings, interests, and synergistic relationships.[38] Put differently, the scope and application of the judicial role is better appreciated by tracking the common law's development of its key constitutional law precedents, as shaped by the governing political environment over time. This is true even if the constitutionalism is qualitatively characterized by court rulings that do not proceed in a straight line and, instead, can only be adjudged to be messy at best and contradictory at worse. Regardless, outlining federalism's uneven but steady progress allows for a deeper appreciation of illustrative rulings and political events that signify the nature of unionism, the interests of state sovereignty, and the ideological contestations defining federalism jurisprudence. While by no means an exhaustive list or chronology, the next section conveys several crucial moments in representative eras, up to the present.

The Founding and Nascent Nationalism

The 1780s American confederacy is defined by state-centric decentralization. In contrast, the new constitutional framework expressed an evolving commitment to consolidation as the nation matured. While the framers agreed to form the U.S. Supreme Court as a court of last resort, no consensus emerged in Philadelphia to grant state courts federal authority or to establish federal courts; thus Congress had to resolve these issues after the convention, ostensibly through the passage of the 1789 Judiciary Act. In an era of growing centralization, the fault lines for early federalism contests thus were exposed by congressional decisions to create lower federal courts, to vest them with power over cases affecting state courts, and to situate the continuing relevance of English law in American jurisprudence and separation of powers theory (i.e., if English law granted federal courts common law authority over the states and the scope of coterminous tripartite federal power). Not only do these issues manifest the colonial legal culture's influence on modern federalism principles, they also represent one of the first landmark rulings of the first Supreme Court and historically "part of the high drama of public affairs" of the time.[39]

In *Chisholm v. Georgia*,[40] the justices ruled Georgia could be sued in federal court by a private out-of-state citizen seeking contract damages for supplies delivered but not paid for during the Revolution. In opposition,

Justice James Iredell's dissent urged the states cannot be sued without their consent under common law sovereign immunity rules; thus Georgia did not have to defend itself against a private federal court action. The intense public outcry in response to *Chisholm* aligned itself with Iredell's views. By January 1798 the states had ratified the Eleventh Amendment principle that federal courts are divested from hearing similar lawsuits. As a result, *Chisholm* is a historical marker to explain what was beneath the states' motivation to use the amendment process to overrule, for the first time, a U.S. Supreme Court outcome. It also raised the persistent issue of whether the *Chisholm* majority—consisting of delegates to the convention (John Blair, James Wilson) and key figures in state ratifying conventions and in writing the Federalist Papers (William Cushing, John Jay)—correctly captured the founders' intent in giving to the Supreme Court jurisdictional and national power over the states under the Eleventh Amendment. Enduring until the Civil War and sporadically afterward, *Chisholm*'s impact would serve to complicate the meaning of federalism and sovereignty, thus reflecting a constitutional truth that the amendment's meaning has never been truly settled and, as such, remains a vexing source of judicial conflict and political controversy.[41]

Wrestling with *Chisholm*'s federalism implications must account for framing intent, its ideological context, and the effect of both on the judicial function. The political unrest caused by what many founders thought was the abuse of state legislative authority (a key reason behind the call for a constitutional convention) was soon eclipsed by persistent jurisdictional struggles to determine the judicial role of all federal courts when situated against state courts in the aftermath of the Constitution's ratification. The 1789 Judiciary Act, establishing inferior (district and circuit) federal courts, and the Judiciary Act of 1801, reforming circuit court operations and enlarging federal legal authority over state courts (but repealed one year later), generated several pivotal controversies of judicial federalism (the proper relationship between federal and state courts) that defined the nation's early judicial history. Whereas the conflicts illustrate a general reluctance to trust centralized power, they also highlight the tenacity of partisanship between the Federalists (favoring centralization and creditor interests) and the Jeffersonian Republicans (supporting state and debtor interests) over land speculation litigation, the punitive effect of seditious libel laws under the Alien and Sedition Acts (laws criminalizing political dissent against the government), the wisdom of foreign trade and oceanic commercial policy, and the ambiguity of the Supreme Court's appellate jurisdiction over state law interpretations.[42]

One facet of federalism involved ongoing attempts by states and their judiciaries to attack the Supreme Court's Article III and Section 25 (of the 1789 Judiciary Act) power to review state laws. As *Chisholm* symbolized, such challenges began at the Court's inception and continued apace until the Civil War and afterward. A variety of institutional developments, including the paltry nature of federal court jurisdiction, the travails of circuit riding, and the narrow scope of subject matter the courts heard, combined to tie the federal courts to local geographical regions and preferences, thereby significantly reducing their legal or policymaking influence over national affairs. Moreover, the Supreme Court's beginning was greatly affected by the ideological ramifications of the new society and its untested culture. The conventional labels typically used to describe the judiciary—including definitions of nationalism, federalism, and chief justice orientations—reflect the reality that "ideology continually confronts, reshapes, and is reshaped by cultural experience, and the presence of potentially competitive ideologies in the same time frame." As such, the "ideological ethos" of early America is "most accurately described as an amalgamation of republican and liberal ideologies, with other ingredients, such as the belief that America was an exceptional and unique culture." In this light the Supreme Court is perhaps best perceived as nothing more than "an institution responding to contradictions in the culture of its time."[43]

These dynamics appear in several Marshall Court (1801–1835) opinions, among them *Marbury v. Madison,* the case fortifying the power of judicial review.[44] The opinions showcase that it was up to the task of building its political reputation and institutional legitimacy as a coequal branch of government in the postfounding period. It did so in spite of the partisan strain caused by the nation's first political parties, the pro-centralization Federalists and states' rights Republicans, and the bitterly contested 1800 presidential election, won by Republican Thomas Jefferson. In a few short years the events leading to the beginning and resolution of the War of 1812 with Great Britain created some common ground that was used to strike a balance between the needs of the nation and parochial preferences. Under Marshall's Federalist leadership and with his talent for consensus building, the Court thus positioned itself to become politically legitimate, even though over time, as the bench's composition changed with at least five appointments from Presidents Thomas Jefferson and James Madison, presumably the Court would become less nationalistic.[45] The Court's salience grew when it granted Congress broad powers to regulate the economy under Article I's commerce (*Gibbons v. Ogden,* 1824) and necessary and proper clauses (*McCulloch v. Maryland,* 1819). With *Gibbons,* Marshall's somewhat ambiguous language suggested that states had some role in regulating the political economy so long as they did not interfere with Congress's ability to control interstate or foreign commerce, and in *McCulloch* Marshall equipped the federal government with the means to assert its supremacy over the states if Congress was acting within the scope of its enumerated powers. For legal historian William Wiecek, *McCulloch* especially is relevant because it is a trilogy of Marshall Court cases that earmarked the Supreme Court as the final authority in constitutional law governing the political branches and the states.[46] In still other cases, including *Martin v. Hunter's Lessee* and *Cohens v. Virginia*, the Court armed itself with ample authority to review state court civil and criminal laws. For legal historian G. Edward White, this cluster of cases actuated the worst fears of anti-consolidationists, who believed the justices eventually would exceed their constitutional authority on the basis that "every extension of federal legislative power would yield a comparable extension of federal judicial power."[47]

Whereas *Marbury*, *Gibbons*, and *McCulloch* supplied the federal courts with the necessary authority to put affirmative constitutional limitations on the states, *Martin v. Hunter's Lessee* and *Cohens v. Virginia* are heralded as comprising some of the "great foundational 'federalism' decisions of the Marshall Court," ostensibly because they marked the constitutional boundaries of federal court jurisdiction over the states.[48] *Martin*'s ruling by Justice Joseph Story (Chief Justice Marshall recused himself) rejected on constitutional grounds a Virginia appeals court's refusal to follow Section 25 of the 1789 Judiciary Act. In a second appeal to the high court, Martin's ownership rights to land he inherited from a British loyalist, and whose title was protected by the 1783 Peace and 1794 Jay treaties, were vindicated—thereby trumping Virginia's assertion that it acquired the property through its alien inheritance confiscation laws. Justice Story insisted the Constitution is a constitutive act of the people and, at times, expressly impairs state sovereignty. While Section 25 properly conferred concurrent jurisdiction, federal courts also enjoyed appellate authority over state determinations, principally to harmonize conflicting interpretations and to create a uniform body of law. As he wrote, "The courts of the United States can, without question, revise the proceedings of the executive and legislative authorities of the states, and if they are found to be contrary to the constitution, may declare them to be of no legal validity"; the same principle, he continued, applied to state court judgments.[49] Under this view, the Constitution, and Congress's Section 25, meant the Supreme Court was fully empowered to review state civil cases under its appellate powers.

Martin's importance lay too in showing the Court was willing to at least temporarily dismantle the compact theory—the antinationalist argument asserting the states did not relinquish sovereignty when the nation was created. *Martin* put few limits on centralization while "relegat[ing] the states to little more than administrative units."[50] Later Chief Justice John Marshall extended Story's reasoning in *Cohens v. Virginia*, but this time to state court criminal matters. *Cohens* tested the Supreme Court's authority to evaluate the criminal convictions of defendants for illegally selling lottery tickets under state law. On appeal, they claimed immunity from prosecution because a federal law enacted in the District of Columbia legally sanctioned what Virginia outlawed. Restated, they directly asserted that federal courts could not exercise dominion over state sovereignty, either generally or specifically under the Eleventh Amendment, notwithstanding Section 25's opposite suggestion.[51]

While Marshall deflated any state rights' opposition by ruling for Virginia on the grounds that the congressional anti-lottery prohibition only applied to the district, he rebuffed Virginia's principal claims by reasserting national *and* judicial authority under the supremacy clause. In his words, the Court's "judicial power as originally given, extends to all cases arising under the constitution or a law of the United States, whoever may be the parties." Virginia's status as a party did not divest federal courts of their appellate jurisdiction. Further, the Court could review state court rulings because "in a government acknowledgedly supreme, with respect to objects of vital interest to the nation . . . the exercise of the appellate power over those judgments of the State tribunals which may contravene the constitution or laws of the United States, is . . . essential to the attainment of those objects." Marshall swept aside the Eleventh Amendment argument by observing federal courts were only barred from hearing lawsuits from citizens without state consent, but reviewing federal law was permissible when the state initiated criminal prosecution, and it was not commenced "by a citizen of another State, or by a citizen or subject of any foreign State." Like the *Martin* case before it, *Cohens* signaled that naked claims to state sovereignty were not going to stop federal courts from weighing in on the constitutionality of state court proceedings or judgments. In fact, each ruling stressed the need for the highest court in the land to bring uniformity to constitutional interpretations of international and domestic law, including the extent to which the nation is bound by its treaty obligations and in commercial cases. Both cases thus helped to fuse federalism theory with the permissible exercise of appellate jurisdiction within "contested terrains of constitutional discourse," therefore creating a "bold vision of federal judicial supremacy."[52]

The rise of federal judicial power and the drift toward centralization were opposed by detractors centered in local cultures, attachments, and interests. The localism spirit, closely aligned with states' rights, dates back to the Revolution and remains pervasive. Several political events, chief among them Thomas Jefferson's Republican victory over Federalist John Adams as president in 1800, polarized sectional differences as national and state leaders fought over what the judiciary's role should be in governing the nation. Ultimately, that question became subsumed by other political battles involving the scope and application of the Alien and Sedition Acts, the Kentucky and Virginia Resolutions, chartering a National Bank, federal court reform, the impeachment of federal judges, western land development (spurred on by the Louisiana Purchase), the expansion of slavery, and sundry diplomatic or national security disruptions.[53]

These developments coincided with a growing national economy. The Supreme Court encouraged expansion by granting Congress broad regulatory powers while simultaneously limiting state interference through Article I, Section 10, those constitutional restraints preventing states from impairing private contracts, coining money, or levying duties on imports or exports. By 1825, over a thirty-four-year period, the Marshall Court had nullified almost a dozen state laws for constitutional reasons. The judicial activity illustrates that the coexistence between levels of government was regularly being tested: it was increasingly unclear if a "nation-centered or states-centered theory of federalism would prevail."[54] Persistent objections to centralization helped bracket other federalism moments between Jacksonian democracy and the Civil War.

The Nullification Crisis of 1832–1833, caused by South Carolina's refusal to comply with the federal tariff supported by President Andrew Jackson and the Congress, combined with rising sectional differences over slavery to foreshadow dramatic legal and policy change that included an implied right of southern secession from the Union. The Era of Good Feelings, a snapshot in time marked by the rise of the philosophy of legal science and the legal profession and by a striving for the development of an orderly balance of legal principles, also reflected a period of national harmony and less political strife in the patriotic aftermath of the War of 1812, but it stood firm only so long as the provocative issues of the day (slavery, western progress, and the economy) were kept submerged.[55] Soon, however, these questions dominated political affairs. The president sparred with Congress over the parochial and moral consequences of chartering a Second National Bank, securing Indian removal, and slave ownership.[56] In contrast to the nationalist Marshall Court, South Carolinian John Calhoun's advocacy of a state-centric compact theory during the Nullification Crisis raised credible fears of southern secession.

The apprehension fueled many of the Taney Court's (1836–1864) federalism contributions, but other factors were at work as well. The antebellum period featured increased state court activism, where judges confidently used private tort, contract, and natural law principles to adopt Jacksonian reforms and further the interests of capitalists.[57] The U.S. Constitution, however, seemed to veer in a different jurisprudential direction because it granted Congress powers over new state admission, legal governance in the territories (Art. IV, sect. 3), and slave importation (Art. I, sect. 9). Interpreting these and other constitutional provisions (e.g., the republican guaranty to state governments, privileges and immunities, and full faith or credit) proved to be a highly fluid enterprise and increasingly divisive for the courts and country. Lingering but unresolved questions over the meaning of the three-fifths clause and the apportionment distortion it created in favor of southern political representation (or in deciding if territories could be admitted into the Union as slaveholding or free states) added to a growing disunion sentiment that took root and continued to grow shortly after the Louisiana Purchase.[58]

Apart from the interpretative challenges facing the judiciary, the political age was volatile. The 1858 congressional and 1860 presidential elections, together with the coalescence of several southerners (and slaveholders) on the bench, created a political climate that made it difficult for judges to separate their partisanship from their judicial behavior and, by definition, the neutral and independent discharge of their official duties. This was true of the Taney Court as well, for its "members . . . were predominately politicians, appointed for political reasons in an intensely political age, and their partisanship, though it might be muted, was never entirely smothered by the proprieties of judicial office."[59] Taney's elevation from secretary of the Treasury in the Jackson administration to Supreme Court justice is illustrative, prompting an aging John Quincy Adams to muse that the Maryland native was a "convert from the ranks of federalism to rank democracy and a man of exceedingly doubtful moral principle."[60] The partisan invectives register the difficulties of measuring the Taney Court's federalism legacy in light of its ambivalent decision-making: it ratified state-centric slaveholder interests in *Dred Scott v. Sandford* while simultaneously advancing economic consolidation in landmarks such as *Propeller Genesee Chief v. Fitzhugh* (extending admiralty federal court jurisdiction) and *Swift v. Tyson* (allowing the federal judiciary to create federal common law in commercial matters without following state court rulings). Until it was later overruled in 1938, *Swift* eventually let federal judges craft centralizing rulings in a variety of private law realms, including wills, torts, contracts, and damages.[61]

Still, while Chief Justice Roger B. Taney's constitutionalism paralleled many Marshall Court precedents, it nonetheless maintained a healthy respect for strict construction and judicial restraint—at least insofar as placing affirmative limits on the federal government's capability to obstruct state autonomy, particularly in slavery cases, was concerned. His rather schizophrenic reputation as a former Federalist, a southern slaveholder, and political hack tends to obscure reasonable attempts to decipher the constitutional meaning of Taney's commitment to national goals, dual federalism principles, and the entrenchment of slavery as a political institution.[62] Several opinions—among them *Charles River Bridge v. Warren* (ruling a state legislative charter did not impair a contract of a monopolistic corporation that had unrestricted rights to collect bridge tolls), *Briscoe v. Bank of Kentucky* (sanctioning paper money issuance by a state-owned bank), the *License Cases* (permitting state regulation of local liquor sales), *Strader v. Graham* (affirming slave status by residency and not temporal employment or residence in a free state), and *Cooley v. Board of Wardens of the Port of Philadelphia* (creating a doctrine of selective exclusiveness protecting the exercise of intrastate dormant commerce power in the absence of federal law)—exemplify the balance the Taney Court tried to achieve in federalism cases. Of those cases and others involving interpretations of the contract clause, the political questions doctrine, and the scope of state police powers, *Cooley* arguably was highly significant because it gave the states the flexibility of protecting their own commercial affairs from federal encroachment if Congress had not legislated in the area, thus illustrating its consistency with dual federalism ideals.[63]

Justice Story, a nationalist from the Marshall Court, paradoxically was at the center of some of the key federalism disputes that distinguished Taney and his Court's work. Their differences are displayed in Chief Justice Taney's disagreement (in a concurring opinion) in *Prigg v. Pennsylvania*,[64] a Story-penned majority opinion that upheld the federal Fugitive Slave Act of 1793, identifying it as an exclusively federal, not state, enforcement remedy. In doing so it struck down Pennsylvania's Personal Liberty Law and all others that were designed to protect runaway slaves from slave owners who kidnapped and returned them to bondage without any sort of legal process. Yet the decision was profitable to slave interests because the Taney Court gave masters and states the constitutional freedom to recapture their slave property in a state other than that where the slave had established domicile, which meant they did not have to worry about abolitionist-minded interference from state officials. But in upholding the federal law, and impliedly ceding to Congress all regulatory enforcement powers over slave property, *Prigg* also gave federal officials unfettered discretion to apply or disregard the federal recapture law, thus undermining southern interests as well. That is why Taney concurred in the result but disagreed with the Court's rationale. Under Taney's pro-slavery view, the constraints of federal law displaced state sovereignty by preventing states from taking advantage of their own laws to enforce the terms of slave recapture. Regardless, it stands to reason that *Prigg* is arguably analogous to Story's attempt to follow the commercial law principles of *Swift v. Tyson* (1842), which earlier in the same term set the controversial precedent of nationalizing federal common law while ignoring state law; in doing so, however, it resulted in an outcome that never completely satisfied anybody in the debate over slavery.[65]

A similar irony was in play in grasping how a key nullification and compact theory principle—the one insisting that federal courts are powerless to construe federal law against the states—became the crux of the Supreme Court's decision in *Dred Scott v. Sandford*.[66] In traveling and residing in a free state (Illinois) and a territory in Upper Louisiana (north of Missouri) with his master, Dred Scott thought he was liberated from bondage and entitled to full U.S. citizenship rights under Congress's 1820 Missouri Compromise, which admitted two states, Missouri (slave) and Maine (free), and imposed a ban on slavery in territories above parallel 36°30' north. In a 7–2 vote each legal argument was rejected.

On the citizenship question, Taney's opinion reasoned that the Constitution did not intend to give slaves (and free blacks born in the United States) citizenship rights because they are "considered as a subordinate and inferior class of beings who had been subjugated by the dominant race, and, whether emancipated or not, yet remained subject to their authority, and had no rights or privileges but such as those who held the power and the Government might choose to grant them." As such, Congress had exclusive naturalization authority, and states were powerless to make slaves U.S. citizens, no matter where they resided. Taney added that slaves at the founding were never a part of the political community of free people given "the legislation and histories of the times, and the language used in the Declaration of Independence"—partially because slaves always have "been regarded as beings of an inferior order, and altogether unfit to associate with the white race either in social or political relations, and so far inferior that they had no rights which the white man was bound to respect, and that the negro might justly and lawfully be reduced to slavery for his benefit."[67]

Whereas some social scientists imply the historical precedents of the time meant the judiciary could never consider slaves as constitutional citizens, law professor Earl Maltz is more circumspect, saying the Taney Court did not speak with one voice on the issue because three of the seven justices in the majority (John Campbell, Samuel Nelson, and John Catron) did not address the issue.[68] While most in the majority agreed on the result, only four justices (Taney, Daniel, Campbell, and Catron) specifically weighed in on the Missouri Compromise's constitutionality, and Taney's discussion is plausibly nonbinding obiter dictum. For identical reasons, what the Court precisely held in the whole judgment, and specifically that aspect of the ruling leading to the judicial nullification of the Missouri Compromise, is equally problematic as the precedents Taney was construing appeared to favor its affirmation.[69] Nevertheless, in concluding Congress is drained of delegated authority to ban slavery in the territories, the chief justice wrote that the "right to property in a slave is distinctly and expressly affirmed in the Constitution." In reducing human slaves to objects of property and linking the Fifth Amendment's due process clause (safeguarding life, liberty, and property rights) with the Article IV, Section 3 fugitive slave clause (affirming the right to import slaves until 1808) as textual support, he declared that Congress's Article IV, Section 3 powers to supply "all needful Rules and Regulations" for territories and to admit states could not trump a slaveholder's right to bring property into areas governed by the Louisiana Purchase. Congress's authority, in fact, is granted only to insure that slaveholders are allowed to defend their rights and interests in slave property. While the remaining justices supporting Taney differed with his rationale, they agreed that the preservation of state sovereignty and the property rights of slave owners were superior interests that outweighed any opposing congressional powers to settle the slavery issue independently of the Court.[70]

Dred Scott is a landmark for many reasons. Dred Scott's plea for freedom was eclipsed by the Court's political decision to impose a judicial solution to a problem that the people's deliberative chamber had tried to fix with its own laws. Court watchers have long acknowledged that the case could have been settled on jurisdictional grounds without reaching the constitutional question raised by the Missouri Compromise. While some defend the Taney Court in light of the totality of its jurisprudence, critics assert the Court's intervention was ill-advised because the outcome could not be separated from a state-centered view of nationalism, thus adding to the growing perception that the bench was highly politicized and weakening the holding's judicial plausibility.[71] Also, *Dred Scott* intensified sectional and partisan divisions that were already at a boiling point over many issues, among them whether Kansas should be admitted into the Union as a free or slave state. Consequently, the opinion and the reaction to it soon became instrumental in framing the famous debates between Illinois senator Stephen Douglas and the contender for his seat, Abraham Lincoln, thus becoming a harbinger of Lincoln's 1858 senatorial defeat and his 1860 presidential victory. Moreover, it is symbolically linked with the Court's pro-slavery jurisprudence in the 1870s and afterward, which had the effect of reinterpreting the Civil War Amendments largely to remove, and not enhance, freedmen's equality, as most conspicuously evidenced in *Plessy v. Ferguson* and its endorsement of the separate but equal doctrine. So while slaveholders and their supporters applauded the result in *Dred Scott*, the outcome contributed to a different understanding of federalism that seriously diminished the Court's legitimacy and disrupted the body politic.[72]

While these historical perspectives and scholarly judgments are powerful signs that the Taney Court bears some responsibility for politicizing the Court and slavery as a national issue, the Court's southern cast did not rapidly or wholesale overturn what the Marshall Court is credited with doing in the name of the Union. A common perception appears to support legal scholar Martin Siegel's conclusion that "Chief Justice

Taney, instead of demolishing the legal federalism of his great predecessor, stressed a 'divided sovereignty,' and actually led the way to the enhancement of the power of the federal judiciary while protecting property rights, maintaining the sanctity of the contract clause, and furthering capitalist development." The salient political order and norms of the time, along with Taney's increasing rigidity in defending the South aggressively with judicial power as he aged on the bench, therefore register a recurring theme of federalism that remains wedded to the concept of judicial supremacy and the role it plays in creating political synergies between the federal government and the states.[73] The continuing interplay between what the Supreme Court did before and in response to the Civil War and its growing judicial activism in interpreting federalism principles that ultimately favored economic nationalism are analyzed next.

The Civil War, Dual Federalism, and the Rise of Economic Nationalism

Although *Dred Scott*'s federalism contribution may rest on the disunion it came to symbolize, the Civil War ended any ongoing threats of nullification or outright secession.[74] *Texas v. White*, a Chase Court (1864–1873) ruling, supplied a judicial endorsement of the message. At issue was whether Texas could reclaim bonds that the United States agreed to pay as compensation to settle boundary issues relating to Texas's admission into the Union in 1850, even though Texas seceded in 1861. The justices responded by clarifying the nature of the Union principally as a political community comprised of states. As Chief Justice Salmon P. Chase's majority opinion explained,

> The Union of the States [was] confirmed and strengthened by the necessities of war, and received definite form and character and sanction from the Articles of Confederation. By these, the Union was solemnly declared to "be perpetual." And when these Articles were found to be inadequate to the exigencies of the country, the Constitution was ordained "to form a more perfect Union." . . . But the perpetuity and indissolubility of the Union by no means implies the loss of distinct and individual existence, or of the right of self-government, by the States. Under the Articles of Confederation, each State retained its sovereignty, freedom, and independence, and every power, jurisdiction, and right not expressly delegated to the United States. Under the Constitution, though the powers of the States were much restricted, still all powers not delegated to the United States nor prohibited to the States, are reserved to the States respectively, or to the people. . . . [It is therefore reasonable to think that] the preservation of the States, and the maintenance of their governments, are as much within the design and care of the Consti-

tution as the preservation of the Union and the maintenance of the National government.[75]

Texas could reclaim the bonds because its status as a state was never destroyed in a Union that is perpetual. So, Chase concluded, "the Constitution, in all its provisions, looks to an indestructible Union composed of indestructible states." *Texas* openly ratified President Lincoln's view of American constitutionalism (that secession was a nullity because the states never left the Union) and, in doing so, reinforced the basic tenets of dual federalism theory.[76]

Settling vexing constitutional issues of postsecession admission of states and discovering the nature of emancipated slave political liberty allowed courts to sort out Reconstruction's federalism implications. Up through 1875 federal courts received additional jurisdictional and removal powers to review habeas corpus petitions involving violation of national laws that might otherwise be heard in state courts with local biases. They also were asked by the legislature to adjudicate a rising number of civil rights transgressions and prosecutions. Further, Congress reconfigured federal court organization by changing the judiciary's geographical circuit boundaries and increasing the size of the Supreme Court, mainly to give federal courts the tools they needed to mute southern influence and to handle the pressures of Supreme Court justices riding circuit.[77] These congressional actions complemented new constitutional law protections in the Civil War Amendments and other key civil rights laws.

Reconstruction witnessed a bevy of Republican-led initiatives that altered the constitutional landscape and augmented federal court power. Longtime opponents of slavery, mainly northern political elites of the 39th Congress, quickly realized in light of these developments that the Union victory had spawned a rare moment in time to write their preferences into law.[78] At the same time, there was a rapid proliferation of discriminatory black codes in many southern states after Robert E. Lee's surrender at Appomattox. So, between 1865 and 1875, Congress tried to strike an acceptable political balance between maintaining federal control, allowing ex-Confederate states back into the Union, and enlarging the civil rights and liberties of emancipated slaves. The latter objective was the focus of three key Civil War Amendments and a slew of key civil rights enforcement statutes. The Thirteenth and Fifteenth Amendments abolished slavery and put into place antidiscriminatory safeguards in securing equal voting rights. The Fourteenth Amendment offered the promise of achieving three key personal liberties by constraining state action in Section 1, including a guaranty of citizen privileges and immunities; due process rights relative to life, liberty, or property interests;

and antidiscrimination proscriptions requiring equal protection of the laws. The Fourteenth Amendment's Section 5 also gave Congress wide latitude to "enforce by appropriate legislation" the Section 1 proscriptions. Enforcement was bolstered by several civil rights statutes.[79]

Then and now the amendment's textual ambiguity remains an open invitation for the legislature or judiciary to extend its protections beyond the initial goal of strengthening ex-slave civil rights and liberties. Although historians, lawyers, and judges have long wrestled with the amendment's historical significance, there is consensus that it did not immediately change the way state judges interpreted their own police powers. In that sense the amendment did not spell major change for its judicial interpreters, at least in the short term. Nonetheless, the increasing salience of the Supreme Court's precedents became apparent as they fashioned the operative rules for federalism judicial interpretations in the industrial post–Civil War period.[80] At least two strands of constitutional interpretation assume special relevance in appreciating the Fourteenth Amendment's pivotal effect on federalism principles over time.

The first involves the judicial supervision of state action and racial discrimination politics. The second relates to judicial review of the exercise of state police powers and its effect on commercial rights during an era of growing laissez-faire capitalism and centralization, as shaped by Reconstruction politics, the Industrial Revolution, and the Progressive Age of Reform. Whereas state and lower federal courts after 1868 began to struggle with the amendment in some social justice cases of segregation, interracial marriage, and political voting rights, the Supreme Court's post-Reconstruction jurisprudence retooled federalism principles in both areas, beginning with the *Slaughterhouse Cases*.[81]

At issue was a Louisiana law granting to a corporation a twenty-five-year exclusive right to maintain a slaughterhouse in a centralized location in the Crescent City. Under the franchise the corporation built the abattoir and leased out its use for a fee to white New Orleans butchers who wanted to process their meat products for consumption. For the Louisiana assembly, the measure politically effectuated sanitation reform; the law became a priority because the city had a long history of neglect and unregulated disposal of animal waste products that increasingly put public health at risk. The aggrieved butchers thought differently, arguing the state law compromised property and labor rights as defined by Section 1 of the Fourteenth Amendment. The differences of opinion raised a basic federalism question: Did the Fourteenth Amendment give the butchers the freedom to ply their trade by stopping Louisiana from using its police powers to regulate slaughterhouses in the public interest of promoting citizen health?[82]

The Court did not think so. By a one-vote margin the justices upheld Louisiana's use of its police powers. Speaking for five justices, Samuel F. Miller reasoned the public interest regulation merely confined carcass disposal to one centralized location, thereby affecting only the manner in which livestock was butchered; the basic right to engage in the trade was left alone. Exercising the state's police power, he continued, is not limited by the Fourteenth Amendment's text because its privileges and immunities do not identically protect United States and state citizens. Only U.S. citizens are sheltered against state action as the federal Constitution applies to nationally derived freedoms, such as a citizen's right to assemble peaceably, to petition the government, or to petition for a writ of habeas corpus. Insisting, as the butchers did, that property or labor freedoms must be respected as federal safeguards was not credible. If such freedoms were in play at all, the butchers must sue for their legal recognition in state courts as state citizens. To hold otherwise would wrongfully permit Congress to usurp state policy or to transform the Court into a "perpetual censor upon legislation of the States on the civil rights of their own citizens," thereby "radically chang[ing] the whole theory of the relations of the State and Federal governments to each other and of both these governments to the people." The Court summarily dismissed the butchers' due process argument as well, noting that the rights they were asking for had never been known to be "a deprivation of property within the meaning of that provision." Justice Miller was also unmoved by the butchers' claims of discrimination, strongly asserting in dicta that only bigoted state laws totally directed at "negroes as a class, or on account of their race," were actionable equal protection grievances.[83]

Justice Stephen Field's lead dissent argued in vain that corporate elites were bestowed with special monopolistic privileges by legislative fiat. He objected to the creation of a constitutional distinction between national and state citizenship rights. In drawing extra meaning from Article IV, Section 2 and other precedents, he argued the Fourteenth Amendment broadly encompassed fundamental liberties like the butchers' right "to pursue a lawful employment in a lawful manner without regulatory interference."[84] Although Justice Miller's *Slaughterhouse* reasoning finds support as a matter of political history and constitutional interpretation, court watchers tend to be more critical, arguing that he reduced the guaranty of equal protection to insignificance.[85] Accordingly, critics similarly assert that with few exceptions[86] the Supreme Court constricted the Fourteenth Amendment's substantive meaning in a series of cases after *Slaughterhouse*. With *United States v. Cruikshank* the Court interpreted the 1870 Enforcement Act as a nullity, excusing the harm white defendants violently inflicted on blacks at a Colfax, Louisiana, courthouse during a political rally. In *United States v. Harris* federal prosecutions under the 1871 Ku Klux Klan Act were declared unconstitutional, thus undermining the legislation's purpose of stopping private conspiracies from interfering with black civil rights.[87] Another precedent from Chief Justice Morrison Waite's Court (1874–1888), the *Civil Rights Cases*, drained Congress's Section 5 (of the Fourteenth Amendment) power to penalize discriminatory state action.[88]

Specifically, *Civil Rights* invalidated the Civil Rights Act of 1875, a federal law outlawing discrimination in public accommodations. Justice Joseph P. Bradley's majority opinion ruled the Fourteenth Amendment only protects against "State action of a particular character." Consequently, it did not apply to punishing "individual invasion[s] of individual rights [which are not within] the subject matter of the amendment." Section 5, the Court reasoned, delegates to Congress the limited authority "to adopt appropriate legislation for correcting the effects of such prohibited State laws and State acts." Although Congress may create a law that "in advance . . . meet[s] the exigency when it arises," the legislation's purpose "should be adapted to the mischief and wrong which the amendment was intended to provide against; and that is, State laws, or State action of some kind, adverse to the rights of the citizen secured by the amendment." Corrective legislation, which did not include the 1875 Civil Rights Act, said the Court, "may be necessary and proper for counteracting such laws as the States may adopt or enforce, and which, by the [Fourteenth] amendment, they are prohibited from making or enforcing."[89]

Civil Rights unmistakably undercut efforts by federal officials to enforce civil rights in the critical area of private discrimination. Some commentators nonetheless argue the Waite Court justices behaved as political centrists who shared the Republican ideology of giving to African Americans a body of rights equal to that white "free laborers" enjoyed under the state neglect doctrine (allowing federal officials to enforce some property, contract, and physical security rights instead of completely denying them).[90] Still, by embracing the state action concept the Supreme Court accomplished conflicting goals: it constructed common law designed to end state-sponsored discrimination while simultaneously affording private entities multiple opportunities to evade the law and abuse civil rights without fear of judicial sanction. On top of that, the *Civil Rights Cases* greatly cabins congressional power by requiring that the legislation's validity turn on whether it meets a judicially imposed and elevated standard of judicial scrutiny. By forcing Congress to write legislation to correct specific state law violations, the Waite Court engaged in a variation of contemporary clear statement analysis (discussed generally in the next chapter), a legal principle used in statutory cases to lessen federal interference with state autonomy. The legal standard set by the *Civil Rights Cases* also infers that the enactment of "general" legislation, or corrective laws that are not specific enough, may invite Tenth Amendment challenges that further weaken federal civil rights enforcement.[91]

Such cases record the way the justices manipulate legal doctrine to achieve federalism ends. They register as well the vagaries of breathing life into the race-based applications of the Fourteenth Amendment that are only destined to "unfold on a case-by-case basis through what was doubtless an evolutionary process mediated by political and institutional factors."[92] Political scientist Howard Gillman counts among those influences President Ulysses Grant's reluctance to continue civil rights enforcement by 1873, the disintegration of Freedmen's Aid Societies and increased racism in the North, the president's delivery of patronage appointments to select southern Democrats, and the pardons of convicted Klansmen. By the mid-1880s the verve for reconstructing freedmen's political and civil rights was sharply diminished, only to be replaced by another legal movement in federalism.[93] Justice Miller's *Slaughterhouse* "race theory interpretation," which limited the Fourteenth Amendment to cases involving African Americans and the nonrecognition of other fundamental rights for fear of disturbing the traditional balance of federal power, began to yield to more permissive renditions of economic freedom favoring national commercial interests, an agenda item of growing salience to the Republican Party.[94]

The growth of federal court influence, brought on by Congress's legislative decisions to remove more criminal and civil cases from state courts in certain cases, was matched by a steady diet of judicial appointments controlled by Republican presidents and the Senate from 1875 to 1891. That trend ran counter to the rise of a grassroots progressive movement that was spearheaded by disaffected groups of farmers, labor organizations, industrial workers, urban consumers, and social reformers pressing state legislatures and courts to regulate the abuses of big businesses. In response, and often at the behest of corporate interests seeking business-friendly outcomes, federal courts frequently reviewed disputes challenging the regulation of railroad and utility rates, out-of-state insurance contracts, tariff protections, antitrust laws, internal improvements, and monetary policies. Notably, this coincided with the passage of the Evarts Act of 1891, key legislation that added a layer of middle-tier appellate circuit courts to the federal judiciary. Its enactment signaled an end to circuit riding and helped ease the pressures of a burgeoning Supreme Court caseload, further reducing localized influences on the high court and facilitating its national institutionalization.[95] As judicial review of the constitutionality of state economic and interstate commerce regulation ticked upward, so did the opportunities for federal court monitoring.

Up to the beginning of the twentieth century, the Supreme Court struck down state and federal laws at a level far outpacing any previous judicial activity from the antebellum period. Between 1888 and 1918, over seven hundred Fourteenth Amendment cases were litigated, a sharp increase from the preceding fifteen-year period. In the two decades before 1900, the Supreme Court also struck down in whole or in part state laws interfering with the federal commerce clause in nineteen states. This judicial behavior put the high court in a position to almost single-handedly develop the national marketplace through its commerce clause adjudications.[96] At first the justices were tolerant of legislative decisions interfering with private property rights so long as the regulation was in the public interest. In *Munn v. Illinois* an Illinois law setting prices for grain storage elevators was challenged on the grounds that it was a violation of due process and property rights because grain operators could not freely set prices in the private marketplace. The law's enactment was inspired by the Granger (farmer) labor movement in order to stop exorbitant pricing by a few industry firms. Siding with Illinois, the Court thought that the law was legitimate under the state's police powers because the nature of the property at issue was "clothed with a public interest [and it was] used in a manner to make it of public consequence and affect the community at large." Hence fixing storage rates could be "controlled by the public for the common good," and the grain operators lost. In stressing the validity of state police powers and deemphasizing the Fourteenth Amendment, Chief Justice Waite's majority opinion deferred to the legislature, insisting that any abuse of legislative discretion must be corrected by the political process and not by judicial fiat. Still, the opinion also said that states could not expect to regulate property across state lines, even if it was in the public interest, because in those situations the operation of the federal commerce clause would trump the state's regulation.[97]

In only a few short years, *Munn* would be replaced by its inverse principle and minor premise—namely, that private property interests should receive extra judicial oversight in guarding against overzealous state regulations. In *Chicago, Milwaukee and State Pacific Railway v. Minnesota,* the Fuller Court (1888–1910) rejected a law letting a state commission fix railroad rates without giving the affected companies notice and an opportunity to contest rate decisions or their reasonableness in court. In finding a procedural due process violation that compromised the company's property rights, the justices gave themselves frontline policymaking responsibility to weigh the reasonableness of rates and whether the legislation was in the public interest, a traditional function of state police power. The Fuller Court, with an influx of new judicial appointments favoring corporate interests and railroads, retooled due process and federal law to make both tantamount to a substantive defense of property rights in a series of later cases that, among other things, disallowed a national income tax, permitted corporations to sue as "persons" under the Fourteenth Amendment, condoned the use of injunctions to stop labor disputes, and disrupted antitrust legislation that sought to achieve competitive fairness in the marketplace.[98]

The outer limit of conservative judicial activism in the period is conventionally associated with *Lochner v. New York*. New York used a health measure to protect bakery employees from the harm of ingesting flour dust in unventilated work spaces by setting the maximum hours they could work. The Supreme Court, led by Justice Rufus Peckham, construed the law to be a breach of a liberty of contract (between the employer and employee) that is part of due process. Peckham's logic drew from *Allgeyer v. Louisiana*, an earlier precedent establishing that

> the "liberty" [in the Fourteenth Amendment] . . . is deemed to embrace the right of the citizen to be free in the employment of all his faculties; to be free to use them in all lawful ways; to live and work where he will; to earn his livelihood by any lawful calling; to pursue any livelihood or avocation; and for that purpose to enter into all contracts which may be proper, necessary, and essential to his carrying out to a successful resolution the purposes above mentioned.[99]

Lochner led to universal condemnation rooted in accusations of judicial activism, a point reinforced by Justice Oliver W. Holmes's famous dissent castigating the Court. Holmes wrote that the "Fourteenth Amendment does not enact Mr. Herbert Spencer's *Social Statics* [because] . . . a constitution is not intended to embody a particular economic theory," a position reiterating the view that laissez-faire was creatively etched into constitutional law. The due process clause now was enveloped in the philosophical tradition of Spencer: only nongovernmental interference with economic transactions, with the freedom of individuals to bargain equally with each other in the marketplace, that showed little concern about equitably redistributing available resources would be tolerated by the courts.[100]

Whereas *Lochner* contributed to developing the doctrine of substantive due process that drew strength from both the Fourteenth and Fifth Amendments, the precedent merely complemented other interpretative devices that the Supreme Court developed to augment its own authority and to give the lower federal courts a freer hand to promote industrial capitalism. The reach of several judicial doctrines was extended to limit state regulatory powers, including using due process to incorporate the Fifth Amendment's takings clause and applying it against state actions; letting corporations be protected against illegal Fourth Amendment searches and seizures; using the preemption doctrine to allow Congress instead of the states to control a commercial area of regulation; interpreting the Eleventh Amendment so as to diminish its force as a bar to federal lawsuits directed against state officers; and revamping federal jurisdictional and procedural laws to increase lower federal court review of federal economic cases and state-based challenges. In sum, the inculcation of laissez-faire, built on dual federalism principles, creative interpretations of federal law, and celebrating "individualism as a moral and economic ideal," had become "a product of the courts."[101]

The Rise of the Democratic Welfare State through Cooperative Federalism

At the turn of the twentieth century, dual federalism was still intact, and the Supreme Court regularly monitored state and federal legislation in accordance with that theory. Yet rapid expansion westward, population increases, new technological innovations, increasing urbanization, and the gradual transition in the post–Civil War political economy from an agrarian to an industrialized state all combined to alter the size and scope of national power over business, transportation, interstate commerce, and occasionally social affairs. Nationalism was increased during the Progressive Era with the ratification of the Sixteenth and Seventeenth Amendments, which respectively instituted the federal income tax and replaced the role that state legislatures played in electing U.S. senators with direct popular election. Having an independent and regular source of revenue allowed legislators to govern national constituencies; similarly, direct elections freed Congress from the growing perception that the Senate was beholden to corporate interests, beset with political corruption, and controlled by the rule of political parties. Moreover, the creation of the Interstate Commerce Commission in 1887 allowed the federal government more regulatory power over commercial transactions.[102]

Still, while federal courts at times reigned in regulatory initiatives correlated to the dynamics of a nation in flux, state governments managed their internal affairs through a reasonable exercise of police powers, particularly if the lawmaking was in the public interest and did not blatantly cross state lines. Judges, ever mindful of republicanism ideology, deciphered the founding document and statutes by differentiating between the "will of the law and the will of the judge." Despite the increasing availability of substantive due process, up until the 1930s the judiciary arguably evidenced more of a declaratory role than a lawmaking one—this meant that legal principles were developed through the exercise of a guardian form of essentialist review, an orthodoxy built on static conceptions of what constitutional text means in light of fluctuating social conditions.[103] That judicial commitment, regardless, was tested and ultimately expressed by Supreme Court rulings, such as *Lochner v. New York* and *Munn v. Illinois*, which struggled to identify the constitutional point of departure at which the public interest outweighed the affirmation of private rights.

Yet the relative balance that judiciaries fostered among peripheral governments was strained by the onset and repercussions of World Wars I and II and a U.S. economic crisis of the first magnitude, the 1929 stock market crash and ensuing Great Depression. The rise of communism and fascism in central Europe and the threats they posed to U.S. national security, in conjunction with the domestic dysfunction caused by declining prices, rising bank failures, pervasive mortgage foreclosures, increasing unemployment, and growing poverty, in time worked to stultify the states and paralyze the nation. In the midst of these changes the era of economic nationalism began to dissipate with the emergence of congressional "statutorification," or the creation of federal statutes and related bureaucratic structures that led to the development of a new administrative welfare state during the 1930s New Deal.[104] As the Supreme Court's docket moved away from cases testing the restrictions of laissez-faire economics and business protectionism, the justices became immersed in new regulatory challenges that centered on the scope of congressional commerce power, the limits (if any) placed on the exercise of federal authority by the Tenth Amendment, and whether Congress appropriately delegated its lawmaking powers to federal agencies. Doctrinally this meant that judges had to detach themselves from a priori assumptions governing separation of powers (with strict departmentalism in place to avoid undue concentration of powers in one branch) and federalism (cabining federal powers through express delegation while respecting reserved state powers) analyses. Untangling this line of jurisprudence raised supplementary intergovernmental concerns about whether the Supreme Court would use its discretion to place new restraints on the exercise of congressional authority or, concomitantly, negate its own jurisdiction while actively policing federalism boundaries.[105]

The instability and uncertainties of the nascent political regime led to a political and judicial response that ushered in a different era of cooperative (instead of dual) federalism. As its name implies, its orientation is more fluid and sharing, so the lines of state-federal collaboration are less rigid and more decentralized.[106] Much of the synergy resulted from the infusion of federal grant-in-aid monies, borne out of the relief and reform exigencies of the times. Beginning in the 1930s and extending to the 1960s, there were large increases in state aid to localities, often on a conditional basis: grant monies had to be spent for a specific legislative purpose or in accordance with a predetermined allocation or formula, and the like. The same was true for federal aid, at least in terms of its exponential growth, so much so that political scientist David Walker characterizes its availability as both "a turning point in the history of U.S. intergovernmental relations" and a linchpin of centralizing initiatives driven by the requirements of "relief, reform, and economic recovery and then . . . defense and postwar rehabilitation."[107]

But Walker also acknowledges that the "basic shift in the development of American federalism would not have persisted [until the 1960s] without judicial sanction." Legal historian G. Edward White adds that a changing international order, in combination with traditional objections disfavoring the institutionalization of a new agency form (with its emphasis on specialization and a melding of legislative, executive, and judicial functions), facilitated the need for greater judicial supervision.[108] Courts had transformed their function to gauge solely when it was appropriate to give the executive full constitutional authority to defend the nation while determining when it was best to check the arbitrary exercise of agency power. Just as significantly, after the New Deal and by the end of World War II, the Supreme Court was prepared to extend national power beyond the economic realm to use, progressively, the due process and equal protection clauses of the federal Constitution as the underpinning for protecting civil rights and liberties against state action in social legislation cases. While New Deal politics, including Franklin D. Roosevelt's much maligned "court packing plan" (Roosevelt's proposal to fill the bench with New Deal supporters) and the Supreme Court's so-called switch in time that saved nine (a change in membership supporting the New Deal) routinely are cited as the impetus behind the changes in constitutional doctrine, critics downplay their significance as causal elements explaining the rise of the new order.[109] Nevertheless, the doctrinal shift did occur and four cases (*Steward Machine Company v. Davis, United States v. Darby, Wickard v. Filburn,* and *Palko v. Connecticut*) contributed to the passing of dual federalism and thus exemplify some of the commercial and personal liberty implications of cooperative federalism.

The political rationale and context supporting centralization, and surrounding *Steward Machine,* aid in situating the Supreme Court's initial response to the unprecedented action taken by President Roosevelt and Congress to bring the country out the Depression. During President Herbert Hoover's administration, the federal government, working through the Department of Commerce, the Federal Trade Commission, and the Department of Justice, encouraged competing businesses to promote their interests in collaborative, voluntary trade associations. The associations fostered a network between government, business, and labor. Soon after Roosevelt's inauguration the White House and Congress revised the model to give the federal government a much more proactive role in those areas, even though states traditionally functioned well to provide general welfare initiatives. A variety of legislation, including the National Industrial Recovery Act, the Agricultural Adjustment Act, and the National Labor Relations Act, to name only a few, displayed an official commitment to rely less on corporations as frontline actors and more on administrative agencies to spearhead economic recovery.[110]

The Social Security Act of 1935 was part of this resourcefulness. With input from the Social Security Administration, it partnered the states with the federal government to supply pension benefits and unemployment compensation to elderly and out-of-work citizens. Financing the latter part of the program was partially accomplished by a federal excise tax levied on employers, but with some tax credit relief afforded to states having their own unemployment compensation system. The tax was challenged in *Steward Machine* on Fifth Amendment grounds; plus it was labeled as a coercive and unlawful encroachment on powers reserved to state governments under the Tenth Amendment. Justice Benjamin Cardozo's response, in a 5–4 ruling, upheld the tax. In turning aside these objections, Cardozo interpreted Congress's Article I power to tax and spend broadly, finding as well no proof behind the claim that the program's "dominant end and aim is to drive the state legislatures under the whip of economic pressure into the enactment of unemployment compensation laws at the bidding of the central government." Instead, he reasoned, there is little federal coercion because "the Social Security Act is an attempt to find a method by which all these [federal and state] public agencies may work together to a common end." As a gentle nudge instead of a sledge hammering, the justices signaled that Congress is fully vested to use its taxing powers to spend in the general welfare—a point Cardozo reinforced by citing statistics presented in the government's brief showing that the law was a much-needed fix to correct a growing national emergency that also gripped the states. Notably, in the separate dissents recorded by Justices James McReynolds, George Sutherland (joined by Willis Van Devanter), and Pierce Butler, the act was compulsory in dictating how the states administered their own unemployment compensation schemes, in contravention to the Tenth Amendment or the principles of dual sovereignty established by *Texas v. White* (as McReynolds stressed).[111]

The dissents were in line with the previous views the justices expressed collectively as the so-called four horsemen of (conservative) reaction, a key bloc largely responsible for obstructing the New Deal in cases like *Panama Refining Company v. Ryan*, *Schechter Poultry Corporation v. United States*, *United States v. Butler*, and *Carter v. Carter Coal Company*, which wholly or partially invalidated, on a mixture of anti-delegation, commerce clause, or Tenth Amendment grounds, the National Industrial Recovery Act, the Agricultural Adjustment Act, and the Bituminous Coal Act. But by the time *United States v. Darby* and *Wickard v. Filburn* were delivered, the Court's composition had changed with new Roosevelt appointments. Several progressive-minded justices, among them Hugo Black, Stanley Reed, Felix Frankfurter, and William O. Douglas, coalesced on the bench to dismantle incrementally the outgoing regime's jurisprudence.[112] While both are commerce clause cases, their distinctive contributions make *Darby* and *Wickard* significant federalism decisions that deepened the federal government's involvement in national marketplace regulation.

Through the Fair Labor Standards Act of 1938, Congress set the minimum wages and maximum hours of workers toiling to manufacture products and then ship them across state lines. Part of the legislative goal, backed by criminal sanctions and a mandatory record-keeping process, was to cultivate the free commercial flow of goods by encouraging companies to produce them in optimal, and not subpar, labor conditions. A Georgia lumber company that failed to comply with the law challenged the criminal indictment that the federal government used as a basis for prosecution. *Hammer v. Dagenhart*, which declared the national legislature did not have constitutional license to exclude child labor merchandise from interstate commerce, appeared to immunize the local manufacture of goods under the commerce power as well—so the lower court quashed the indictment. But in a unanimous decision by Justice Harlan Fiske Stone, in *Darby* the Supreme Court reversed.[113]

Drawing heavily on the Marshall Court's *Gibbons v. Ogden* and *McCulloch v. Maryland* as controlling precedents, Stone confirmed that Congress has full discretion to "exclude from the commerce articles whose use in the states for which they are destined it may conceive to be injurious to the public health, morals or welfare, even though the state has not sought to regulate their use." Indigenous lumber production and its interstate distribution are within the reach of Congress, for

> the power of Congress over interstate commerce is not confined to the regulation of commerce among the states. It extends to those activities intrastate which so affect interstate commerce or the exercise of the power of Congress over it as to make regulation of them appropriate means to the attainment of a legitimate end, the exercise of the granted power of Congress to regulate interstate commerce.[114]

The Tenth Amendment, he continued, was not an impediment either because it was not construed to be an independent check on national power. In fact, it was merely "a truism" asserting "all is retained which has not been surrendered." As it stood for nothing more than being "declaratory of the relationship between the national and state governments," it was innocuous: historically its purpose was only "to allay fears that the new national government might seek to exercise powers not granted, and that the states might not be able to exercise fully their reserved powers." Accordingly, *Hammer* was overruled, the act was sustained, and all the pre-*Darby* categorical formalistic interpretations that were in play only to insulate states from the exercise of congressional commerce power were largely swept away.[115]

The following year, in *Wickard v. Filburn*, the Supreme Court unanimously turned back an Ohio wheat farmer's claim that Congress could not assess a financial penalty for exceeding a national production quota in violation of the Agricultural Adjustment Act of 1938. The quota was in place to raise wheat prices by preventing an oversupply that would drive them down. The farmer argued that the wheat he harvested over quota was locally done; therefore it was intrastate production activity and immune from federal regulation. For Justice Robert Jackson, it did not matter if it was local: "That [the farmer's] own contribution to the demand for wheat may be trivial by itself is not enough to remove him from the scope of federal regulation where, as here, his contribution, taken together with that of many others similarly situated, is far from trivial." In other words, "even if [the farmer's] activity be local, and though it may not be regarded as commerce, it may still, whatever its nature, be reached by Congress if it exerts a substantial economic effect on interstate commerce, and this irrespective of whether such effect is what might at some earlier time have been defined as 'direct' or 'indirect.'" Jackson concluded by saying there was "no doubt that Congress may properly have considered that wheat consumed on the farm where grown, if wholly outside the scheme of regulation, would have a substantial effect in defeating and obstructing its purpose to stimulate trade therein at increased prices." These statements created *Wickard*'s aggregation principle, thus giving the legislature a free hand to control all types of economic activities under the commerce clause. In addition to helping to bury dual federalism and its formalistic approach to constitutional interpretation, *Wickard* ushered in a new paradigm of judicial deference to Congress in commerce clause, political economy cases.[116]

Nationally, the effect of *Steward Machine*, *Darby*, and *Wickard* was to let the political process, instead of the federal judiciary, dictate the terms of commercial progress and related interstate activities. The lack of judicial presence had an opposite result on the subnational level, since states had a freer hand with the infusion of federally derived grant monies to use their police powers to control internal affairs, including education, health care, public safety, and local utilities or related public services.[117] The federal judicial abandonment of economic protectionism, in conjunction with the Supreme Court's approval of the centralization accompanying the new democratic welfare state, coincided with yet again another doctrinal shift in constitutional law during the new era of cooperative federalism:

the nationalization of the federal Bill of Rights through the doctrine of selective incorporation under the Fourteenth Amendment.

The leading case is *Palko v. Connecticut*. Prior to *Palko*, the Marshall Court, under *Barron v. Baltimore*, refused to apply specific federal civil rights and liberties against state action. Thirty-five years later the Fourteenth Amendment's ratification, with its explicit prohibition that "no State shall" deprive citizens of due process, helped change that interpretative calculus. As the nineteenth century drew to a close and up until 1937, the justices remained divided about what process is due, insofar as absorbing Bill of Rights guarantees into the amendment and applying them against the states. In fact, they only recognized a few exceptions to the anti-incorporation principle set in *Barron*—and those involved the Fifth Amendment's takings clause, the Sixth Amendment's right to counsel and fair trial protections, and the First Amendment's free speech and press provisions.[118]

Yet, in *Palko*, a case in which a convicted cop killer argued that he was placed in double jeopardy when Connecticut prosecutors used state law to retry him on his offenses so he could face the death penalty instead of a life sentence, the Supreme Court established a new pro-incorporation standard. Although the Court ruled against the defendant, Justice Benjamin Cardozo's majority opinion stated there were certain fundamental rights, which did not include the defendant's purported Fifth Amendment right, that deserved due process recognition and therefore constituted bars against unconstitutional state actions. To be judicially acknowledged, Cardozo reasoned, such rights were "implicit in the concept of ordered liberty, and thus, through the Fourteenth Amendment, become valid as against the states." He inferred that it would be up to the Court to determine, through a "process of absorption," which liberties qualified and could be ranked "as fundamental." Transgressions against fundamental rights, in the Court's mind, had to "violate a 'principle of justice so rooted in the traditions and conscience of our people.'" With these words the Supreme Court put in motion the preferred freedoms doctrine, a legal standard empowering the justices to determine, on an ad hoc basis, which specific guarantees of the federal Bill of Rights could be selected for incorporation and made actionable against the states as part of Fourteenth Amendment due process.[119]

The trajectory of federalism opinions from the Supreme Court was never straight or consistent from the founding to the New Deal period. Consequently, as a political argument, it is an oversimplification to view the Court's work product as simply favoring centralization or states' rights in one period or another. The previous two sections suggest otherwise. While federalism questions are typically framed by reference to the institutional behavior of the political branches, the Supreme Court supervised the constitutionality of actions by peripheral governments with outcomes that were strongly influenced by the prevailing norms and nuances of the operative political regime. As one scholar put it, "Any notions that the federal principle and judges deal with the former but exert little impact on the latter, are swept aside by the Supreme Court's record,"[120] and that is true from the founding to the New Deal. The next, concluding section likewise surveys Supreme Court decision-making after World War II and up to the 1960s, a time when cooperative federalism politically morphed into new federalism, a distinct phase of intergovernmental behavior that is often associated with conservative states' rights political rhetoric.

THE JUDICIAL ROLE IN NEW FEDERALISM POLITICS

Early in the first term of President Richard Nixon's presidency, "New Federalist Paper No. 1" was circulated to White House insiders for debate. Using the pseudonym "Publius," the real author, Special Assistant to the President William Safire, wrote the white paper as a template for the administration's policy on achieving federalism reform. Therein Publius concedes that the federal government must oversee monetary policy and foreign affairs, as well as superintend additional national areas of regulation, such as "rais[ing] revenues, borrow[ing] money, [or] handl[ing] massive mechanical chores such as mailing Social Security checks." Within their own spheres, states and cities must also ideally "reflect flexibility in administration, respond to local custom and idiosyncrasy, and experiment without being intimidated by the danger of colossal failure." Delimiting sovereign authority in this fashion is fruitful because it fosters political liberty, for "the individual [can] do what he does best by doing what is best for himself."[121]

Yet Publius's perspective was fused with the more somber reflection that post–New Deal centralization has served to "de-humanized government, to separate the citizen from the centers of decisions affecting his life" on the local level. That atomization, he argued, calls for the creation of a new federalism. Doing so overcomes the contradictory demands of dual sovereigns trying to coexist in one polity. Establishing a different kind of governing philosophy is imperative for another reason: it permits ordinary citizens to "regain control" over government through a new order of "national localism." With national localism, the control that is lost will be returned through a corollary principle of "selective decentralization, or a new distribution of administrative power." Conceptually, at least in the Nixon formulation, new federalism thus respects the reality of centralization while simultaneously honoring the citizen's basic choice to administer local affairs without meddlesome federal interference. In this way political participation, individual liberty, and fairness are simultaneously enhanced.[122]

"New Federalist Paper No. 1" offered several illustrations to demonstrate the new federalism's practical operation. The Nixon White House later proposed many of them as legislation designed to implement block grants, revenue sharing, and welfare reform—albeit with only limited success. The initiatives, it was thought, would strengthen democratic government by empowering citizens with the freedom of choice to accept the benefits of national rule (or funding) or not. In this way the needs of the nation and its goals are met by tapping into the energy of state and local action.[123] This dynamic lets the new federalism's purpose be realized, which thus strikes a workable balance between opposites while trying to achieve national goals and decentralization; that is, (1) securing "*both* national unity and local diversity," and (2) safeguarding "*both* individual equality at the national level and individual uniqueness at the local level." While even administrative insiders were confused by the contradictory and confusing nature of the president's domestic policies,[124] at least in theory reconciling the contradictions also bridged the gap between the old and new conceptions of federalism—those ideas are enshrined by framing intent but diminished by the arbitrariness of administrative practices that consume the modern welfare state. Accordingly, Publius concludes that "part of what is 'new' in the new Federalism—is that *'States' rights' have now become rights of first refusal*." In other words, "local authority will now regain the right to meet local needs itself, and gain an additional right to Federal financial help; but it will not regain the right it once held to neglect the needs of its citizens."[125]

Suggesting there is an affirmative right of state sovereigns to limit national authority has always been historically and politically salient in federalism analyses. Still, while Publius insists new federalism's object "is not to wrap liberal principles in conservative clothing, or vice versa," there is little doubt it is routinely cast in a distinct mold of partisanship. Mostly in rhetoric but sometimes in actionable successes or failures, it was the basis of Nixon's governing philosophy and, less so, the point of departure for the devolutionary politics chiefly associated with the Reagan presidency and the 104th Congress (led by Newt Gingrich and the Contract with America platform). That Nixon, Reagan, and subsequent conservatives wavered in their commitment to adopting Nixon's managerial solution to reforming government—as seen by Publius's and later the president's key endorsement of the welfare state, including a rather radical Family Assistance Plan that guaranteed a yearly federal minimum income payment of $1,600 to a family of four—underscores the fact that even conservatives cannot agree on the basic ideological question of establishing limits to the federal government and how far it can properly go in touching the lives of ordinary citizens. On this point, another conservative, under the pseudonym "Cato," published a vitriolic response to "New Federalist Paper No. 1" at the time it came out, mocking the new federalism as actually being a "new nationalism" that, if adopted, would betray the true historic conception of federalism and the founding.[126] As a result, it is not surprising to see that the new federalism's political message was sent and received in most of the liberal or conservative post-Reagan presidencies and that it still resonates today in the Tea Party movement, health-care reform, the 2010 midterm elections, and the presidential contest in 2012. Indeed, the existence and strategic use of such ideological disagreements have always formed a running theme of the old, new, and progressive trends of American federalism politics and policies.

Put differently, new federalism captures an erstwhile policy concern about the proper scope and limits of sovereignty in the American republic—or, in the rhetorical terms used to describe its impact in the 1960s, whether it is politically appropriate in light of centralization to "cease viewing the state governments as separate, sovereign and equal, [or] to view them as dependent, subordinate, and inferior."[127] Yet arguing that it is either a fixed conception of constitutional structure, a pliable instrument of public policy politics, or both only raises the question of what new federalism really is and which political institution is best suited to striking the proper balance between dual sovereigns. That issue was raised in Cato's critique of Publius and in "New Federalist Paper No. 1" by the declaration that "the freedom of the individual requires Federal and judicial *checks on any unfairness* inflicted by local government or private enterprise, and local flexibility on unfairness inflicted by national policies or the letter of Federal law."[128] As in all the relevant federalism eras, what ultimately becomes an unfair and unconstitutional exercise of sovereign power has from the founding remained within the realm of the bench to decide, and that reality informs and colors the perception that the federal courts are using their discretion to act either as neutral umpires or aggressive enforcers of federalism theories, principles, ideas, and restraints. In this sense, in the 1960s as well as in the past, present, and future, "the ambiguous language of the Constitution has welcomed many 'new federalisms.'"[129]

By 1942, arguably there were few constitutionally interpreted rights of first refusal (in the new federalism sense) that the states could look to for judicial relief. The Tenth Amendment had been reduced to a truism, and the Supreme Court gave its blessing to Congress to regulate state affairs with an expansive interpretation of commerce and spending powers. Even so, open questions persisted as to what the Court's position would be in applying federal due process and equal protection rights to areas of domestic lawmaking that traditionally were managed by the states with police powers (i.e., crime, education, and labor policies). A 1938 case, *United States v. Carolene Products Co.*, suggested an answer in its famous Footnote Four. The Court's actual holding—which upheld the constitutionality of regulating the shipment of filled milk under the commerce clause—has been overshadowed by the footnote's obiter dictum, which signaled that the Supreme Court would aggressively protect politically marginalized citizens in trying to secure their fundamental rights when oppressive laws threatened to take them away. While the Court reaffirmed it would give deferential review to Congress in cases involving economic regulation, the footnote strongly implied that more rigorous judicial scrutiny applies in noneconomic, or social legislation, litigation. *Carolene Products* thus established an interpretative "double standard" for Fourteenth Amendment cases. In the process, it foreshadowed the Supreme Court's progressive rulings issued under the leadership of Chief Justice Earl Warren from 1953 to 1969. The Warren Court due process and egalitarian revolutions produced a gamut of political, social, and legal issues that were part of the national political agenda due to a convergence of several political happenings, among them *Brown v. Board of Education*, the Vietnam War, President John F. Kennedy's and Martin Luther King Jr.'s assassinations, Lyndon Johnson's Great Society and the War on Poverty, and the civil rights movement.[130]

The *Brown* decision, which established a judicial mandate to end public school racial segregation under the equal protection clause, in conjunction with Johnson's "creative federalism" under the Great Society program, greatly enhanced the federal government's regulatory presence in local policy areas that previously had not been the subject of aggressive monitoring.[131] Through *Brown*, federal courts became active leaders in dismantling racial discrimination that persisted under state Jim Crow laws, with those judges ultimately issuing integration orders that required forced busing, a tactic designed to help compliance but that wound up producing a political backlash against judges and the Warren Court, particularly in the South. As the Warren Court gelled in its liberal composition in the mid-1960s, in a series of controversial landmark decisions the justices applied the Fourteenth Amendment to state laws addressing free speech and religious freedom; police and prosecutorial crime policies in defining defendants' rights relative to the exclusion of trial evidence, search and seizure, self-incrimination, and the right to counsel; political decisions relating to the apportionment of legislative districts, representation, and voting rights; and personal autonomy and privacy rights. In response, critics linked Warren Court activism to federalism concerns, claiming that the federal government's regulatory growth transformed the states into "objects of federal regulations, rather than independent partners in a system of dual sovereignty."[132]

For the New Federalists, the political climate was conducive to claiming, as the Nixon administration did, that the federal government was spiraling out of control and unduly trampling states' rights. A similar argument was later adopted by Ronald Reagan, but his administration's federalism reform was more directed at taking actions that greatly scaled back government intervention at all levels.[133] As the next chapter explains, the politics underlying the rhetoric and proposals to enact new state-based federalism reforms were the basis for questioning if the Supreme Court ought to use its authority to reverse the trend of centralization in a political process that seemed to offer no protection for the states. Put differently, if the constitutional structure of federalism and its built-in political safeguards fail to help the states remain sovereign and free from national regulation, should the justices step in and use the principles of new federalism to safeguard their rights by imposing limits on congressional or judicial power? As the Supreme Court's composition was altered to reflect the conservative preferences of Presidents Nixon and Reagan, the answer came in the new federalism jurisprudence of the Supreme Court under the leadership of Chief Justice William H. Rehnquist.

NOTES

1. "The Affordable Care Act," White House, 2010, www.whitehouse.gov/healthreform/healthcare-overview#healthcare-menu (accessed June 9, 2011).

2. Dahlia Lithwick, "Lawyers vs. Health Reform: Why the Court Challenges Will Fail," *Newsweek*, April 5, 2010, 25.

3. *State of Florida v. U.S. Department of Health and Human Services*, 648 F.3d 1235 (11th Cir. 2011). See also *State of Florida v. U.S. Department of Health and Human Services*, 780 F. Supp. 2d 1256 (N.D. Fla. 2011); N. C. Aizenman and Amy Goldstein, "Judge Strikes Down Entire New Health-Care Law" *Washington Post* (February 1, 2011).

4. Adam Liptak, "Justices to Hear Health Care Case as Race Heats Up," *New York Times* (November 14, 2011), at www.nytimes.com/2011/11/15/us/supreme-court-to-hear-case-challenging-health-law.html?pagewanted=all (accessed May 6, 2012). See also David G. Savage and Noam N. Levey, "Federal Appeals Court Strikes Down Insurance Mandate," *L.A. Times* (August 12, 2011).

5. Independent Women's Forum, 2011, "Health Care Lawsuits," www.healthcarelawsuits.org (accessed August 13, 2011); ACA Litigation Blog, August 12, 2011, http://acalitigationblog.blogspot.com (accessed August 13, 2011).

6. David G. Savage, "Supreme Court Refuses to Skip Lower Courts on Healthcare Reform Law," *L.A. Times*, April 25, 2011; Steve Chapman, "Healthy

Constitutional Commerce," *Akron Beacon Journal*, April 17, 2011; Kevin Sack, "Health Suits Stir Concerns on Court Partisanship," *New York Times*, December 16, 2010, A26.

7. Richard A. Epstein, "Obama's Constitution: The Passive Virtues Writ Large," *Constitutional Commentary* 26 (Spring 2010): 183.

8. Michael B. Rappaport, "The Obama Administration, Fundamental Institutional Change, and the Constitutional Lawmaking System," *Constitutional Commentary* 26 (Spring 2010): 216; John Dinan and Shama Gamkhar, "The State of American Federalism, 2008–2009: The Presidential Election, the Economic Downturn, and the Consequences for Federalism," *Publius: The Journal of Federalism* 39, no. 3 (2009): 378.

9. Michael D. Tanner, "Bad Medicine: A Guide to the Real Costs and Consequences of the New Health Care Law (White Paper)" (Washington, DC: Cato Institute, 2010); Paul D. Clement et al., "The Roberts Court and Federalism," *New York University Journal of Law and Liberty* 4 (2009): 357.

10. Pew Center on the States, *State of the States 2010: How the Recession Might Change States* (Washington, DC: Pew Center on the States, 2010), www.pewstates.org/uploadedFiles/PCS_Assets/2010/2010_State%20of%20the%20States_web.pdf (accessed October 7, 2010); John Dinan, "The State of American Federalism, 2007–2008: Resurgent State Influence in the National Policy Process and Continued State Policy Innovation," *Publius: The Journal of Federalism* 38, no. 3 (2008): 381–415; Tim Conlan and John Dinan, "Federalism, the Bush Administration, and the Transformation of American Conservatism," *Publius: The Journal of Federalism* 37, no. 3 (2007): 279–303.

11. Robert A. Shapiro, "Not Old or Borrowed: The Truly New Blue Federalism," *Harvard Law and Policy Review* 3 (Winter 2009): 33–57.

12. 347 U.S. 483.

13. Shapiro, "Not Old or Borrowed," 34.

14. Shapiro, "Not Old or Borrowed," 34. See also Andrew P. Napolitano, *The Constitution in Exile: How the Federal Government Has Seized Power by Rewriting the Supreme Law of the Land* (Nashville, TN: Nelson Current, 2006).

15. Shapiro, "Not Old or Borrowed," 35.

16. Michael Hail and Stephen Lange, "Federalism and Representation in the Theory of the Founding Fathers: A Comparative Study of U.S. and Canadian Constitutional Thought," *Publius: The Journal of Federalism* 40, no. 3 (2010): 366, 371; Alison L. LaCroix, *The Ideological Origins of American Federalism* (Cambridge, MA: Harvard University Press, 2010).

17. Jack N. Rakove, *Original Meanings: Politics and Ideas in the Making of the Constitution* (New York: Vintage Books, 1996), 25–26, 44; Edward A. Purcell Jr., *Originalism, Federalism, and the American Constitutional Enterprise: A Historical Inquiry* (New Haven, CT: Yale University Press, 2007), 22.

18. Hail and Lange, "Federalism and Representation in the Theory of the Founding Fathers," 360, 370. See also Raoul Berger, *Federalism: The Founders' Design* (Norman: University of Oklahoma Press, 1987), 46.

19. Paul A. Rahe, *Republics Ancient and Modern: Classical Republicanism and the American Revolution* (Chapel Hill: University of North Carolina Press, 1992), 579. See also Samuel H. Beer, "Federalism, Nationalism, and Democracy in America,"

American Political Science Review 72, no. 1 (1978): 12–15; Hail and Lange, "Federalism and Representation in the Theory of the Founding Fathers," 372; and David Brian Robertson, "Madison's Opponents and Constitutional Design," *American Political Science Review* 99, no. 2 (2005): 226. For analyses of whether the framers, as elites, were motivated by their own economic self-interests, see Charles A. Beard, *An Economic Interpretation of the Constitution of the United States* (New York: Macmillan Co., 1913); Jack C. Heckelman and Keith L. Dougherty, "An Economic Interpretation of the Constitutional Convention Revisited," *Journal of Economic History* 67, no. 4 (2007): 829–48; and Robert McGuire, *To Form a More Perfect Union: A New Economic Interpretation of the United States Constitution* (New York: Oxford University Press, 2003).

20. James Madison, "Vices of the Political System of the United States, April 1787," in *Selected Writings of James Madison*, ed. Ralph Ketcham, American Heritage Series (Indianapolis: Hackett Publishing Company, 2006), 39.

21. Richard K. Matthews, *If Men Were Angels: James Madison and the Heartless Empire of Reason* (Lawrence: University Press of Kansas, 1995), 176. See also Rakove, *Original Meanings*, 46–49; David M. O'Brien, "The Framer's Muse on Republicanism, the Supreme Court, and Pragmatic Constitutional Interpretivism," *Review of Politics* 53, no. 2 (1991): 262–63, 258.

22. Rahe, *Republics Ancient and Modern*, 588–90 and 596; Beer, "Federalism, Nationalism, and Democracy in America," 13. See also James Madison, "The Union as a Safeguard against Faction: *Federalist* No. 10 [1787]," in Ketcham, *Selected Writings of James Madison*, 83–89.

23. James Madison, "Letter to George Washington, April 16, 1787," in Ketcham, *Selected Writings of James Madison*, 42; James Madison, "Explanation of Checks and Balances Concluded: *Federalist* No. 51, February 6, 1788," in Ketcham, *Selected Writings of James Madison*, 121. See also Martin Diamond, "*The Federalist* on Federalism: 'Neither a National nor a Federal Constitution, but a Composition of Both,'" in *Federalism: A Nation of States*, ed. Kermit L. Hall, United States Constitutional and Legal History Series (New York: Garland Publishing, 1987), 95; Rakove, *Original Meanings*, 51.

24. LaCroix, *The Ideological Origins of Federalism*, 148–49.

25. James Madison, "Letter from James Madison to Thomas Jefferson (March 18, 1787)," in *The Writings of James Madison: Comprising His Public Papers and His Private Correspondence, Including Numerous Letters and Documents Now for the First Time Printed*, Vol. 2: *1793–1787* (New York: G. P. Putnam's Sons, 1901): 324, 326. See also Charles F. Hobson, "The Negative on State Law: James Madison, the Constitution, and the Crisis of Republican Government," *William & Mary Law Review* 36, no. 2 (1979): 215–35.

26. LaCroix, *The Ideological Origins of American Federalism*, 139–40, 145; Mary Sarah Bilder, *The Transatlantic Constitution: Colonial Legal Culture and the Empire* (Cambridge, MA: Harvard University Press, 2004).

27. Rahe, *Republics Ancient and Modern*, 597; LaCroix, *The Ideological Origins of American Federalism*, 167–68.

28. Forrest McDonald, *States' Rights and the Union: Imperium in Imperio, 1776–1876* (Lawrence: University Press of Kansas, 2000), 17; LaCroix, *The Ideological Origins of American Federalism*, 150.

29. Madison expressed these views in his personal correspondence with Thomas Jefferson. See James Madison, "State and Federal Power and the Public Good; Letter to Thomas Jefferson, October 24, 1787," in Ketcham, *Selected Writings of James Madison*, 77. See also Walter P. Murphy, *The Triumph of Nationalism: State Sovereignty, the Founding Fathers and the Making of the Constitution* (Chicago: Quadrangle Books, 1967), 214; LaCroix, *The Ideological Origins of American Federalism*, 173; Forrest McDonald, *Novus Ordo Seclorum: The Intellectual Origins of the Constitution* (Lawrence: University Press of Kansas, 1985), 275–76.

30. Law professor Johnson observes that when the Bill of Rights was passed, Madison himself appeared willing to think of a judicial remedy as being an acceptable devise for securing liberty (instead of the negative). See Calvin H. Johnson, *Righteous Anger at the Wicked States: The Meaning of the Founders' Constitution* (New York: Cambridge University Press, 2005), 1150. The ideological transformation of American federalism and its emphasis on federal courts is analyzed in LaCroix, *The Ideological Origins of American Federalism*, 168–69. See also Purcell, *Originalism, Federalism, and the American Constitutional Enterprise.*

31. LaCroix, *The Ideological Origins of American Federalism*, 173.

32. McDonald, *Novus Ordo Seclorum*, 276.

33. McDonald, *Novus Ordo Seclorum*, 276. See also LaCroix, *The Ideological Origins of American Federalism*, 173; Rakove, *Original Meanings*, 175–76.

34. James Madison, "Combining National and Federal Forms: *Federalist* No. 39, January 16, 1788," in Ketcham, *Selected Writings of James Madison*, 99.

35. Compare Malcolm M. Feeley and Edward Rubin, *Federalism: Political Identity and Tragic Compromise* (Ann Arbor: University of Michigan Press, 2008), 2; Purcell, *Originalism, Federalism, and the American Constitutional Enterprise*, 181; John D. Nugent, *Safeguarding Federalism: How States Protect Their Interests in National Policymaking* (Norman: University of Oklahoma Press, 2009), 7.

36. LaCroix, *The Ideological Origins of American Federalism*, 221.

37. David B. Walker, *The Rebirth of Federalism: Slouching Toward Washington*, 2nd ed. (New York: Chatham House Publishers, 2000), 65. See also ibid., chs. 5 and 6.

38. Jenna Bednar, *The Robust Federation: Principles of Design* (New York: Cambridge University Press, 2009), 96.

39. John V. Orth, *The Judicial Power of the United States: The Eleventh Amendment in American History* (New York: Oxford University Press, 1987), 19. See also Bilder, *The Transatlantic Constitution*, 1, 11; Maeva Marcus and Natalie Wexler, "The Judiciary Act of 1789: Political Compromise or Constitutional Interpretation?," in *Origins of the Federal Judiciary: Essays on the Judiciary Act of 1789*, ed. Maeva Marcus (New York: Oxford University Press, 1992), 13–39.

40. 2 U.S. 419 (1793).

41. Orth, *The Judicial Power of the United States*, 22–23.

42. LaCroix, *The Ideological Origins of American Federalism*, 175–77; McDonald, *States' Rights and the Union*, 52–53. See also William M. Wieck, "*Murdoch v. Memphis:* Section 25 of the 1789 Judiciary Act," in Marcus, *Origins of the Federal Judiciary*, 223–47.

43. G. Edward White (with the aid of Gerald Gunther), *The Marshall Court and Cultural Change, 1815–35*, Vols. 3 and 4: *The Oliver Wendell Holmes Devise: History of*

the Supreme Court of the United States, ed. Daniel J. Boorstin (New York: Cambridge University Press, 2010), 2–3, 10. See also Howard Gillman, "How Political Parties Can Use the Courts to Advance Their Agendas: Federal Courts in the United States, 1875–1891," *American Political Science Review* 96, no. 3 (2002): 511–24.

44. 5 U.S. 137 (1803).

45. Michael J. Klarman, "How Great Were the 'Great' Marshall Court Decisions?," *Virginia Law Review* 87 (October 2001): 1171–72. See also Melvin Urofsky, *A March of Liberty: A Constitutional History of the United States* (New York: Alfred A. Knopf, 1988), 221.

46. The other cases are *Dartmouth College v. Woodward*, 17 U.S. (4 Wheat.) 518 (1819) and *Sturges v. Crowninshield*, 17 U.S. (4 Wheat) 122 (1819), both strengthening the national constraints the constitution puts on states not to interfere with private contracts or property rights. William M. Wiecek, *The Lost World of Classical Legal Thought: Law and Ideology in America, 1886–1937* (New York: Oxford University Press, 1998), 34–37. See also Herbert A. Johnson, *Gibbons v. Ogden: John Marshall, Steamboats, and the Commerce Clause* (Lawrence: University Press of Kansas, 2010), 108, 132–33.

47. G. Edward White, "Recovering Coterminous Power Theory: The Lost Dimension of Marshall Court Sovereignty Cases," in Marcus, *Origins of the Federal Judiciary*, 97. See also *Gibbons v. Ogden*, 22 U.S. 1 (1824); *McCulloch v. Maryland*, 17 U.S. 319 (1819); *Martin v. Hunter's Lessee*, 14 U.S. 304 (1816); and *Cohens v. Virginia*, 19 U.S. 264 (1821).

48. Purcell, *Originalism, Federalism, and the American Constitutional Enterprise*, 45.

49. *Martin v. Hunter's Lessee*, 344.

50. Urofsky, *A March of Liberty*, 173, 209.

51. Urofsky, *A March of Liberty*, 215.

52. LaCroix, *The Ideological Origins of American Federalism*, 212, 219. See also Johnson, *Gibbons v. Ogden*, 62–63; *Cohens v. Virginia*, 19 U.S. 264, 392, 412, 415 (1821).

53. McDonald, *States' Rights and the Union*, 27–70. See also Richard A. Ellis, *The Jeffersonian Crisis: Courts and Politics in the Young Republic* (New York: Oxford University Press).

54. Walker, *The Rebirth of Federalism*, 73. See also McDonald, *States' Rights and the Union*, 86–87; Urofsky, *A March of Liberty*, 220, 226.

55. Paul Finkelman and Donald R. Kennon, eds. *Congress and the Emergence of Sectionalism: From the Missouri Compromise to the Age of Jackson* (Athens: Ohio University Press, 2008), 3. See also Harold M. Hyman and William M. Wiecek, *Equal Justice under Law: Constitutional Development, 1835–1875* (New York: Harper and Row Publishers, 1982), 13; Wiecek, *The Lost World of Classical Legal Thought*, 38–39.

56. Tim Alan Garrison, "United States Indian Policy in Sectional Crisis: Georgia's Exploitation of the Compact of 1802," in *Congress and the Emergence of Sectionalism: From the Missouri Compromise to the Age of Jackson*, ed. Paul Finkelman and Donald R. Kennon (Athens: Ohio University Press, 2008), 97–124; Tim Alan Garrison, "The Devil and Andrew Jackson: Historians and Jackson's Role in the Indian Removal Crisis," in Finkelman and Kennon, *Congress and the Emergence of Sectionalism*, 221–57.

57. Hyman and Wiecek, *Equal Justice under Law*, ch. 2.

58. William M. Wieck, *The Sources of Antislavery Constitutionalism in America, 1780–1848* (Ithaca, NY: Cornell University Press, 1977), 105–8, 119. See also Paul Finkelman, *An Imperfect Union: Slavery, Federalism, and Comity* (Chapel Hill: University of North Carolina Press, 1981), 21.

59. Don E. Fehrenbacher, *The Dred Scott Case: Its Significance in American Law and Politics* (New York: Oxford University Press, 1978), 233. See also Hyman and Wiecek, *Equal Justice under Law*, 62.

60. Martin Siegel, "The Taney Court: 1836–1864," in *The Supreme Court in American Life*, ed. George J. Lankevich (Millwood, NY: Associated Faculty Press, 1986), 3:5.

61. *Swift v. Tyson*, 41 U.S. 1 (1842), was overturned by *Erie Railroad v. Tompkins*, 304 U.S. 64 (1938). Hyman and Wiecek, *Equal Justice under Law*, 73. See also *Dred Scott v. Sandford*, 60 U.S. 393 (1857), and *Propeller Genesee Chief v. Fitzhugh*, 53 U.S. 443 (1852).

62. Robert J. Harris, "Chief Justice Taney: Prophet of Reform and Reaction," in *American Constitutional Law: Historical Essays*, ed. Leonard W. Levy (New York: Harper and Row, 1966), 95–96. See also Fehrenbacher, who states that "from the Whig point of view . . . [Taney] reeked of partisanship, having served as [President] Jackson's hatchet man in the Bank War." Fehrenbacher, *The Dred Scott Case*, 227.

63. Compare Harris, "Chief Justice Taney: Prophet of Reform and Reaction," 97–98, with Hyman and Wiecek, *Equal Justice under Law*, 84. See also *Charles River Bridge v. Warren*, 36 U.S. 420 (1837); *Briscoe v. Bank of Kentucky*, 11 Pet. (36 U.S.) 257 (1837); *The License Cases*, 46 U.S. 504 (1847); *Strader v. Graham*, 51 U.S. 82 (1851); and *Cooley v. Board of Wardens of the Port of Philadelphia*, 53 U.S. 229 (1851).

64. 41 U.S. 539 (1842).

65. See Hyman and Wiecek, *Equal Justice under Law*, 108. See also Paul Finkelman, "The Taney Court (1836–1864): The Jurisprudence of Slavery and the Crisis of the Union," in *The United States Supreme Court: The Pursuit of Justice*, ed. Christopher Tomlins (Boston: Houghton Mifflin Company, 2005), 75–99; James F. Simon, *Lincoln and Chief Justice Taney: Slavery, Secession, and the President's War Powers* (New York: Simon & Shuster, 2006); Tony Freyer, *Harmony and Dissonance: The Swift and Erie Cases in American Federalism*, Linden Studies in American Legal History (New York: New York University Press, 1981).

66. 60 U.S. 393 (1857).

67. 60 U.S. 393, 405, 406, and 407–8 (1857).

68. Earl M. Maltz, *Slavery and the Supreme Court, 1825–1861* (Lawrence: University Press of Kansas, 2009), 266. See also Mark A. Graber, *Dred Scott and the Problem of Constitutional Evil*, Cambridge Studies on the American Constitution (Cambridge: Cambridge University Press, 2006), 53–54.

69. Hyman and Wiecek, *Equal Justice under Law*, 180, 184. See also Maltz, *Slavery and the Supreme Court, 1825–1861*, 248–55; and Graber, *Dred Scott and the Problem of Constitutional Evil*, 19.

70. See Maltz, *Slavery and the Supreme Court, 1825–1861*, 249–55; Paul Finkelman, "The Taney Court (1836–1864)," 89; Graber, *Dred Scott and the Problem of Constitutional Evil*, 19–20; and *Dred Scott v. Sandford*, 60 U.S. 393 (1857).

71. The extrajudicial contact that some of the justices had with pro-slavery President James Buchanan before the decision was reached, along with the alleged taint that was put on the Supreme Court because of its involvement in the 1877 Electoral Commission that gave Republican Rutherford Hayes a victory in the controversial presidential election, contributed to that view. *Dred Scott* also caused a breakdown in collegiality on the Court itself, as after it was announced, but before Taney filed his opinion and without his consent, Justice Benjamin Curtis distributed his dissent to a Boston newspaper. That decision strengthened the abolitionist will and put Taney on the defensive in trying to deflect charges that his original opinion was being changed in order to rebut what Curtis had written about the historical shortcomings of the Taney ruling. Amid accusations of dishonesty and breaches of judicial ethics, collegiality evaporated and hard feelings ensued, causing Curtis to resign. The vacancy was quickly filled with a Buchanan appointee (Nathan Clifford), who sympathized with the South. See Maltz, *Slavery and the Supreme Court, 1825–1861*, 268–69; Fehrenbacher, *The Dred Scott Case*, 308–9, 315–21; Paul Finkelman, "The Taney Court (1836–1864)," 97–98; and Hyman and Wiecek, *Equal Justice under Law*, 178, 493.

72. Hyman and Wiecek, *Equal Justice under Law*, 493, 500–1; Paul Finkelman, "The Taney Court (1836–1864)," 94–98; Maltz, *Slavery and the Supreme Court, 1825–1861*, 268–72; Fehrenbacher, *The Dred Scott Case*, 315–21. See also *Plessy v. Ferguson*, 163 U.S. 537 (1896).

73. For Siegel's assessment of the Taney Court, see Siegel, "The Taney Court: 1836–1864," in *The Supreme Court in American Life*, ix–x. See also Walker, *The Rebirth of Federalism*, 67.

74. J. G. Randall, *Constitutional Problems under Lincoln*, rev. ed. (Urbana: University of Illinois, 1964), 522.

75. 74 U.S. 700, 726 (1869).

76. Walker, *The Rebirth of Federalism*, 74.

77. Gillman, "How Political Parties Can Use the Courts to Advance Their Agendas," 515; William E. Nelson, *The Fourteenth Amendment* (Cambridge, MA: Harvard University Press, 1988), 61–63.

78. Nelson, *The Fourteenth Amendment*, 44–48. See also Gillman, "How Political Parties Can Use the Courts to Advance Their Agendas," 515; Michael Les Benedict, *A Compromise of Principle: Congressional Republicans and Reconstruction, 1863–1869* (New York: Norton, 1974).

79. The legislative response to the Civil War Amendments comprise the following: The Civil Rights Act of 1866, 14 Stat. L. 27; the first Enforcement Act (May 31, 1870), 16 Stat. L. 140; the second Enforcement Act (February 28, 1871), 16 Stat. L. 433, and the third Enforcement Act (or Ku Klux Klan Act) (April 20, 1871), 17 Stat. L. 13. The 1866 Civil Rights Act, enacted despite President Andrew Johnson's veto, followed the Thirteenth Amendment by reversing southern black codes restrictions and set criminal penalties against anyone acting under "color of law" who denied them. The first and second Enforcement Acts enforced Fifteenth Amendment principles, including establishing criminal penalties against black voting rights violations, and the third Enforcement Act curbed private conspiracies that often, with the use of violence, curtailed black civil rights. See also Robert J. Kaczorowski, "Revolutionary Constitutionalism in the Era of the Civil War

and Reconstruction," *New York University Law Review* 61 (1986): 871–900; Eugene Gressman, "Unhappy History of Civil Rights Legislation," *Michigan Law Review* 50 (1951): 1323–58.

80. Richard Franklin Bensel, *The Political Economy of American Industrialization, 1877–1900* (Cambridge: Cambridge University Press, 2000), 321–54. See also Wayne D. Moore, "(Re)Construction of Constitutional Authority and Meaning: The Fourteenth Amendment and Slaughterhouse Cases," in *The Supreme Court and American Political Development*, eds. Ronald Kahn and Ken I. Kersch (Lawrence: University Press of Kansas), 250; Ronald M. Labbe and Jonathan Lurie, *The Slaughterhouse Cases: Regulation, Reconstruction, and the Fourteenth Amendment* (Lawrence: University Press of Kansas, 2003), 406.

81. 83 U.S. 36 (1873). See also Hyman and Wiecek, *Equal Justice under Law*, 80; Nelson, *The Fourteenth Amendment*, 151–55.

82. Labbe and Lurie, *The Slaughterhouse Cases*, 101.

83. *Slaughterhouse Cases*, 83 U.S. 36, at 61, 74, 77, 81.

84. Ibid., 88, 95, 98.

85. Labbe and Lurie, in *The Slaughterhouse Cases*, moderately defend Miller's legal rationale, and Gillman explains that prior state court police powers' precedents, along with prevailing norms and ideologies that shaped class conflict and capitalism, framed the Supreme Court's understanding of the legal issues presented by the case and its outcome. Howard Gillman, *The Constitution Besieged: The Rise and Demise of Lochner Era Police Powers Jurisprudence* (Durham, NC: Duke University Press, 1993), 61–67. Others are less charitable toward Miller, the whole opinion, and the Supreme Court's general interpretative approach. See Phillip S. Paudlin, *A Covenant with Death: The Constitution, Law, and Equality in the Civil War Era* (Urbana: University of Illinois Press, 1975), 55–58; and Michael Vorenberg, "The Chase Court (1864–1873): Cautious Reconstruction," in Tomlins, *The United States Supreme Court*, 118–19.

86. Such as *Ex Parte Virginia*, ruling that a state judge who excluded blacks from jury service could be criminally indicted under enforcement legislation. Justice William Strong's majority opinion declared that a "great purpose" of the Thirteenth and Fourteenth Amendments is to achieve a "perfect equality of civil rights" among all persons in the states. *Ex Parte Virginia*, 100 U.S. 339, 344–45 (1879). Section 5, the enforcement clause, gave the amendments "much of their force" since it "enlarged" Congress's power to enact appropriate legislation that made "the Amendments fully effective," reasoning "such enforcement is no invasion of State sovereignty" because Congress is acting pursuant to its delegated authority. *Ex Parte Virginia*, 100 U.S. 339, 345–46 (1879).

87. See also Gressman, "Unhappy History of Civil Rights Legislation," 1336–43; Hyman and Wiecek, *Equal Justice under Law*, 515; Vorenberg, "The Chase Court (1864–1873)," 119.

88. *The Civil Rights Cases*, 109 U.S. 3 (1883); *United States v. Harris*, 106 U.S. 629 (1883); and *United States v. Cruikshank*, 92 U.S. 542 (1876).

89. 109 U.S. 3, 11, 13–14.

90. Brandwein asserts, "The decision permits broader federal protections for civil rights than has been recognized." Pamela Brandwein, "The Civil Rights

Cases and the Lost Language of State Neglect," in Kahn and Kersch, *The Supreme Court and American Political Development*, 275.

91. Clear statement rules and Tenth Amendment analysis have been used by the Rehnquist Court (1986–2005) to limit federal power. Ernest A. Young, "The Story of *Gregory v. Ashcroft*: Clear Statement Rules and the Statutory Constitution of American Federalism," in *Statutory Interpretation Stories*, ed. William N. Eskridge Jr., Philip P. Frickey, and Elizabeth Garrett (New York: Foundation Press, 2011), 197–225. See also Christopher P. Banks, "The Constitutional Politics of Interpreting Section 5 of the Fourteenth Amendment," *University of Akron Law Review* 36, no. 3 (2003): 427–73.

92. Moore, "(Re)Construction of Constitutional Authority and Meaning," 242.

93. Gillman, "How Political Parties Can Use the Courts to Advance Their Agendas," 516.

94. Gillman, "How Political Parties Can Use the Courts to Advance Their Agendas," 516; Morton J. Horwitz, *The Transformation of American Law, 1870–1960: The Crisis of Legal Orthodoxy* (New York: Oxford University Press, 1992), 69.

95. Edward A. Purcell, *Brandeis and the Progressive Constitution: Erie, the Judicial Power, and the Politics of the Federal Courts in Twentieth-Century America* (New Haven, CT: Yale University Press, 2000), 11–16; Gillman, "How Political Parties Can Use the Courts to Advance Their Agendas," 517, 521.

96. Howard Gillman, "The Waite Court (1874–1888): The Collapse of Reconstruction and the Transition to Conservative Constitutionalism," in Tomlins, *The United States Supreme Court*, 136; Gillman, "How Political Parties Can Use the Courts to Advance Their Agendas," 512; Bensel, *The Political Economy of American Industrialization, 1877–1900*, 326–33, 512.

97. *Munn v. Illinois*, 94 U.S. 113 (1877), 126. See also Kermit L. Hall, *The Magic Mirror: Law in American History* (New York: Oxford University Press, 1989), 234.

98. See *Pollock v. Farmers' Loan & Trust Co.*, 158 U.S 601 (1895) (nullifying income tax); *County of Santa Clara v. Southern Pacific R.R. Co.*, 118 U.S. 394 (1886) (recognizing corporations as Fourteenth Amendment "persons"); *In re Debs*, 158 U.S. 564 (1895) (affirming use of labor injunctions); *U.S. v. E.C. Knight Co.*, 156 U.S. 1 (1895) (authorizing sugar monopoly); and *Chicago, Milwaukee & State Pacific Railway v. Minnesota*, 134 U.S. 118 (1890). See also Bensel, *The Political Economy of American Industrialization, 1877–1900*, 344–47; Gillman, *The Constitution Besieged*, 2–4; Horwitz, *The Transformation of American Law, 1870–1960*, 66–67.

99. *Allgeyer v. Louisiana*, 165 U.S. 578 (1897), 590. See also *Lochner v. New York*, 198 U.S. 45 (1905).

100. Neil Duxbury, *Patterns of American Jurisprudence* (New York: Oxford University Press), 27. See also *Lochner* (Holmes, J., dissenting).

101. Duxbury, *Patterns of American Jurisprudence*, 25–26. See also Purcell, *Brandeis and the Progressive Constitution*, 41–43.

102. Purcell, *Brandeis and the Progressive Constitution*, 146–48; Patrick M. Garry, *An Entrenched Legacy: How the New Deal Constitutional Revolution Continues to Shape the Role of the Supreme Court* (University Park: Pennsylvania State University Press, 2008), 91; Kimberley S. Johnson, *Governing the American State: Congress and the New Federalism, 1877–1929* (Princeton, NJ: Princeton University Press, 2007), 31.

103. G. Edward White, *The Constitution and the New Deal* (Cambridge, MA: Harvard University Press, 2000), 205–6 (quoting Chief Justice John Marshall in *Osborne v. Bank*, 4 Wheat. 316 [1824]). See also Walker, *The Rebirth of Federalism*, 81, 87–88.

104. Duxbury, *Patterns of American Jurisprudence*, 150; Lucas A. Powe Jr., *The Supreme Court and the American Elite, 1789–2008* (Cambridge, MA: Harvard University Press, 2009), 201.

105. Erwin Chemerinsky, *Enhancing Government: Federalism in the 21st Century* (Stanford, CA: Stanford University Press, 2008); White, *The Constitution and the New Deal*, 70–71, 125.

106. Walker, *The Rebirth of Federalism*, 89–90; Johnson, *Governing the American State*, 163.

107. Walker, *The Rebirth of Federalism*, 98.

108. White, *The Constitution and the New Deal*, 93, 97; Walker, *The Rebirth of Federalism*, 90.

109. The conventional linkages are presented in Garry, *An Entrenched Legacy*, 17. More critical analyses are found in White, *The Constitution and the New Deal*, or Ken I. Kersch, "The New Deal Triumph as the End of History? The Judicial Negotiation of Labor Rights and Civil Rights," in Kahn and Kersch, *The Supreme Court and American Political Development*, 169–226.

110. Hall, *The Magic Mirror*, 271–75; Walker, *The Rebirth of Federalism*, 112; Sylvia Snowiss, "Presidential Leadership of Congress: An Analysis of Roosevelt's First Hundred Days," *Publius: The Journal of Federalism* 1, no. 1 (1971): 59–87.

111. *Steward Machine Co. v. Davis*, 301 U.S. 548 (1937), 586–88. See also Hall, *The Magic Mirror*, 276.

112. Purcell, *Brandeis and the Progressive Constitution*, 218–31, 233. See also *Panama Refining Company v. Ryan*, 293 U.S. 388 (1935); *Schechter Poultry Corporation v. United States*, 295 U.S. 495 (1935); *United States v. Butler*, 297 U.S. 1 (1936); and *Carter v. Carter Coal Company*, 298 U.S. 238 (1936).

113. *United States v. Darby*, 312 U.S. 100 (1941). See also *Hammer v. Dagenhart*, 247 U.S. 251 (1918).

114. *United States v. Darby*, 312 U.S. 100, 119 (1941). See also *Darby* at 114.

115. White, *The Constitution and the New Deal*, 227. See also *United States v. Darby*, 312 U.S. 100, 124 (1941).

116. White, *The Constitution and the New Deal*, 232; Walker, *The Rebirth of Federalism*, 92–93. See also *Wickard v. Filburn*, 317 U.S. 111, 125, 128–29 (1942); Jim Chen, "The Story of *Wickard v. Filburn*: Agriculture, Aggregation, and Commerce," in *Constitutional Law Stories*, ed. Michael C. Dorf (New York: Foundation Press, 2009), 69–118.

117. Walker, *The Rebirth of Federalism*, 81, 94.

118. Hall, *The Magic Mirror*, 313–32. See also *Palko v. Connecticut*, 302 U.S. 319 (1937), and *Barron v. Baltimore*, 32 U.S. 243 (1833).

119. Hall, *The Magic Mirror*, 313. See also *Palko v. Connecticut*, 302 U.S. 319, 325 (1937).

120. Walker, *The Rebirth of Federalism*, 175.

121. Publius, "New Federalist Paper No. 1," *Publius: The Journal of Federalism* 2, no. 1 (1972): 99 and 101. See also Daniel Elazer, "Editor's Introduction," *Publius:*

The Journal of Federalism 2, no. 1 (1972): 95–97; Timothy Conlan, *New Federalism: Intergovernmental Reform from Nixon to Reagan* (with an introduction by Samuel H. Beer) (Washington, DC: Brookings Institution, 1988); Timothy Conlan, *From New Federalism to Devolution: Twenty-Five Years of Intergovernmental Reform* (Washington, DC: Brookings Institution Press, 1998).

122. Publius, "New Federalist Paper No. 1," 89, 100, and 103.

123. Samuel H. Beer, "Introduction," in Conlan, *New Federalism*, xv and xxii. See also Conlan, *From New Federalism to Devolution.*

124. Kevin J. McMahon, *Nixon's Court: His Challenge to Judicial Liberalism and Its Political Consequences* (Chicago: University of Chicago Press, 2011), 66.

125. Publius, "New Federalist Paper No. 1," 99 (emphasis in original).

126. See Cato, "Federalism: Old and New," *Publius: The Journal of Federalism* 2, no. 1 (1972): 116–31. See also Conlan, *New Federalism*, and Conlan, *From New Federalism to Devolution.* An updated assessment of some of the old and new ideological conflicts related to new federalism ideas, as presented in an evaluation of federalism case law from the U.S. Supreme Court under the leadership of Chief Justice John Roberts, is found in Clement et al., "The Roberts Court and Federalism."

127. Martha Derthick, "Crossing Thresholds: Federalism in the 1960s," in *Integrating the Sixties: The Origins, Structures, and Legitimacy of Public Policy in a Turbulent Decade*, ed. Brian Balogh (University Park: Pennsylvania State University Press), 77.

128. Publius, "New Federalist Paper No. 1," 112 (emphasis in original). See also Cato, "Federalism: Old and New," 117, suggesting Publius "has no quarrel" with letting federal judges apply new federalism principles in accordance of with "living Constitution" judicial philosophies.

129. Beer, "Introduction," in Conlan, *New Federalism*, xiii. Political scientist Kevin McMahon underscores the point as well that Nixon's presidency and what it represented ought to be judged by "the tumultuous nature of the times" and perhaps "not someone who was defined by his steadfast belief in a particular set of ideological principles despite its consequences." McMahon, *Nixon's Court*, 67.

130. Hall, *The Magic Mirror*, 313–32. See also Powe, *The Supreme Court and the American Elite, 1789–2008.* See *United States v. Carolene Products Co.*, 304 U.S. 144 (1938); *Brown v. Board of Education*, 347 U.S. 483 (1954). The significance of *Brown* and what it means are debated in *What "Brown v. Board of Education" Should Have Said: The Nation's Top Legal Experts Rewrite America's Landmark Civil Rights Decision*, ed. Jack M. Balkin (New York: New York University Press, 2001).

131. Creative federalism extends the cooperative model by stressing direct federal-city relationships that avoid the states and takes advantage of contractual arrangements between federal agencies and nongovernmental agencies, such as community action groups. Michael D. Reagan, *The New Federalism* (New York: Oxford University Press, 1972), 23.

132. Garry, *An Entrenched Legacy*, 93. See also Morton J. Horwitz, *The Warren Court and the Pursuit of Justice: A Critical Issue* (New York: Hill and Wang, 1998).

133. Conlan, *From New Federalism to Devolution.*

3

The Rehnquist Court, New Federalism, and States' Rights

At the time he was appointed sixteenth chief justice of the United States, William Rehnquist had established himself as the type of throwback conservative attractive to the Reagan administration. Rehnquist earned his Republican credentials as Arizona senator Barry Goldwater's speechwriter and legal adviser during the 1964 presidential campaign. His political activities and prior law clerk experience for Justice Robert Jackson showed he was an ardent critic of the Warren Court's judicial activism, especially its civil rights decisions. In time he became a significant part of Goldwater's political strategy to recast the Republican Party (GOP) as an organization aligned with slowing down the pace of achieving racial equality in the South. Also, before Nixon put him on the federal bench, the president appointed him to lead the Department of Justice's Office of Legal Counsel, which is widely known to "have a major impact on the shape of every administration's legal and constitutional policy." In learning the art of strategic legal policymaking, he was part of the political regime's support structure responsible for determining constitutional change.[1]

Nixon's decision to elevate Rehnquist to the Supreme Court in 1971 comfortably fit with the president's Southern Strategy attacking the Warren Court's liberal judicial politics. Yet it may have been at odds with Nixon's new federalism and its acceptance of the modern welfare state, which Rehnquist opposed as a political and judicial conservative.[2] As this chapter shows, the early formation of Rehnquist's legal jurisprudence probably had a better connection to the type of new federalism Ronald Reagan offered, especially in its repudiation of the expansive role the federal government played after the New Deal. The Reagan Revolution, favoring decentralization and advancing traditional social values, made it possible for the Rehnquist Court to find its voice as a judicial leader and protector of state sovereignty.

While the political science and legal academies generally agree the Rehnquist Court (1986–2005) broke new ground in setting limits on congressional power and insulating state governments from federal intrusiveness, the salience, causes, and consequences of the federalism revival still remain unclear. Scholars divide sharply on the revival's motivations, whether it accomplished much, and if it will endure as a constitutional or political revolution. Another issue concerns whether the Rehnquist Court acted any differently from past Supreme Courts in aggressively pursuing a states' rights agenda or merely "opened the door for a later Court" to implement the type of federalism revolution that would change "the actual scope of national power."[3]

This chapter first traces the political development of new federalism during the Nixon and Reagan presidencies and then in the Rehnquist Court. The analysis next centers on William Rehnquist's theory of state sovereignty in respect to establishing limits on the use of the federal government's delegated powers and reducing federal court jurisdiction to entertain private lawsuits against the states. His jurisprudence is measured in light of his judicial opinions written as a Burger Court (1969–1985) associate justice and as chief justice in his own court (1986–2005). Of special focus is determining whether the accomplishments and failures of the new federalism revival are diminished by the paradox and reality that the justices often turn against the states in endorsing federal supremacy in select types of cases. Thus the third section outlines the revolutionary and counterrevolutionary trends in the federalist revival and the degree to which the Rehnquist Court expanded the use of process-based rules and substantive constitutional principles to enforce its new federalism vision, particularly in the context of dormant commerce clause and clear statement rules cases. The conclusion offers its own assessment of Rehnquist Court new federalism as a precursor to the case studies and analyses in the next three chapters: its implications for Justice Clarence Thomas's federalism in religion cases, the role the states play in foreign policy preemption cases, and whether the Roberts Court is likely to continue Rehnquist Court new federalism or steer its own path as an umpire of state-federal relationships.

THE POLITICS OF NEW FEDERALISM

The term "new federalism" is associated with a revival or reassertion of pre–Civil War federalism principles by the Rehnquist Court. That initiative supposedly placed a series of aggressive and affirmative constitutional limits on the central government while protecting the sovereignty, autonomy, or rights of state governments. While scholars disagree about the use of judicial authority or its impact on creating or sustaining the revival, clearly the construction of a new federalism paradigm is closely tied to the synergy created between constitutive elements of the governing political regime, as informed (but not necessarily dictated) by ideology across different time periods.[4] Thus it cannot be perceived solely as a judicial doctrine that materializes in isolation from the rest of the polity and its prevailing ideological coalitions, preferences, or conflicts. Of vital importance in understanding the model's significance are the agendas and policies resulting from the interplay between presidential administrations, congressional representatives, political parties and bureaucrats, interest groups, professional associations, intergovernmental lobbyists, and the public. In this respect Richard Nathan, an architect of the Nixon administration's early domestic agenda, aptly echoes social scientist Samuel Beer's position that "there will always be a New Federalism," since American federalism is perpetually "opportunistic," "dynamic," "cyclical," and "pro-government."[5]

For this reason Nathan tried to, but could not, come up with a clear-cut method of classifying or "characterizing new federalisms over time," because "the determining conditions are so changeable." One of the many examples he cites is then Speaker of the House Newt Gingrich's program favoring block grants to the states for Medicaid and welfare while paradoxically sustaining a centralist regulatory approach on environmental or business issues. Another is New York attorney general Eliot Spitzer's conversion to a "fervent federalist" who aggressively threw the powers of his office behind efforts to thwart conservative business and corporate interests in the aftermath of Reagan's 1980 presidential election. These illustrations and countless others show that rarely do the issues of new federalism remain apolitical, policy neutral, or value-free.[6]

As a source of contemporary public policy or institutional power, the new federalism's ideological direction and its priorities are usually best conceived of as an exercise in pragmatism and political opportunism; depending upon the issue and who is in charge or influential in the principal regime, it discernibly tilts to the political Right or Left and sometimes points somewhere in between. The efforts made by national political parties to pursue larger concerns of strategic governmental or issue reform in federalism areas are instructive. Under the heading "Crisis of the Cities," the official Republican Party platform in 1968 declared a conservative preference for presidential leadership that would "buttress state and local governments," and it expressed "vigorous federal support" for the development of "innovative state programs." But, under the subtitle "Government Reorganization," the 1980 GOP platform reflected a strident ideological commitment to achieve "decentralization of the federal government," and under the heading "Government Reform," it showed support for federal agency consolidation while making a "pledge to eliminate bureaucratic red tape" and to "conduct cost-benefit analyses" to identify adverse regulatory effects on state and local governments. Not surprisingly the 1968 platform tracks Nixon's tempered brand of new federalism that fostered centralization by encouraging cooperative relationships between the federal government and states, whereas the 1980 platform aligns with a fervent pursuit of Reagan's new federalism, which provocatively advanced an agenda of wholesale retrenchment of centralized authority in the course of enhancing state government autonomy.[7]

Identical new federalism platforms in the past and present attract White House attention as well. President Barack Obama's May 20, 2009, executive memorandum on preemption (discussed in chapter 1), reversing the policy in William Clinton's August 4, 1999, Executive Order 13132 encouraging agencies to engage in regulatory preemption, falls to the left of Clinton's moderate position that theoretically permits the federal bureaucracy to override tort lawsuits filed in state courts under state laws on an implied basis.[8] While Obama's shift in policy alters agency practice, as a federalism matter it visibly relates only to preemption, a topic consistently addressed in prior years by executive orders from Presidents G. H. W. Bush and Ronald Reagan. Before September 11, by executive order President G. W. Bush formed an Interagency Working Group on Federalism, whose mission was to disclose "federal endeavors" that "may more appropriately be carried out by State or local authorities" and to locate "measures for improving Federal responsiveness to State and local concerns."[9] As the 1980 GOP platform suggests, in other instances presidents have been more assertive in making wholesale federalism reform a domestic priority that aimed to reconfigure the federal government's basic substantive relationship to the states. Such is the case with President Reagan's new federalism policy agenda and, before him (but with less ideological vigor endorsing progressive goals), President Richard Nixon's new federalism.

The political differences between Nixon's and Reagan's new federalism link to the Supreme Court's states' rights initiatives under Chief Justice Rehnquist. The Nixon White House perceived the progressive President Lyndon Johnson's Great Society domestic program as worthy of implementation but poorly executed and carried out by federal agencies. By one account, Nixon inherited a bloated and unwieldy federal bureaucracy composed of roughly 150 agencies, 400 regional and field offices, and 456 "program channels" servicing a vast regulatory network.[10] As a fix he sought to establish a workable plan of welfare aid to families in need and to improve the intergovernmental managerial processes of delivering federal aid to the states by using a variety of block grants and a series of pathbreaking special revenue-sharing reforms. Still, Congress rejected Nixon's family aid plan, and the president had only marginal success in improving administrative grant efficiencies. Although states were given additional grant-management control, Nixon's programmatic accomplishments were offset by the countervailing effects of making his new federalism a political reality: it resulted in increasing domestic spending and more entitlements programs and, in general, led to the entrenchment of centralization. Starting with Nixon, there was a sharp uptick in the creation of social legislation featuring new environmental, energy, health and safety, and conservation regulations, all of which greatly impacted states and localities.[11]

Nixon's political acumen and his responses to Congress and the electorate are significant as well. Instead of zealously working with his party to achieve federalism reforms, his 1968 presidential campaign was more candidate centered and focused on keeping a "law and order" pledge that he had made to the American people. That promise was intimately linked with tapping into his campaign's Southern Strategy, an attempt to attract support from conservatives representing the South who detested the cultural and race implications of the Warren Court's *Brown* ruling. It was also a reaction to the social, economic, and political upheavals that the country was experiencing due to rampant street crime and civil disorder, racial tensions underlying the civil rights movement, and the country's protracted involvement in the unpopular Vietnam War. The conservative antipathy toward liberal courts, whose decisions were seen as more a cause of than a solution to the problem of street crime, infused the national political dialogue and Nixon's campaign strategy.[12] While Nixon extolled the rule of law, the inroads and controversies originating from the school desegregation decision in *Brown v. Board of Education* (1954) were accompanied by fierce criticisms of the Warren Court's criminal procedure rulings, including *Mapp v. Ohio* (expanding the exclusionary rule and preventing incriminating evidence from being heard by juries), *Gideon v. Wainright* (guaranteeing the right to appointed legal counsel for indigent defendants), and *Miranda v. Arizona* (protecting defendants from coercive police interrogations). So, for reasons of political expediency (and with South Carolina's Strom Thurmond's endorsement), Nixon's anti-crime election strategy included a frontal attack on the liberal Warren Court for expanding the rights of the criminally accused and risking public safety, and the candidate vowed to put an end to it. That message was loudly sent in his GOP convention nomination acceptance speech in August 1968, in which he said, "Let us always respect, as I do, our courts and those who serve on them, but let us also recognize that some of our courts in their decisions have gone too far in weakening the peace forces as against the criminal forces in this country."[13]

Nixon's political rhetoric was a thinly veiled assault on the U.S. Supreme Court and its perceived ally, the U.S. Court of Appeals for the District of Columbia Circuit (DC Circuit), led by Chief Justice David Bazelon and his liberal cohorts. The court of appeals increasingly irked conservatives for its own brand of liberal activism, and it too wound up in the crosshairs of congressional and executive retaliatory action. Even before Nixon was put in the White House, the Democratically controlled Congress, feeling the pressures of the times, enacted the Omnibus Crime Control and Safe Streets Act of 1968 (Safe Streets Act), a comprehensive crime bill that used block grants to give states and cities more control in battling street crime. It also liberalized the existing rules of evidence to allow more confessions by defendants to be considered by juries and expanded the use of wiretapping by law enforcement without judicial interference, while tightening up licensing requirements for firearms sales. As the 1970 midterm elections neared, the Safe Streets Act became the crux for enacting the Nixon administration's proposals to let the police use "no-knock searches" and "preventive detention" measures to fight criminals in the District of Columbia, ideas that were too politically extreme to be put into the act's original design. But those provisions soon found a home in the District of Columbia Court Reform and Criminal Procedure Act of 1970 (DC Crime Bill), a bill passed by Congress but drafted by Nixon's Department of Justice shortly after the president's election.[14]

The DC Crime Bill accomplished two conservative ends in the context of Nixon's partisan agenda. Not only was it politically in tune with fighting the soaring crime rate in the district, but it also displaced the DC Circuit's jurisdiction to handle local criminal appeals, a move designed to stop that court's "mollycoddling judges" from "dream[ing] up ingenious excuses to free criminals from jail."[15] While Congress and President Nixon scored a victory in helping to deflate DC Circuit liberal activism, fixing the federal bureaucracy and stopping the Warren Court proved to be more difficult. To detractors, reform coming from the president responsible for pushing for the Family Assistance Plan must have appeared to be fanciful.[16] Congress also actually rejected Nixon's new federalism Family Assistance Plan, and the president's attempts to achieve better intergovernmental efficiency with less federal omnipotence yielded only mixed and marginal policy results.[17]

Nixon ultimately fared better, however, in resisting the Supreme Court and its liberal composition, including the formidable William Brennan, a staunch ally of Earl Warren. But by 1969, the chief justice had retired, and his departure was followed by three others in quick succession (created by the vacancies of Justices Abe Fortas, Hugo Black, and John Marshall

Harlan). Warren Burger, a judge on the DC Circuit and strident critic of liberal judicial politics, was tapped to become the next chief justice. Whereas Burger's appointment satisfied supporters of Nixon's criminal justice platform, the president's next choices—Clement Haynsworth Jr. and G. Harrold Carswell—doggedly aimed to enhance the Republican Party's place in southern politics, but the Democratically controlled Senate refused to cooperate, ostensibly because the first nominee could not get past questions of legal ethics, and the second was deemed incompetent and racist. After the Senate rejected both, a fellow Minnesotan, Harry Blackmun, was confirmed in 1970. Next in line was a lifelong but moderate Democrat from Virginia, Lewis Powell, a well-respected former president of the American Bar Association who, by 1972, had also achieved some credibility in the Nixon White House for supporting law enforcement and chiding the Supreme Court for its criminal justice rulings. And lastly, in the same year, Nixon sought and received confirmation of a conservative from Attorney General John Mitchell's U.S. Department of Justice, William H. Rehnquist. Thus, within a span of four years, Nixon was able to appoint a fresh batch of new justices who all appeared poised to seize upon the promise of retrenching the Warren Court and its criminal due process revolution.[18]

The social and political fabric, as well as the short-lived consensus of 1960s legal liberalism propelled by President John F. Kennedy's assassination and the onset of Lyndon Johnson's Great Society, began to unravel during the Nixon presidency. That disintegration was hastened by cultural disruptions in the 1970s that were punctuated by the fading civil rights movement, the end of the Vietnam War, the Watergate scandal and Nixon's resignation, and the onset of an era of burgeoning federal regulation featuring a large influx of environmental, workplace, and consumer-protection legislation. When Republican vice president Gerald Ford took over the presidency in 1974, the next year he got the chance to appoint John Paul Stevens, from the U.S. Court of Appeals for the Seventh Circuit, to the bench as a replacement for liberal William O. Douglas, who retired due to illness after thirty-six years of service.

Even though the high court's membership moved to the right in the 1970s with new appointments favoring a strict construction of the U.S. Constitution, to the dismay of some the Burger Court did not dramatically reverse many Warren Court precedents. If anything, it used its predecessor's precedents to make only relatively modest adjustments to constitutional doctrine in certain areas like criminal justice, whereas it either stayed the course or broke new ground, often in a progressive direction, in deciding issues of school desegregation (*Swann v. Charlottes-Mecklenburg Board of Education*, 1971), personal autonomy and abortion (*Roe v. Wade*, 1973), women's equality rights (*Reed v. Reed*, 1971), the death penalty (*Furman v. Georgia*, 1976), and affirmative action (*University of California v. Bakke*, 1978). Moreover, in key areas of federalism, such as interstate commerce, conditional spending, taxation, and preemption or supremacy clause regulation, with very few exceptions the Burger Court erred on the side of nationalizing power.[19] Critics expecting more conservatism from the Burger Court would have to wait until the political climate and the Court's composition changed further, and that transformation was soon to arrive with Californian governor Ronald Reagan's election to the presidency in 1980.

In the eight years of the Reagan Revolution, the president was able to make several new Supreme Court appointments. As will be discussed shortly, Reagan's judicial choices were cast in the same ideological mold of strict construction that Richard Nixon preferred[20]; as opposed to earlier 1960s and 1970s governing regimes, however, the conservatives on the bench dealt with a different 1980s political environment that was heavily influenced by Ronald Reagan's ideological fervor and his intergovernmental version of new federalism. His platform was shaped early on by a weakened presidency (due to Nixon's resignation and a perceived lack of strong leadership in the Carter administration), a decentralized Congress featuring an increasingly influential network of committees and party leadership, an influx of new organized interests and campaign cash generated by political action committees, and a weak economy held captive by a foreign oil cartel and domestic stagnation due to rising deficits, inflation, and interest rates. Another institutional development related to the sharp increase in federal grants to the states. Roughly $7 billion was filtered to subgovernments though 130 grant programs in 1960; in the ensuing two decades the figures were $90 billion with over four hundred grant programs, representing a 15 percent increase in state and local spending. By 1980, these elements registered an electoral mood that made it easy for candidate Reagan to attack the federal government because "it combined the worst of two worlds: it had become excessively intrusive and overbearing and at the same time unmanageable and inept."[21]

State governments also played a key role in administering the policy goals of the centralized regime, although for some scholars it seemed "cooptation as much as cooperation frequently characterized the intergovernmental relationships in various program areas."[22] As a result, in his first inaugural address President Reagan announced his intention to roll back the federal government, for the time had come to reinstate the historic equilibrium in government by "returning power to the states." Almost immediately the rhetoric was matched by executive action and new legislative proposals. One example is Executive Order 12372, which conceptually linked new federalism philosophy with the goal of achieving tangible on-the-ground results. By issuing it the president aimed to defuse federal intrusiveness and to bolster intergovernmental coordination by giving state officials more control over which federally subsidized projects they had to administer. Scaling back the federal presence meant the president was committed to reducing categorical grants, devolving program responsibilities to the states with additional block grants and increased managerial supervision over regulatory initiatives, and slashing federal regulations. Despite securing some early successes, Reagan's new federalism exponentially increased federal spending, with outlays rising in the billions from 1981 to 1988, and that was a pattern of growing spending that was occurring in the states over an identical period.[23]

In respect to intergovernmental reform, the major difference in the new federalisms of Reagan and Nixon is that Reagan defined and acted upon the philosophy of governance as a federalist ideology, whereas Nixon's allegiance was more akin to a secondary and less ideologically driven exercise in pragmatic governance. Unlike Nixon, Reagan was not that interested in improving the managerial efficiencies of administration; rather, in his public posturing he boldly "sought to redefine and restructure the responsibilities of governments in the federal system while significantly lowering the overall commitment of the federal government to providing financial aid to local governments."[24] To be sure, to different degrees both Nixon and Reagan achieved similar accomplishments in altering at least the mind-set and expectations about what the role of government is by de-emphasizing federal omnipotence and trying to shift the balance of decision-making toward states, cities, and localities. As with Nixon's new federalism, too, the concrete benefits the Reagan administration garnered only produced a policy track record of paradoxes and ironies that yielded mixed results and modest successes. It is plausible that Reagan, whenever he found it politically necessary, did not hesitate to subordinate the goal of returning power back to the states to the larger aims of reducing federal predominance in the course of preserving free competition in the private marketplace and reinforcing the inculcation of traditional conservative social values, especially in beating back the advancement of abortion rights.[25]

Perhaps the most lasting philosophical impact, then, of Reagan's new federalism relates not to achieving intergovernmental reform but instead rests with the way it rhetorically framed the ideological debate surrounding the use of official power by political institutions, especially the judiciary.[26] In this sense, Reagan's new federalism readily connects to judicial philosophies favoring strict construction and, in regard to federalism cases, the predilections of jurists who were thought to embrace the idea of dual federalism as a matter of legal principle. Although Presidents Reagan and Nixon both sought justices who were committed to strict construction and judicial restraint, Reagan's appointments can be differentiated because, as a political tool, they were generally perceived as potential advocates of the president's new federalism agenda favoring a potent ideological mix of decentralization, judicial restraint, and traditional social values. In contrast, President Nixon's Supreme Court justices were conservatives who more closely aligned with battling the Warren Court and its liberal criminal justice activism instead of advocating a strident return of authority back to the states.[27]

The Reagan selection process reinforced the distinction. While both presidents used a Republican ideological selection model to frame their judicial choices as symbolic instruments of presidential authority, in bureaucratic fashion and with a hands-off approach Reagan delegated to subordinates the task of staffing the courts with conservative ideologues. His nominees were screened from an elaborate political network of insiders from within the executive branch, including members of his Committee on Federal Judicial Selection, chaired by the White House counsel and administered with the cooperation of key advisers and the Department of Justice. The latter's Office of Legal Policy helped vet possible nominees by filtering the final selections though an intensive ideological lens, measuring their commitment to the president's political agenda through interviews, a detailed examination of their past record, writings, and political activities, and the like. Like Nixon, Reagan's team targeted the Supreme Court for criticism, but it also widened the applicant pool and the conservative net of social values that prospective justices ought to emulate. Consequently, the president sought nominees who shared his outrage over the judiciary's rulings that extended abortion rights, supported racial integration through busing, restricted religious activities in public schools, and favored affirmative action. Moreover, the preexisting convention of allowing the American Bar Association (as a liaison to the legal profession) to add its own assessment of nominees apart from the White House was diminished, thus allowing the judicial selection process to become highly ideological and centralized within the executive branch and inside the White House.[28]

In comparison to the Nixon White House, Reagan's judicial nominees to the Supreme Court focused less on criminal justice and more on returning power back to the states as a matter of federalism theory, judicial power, and political rhetoric. With a corresponding infusion and growth of a conservative intelligentsia in the 1980s and afterward, which encompassed governmental officials in the executive branch as well as additional influences from think tanks and interest groups like the Federalist Society, the Heritage Foundation, the American Enterprise Institute, and the U.S. Chamber of Commerce, the Reagan White House's first three Supreme Court selections were thought to be good ideological fits with the conservative legal agenda embracing the strategic use of public interest litigation. In 1981, with the strong backing of Attorney General William French Smith, the president was able to keep his campaign promise to put the first woman on the high court with Sandra Day O'Connor when Justice Potter Stewart left the bench. O'Connor's background as an Arizona legislator and state judge, along with her perceived commitment to judicial restraint, criminal justice reform, and abortion rights, assisted Reagan in fulfilling that promise.[29]

The president's next two choices were even more ideologically driven, in large part because after his reelection William French Smith was replaced by Edwin Meese as attorney general. Meese, an ideologue strongly interested in packing federal courts with conservatives favoring strict construction and judicial restraint, seized the political moment when he learned that Chief Justice Warren Burger intended to retire. By the time Burger actually left the Court, Meese and key Department of Justice insiders had ample time to vet nominees ahead of the announcement with specific ideological criteria in mind. Those benchmarks were later etched into a pamphlet prepared by the Justice Department's Office of Legal Policy that reflected a conservative interpretation of constitutional principles (including Section 4, titled "Guidelines on Respecting the Limited Power Granted to the Federal Government"). For the Reagan judicial selection team, it was a precondition for nominees to share the president's preference for judicial restraint, but they also were judged by other factors specifically relating to federalism, such as showing "deference to states in their spheres" and understanding that "the federal government is one of enumerated powers." In those respects, and in showing a conservative sensitivity to religion, criminal justice, civil rights, and free speech issues, William H. Rehnquist (already a justice first elevated to the bench by Richard Nixon in 1972) was tapped for chief justice. At the same time, Rehnquist's seat was filled by another strict constructionist from the DC Circuit, Antonin Scalia, who was described by Washington insiders as "a brilliant conservative."[30]

The presidential appointments of O'Connor, Rehnquist and Scalia, plus the additions of Anthony Kennedy (a Reagan appointee replacing moderate Lewis Powell) and Clarence Thomas (a G. H. W. Bush appointee taking liberal Thurgood Marshall's seat), allowed the Supreme Court to coalesce into a "federalism five" majority that scholars identify as launching the federalism revival in ensuing years. A full appreciation of the role Rehnquist played in moving the coalition and Court in that direction involves understanding his jurisprudence when he was a Burger Court associate justice. As discussed next, key elements of Rehnquist's new federalism are disclosed by several dissenting opinions he authored, plus other Rehnquist majority rulings, including *National League of Cities v. Usery* (1976), a 5–4 decision rejecting a political (and endorsing a judicial) safeguards approach to federalism. As will be seen, the judicial safeguards view had a short precedential shelf life, a reality that arguably presented new opportunities for Rehnquist new federalism to flourish in other doctrinal areas of constitutional law favoring state autonomy.

REHNQUIST NEW FEDERALISM

The political agendas and judicial appointments of the Nixon and Reagan administrations are vital sources for understanding Supreme Court new federalism politics after William Rehnquist was elevated from associate to chief justice. While all Rehnquist Court justices did not follow all of the chief justice's legal positions, Rehnquist's judicial record while serving on the Burger Court is some indicia of whether his legal positions were joined by others or remained constant over time. His reputation for being a lone dissenter on the Burger Court was thought to be a factor in how he would decide cases later. As one legal commentator put it, "Rehnquist is somebody with a long vision. His opinions oftentimes are prophetic of what's going to happen if he gets the votes."[31] Illustrative Rehnquist judicial opinions may register "path dependence," a concept used by scholars to measure Rehnquist Court new federalism jurisprudence.[32] Such evidence aids in constructing a legal roadmap of Rehnquist's strategic behavior and the doctrinal path he wanted to take the Court on in later years, provided he could get support from his colleagues, and it gauges his understanding of the judicial role whenever the federal courts were asked to police the structural boundaries of constitutional federalism. This last issue, framed by political scientists and law scholars as the political safeguards debate, remains central to comprehending the ideological conceptions of new federalism and how those ideas are filtered into court outcomes and public policy.[33]

Rehnquist's basic judicial philosophy is purportedly defined by restraint and showing respect for majority rule through strict textually based interpretations of the constitutional document. As he famously said in a 1976 *Texas Law Review* article, he disavowed allegiance to the notion of a living constitution that adapts to the times. That approach, he asserts, impermissibly lets judges concoct "a formula for an end run around popular government" because they would be inclined to write their own policy preferences into law without regard to following founding intent.[34] Although remaining faithful to the constitutional text undergirds his judicial philosophy, Rehnquist's line drawing indicates he adopted a more flexible, structurally based approach to judicial decision-making in federalism cases—one that arguably is set loose from textual constitutional moorings.[35] Under this view, the Constitution's overall structural design or plan orients judicial decision-making by giving judges the requisite authority to protect federalism values that enhance state autonomy while diminishing the threat of excessive federal interference.

An analysis of Rehnquist's judicial behavior suggests a relatively consistent solicitude and respect for state autonomy. That finding originates from a sample of cases from the Supreme Court Database linked to four issues of constitutional federalism that are commonly associated with the Rehnquist Court's state-centered revival: Congress's power to regulate state activities under the commerce clause of Article I, Section 8; whether the Tenth Amendment is a constraint on federal power; the scope of Congress's authority to enforce federal law against the states under Section 5 of the Fourteenth Amendment; and whether the Eleventh Amendment bars federal courts from reviewing lawsuits commenced against state governments.[36] Sixty-six cases are analyzed, with a majority (52 percent) dealing with state tax and regulation issues spanning eighteen areas of federal-state law. Regarding those issues, Rehnquist elected to write dissenting opinions (instead of silently joining others) in 59 percent of the cases.[37] For illustrative purposes, select dissenting and majority opinions are reviewed from within that sample to provide a sense of Rehnquist's construction of the founding document relative to key federalism areas.

Legal scholars and social scientists often refer to Rehnquist's lone dissent in *Fry v. United States* as a basis of Rehnquist's new federalism.[38] At issue was the viability of *Maryland v. Wirtz*, a precedent establishing that states were obliged to abide by the wage and hour provisions of the Federal Labor Standards Act. In *Fry* the scope of Congress's authority and whether it extended to preventing Ohio from giving its employees wage increases beyond what federal law allowed in the Economic Stabilization Act of 1970 was considered by the justices. The 1970 law was a temporary stopgap designed to stem the tide of runaway inflation, which Congress perceived as a national emergency. In dissenting from the majority's decision to uphold the law, Rehnquist claimed it forced state officials to pay its workers a set wage, a violation of state sovereignty. Rehnquist was unconvinced that *Wirtz* meant Congress could use its commerce power to regulate the states in the same way that it could regulate corporations or private individuals. For Rehnquist, the difference was critical because the law reached too far in controlling Ohio's decision to establish compensation, a traditional governmental function. As a result, extending the commerce power improperly let the legislature regulate Ohio "as a state" (i.e., when it acts in the capacity of a sovereign). The dissenter, as well, embraced a structural view of the Constitution to defend his reasoning. Under that view, Ohio, as a sovereign, can ask the Court to invoke the "principles of federalism" in the Tenth Amendment as a "constitutional counterweight" to defend itself against federal overreaching under the

Table 3.1. Rehnquist Dissents in Key Federalism Areas, 1971–1986

Case	*Issue/Legal Provision*	*Ideological Direction/ Vote (Full Court)*	*Ideological Direction/ Vote (Rehnquist Dissent)*
Written Opinion in Expected Direction			
Allenberg Cotton Co. v. Pittman (1974)	Federalism/Constitution (Interstate Commerce)	Liberal (8–1)	Conservative
Fry v. United States (1975)	Federalism/Constitution (Interstate Commerce)	Liberal (7–1)	Conservative
City of Philadelphia v. N.J. (1978)	Econ. Activity/Constitution (Interstate Commerce)	Liberal (7–2)	Conservative
Hughes v. Oklahoma (1979)	Econ. Activity/Constitution (Interstate Commerce)	Liberal (7–2)	Conservative
Nevada v. Hall (1979)	Econ. Activity/Const. Am. (Eleventh Amendment)	Liberal (6–3)	Conservative
City of Rome v. United States (1980)+	Section Five (Fourteenth Amendment)	Liberal (6–3)	Conservative
Kassel v. Consolidated Freightways (1981)	Econ. Activity/Constitution (Interstate Commerce)	Liberal (6–3)	Conservative
Sporhase v. Nebraska (1982)	Federalism/Constitution (Interstate Commerce)	Liberal (7–2)	Conservative
South-Central Dev. v. Wunnicke (1984)	Federalism/Constitution (Interstate Commerce)	Liberal (6–2)	Conservative
Written Opinion Not in Expected Direction			
Edgar v. Mite Corporation (1982)	Econ. Activity/Constitution (Interstate Commerce)	Conservative (6–3)	Liberal
	Econ. Activity/Constitution (Case/Controversy)	Conservative (6–3)	Liberal
Armco, Inc. v. Hardesty (1984)	Econ. Activity/Constitution (Interstate Commerce)	Conservative (8–1)	Liberal

Source: The Supreme Court Dataset, 1953–2011 terms, at http://scdb.wustl.edu/analysis.php (using Data Release SCDB_2011_01).
Note: +Added and coded by authors using coding protocols established by dataset.

commerce clause. Lastly, he suggested that the Eleventh Amendment offered a similar protection to prevent states from being hauled into federal court when they are sued.[39]

Other dissents in table 3.1 index Rehnquist's narrow construction of the Fourteenth Amendment's enforcement clause, which, if broadly construed, could negatively impact state autonomy whenever states tried to control their own electoral processes. Earlier Warren Court precedents broadly interpreted Congress's enforcement power to ensure states would not discriminate against minorities trying to exercise their voting rights, a key problem in the South. As a constitutional matter this meant that under the 1965 Voting Rights Act states had to preclear, or get advance approval, from the federal government if it wanted to change the methods by which voting took place in states or cities. One of the federalism purposes of preclearance was to prevent any locality from bypassing the federal mandate (of providing equality in voting) if it chose to disenfranchise minorities through its own laws, especially if it had a track record of doing that in the past. When the city of Rome, Georgia, altered its electoral processes, it challenged whether it had to go through the federal government to do so, claiming Congress lacked the authority to require preclearance under the enforcement powers granted by the Civil War Amendments (under Sections 2 and 5 of the Thirteenth and Fourteenth Amendments, permitting Congress to enforce, with appropriate legislation, voting and equality rights).

Thus in *City of Rome v. United States* the Supreme Court upheld the U.S. attorney general's authority to refuse to preclear the city's redistricting changes in compliance with the 1965 Voting Rights Act's goal of achieving equal political representation. Rehnquist's dissent construed Congress's enforcement authority differently, arguing that the Court misapplied it to let Congress, instead of the judiciary, judge if voting rights were substantively taken away by the city by its actions. As he explained,

> To permit congressional power to prohibit the conduct challenged in this case requires state and local governments to cede far more of their powers to the Federal Government than the Civil War Amendments ever envisioned; and it requires the judiciary to cede far more of its power to interpret and enforce the Constitution than ever envisioned. The intrusion is all the more offensive to our constitutional system when it is recognized that the only values fostered are debatable assumptions about political theory which should properly be left to the local democratic process.[40]

As an issue of democratic theory, he reasoned that the city ought not to be questioned about its representation decision processes because evidence was lacking to show that it committed unconstitutional violations diminishing equality. In constricting Congress's enforcement power, he insisted that the judiciary has a duty to first "carefully scrutinize the alleged source of congressional power" and explore why it must use it "to intrude so deeply in the government structure of the municipal corporations created by some of the 50 States." In this instance, the Court improperly invoked a remedy to fix a violation without first establishing that there was a constitutional wrong to rectify. Not only did the Court ignore the lower court's findings that the city did not act with a discriminatory purpose, the Court forced the city of Rome to "structure its political system" without the necessary evidence in place to justify federal interference. Because "the enforcement provisions of the Civil War Amendments were not premised on the notion that Congress could empower a later generation of blacks to 'get even' for wrongs inflicted on their forebears," the Court displaced the city's prerogatives to make its own decisions about political representation. The crux of Rehnquist's objection is his refusal to let Congress create substantive rights under the Fourteenth Amendment using its enforcement powers; in other words, those basic political decisions should be instead left to popular will at the state level. This meant that the judiciary should step in only to fix documented instances of voting rights' violations in the states.[41]

The preference Rehnquist exhibits for insulating state governments from federal oversight extends to commercial interactions involving the dormant commerce clause (implicitly letting states regulate mercantile transactions in the absence of controlling federal law). Three rulings—*City of Philadelphia v. New Jersey* (striking down local law regulating importation of solid waste), *Hughes v. Oklahoma* (striking down prohibition on out-of-state distribution of minnows), and *Kassel v. Consolidated Freightways* (striking down state law restricting truck lengths on highways)—are illustrative. Among them, *Kassel* is unique because it represented an ideological standard for legal policies adopted by the Department of Justice under Attorney General Meese's supervision in the late 1980s. Specifically, lawyers from the Office of Legal Policy cited it as one of several Rehnquist-authored opinions that correctly interpreted the Constitution in favor of the states.[42] Notably, those cases, as well as the others listed in table 3.1, represent the expected ideological direction. Yet some of his federalism outcomes are not moderated by ideology, which, for some scholars, is an aspect of judicial behavior that may supply a benchmark for determining the integrity and consistency of state sovereignty theory.[43]

Armco, Inc. v. Hardesty is arguably one instance. Armco, Inc., an Ohio steel manufacturer doing business in West Virginia, challenged West Virginia's wholesale product tax exemption for local manufacturers as running afoul of the interstate commerce clause since it discriminated against out-of-state businesses. In a lone dissent, Rehnquist argued the Court wrongly struck the tax down because its decision was not supported by the evidence. Since the record was silent, he voted in favor of West Virginia's claim. As a state tax case involving an economic activity, the Supreme Court Dataset (1953–2011 terms) used to compile the cases deemed the dissent a liberal outcome, or, restated, as pro-state or anti-business. It is plausible that the coding decision was based on Rehnquist's decision to express his pro-state preference to give West Virginia the choice to use a tax exemption without federal interference; alternatively, from an anti-business perspective, he may have thought that West Virginian businesses were harmed by not being able to take advantage of the tax break. In federalism terms the liberal outcome in his dissent may still be *ideologically* aligned with his vote in the sense that he chose to defer to, or to show respect for, West Virginia's policy choice to give local businesses special consideration in certain tax matters. On the other hand, the decision to support West Virginia's tax policy meant that Ohio manufacturers had to pay more taxes, an outcome that could also be considered anti-business and, as such, makes the coding decision more ambiguous.

Other characteristics of Rehnquist's new federalism surface when he speaks on behalf of the full court in majority opinions. *National League of Cities v. Usery* is the leading example (see table 3.2). At issue was whether Congress could apply the federal Fair Labor Standards Act (FLSA) and its minimum wage and maximum hour requirements to state employees under the commerce clause. In spite of precedents suggesting otherwise, the Court returned power back to the states by limiting Congress's regulation of the economy. In a 5–4 ruling, Rehnquist argued Congress overreached because it sought to control "functions [that are] essential to [the states'] separate and independent existence," an error degrading their "independent authority," if not their "necessary existence." Permitting the regulation to stand would interfere with "attributes of sovereignty attaching to every state government," disrupting the basic choices states make "as States." The Tenth Amendment, as well, is an affirmative limitation on irregularly exercised national power. The constitutional structure, which Rehnquist construed holistically and without regard to specific textual clause references, gives state officials the latitude to govern "traditional aspects" of state sovereignty, including those relating to employee compensation.[44]

Speaking for the dissent, Justice William Brennan raised an ongoing issue that continues to surface in contemporary federalism debates: whether the Supreme Court is obliged to exercise judicial review to protect state governments from federal omnipotence. For Brennan, Congress acted within the proper scope of its delegated commercial powers in applying the FLSA to state governments in *Usery*. Regardless, he reasoned, the states are adequately safeguarded by the Constitution's original design,

Table 3.2. Rehnquist Majority Opinions in Key Federalism Areas, 1971–1986

Case	*Issue/Legal Provision*	*Ideological Direction/Vote*
Written Majority Opinion in Expected Direction		
Edelman v. Jordan (1974)	Civil Rights/Eleventh Amendment	Conservative (5–4)
National League of Cities v. Usery (1976)	Unions/Constitution (Interstate Commerce)	Conservative (5–4)
Mt. Healthy City School Dist. v. Doyle (1977)	Civil Rights/Eleventh Amendment	Conservative (9–0)
Arizona Public Service v. Snead (1979)	Economic Activity/Constitution (Interstate Commerce)	Conservative (9–0)
Quern v. Jordan (1979)	Civil Rights/Eleventh Amendment	Conservative (9–0)
Green v. Michigan Dep't of Soc. Services (1985)	Civil Rights/Eleventh Amendment	Conservative (5–4)
Written Majority Opinion Not in Expected Direction		
United States v. Mauzrie (1975)	Civil Rights/Constitution (Interstate Commerce)	Liberal (5–4)
Fitzpatrick v. Bitzer (1976)	Civil Rights/Const. Am. (Sect. 5, Fourteenth Amendment)	Liberal (9–0)
White v. Massachusetts Council (1983)	Economic Activity/Constitution (Interstate Commerce)	Liberal (7–2)

Source: The Supreme Court Dataset, 1953–2011 terms, at http://scdb.wustl.edu/analysis.php (using Data Release SCDB_2011_01).

which makes them integral in electing the president and congressional representatives. As a result, any threats to state sovereignty are reduced by the normal operation of democratic politics, which automatically take into account state interests whenever policies and laws are created in the deliberative process. So long as the political process, and the procedural safeguards therein, preserve the states, it is unnecessary for courts to do so by exercising judicial review. For Brennan, only activist judges substitute their own judgment for those produced by the political process in opting to defend the states, mainly because the constitutional structure is a sufficient check on federal powers.[45]

The judicial conflict between Justices Rehnquist and Brennan presaged later struggles over the constitutional limits of national power that, in time, led to the judiciary's frustration with trying to figure out what kinds of state activity fall on the state-protected side of the constitutional line in federalism cases handed down over the next decade. The ambiguity of knowing exactly when federal obtrusiveness upset traditional state functions to the point of a constitutional violation caused the Supreme Court to reverse *Usery* in *Garcia v. San Antonio Metropolitan Transit Authority*, a ruling marked by Justice Harry Blackmun's decision to switch sides and join the *Usery* dissenters and their political safeguards rationale. *Garcia*, decided in a close 5–4 vote, effectively wrote law professor Herbert Wechsler's political safeguards argument (set forth in a 1954 *Harvard Law Review* article) into constitutional law; more significantly, it also meant that the justices interested in establishing stricter federal limits and preserving state autonomy through judicial review would have to do it in other ways.[46] One possibility sought to restrict federal courts from hearing lawsuits against state governments, a topic Rehnquist visited several times in Eleventh Amendment majority opinions (see table 3.2).

By its words the Eleventh Amendment only forecloses lawsuits in federal courts that are started against a state by citizens from another state. Still, as Rehnquist stated in *Edelman v. Jordan*, state immunity also extended to actions by state citizens against their own state under an earlier precedent, *Hans v. Louisiana*. These rules and whether there were any exceptions to their operation were tested in *Edelman*, a lawsuit brought by an Illinois citizen (representing a class of litigants) against Illinois officials for improperly administering a federal categorical grant program (Aid to the Aged, Blind, and Disabled [AABD]) authorized under the Social Security Act and federal regulations. Under the program, states agreeing to participate can use federal monies to help pay for benefits given to eligible recipients, but only if they agreed to follow federal guidelines in administering the program. Illinois took part in the jointly funded cooperative arrangement, but in applying the state's own regulations, state officials failed to comply with the federal guidelines, which caused the petitioners to have their own benefits wrongfully withheld. They sued to recover the payments they should have received had state officials correctly processed aid applications under controlling federal law, a form of retroactive relief. Still, the *Edelman* five-justice majority refused to accept their position in accordance with what they thought the Eleventh Amendment meant.

Through Rehnquist the Court expanded state immunity by narrowly interpreting two instances in which the Eleventh Amendment might not work to foreclose private actions in federal courts. In *Edelman*, both were raised as arguments to overcome state immunity. The first concerned *Ex Parte Young*, a precedent the lower federal court used with equitable restitution principles to permit the recovery of monies from state treasuries that were wrongfully withheld by state officials. In reversing the lower court, Rehnquist reasoned *Ex Parte Young* only authorized lawsuits to stop prospective (and not retroactive) violations of federal law, a result immunizing Illinois from the liability of having to account for paying benefits as compensation to those who should have received them in the past under federal mandates.

The alternative argument, centering on whether Illinois impliedly waived its immunity by consenting to the lawsuit through its voluntary participation in the AABD program under federal conditions, was equally unavailing. In rejecting it Rehnquist argued that Illinois's cooperation in the federal program did not supply a clear indication that it consented to be sued in a private action. Likewise, he did not see anything in the Social Security Act indicating that Congress intended to authorize private lawsuits and abrogate state immunity. He emphasized that the judiciary is hard pressed to find that a state ordinarily chooses to give up its constitutional rights (and immunity). So he required that a waiver must be judicially identified "by the most express language or by such overwhelming implications from the text as (will) leave no room for any other reasonable construction" by judges. In applying the standard, Rehnquist was unmoved by dissenting Justice Thurgood Marshall's claim that a combination of factors—including the fact that another civil rights statute, 42 U.S.C. § 1983, created a private cause of action and could be used to sue Illinois—showed that Congress unequivocally intended to displace state immunity.[47]

While the dissents and majority opinions are not representative of all the different facets of Rehnquist's new federalism, they nonetheless signify basic contours of an evolving theory of state sovereignty.[48] For Rehnquist, the aspect of state sovereignty most worthy of intensified judicial protection appears to be rooted in a closely related concept of state autonomy. His *Fry*, *City of Rome*, and dormant commerce clause dissents, as well as the *Usery* majority opinion, all reflect an acute preference for protecting the capacity of state officials to make autonomous policy choices about how to manage essential government functions. While his judicial philosophy is based in restraint, his new federalism is paradoxically oriented from a structural interpretation of the constitutional framework that is suspicious about whether the political process itself can adequately safeguard the states: democratic majority rule must be respected whenever feasible, and the federal government can act—and must stay within—the realm of its delegated powers, but the court is free and often supreme in constructing principles of federalism that are not necessarily anchored to specific clauses or text. Under that view, judges can justify using an aggressive form of judicial review to ensure that the political branches are reigned in while simultaneously giving state officials the autonomy to make unconstrained governance choices that best preserve state sovereignty in a dual federalism paradigm.[49] While sometimes he is amendable to granting federal officials deference, *City of Rome* suggests little tolerance for letting the federal government create substantive rights that displace state regulation; for federal law to trump state law, there must be clear proof that the former corrects the problems caused by the latter's unconstitutionality. The state immunity cases are insightful for an identical reason. While state officials may be subject to federal jurisdiction to stop violations of federal law in the future, states must generally consent to the legal process. Ambiguously defined sources of constitutional text or statutes cannot be the basis for federal judicial action that increases the likelihood that states, as sovereign units in the constitutional system (and figuratively unlike regular citizens), will be subject to being sued in lawsuits by private parties, so Rehnquist insists that any consent (to being sued) or waiver of state immunity must be supported by clear statutory intent because, otherwise, courts do not have the authority to act in the federal interest. The extent to which these principles were consistently applied by the conservative justices who seemed inclined to favor states' rights positions in the Rehnquist Court federalism revival is considered next.

REVOLUTIONARY AND COUNTERREVOLUTIONARY TRENDS

By the time Rehnquist became chief justice in 1986, he had built the foundation for his state sovereignty theory in many of his Burger Court opinions. Yet it was uncertain if he could succeed in convincing his colleagues that his vision of new federalism was worthy of judicial implementation. Court watchers evaluating the Rehnquist Court, lasting from 1986 to 2005, tend to agree that it consisted of at least two, and possibly three, Courts within a Court, each of which left a different federalist legacy that did not uniformly protect states. The first, from October 1986 to July 1994, is characterized by relatively rapid membership flux, few doctrinal advances, and a bench divided against itself as it struggled with an agenda that was top-heavy with hot-button social legislation cases (i.e., abortion, right to die, affirmative action, and certain religious freedoms) instead of federalism disputes. The second Rehnquist Court, greatly impacted by a reconfiguration of ideologically opposed voting blocs due principally to the arrival of Clarence Thomas and the departure of Byron White, lasted from October 1994 to July 2003. That period saw a return to federalism cases, with better internal cohesion among the conservative justices favoring federalist jurisprudence, fewer social legislation cases, and more doctrinal innovations in federalism precedents. The last Rehnquist Court, linked with the last years of the chief justice's stewardship, is known for achieving a federalist retreat of sorts, marked by increasing judicial conflict within the five-justice conservative bloc that had the effect of vitiating pro-state precedents established in the earlier period. As pundit Linda Greenhouse suggests, the last segment may symbolize the chief justice's waning influence as the leader of the federalist coalition, perhaps putting the revival's constitutional significance at risk.[50]

With few exceptions, scholars conclude the Rehnquist Court's new federalism impact or legacy is generally modest at best, or overstated at worst, and may not even be a legacy attributable to Rehnquist.[51] An investigation of those possibilities and consideration of another—that the revival might have more significance than is acknowledged—begins with a survey of some aggregate trends in federalism litigation data. Table 3.3, accordingly, offers a rough approximation of the Rehnquist Court's treatment of federalism cases in comparison to the Warren and Burger Courts. The empirics therein collect and ideologically code only "federalism" cases; within that sample, decisional trends are observed relative to striking down federal or state regulation, or in changing precedent.[52]

Comparing the dockets across the Warren, Burger, and Rehnquist Courts shows that each spanned roughly the same time period, ranging between fifteen and eighteen terms, with each yielding a similar number of federalism cases, from 94 to 124. Predictably, the percentage of liberal anti-state outcomes was highest in the Warren Court; thereafter, there is a sharp decline to the lowest percentage registered in the Rehnquist Court (from 71 to 54 percent). Although overall the justices in all eras consistently voted in favor of national power, the 17 percent decline in liberal outcomes reflects a decreasing trend toward centralization in the two conservative Burger and Rehnquist Courts, with the latter (46 percent) exhibiting a record of supporting a greater rate of conservative pro-state results as compared to its predecessors (27 and 38 percent). Similarly, the Warren Court

Table 3.3. Federalism Decisional Trends, U.S. Supreme Court, 1953–2004

	Warren Court (1953–1968)	*Burger Court (1969–1985)*	*Rehnquist Court (1986–2004)*
Number of Federalism Rulings	94	108	124
Decision Direction			
Liberal	71%	59%	54%
Conservative	27%	38%	46%
Declaration of Unconstitutionality			
None	88%	93%	88%
State Law, Regulation, Constitution	11%	6%	6%
Municipal/Local Ordinance	1%	1%	0%
Congressional Act	0	0	6
Precedent Alteration			
None	98%	98%	96%
Formal Alteration	2%	3%	4%

Source: The Supreme Court Dataset, 1953–2011 terms, at http://scdb.wustl.edu/analysis.php (using Data Release SCDB_2011_01).

records the highest rate of constitutional reversals of state and local laws (11 percent), whereas the Rehnquist Court featured the least (6 percent), again showing solicitude for states. Perhaps the most significant finding relates to judicial review. Unlike either of the earlier Courts, Rehnquist justices nullified congressional legislation, indicating that it was aggressive in checking centralized authority. Moreover, while each Court followed stare decisis at a high level with regard to federalism-coded cases, the Rehnquist Court was unique in departing from it more often than its liberal and conservative counterparts in federalism cases, thus perhaps underscoring an activist inclination to change the law to reach desirable outcomes.

Whereas the revolutionary aspects of the revival conspicuously emerged in several high-profile rulings after 1994, the justices signaled that the approach to deciding federalism cases might be different than in the past. In *South Dakota v. Dole*, a 7–2 decision, Chief Justice Rehnquist's majority opinion confirmed the use of Congress's Article I spending power to condition the receipt of federal highway monies on the adoption of minimum age requirements for alcohol consumption. He reasoned the disparity in drinking ages among the states intensified the problem of drinking and driving across U.S. highways, justifying a national solution serving the general welfare. Conspicuously, he measured the federal law's constitutionality against a judicial finding that Congress must clearly notify the states of the conditions they had to satisfy in order to get the funds, which operated as a procedural protection for states against federal compulsion and overreaching. Although the outcome reaffirmed broad federal spending prerogatives, the mix of constitutional and statutory interpretative elements expressed in *South Dakota*, framed in language favoring antifederal coercion, state-centric volition, and clear statements of notice, can be traced to earlier pre–Rehnquist Court federalism cases favoring state sovereignty.[53] From another perspective *South Dakota* provides insight as it featured the dissenting voice of Sandra Day O'Connor, who, as a prospective ally of Rehnquist in the "federalism five" voting bloc coalescing after 1994 and perhaps by then acting as the Court's leading federalism spokesman, could not conclude, as Rehnquist did, that a drinking age edict is reasonably related to the purposes of federal highway construction and, concomitantly, to the appropriation of federal funds with conditions. The case's other dissenter, liberal Justice Brennan, agreed, sharing O'Connor's view that conditioning the receipt of funds on abstract concerns about highway safety wrongly means that "Congress could effectively regulate almost any area of a State's social, political, or economic life on the theory that use of the interstate transportation system is somehow enhanced," thereby invading the states' reserved powers.[54]

The *South Dakota* implication that the justices might be more receptive to using procedural orientations to gauge their understanding of individual rights and federalism outcomes surfaced in two other 1991 statutory interpretation cases, *Gregory v. Ashcroft* and *Coleman v. Thompson*.[55] By then, a variety of rule-based conceptions with different connotations greatly informed the parameters of federalism judicial enforcement. By 1985 *Garcia*'s political safeguards approach had replaced *Usery*'s 1976 judicial safeguards paradigm, and precedents identifying what process is due, at issue in *Gregory* as a matter of federalism's synergy with age discrimination and germane to *Coleman* with respect to federalism's nexus with criminal justice, increasingly supplied the context for comprehending the scope and application of substantive constitutional rights. In *Gregory* judges serving by gubernatorial appointment and facing mandatory retirement at age seventy under the Missouri constitution claimed that federal law, the Age Discrimination and Employment Act (ADEA) (as well as equal protection under the federal Constitution), displaced state law so that they could remain on the bench past age seventy. Writing for a 7–2 Court, Justice O'Connor disagreed. She observed that the ADEA covers state employees but not appointees on the policymaking level. Critical to the case was the absence of a plain statement by Congress showing that the ADEA applied to the judges in a policymaking capacity, so the Court had to presume its absence meant that Congress did not intend to regulate an area of electoral politics that traditionally fell to the states. As a result the judges were exempt from the ADEA, and they had to retire at seventy under state law.

An identical rationale weaved itself into *Coleman*'s outcome, but this time by imposing a procedural principle that either facilitates or thwarts federal judicial review of criminal appeals. In *Coleman*, a death penalty prisoner was barred from appealing his conviction in state court; so he sought relief and a retrial through a federal habeas corpus petition, arguing he missed the thirty-day appeal deadline because of his attorney's error. Justice O'Connor, speaking for a 6–3 majority, observed the case "was about federalism . . . [and] the respect that federal courts owe the States and the States' procedural rules when reviewing the claims of state prisoners in federal habeas corpus." In that light, she applied a rule of construction and deference to the state court's decision to dismiss the appeal. The judicially crafted canon, derived from an earlier O'Connor majority opinion in *Michigan v. Long* and other analogous Rehnquist-written capital habeas precedents, presumed federal courts have habeas jurisdiction only in the absence of a plain statement that there is an independent and adequate ground in state law that would otherwise prevent the federal court from reviewing the appeal. In *Coleman*, O'Connor concluded the state court's dismissal of the appeal was based on an independent and adequate ground of procedural default under state court rules (i.e., not meeting the thirty-day deadline). Thus the rule's presumption favoring federal jurisdictional review was rebutted, so the petitioner lost his habeas right to have his constitutional claims of error heard in federal court.[56]

Significantly, the new *Coleman* directive was directly at odds with a Warren Court habeas precedent, *Fay v. Noia*, which, as O'Connor concedes, "created a presumption in favor of federal habeas review of claims procedurally defaulted in state court" so long as the prisoner (and not counsel) made the deliberate choice to bypass using state courts for relief. Accordingly, *Fay* was reversed as it was "based on a conception of federal/state relations that undervalued the importance of state procedural rules . . . [and the Court] . . . now recognize[s] the important interest in finality served by state procedural rules, and the significant harm to the States that results from the failure of federal courts to respect them." For one observer, *Coleman*'s analysis and *Fay*'s burial used federalism considerations to assign a higher value to the interest of adhering to state trial process rules while subordinating the interest of allowing state prisoners the chance to use federal courts as venues for fixing alleged constitutional violations.[57]

For supporters, this line of conservative jurisprudence reinforces structural federalism and democratic theory while secondarily giving due respect to individual rights. But liberal detractors argue conservatives have their analysis and constitutional priorities backward.[58] The ideological direction of either perspective, and whether the Court determines it must aggressively police the boundaries of federalism, turns on the quintessential questions posed by *Usery* and *Garcia*: Does the Supreme Court justifiably enforce federalism values if the political processes fail to protect the states (as sovereign units), even though individual rights may suffer? Or, conversely, can the justices legitimately safeguard individual rights without necessarily taking into account the sovereign prerogatives of the states? While these questions are admittedly reductionist, the academic literature mirrors them, often suggesting that the early Rehnquist Court new federalism cases register the same dynamic insofar as they tend to elevate process-based concerns (i.e., whether Congress, courts, or litigants are faithfully or rigorously following the rules) over substantive concerns (i.e., whether discrete individuals are given access to court, constitutional rights, or justice). Moreover, beginning with *Gregory* the application of clear statement rules is a strategic judicial decision: *Garcia*'s political safeguards principle, favoring nonjudicial interference, is doctrinally replaced with a statutory construction norm and obligation to follow procedural safeguards, which, if not complied with, triggers the discretionary judicial choice to check aggressively federal incursions on traditional state functions, including policies touching upon liquor consumption (*Dole*), political representation (*Gregory*), and crime policy (*Coleman*).[59]

A mix of identical issues and charges of judicial activism encompass the reaction to cases decided in the second Rehnquist Court, a time when Justice Byron White left the bench and Justice Clarence Thomas made his presence felt after his 1991 appointment.[60] Starting with *New York v. United States* and its holding that federal law cannot "commandeer" states into making policy choices about how to manage low-level radioactive waste disposal, the Rehnquist Court began to transfigure more assertively constitutional doctrine in favor of dual federalism and state-centric objectives, emphasizing historical and structural constitutional interpretations. In New York, decided by a 6–3 vote, O'Connor's majority opinion invalidated part of the Low-Level Radioactive Waste Management Act Amendments of 1985 as a violation of the states' reserved powers under the Tenth Amendment. Two other legal provisions, offering states financial incentives and access to waste disposal sites upon compliance with federal law, were upheld under the commerce authority. That precedent was extended in *Printz v. United States*, a Scalia opinion for a 5–4 Court applying the Tenth Amendment as a limitation to prevent federal agency officials from requiring state law enforcement personnel to conduct background checks for firearms purchases. The "anti-commandeering" case law conspicuously did not overturn, but implicitly undermined, *Garcia* by looking at the Tenth Amendment as a state sovereignty limitation on the exercise of federal power, a dormant principle originating from *United States v. Darby*'s 1941 declaration that the amendment was a benign "truism" of little force. Furthermore, the anti-commandeering rationale itself was both doctrinally innovative and controversial, with critics observing that the justices created it out of whole cloth from structural and federalism considerations instead of from principles anchored in constitutional text.[61]

In 1995 *United States v. Lopez*, via Chief Justice Rehnquist in a 5–4 decision, nullified the federal Gun-Free School Zones Act because it usurped state law that traditionally regulated crime policy. The Court reasoned that gun possession near local public schools is a noneconomic activity lacking a substantial effect on interstate commerce, a key interpretative issue relating to whether Congress is properly exercising its delegated powers. Thereafter, in *United States v. Morrison*, a bare 5–4 majority extended *Lopez* by striking down part of the federal Violence against Women Act, concluding that the private civil remedy it created to give victims of gender violence a chance to sue their attackers for money damages exceeded Congress's commerce powers and its Fourteenth Amendment, Section 5 enforcement authority. *Morrison* thus dismissed a federal lawsuit by a woman who was sexually assaulted by football players on a team established by a state-run university. Both cases reviewed congressional findings only to reason that each supplied insufficient proof to justify federal interference with state sovereignty. Whereas *Lopez* asserted that the legislative hearings insufficiently showed that regulating gun possession was linked to interstate commerce, *Morrison* observed that the extensive legislative history documenting the problem of gender-based violence in the states did not warrant federal administration of a noneconomic activity that was wrongly aimed at giving victims a damage remedy that punished private parties and not state officials. Besides casting aside several decades of judicial deference to Congress by striking down two federal statutes that ordinarily would have been upheld under the commerce clause, the *Lopez* and *Morrison* rulings indirectly questioned the continued viability of long-standing Warren and Burger Court precedents permitting Congress to use its commerce clause powers to superintend areas of social (noneconomic) regulation involving criminal justice policy and civil rights enforcement in the states.[62]

Additional cases circumscribed Congress's power to enforce substantive civil rights and liberties under the Fourteenth Amendment's Section 5 enforcement clause. Congress used Section 5 to create the Religious Freedom Restoration Act (RFRA) of 1993, legislation overturning an earlier Supreme Court ruling, *Employment Division, Department of Human Resources of Oregon v. Smith*. The RFRA was necessary, Congress reasoned, to restore what the Supreme Court took away in *Smith* when five justices in a Scalia-authored majority opinion replaced long-standing precedents using a flexible "balancing test" (allowing the Court to weigh religious freedom claims against state regulation using a rigorous compelling interest standard of judicial review) with a more rigid general applicability standard (measuring religious freedom claims against neutral laws generally applying to all citizens, without using a compelling interest standard). But Congress's policy judgment to switch constitutional standards in an effort to be more sensitive to religious liberty rights was negated by Justice Anthony Kennedy's majority opinion in a 5–4 ruling in *City of Boerne v. Flores*.[63]

In *Boerne*, a church sued the city under the RFRA after it denied the church's request for a zoning permit that would have reclassified property that the city deemed a historic landmark. After noting there was little in the legislative record to indicate a "widespread pattern of religious discrimination in the country," Kennedy argued the RFRA did not deter or remedy past constitutional violations by state governments; instead, the RFRA incorrectly registered Congress's decision to change the substantive meaning of a constitutional right that the states were obliged to follow, a policy choice that was beyond Congress's enforcement authority. Given the Court's understanding of the constitution's text, structure, and history in a dual sovereignty framework, Congress had exceeded its powers in enacting the RFRA, for it lacked "congruence and proportionality between the injury to be prevented or remedied and the means adapted to that end."[64] The judicial creation of a congruence and proportionality test, which significantly constrains Congress's authority to enforce substantive privileges and immunities, due process, and equality rights found in Section 1 of the Fourteenth Amendment, gave the Rehnquist Court multiple opportunities to limit federal power in subsequent cases addressing regulation of patent enforcement and age discrimination—and all of those cases involved judicial review of congressional findings to ascertain whether Congress's exercise of regulatory power was constitutionally legitimate (see table 3.4).

Still, the Rehnquist Court's extension of Eleventh Amendment immunity to protect states from being sued in federal courts is perceived by many scholars as having the greatest impact on constitutional federalism.[65] In *Seminole Tribe of Florida v. Florida*, Chief Justice Rehnquist, in a 5–4 ruling, overturned *Pennsylvania v. Union Gas Company* in holding Congress could not authorize private lawsuits (by Indian tribes) against states in federal court under the Eleventh Amendment. Florida, the chief justice determined, did not consent to be sued; thus Congress lacked the power to remove the state's Eleventh Amendment immunity to be insulated from defending a federal lawsuit, in spite of Congress's clear intention (as expressed in the legislation) to do so. *Seminole Tribe* is also noteworthy for leaving intact

Table 3.4. Rehnquist Court Doctrinal Innovations in Constitutional Federalism Cases

Case	*Holding*	*Doctrinal Innovation*	*Congressional Statute/ Precedent Overruled or Limited*
New York v. U.S. (1992)	Congress exceeded its power to compel states to enact or administer a federal regulatory program that forces states to take title of low-level radioactive waste	Created anti-commandeering rule to limit commerce power to protect state legislatures using Tenth Amendment and structural dual sovereignty principles	The "take title" provision of Low-Level Radioactive Waste Policy Act Amendments of 1985 (overruled)
Printz v. U.S. (1997)	Congress exceeded its power to compel states to enact or administer a federal regulatory program that forces state officials to conduct background checks for gun purchases	Extended *New York*'s anti-commandeering principles to protect state executive officials	The Brady Handgun Violence Prevention Act (overruled)
U.S. v. Lopez (1995)	Congress exceeded its commerce power to regulate gun possession as non-economic activity in states near school zones	Erected limit on exercise of commerce power by striking down congressional law for the first time since New Deal	Gun-Free School Zones Act (overruled)
U.S. v. Morrison (2000)	Congress exceeded its commerce and Fourteenth Amendment, Section 5 powers to regulate gender-based violence by permitting a civil remedy in law	Added "commercial activities" rationale and limitation in commerce clause analysis	Violence Against Women Act (overruled in part)
City of Boerne v. Flores (1997)	Congress exceeded its commerce and Fourteenth Amendment, Section 5 enforcement powers to regulate First Amendment free exercise claims	Created "congruence and proportionality" standard and limitation in Fourteenth Amendment, Section 5 enforcement cases	Religious Freedom Restoration Act of 1993 (overruled Congress's reclassification of substantive constitutional rights)

(continued)

Table 3.4. (*continued*)

Case	*Holding*	*Doctrinal Innovation*	*Congressional Statute/ Precedent Overruled or Limited*
College Savings Bk. v. Fla. Prepaid Postsecondary Ed. Expense Bd. (1999)	Congress exceeded its power to abrogate state's Eleventh Amendment immunity from federal lawsuits claiming a civil remedy under Section 5 that was not congruent and proportional to targeted problem of patent infringements	Extended *Boerne*'s Section 5 limitation to patent enforcement	Patent and Plant Variety Protection Remedy Clarification Act (limited coverage of statutes to foreclose federal lawsuits) *Parden v. Terminal Railway* (1964) (in part)
Kimel v. Florida Bd. of Regents (2000)	Congress exceeded its power to abrogate states' Eleventh Amendment immunity from federal lawsuits claiming a civil remedy under Section 5 that was not congruent and proportional to targeted problem of age discrimination	Extended *Boerne*'s Section 5 limitation to age discrimination	Age Discrimination in Employment Act (limited coverage of statutes to foreclose federal lawsuits)
Bd. of Trustees v. Garrett (2000)	Congress exceeded its power to abrogate states' Eleventh Amendment immunity from federal lawsuits claiming a civil remedy under Section 5 that was not congruent and proportional to targeted problem of disability rights' violations	Extended *Boerne*'s Section 5 limitation to foreclose federal lawsuits against states claiming disability discrimination	Americans with Disabilities Act (limited coverage of statute to foreclose federal lawsuits)

Seminole Tribe of Florida v. Florida (1996)	Congress exceeded its power to abrogate states' immunity from federal lawsuits under Indian Commerce Clause to prevent Indian Tribe from suing Florida over dispute involving negotiating compacts for Indian tribe gaming activities	Established no abrogation of state immunity under Indian Commerce Clause, with implication that Congress also lacked the power under the Interstate Commerce Clause, in Eleventh Amendment cases	Indian Gaming Regulatory Act (limited coverage of statute to foreclose federal lawsuits) *Pennsylvania v. Union Gas Co.* (1989) (overruled)
Alden v. Maine (1999)	Congress exceeded its power to abrogate states' immunity under Eleventh Amendment to bar state probation officers from suing Maine in state court for violating federal law	Extended *Seminole* no abrogation principle under Eleventh Amendment to state courts as well as federal courts (Article I does not permit Congress to abrogate a state's immunity in its own courts)	Federal Labor Standards Act (limited coverage of statute to foreclose state lawsuits)
Fed. Maritime Comm. v. South Carolina State Ports Authority (2002)	Congress exceeded its power to abrogate states' immunity under Eleventh Amendment to bar private claim in administrative adjudication against South Carolina over berthing cruise ship controversy	Extended *Seminole* no abrogation principle under Eleventh Amendment to federal agency actions or adjudications	Shipping Act (limited coverage of statute to foreclose federal agency actions)

Source: Thomas Merrill, "The Making of the Second Rehnquist Court: A Preliminary Analysis," *Saint Louis University Law Journal* 47 (2003): 569, 585–87

only one of the two remaining bases for Congress to ground its authority to abrogate state sovereignty immunity—namely, the Fourteenth Amendment, Section 5 enforcement power. Thus, the reversal of *Union Gas* meant that Congress could no longer circumvent state immunity by relying on the commerce or supremacy clauses. In addition to cabining congressional authority in the context of Section 5 and Eleventh Amendment cases (discussed earlier), *Seminole Tribe*'s state immunity principle was advanced in *Alden v. Maine* and *Federal Maritime Commission v. South Carolina State Port Authority*, to foreclose federal lawsuits against states as applied to state legislatures and state courts (table 3.4).[66]

Although the scholarship is mixed on the issue, many social science and legal commentators concede that the cases allegedly reviving dual federalism are significant, yet ultimately modest in practical impact or long-term effect.[67] Several cases in particular in the late Rehnquist and early Roberts Courts support that view insofar as they offset the weight of the new precedents or feature pro-centralization outcomes. Such rulings include, for example, *Reno v. Condon* (validating federal restrictions on states to prevent resale distribution of driver license information under the Driver Privacy Protection Act), *Nevada Department of Human Resources v. Katz* (holding the Eleventh Amendment does not bar state governments from being sued under the Family and Medical Leave Act under Section 5 enforcement power), *Tennessee v. Lane* (holding the Eleventh Amendment does not bar state governments from being sued under the Americans with Disabilities Act under Section 5 enforcement power), *Gonzales v. Raich* (upholding Congress's commerce clause authority in regulating medicinal marijuana in the states under the federal Controlled Substances Act), *United States v. Georgia* (holding the Eleventh Amendment does not bar state governments from being sued under Title II of the Americans with Disabilities Act), and *Central Virginia Community College v. Katz* (holding Eleventh Amendment sovereign immunity does not apply in federal bankruptcy court proceedings).[68] Whatever counterinfluence they have must be juxtaposed against the reality that many of the favorable pro-state precedents lost their potency because they resulted from thin 5–4 margins decided along ideological lines and, increasingly, against cantankerous disagreements between justices in the conservative cohort who could not agree on a meaningful theory of state sovereignty or a viable structural view of federalism. Law professor Mark Tushnet's conclusion that the Rehnquist Court failed to topple progressive social programs like the New Deal and the Great Society is strengthened by his depiction of the Supreme Court as a "court divided," a division that plagued any chance the justices had in accomplishing a federalism revolution. Highly respected pundits like *New York Times* reporter Linda Greenhouse also cast doubt on the significance of the Rehnquist

Court's states' rights legacy, inferring that the chief justice had lost his effectiveness by 2005 which, in turn, prevented the Supreme Court from developing a coherent or enduring vision of state sovereignty or dual federalism.[69]

Still, the existence of countervailing centralizing precedents, the persistence of a divided Court rife with 5–4 conflicts, and an inability to speak with one voice have not diminished the view that the Rehnquist Court achieved success with the constitutional doctrinal advances it pushed forward. Although many preexisting precedents were not formally reversed, several were undermined, and additional studies assert that the Rehnquist Court actively changed the law by frequently invalidating federal statutes in pursuit of its dual federalism agenda.[70] For law professor Erwin Chemerinsky, Rehnquist Court federalism decisions represent a "major change in the law," a position echoed by constitutional law scholar Kathleen Sullivan, who describes the "Rehnquist Court's federalism revival [as] theoretically deep even if practically limited."[71] Others in the legal academy, including Ernest Young, John Manning, William Eskridge, and Philip Frickey, acknowledge the salience and significance of the justices' invoking "process federalism" in statutory interpretation cases, ostensibly because it became a quasi-constitutional interpretive device that operated to check congressional power or undermine substantive rights. Young suggests the Court's insistence on having clear statements has become a critical proxy for using the state-centric but repudiated *Usery* judicial safeguards approach, thus allowing process in and of itself to play a "leading role in the Court's federalism jurisprudence" that gives its statutory cases within that subset of law "greater staying power."[72]

The bulk of scholarship evaluating the merits or failings of the Rehnquist Court federalism revival understandably orients its attention toward constitutional cases that have put affirmative limits either on the exercise of Congress's delegated authority (e.g., commerce, Section 5, or Tenth Amendment cases) or, conversely, on judicial review by federal courts (Eleventh Amendment state immunity). Still, other topics within those areas and related issues deserve additional study. One, for example, relates to a subject that has largely escaped the notice of political scientists—namely, whether the Rehnquist Court made an impact in its new federalism cases reviewing the scope and application of the negative, or dormant, commerce clause.[73]

Dormant commerce clause cases, or those instances in which Congress has not enacted a statute that affects commercial regulation that the states are involved in, are especially germane in federalism studies. The absence of federal regulation gives the states free reign to manage their own mercantile activities, and, logically, a pro-federalist bench would support such efforts.[74] That is because they address the core issue of whether the Supreme Court can use its own discretion to regulate the national economy without congressional input. Furthermore, Chief Justice Rehnquist and Justices Scalia and Thomas arguably have used those cases to express their preference for state autonomy; yet there remain important differences in their own respective judicial line drawing, as well as between the legal positions taken by fellow states' rights allies Justices O'Connor and Kennedy. Also, in these and other new federalism cases, the inability of the conservative bloc to unify around a manageable theory of state sovereignty must be juxtaposed against the regular opposition of four liberal justices, Justices Stevens, Ginsburg, Souter, and Breyer, in dissent. Yet only a few studies in political science and law have explored whether the Rehnquist Court advanced a viable theory of state sovereignty or dual federalism in spite of the salient differences between the justices in its dormant commerce clause cases.[75]

An identical justification supports research investigating if Rehnquist Court justices are more successful in advancing dual federalism ideals by using process federalism. The *Usery/Garcia* judicial or political safeguards debate remains a key issue in federalism scholarship, so exploring if the Rehnquist Court has moved toward adopting an activist strategy of using procedure instrumentally to achieve dual federalism goals is worth close attention. Discovering if process federalism operates in lieu of *Usery* and its doctrinal preference for using constitutional law principles to prevent federal overreaching, as either "hard" or "soft" checks on Congress, is an underdeveloped research enterprise, especially in political science.[76] The next section takes up these questions in the context of testing if the Supreme Court has been more solicitous of state autonomy or sovereignty in new federalism cases, particularly at a time when its membership is purported to favor that sort of structural realignment of constitutional federalism.

Dormant Commerce Clause

With few exceptions Congress historically has enjoyed virtually complete power to regulate commerce between the states. Beginning with *Gibbons v. Ogden* (1824) and extending well into the twenty-first century, federal courts have accepted that Congress's Article I power to "regulate commerce with foreign nations, and among the several states, and with the Indian tribes" is not only a source of explicit authority but also a touchstone for implied power. *Gibbons* ambiguously reinforced the principle by giving Congress the capacity to regulate all commercial intercourse "affect[ing] more states than one" while permitting states to police their own economic affairs without federal interference. The uncertainty of its judicial application is highlighted by Chief Justice John Marshall's cryptic statement that "the completely internal commerce of a State . . . may be considered as reserved for the State itself." As a result, the scope of Congress's implied power remains subject to the vagaries of judicial discretion, and there are countless challenges seeking to put limits on the exercise of federal authority. The issue is manifested by the difficulty in trying to draw a meaningful constitutional distinction between permissible interstate activity and illicit intrastate regulation.[77]

Seminal Supreme Court cases, such as the Taney Court's ruling in *Cooley v. Board of Wardens of the Port of Philadelphia* (referenced in chapter 2), strike an uneasy constitutional balance in wrestling with the interstate-intrastate distinction. There, the justices used a cooperative federalism model to anchor their ruling that the centralized and state governments could share regulatory powers in certain types of cases. Yet *Cooley* offered no specific guidance as to where the judicial line should be drawn, leaving it to future courts to decide.[78] Moreover, the leeway that state legislatures claim in regulating their own commercial interest intensifies the interpretive complexity of establishing clear lines of authority. Under dormant commerce clause doctrine, federal courts equip Article I, Section 8 with an alternative meaning measuring what Congress does *not* do in not proactively choosing to regulate a particular area of commerce. When the exercise of congressional power lies in its dormant (or unexercised) state, the clause is afforded a negative, preemptive judicial construction. So, if Congress fails to pass a law specifically preempting state commercial activity, state commercial laws may be negated by federal courts as a violation of the dormant commerce clause. The legal principle's genesis predates even *Cooley*, where Chief Justice Marshall recognized in dicta that a state law could run afoul of the federal "power to regulate commerce in its dormant state."[79]

It is worth noting that the commerce clause's silent effect does not technically turn on the language of Article I, Section 8. Instead, it results from the presumption underlying Congress's choice not to regulate in a commercial area the state wishes to control.[80] Nonetheless, its operation underscores that dormant commerce clause doctrine is solely a judicial creation that encourages federal courts to discover if Congress has overreached in asserting implied powers, or, put differently, whether state commercial regulations are encroaching upon an artificially contrived respect for national authority. Since the federal court is acting without firm congressional guidance the Supreme Court's application of the doctrine only invites accusations of judicial activism from the academic community as well as from the justices themselves.[81]

Regardless of the criticisms the debate surrounding the propriety of the Court's role is oriented from a uniquely defined issue of federalism discrimination. Does state legislation treat out-of-state competitors differently from in-state participants in commercial transactions affecting the national marketplace? Whatever answer the federal courts give is crafted from an antieconomic protectionism standpoint that inquires whether the country would suffer if the states were given free rein to capitalize on their parochial economic interests—a circumstance that if left undisturbed could threaten to balkanize and to disrupt interstate commerce. Accordingly, if the state law in question is not neutrally applied to all interstate and intrastate business activity, or if it is determined to have an illicit discriminatory purpose or effect that harms the free flow of interstate commerce, federal courts are more likely to find discrimination and a constitutional violation.[82]

The search for discrimination in state commercial laws is the focal point for understanding the nuances of the Rehnquist Court's doctrinal approach. Modern cases, such *City of Philadelphia v. New Jersey* (1978) (discussed earlier in this chapter), evaluate the constitutionality of state laws by weighing if they are facially discriminatory (i.e., the law "on its face" is plainly offensive to constitutional text). Hypothetically, it is easy for the justices to conclude that state legislation targeting out-of-state manufacturers with a 50 percent surcharge to protect in-state businesses is plainly discriminatory. But in cases at the constitutional margins, where the motives of the state legislature are less apparent, the Court determines if the state commercial law is neutrally (i.e., even-handedly) applied to all market participants and commercial interests without obvious bias. Neutral laws are typically deemed constitutional so long as the burden that the state law places on commerce does not outweigh the benefits it gives to state and local entities, an analytical approach sanctioned by an earlier Supreme Court precedent, *Pike v. Bruce Church*.[83]

Doctrinally the justices generally use two judicial standards, or tiers, to orient their thinking in reviewing dormant commerce clause cases. Of the two tiers of constitutional analysis, the first (facial discrimination) is a more rigorous principle of judicial review that greatly increases the likelihood that the allegedly protectionist state legislation will be invalidated; as such, it is less generous to the states if the justices opt to use it to decide the case. The 50 percent surcharge example just cited is but one illustration of when the justices may use tier-one analysis to strike down the tax as a protectionist and discriminatory measure. The second tier, which weighs the benefits and burden the state law allegedly places on interstate commerce, requires the justices to engage in an analytical balancing test that naturally provides them with more flexibility and discretion in deciding the case. To illustrate, the justices may find it easier to validate a state law that levies a tax on an out-of-state manufacturer if the tax is imposed to recover the costs of building and maintaining a recycling center that helps to protect citizen health and also to ease pollution levels. Using the second tier to decide cases thus increases the likelihood that the state law under review will be upheld; as such, its judicial application tends to be more generous to the states.[84] Still, regardless of their actual application in cases, the mere existence of both tiers does not diminish the Supreme Court's basic task of nullifying state laws that "discriminate against or unduly burden interstate commerce."[85]

Some general themes emerge in academic studies exploring the Rehnquist Court's dormant commerce clause cases. The most consistent discovery confirms the justices strengthened the scope and application of constitutional restraints that have been imposed against the states in a majority of cases, thus giving the negative dimension of the commerce clause considerable bite. This is not unusual considering the assumption that the Supreme Court's institutional role is perceived to be "more responsive to other national powers than to state legislatures."[86] For example, law professor Bradley Joondeph's study of seventy-six preemption and dormant commerce clause cases decided between October 1991 and September 2005 observes that the Rehnquist Court has not been generous to the states in its rulings, a track record that is also marked by the Court's willingness to overturn precedents and disregard the legal arguments of justices like Thomas and Scalia (or state governments), who routinely ask the Court to abandon its doctrinal approach in this area.[87] Still, the scholarship has produced mixed and sometimes conflicting results in exploring why and to what effect.

Law professor David Day's study of thirteen cases from 1992 to 2005 concluded that the Rehnquist Court was more prone to applying facial discrimination (tier one) in dormant commerce clause cases, which disfavors the states. Day argues the trend is a reflection of the Court's deliberate choice to abandon the *Pike v. Bruce Church* undue burden balancing test, or tier-two analysis. In part he reasons that legal factors, ostensibly the Rehnquist Court's preference for following precedent established by the Burger and earlier Courts, are responsible for the anti-state outcomes, but he also speculates that the Court's majority has opted to defer to Justice Scalia's withering criticism that using the tier-two standard—which allows the justices to balance the competing interests and, therefore, to manipulate the meaning of otherwise plain constitutional text as a matter of judicial philosophy and personal preferences—is an illegitimate exercise of judicial power. Apart from Justice Scalia's interpretation, Day's findings are consistent with Joondeph's observation that in "general terms the [Rehnquist] Court left the doctrines surrounding [preemption and the dormant commerce clause] largely as it found them."[88]

Moreover, the general tendency of invalidating state commercial laws is confirmed by law professor Christopher Drahozal's investigation of sixty-one cases decided from 1970 to 1999. In Drahozal's study, the Supreme

Court was more likely to strike down state regulations when they were challenged by state or local governments (as opposed to private parties); he uses empirical analysis to conclude that, with the possible exceptions of Chief Justice Rehnquist and Warren Burger, "the sorts of 'attitudinal' factors identified in the literature as correlated with a justice's policy preferences have only a slight relationship with how justices vote in dormant Commerce Clause cases."[89] In contrast, Professor Joondeph's analysis and political scientist David O'Brien's study of preemption and dormant commerce clause cases in the Rehnquist Court (up until 1993) find that an amalgam of political and legal factors (based in new institutionalism social science methodology) account for the justices' uneven judicial record in this area. Thus Rehnquist Court dormant commerce clause case outcomes are influenced by factors such as the justices' historical respect for precedent, the Court's membership changes due to appointments from conservative presidents, and external pressures placed on the Court as a national institution in the prevailing political and social environment.[90]

Some of the empirical assumptions, coding decisions, and issues raised in earlier studies are revisited and expanded upon by exploring the effect that certain factors or variables have on Rehnquist Court new federalism decisions interpreting the commerce clause. The data set, consisting initially of Rehnquist Court cases addressing the interstate commerce and supremacy clauses, is compiled from the Supreme Court Database and other sources. Cases on the master list, consisting of sixty-one interstate and commerce clause cases from the database, were reviewed to isolate cases pertaining to dormant commerce clause rulings. The subset of cases was then juxtaposed and reviewed against analogous data sets in the literature, yielding twenty-eight cases for analysis. Working from the general assumption that conservative justices would be more receptive to protecting state regulation affecting commerce in the absence of congressional action, different voting patterns and variables, discussed below, were coded to discover their relationship to case outcomes that either favored the national government or states in dormant commerce clause litigation.[91]

The most conspicuous voting pattern confirms findings from earlier studies showing that the Rehnquist Court decides dormant commerce clause cases in a predominantly liberal (pro-federal or anti–state government) direction.[92] Of the twenty-eight cases, 71.4 percent are liberal, with only 28.6 percent favoring state governments. Table 3.5 summarizes the voting record of individual justices relative to the cases they participated in on the Rehnquist Court. While the small sample size prevents any meaningful comparison of cases that are dissimilar for a variety of reasons, the voting patterns are suggestive that outcomes are not moderated by conventional understandings of judicial ideology that are routinely associated with specific justices. As measured by raw votes supporting the federal or state government, justices thought of as having strong attachment to states' rights positions, such as Anthony Kennedy, Sandra Day O'Connor, Antonin Scalia, and Clarence Thomas, consistently adopt liberal, or anti-state, positions that uniformly outpace their support for state governments, sometimes by significant margins. The most glaring exception is William Rehnquist, who votes in favor of the states by nearly a 3:1 ratio, or 71.4 percent of the time. Likewise, justices perceived to be the most vocal opponents of the dual federalism agenda of their colleagues, such as David Souter, Stephen Breyer, Ruth Bader Ginsburg, and John Paul Stevens, also steadily and predominately vote for the federal government. While the ideological space between the pro-federal and pro–state government positions is narrower with certain justices, such as Thomas or Ginsburg, there appear to be no discernible differences between all of the justices as a majority votes in favor of the federal government most of the time.

Three variables were constructed to measure the nexus between ideology and judicial outcomes using frequencies and cross-tabulation analysis. The first variable counted the number of justices in each case appointed by conservative presidents and juxtaposed this against dormant

Table 3.5. Dormant Commerce Clause Votes, by Justice, 1985–2005

Justice	*Appointing President*	*Liberal (pro-federal)*	*Conservative (pro-state)*
William Brennan	Eisenhower	4 (14.3%)	2 (7.1%)
Harry Blackmun	Nixon	9 (32.1%)	7 (25.0%)
Stephen Breyer	Clinton	7 (25.0%)	4 (14.3%)
Anthony Kennedy	Reagan	18 (64.3%)	8 (28.6%)
Ruth Bader Ginsburg	Clinton	9 (32.1%)	7 (25.0%)
Thurgood Marshall	Johnson	4 (14.3%)	3 (10.7%)
Sandra Day O'Connor	Reagan	17 (60.7%)	11 (39.3%)
Lewis Powell	Nixon	1 (3.6%)	0 (0%)
William Rehnquist	Reagan (for chief justice)	8 (28.6%)	20 (71.4%)
Antonin Scalia	Reagan	16 (57.1%)	12 (42.9%)
David Souter	G. H. W. Bush	14 (50.0%)	7 (25.0%)
John Paul Stevens	Ford	19 (67.9%)	9 (32.1%)
Clarence Thomas	G. H. W. Bush	12 (42.9%)	9 (32.1%)
Byron White	Kennedy	9 (32.1%)	3 (10.7%)

Source: N = 28. The Supreme Court Database, at http://scdb.wustl.edu (Search Reference Code 1101 Ballgame 6238). See also Bradley W. Joondeph, "Federalism, the Rehnquist Court, and the Modern Republican Party," *Oregon Law Review* (2008): 117; David S. Day, "The 'Mature' Rehnquist Court and the Dormant Commerce Clause Doctrine: The Expanded Discrimination Tier," *South Dakota Law Review* 52 (2007): 1; Christopher R. Drahozal, "Preserving the American Common Market: State and Local Governments in the United States Supreme Court," *Supreme Court Economic Review* 7 (1999): 233; and David M. O'Brien, *Constitutional Law and Politics: Civil Rights and Liberties, Volume Two*, 9th edition (New York: W. W. Norton, 2011).

Table 3.6. Votes by Justices Appointed by Conservative Presidents

	Number of Justices Appointed by a Conservative President (each case)		
	6	*7*	*8*
Not Liberal Outcome	1 (3.6%)	7 (25.0%)	0 (0.0%)
Liberal Outcome (pro-national government; anti-state)	1 (3.6%)	10 (35.7%)	9 (32.1%)

commerce case outcomes. The results show that a minimum of six and a maximum of eight conservatively appointed justices participated in each case, and the percentage of liberal (pro-national, anti-state) outcomes becomes greater as the number of conservatively appointed justices increases. For example, table 3.6 shows that 71.4 percent of all twenty-eight cases have a liberal (pro-national, anti-state) outcome when there are six or more conservatively appointed justices present in each case. Because of the small number of cases, the expected count in several categories was less than five, so the number of conservatively appointed justices was recoded into categories to reflect a 2 × 2 table in order to conduct a chi-square test using the Fisher's Exact Test. The categories were defined as seven or fewer conservatively appointed justices in each case or eight or more conservatively appointed justices in each case. The chi-square test using Fisher's produced a significant result at the 0.05 level, suggesting an association between the number of conservatively appointed justices and case outcome. While an imperfect measure that may run the risk of overstatement, the findings support the supposition that the presidential selection of justices, presumably done with the ideological expectation that the appointees' legal judgments will err on the side of allowing states more economic freedom to regulate commercial activities within their own borders, does not translate into reliable pro-state outcomes.

The second variable tests the correlation between the justices' decision to apply legal doctrine in an ideological fashion, a possibility that law professors raise in their own study of dormant commerce clause and federalism cases.[93] In the sample of cases under present review, case outcomes favoring the states were tested against the judicial application of legal standards favoring the federal government (tier one, assessing the constitutionality of state regulations claimed to be per se violations of facial discrimination) or state governments (tier two, assessing the benefits and burdens of state regulations affecting interstate commerce through a balancing test). In terms of frequencies, in the twenty-two cases in which the justices used language indicating that they applied either tier one or tier two as a legal standard, sixteen, or 72.7 percent, applied tier one, whereas only six, or 27.3 percent, used tier two.[94] In the sixteen tier-one cases, 87.5 percent result in a liberal outcome favoring the central government; for the remaining six cases applying tier two, 83.3 percent are conservative outcomes. Using a chi-square test the judicial application of the legal tier variable is statistically significant at the 0.05 level.

Another factor that is evaluated relates to whether the justices are more sympathetic to judicial decisions favoring the states, as measured by the rulings issued by the highest state appeals court, which precede U.S. Supreme Court review. In a study of William Rehnquist's federalism jurisprudence (and not just dormant commerce clause cases), legal scholars Ruth Colker and Kevin M. Scott hypothesized that "a federalist [justice] will be sensitive to the decisions rendered by state courts, particularly when state courts uphold choices made by other branches of state government."[95] As suggested by table 3.5, presented earlier, Colker and Scott confirmed within the scope of their own study that William Rehnquist had strong federalist tendencies—he voted to affirm the lower court decision more often when the court validated state action, and he did so more in comparison to identical rulings from federal appeals courts. By analogy, but in contrast to Colker and Scott's finding (at least in indirect terms), the present analysis finds that the Supreme Court collectively did not show much respect for state court rulings that held in favor of the states in dormant commerce clause challenges. With regard to twenty-one cases decided by the highest state appellate courts with pro-state outcomes, the Supreme Court reversed those decisions in sixteen cases, or 76.2 percent of the time. Similarly, in only five instances, or 23.8 percent of dormant commerce clause cases coming from the highest state appeals courts, did the Supreme Court affirm a pro-state ruling. A chi-square test shows statistical significance at the 0.05 level.

An attempt to explain these admittedly impressionistic findings begins with two perspectives that scholars take in seeking to explain Rehnquist Court judicial behavior. One view, typically offered by legal academicians, suggests that the force of law that is buried within the high court's interpretation of the commerce clause is at the root of understanding why the Court is deferential to Congress's silent intent to stabilize the national marketplace and to prevent economic balkanization. In plain terms, as law the dormant commerce clause has a powerful centralizing effect, one that easily deflects the challenges states routinely pose in trying to regulate their own commercial activities without federal or judicial interference. A second view, intimately tied to the influence legal doctrine wields as an interpretative tool in the hands of a political judiciary, suggests there is something different about federalism cases insofar as explaining court outcomes in ideological terms. Political scientist David

O'Brien admits as much in his own study of Rehnquist Court dormant commerce clause cases, positing that conservative judicial attitudes do a better job of predicting why the Court undercuts civil rights and liberties, a decisional pattern that contrasts with other types of cases that show that conservative judicial preferences are not used to uphold state interests in federalism dormant commerce clause cases.[96]

Also, the basic judicial choice to rest the controlling legal rationale in cases on one of two possible legal standards in dormant commerce clause analysis—tier one, which has a centralizing effect, or tier two, which has an opposite impact—appears to be a significant ideological determinant in knowing whether challenges to allegedly discriminatory state legislation will ultimately succeed or fail. The judicial application of legal standards, in other words, may connect to case outcomes that are either liberal (pro–federal government) or conservative (pro–state government). Still, judicial ideology in and of itself, at least as measured by the proxy of presidential liberal or conservative appointments, has a negligible impact on case outcomes; thus other legal or political factors may be at work, including the application of common law precedents, legal arguments, interest group pressure, or litigant types. What remains unclear is whether the legal standard is intrinsically ideological; if it is, then a justice's choice to use it is evidence that the law is being politically manipulated, something that has been confirmed in legal studies investigating the scope and application of statutory construction rules by federal courts. To illustrate, and as applied to a justice's commitment to using textualism, law professor Frank Cross's research posits, and ultimately finds, that "if textualism were indeed intrinsically conservative, a justice's conservative results could be explained by his or her dedication to a particular legal interpretative approach, not personal ideological preferences."[97] Accordingly, in order to discover what exactly is driving judicial behavior, subsequent research is warranted in order to uncover more fully what is beneath the preliminary empirical observations offered here.

Process Federalism and Clear Statement Rules

The foregoing analysis reiterates that federal judges construe the founding document as a policy instrument to increase national power while restricting discriminatory state regulations, even in new federalism cases that may have a majority coalition committed to states' rights. This chapter's earlier discussion likewise shows that the Rehnquist Court's maturation resulted in discretionary choices that aggressively cabined federal power by invalidating federal actions that were held to infringe upon state interests and transgress constitutional text, structure, or values. Although case outcomes may crosscut along ideological lines, with the power of judicial review the justices interpret constitutional law to produce preferred federalism outcomes that generate at least five votes. Thus in *United States v. Lopez* a federal law prohibiting gun possession near public schools in Texas was annulled on the grounds that Congress went beyond its enumerated capacity to regulate commerce under Article I of the U.S. Constitution. Judicial power, in other words, operates as a "hard" check on legislative prerogatives that only a constitutional amendment can override, thereby dictating how Congress may regulate the intersection of commercial and criminal law at the state level in the future.[98]

Yet principles and precedents of constitutional law are also cultivated by the judicial reading of federal statutes, a topic that is extensively debated in the legal academy but virtually bypassed in political science.[99] At the debate's core is how judicially inspired canons (or principles) of statutory interpretation, among them clear statement rules, become procedural enforcement mechanisms to safeguard judicially protected values of federalism.[100] The different canons judges refer to in deciding what a law means are complex, varied, and inherently controversial. In theory and practice, they consist of interpretative guidelines that govern certain categories of legal usage. "Textualist" canons—like the rule to read each statutory provision by reference to the whole act or another that directs judges to follow dictionary definitions of terms unless the law itself contains a specific meaning—establish grammatical, syntactic, linguistic, or text-based understandings of how to construe ambiguous language. "Extrinsic source" canons, by contrast, let judges refer to sources outside statutory text in order to learn about legislative intent or purpose in trying to discover authoritative meaning. Conventional referents in the extrinsic category may include legislative histories underlying the law's enactment, such as those discovered in committee reports or statements made by representatives in the Congressional Record during floor deliberation, or, if a court is considering the validity of an agency regulation, the referent could be the rule that judges ordinarily defer to the agency's interpretation of a congressional statute unless it is plainly or unreasonably contradicted. "Substantive" canons are more contextual in scope. Judges derive meaning from public policies, legal norms, and conventional understandings that come from the U.S. Constitution, federal statutes, or judge-made common law precedents. The common law rule presuming that a law takes effect on the date of enactment and the due process rule of lenity, which in criminal prosecutions may compel a judge to adopt a less punitive or harsh interpretation of a criminal sanction when the law's meaning is unclear, are common illustrations.[101]

Clear statement rules, or judicial directives that return legislation to Congress which ambiguously convey an otherwise authoritative intent, are a species of canonical statutory construction. While scholars diverge on the issue of whether they are post–ad hoc legal rationalizations or even pretexts for legitimizing judicial preferences, the Rehnquist Court is often characterized by its propensity to use clear statement rules as "quasi-constitutional" principles, a judicial behavioral pattern that gives the rules a potent, if not unevenly applied, substantive policy effect.[102] As a result, some claim their development is one of the most significant contributions of the Rehnquist Court, principally because they operated as "soft" checks on the exercise of federal congressional or executive power.[103] That is, unlike hard checks that invalidate legislation for constitutional reasons and thus may require the subsequent passage of a constitutional amendment to overcome, Congress may choose to respond to a soft check imposed by a clear statement directive by simply reenacting the offending statute that the Court finds deficient because of its vagueness.

The distinction between judicial nullification in constitutional and statutory cases is crucial. Although it is possible that minor revisions to the law will pass constitutional muster, in some instances the imposition of a clear statement rule may require Congress to create an "extraordinarily specific statement on the face of the statute," which in turn carries "very strong presumptions of statutory meaning that can be rebutted only through unambiguous statutory text targeted at the specific problem."[104] Although less congressional heavy lifting is usually required to reenact another statute (rather than passing a constitutional amendment), the extra onus put on Congress to create a law that meets the specificity requirements imposed by the Supreme Court is greater and more difficult to eliminate. When considered in this light, in the form of a clear statement rule, the substantive canon's operation and effect is even more binding because justices are also signaling that the background surrounding the law's enactment, often captured in nontextual sources such as legislative history, are irrelevant as interpretative guides for both the justices and Congress seeking to determine the law's purpose or intent. In other words, the statutory text and its perceived clarity become the sole and unyielding touchstone for judicial analysis, thereby transforming the canon into an irrefutable presumption and policy norm that greatly hampers Congress's legislative capacity to satisfy what is required to make the law judicially acceptable.[105]

The tendency to use clear statement rules in this fashion has been documented in the Rehnquist Court. For example, law professors William Eskridge Jr. and Philip Frickey assert that it departed from past judicial practice, most notably visible in the Burger Court (1969–1985), which typically required offending legislation to be struck down on constitutional grounds through the exercise of judicial review. Instead, they posit, the Rehnquist Court was responsible for creating "super-strong clear statement rules," a dynamic form of judicial activism that gives the justices considerable discretion to read into federal law constitutional values that can only be legislatively challenged by a "clear legislative override" in statutory interpretation cases. Under this view, clear statement rules are an instrumental use of judicial power because they retain substantive policy implications that frame judicial and political behavior. Legal scholars Frank Cross and Emerson Tiller explain that the Court's decision to get Congress's attention by using a clear statement rule is highly rational judicial behavior that is politically significant:

> First, the Court gets its way on the outcome of the case under review. If the Court disapproves of the cause of action, it finds no clear statement, and subsequent decisions in the area should follow. Second, the Court protects itself against congressional retribution. If the contemporary Congress does not particularly care about the invalidated legislation, it will not act and the Court gets its way. If that Congress does care intensely, the clear statement rule invites an override through a new clear statement, rather than some other form of punishment of the Court. The invalidation under the clear statement rule is fundamentally a test of congressional concern for the issue and a deferential submission of the Court, if that concern is sufficiently great. Otherwise, the Court gets its way. Through this approach, the Justices need not guess about congressional preferences and the intensity of those preferences. The doctrine simply tests the congressional preferences and ensures that the Court's preference prevails as the default answer.[106]

Thus, they conclude, "the clear statement rule appears to be a strategic use of doctrine."[107]

As strategic soft checks, clear statement rules are signaling devices that alert the political branches of the constitutional concerns courts have with respect to federal legislation or agency regulations that may subsequently have to satisfy a rudderless discretionary test of court scrutiny. Moreover, they are ideologically malleable. Empirical studies affirm the Rehnquist Court has availed itself of using substantive canons to reach conservative case results; similarly, it often applies language canons to secure liberal case outcomes.[108] This means, as law professor Frank Cross found in his own empirical study of statutory interpretation, that a particular interpretative methodology is inherently ideologically neutral (not liberal or conservative). A liberal justice may resort to using a language canon in a case that results in a conservative outcome; likewise, a liberal outcome may result from a conservative justice's decision to look to an extrinsic source canon, such as a legislative committee report or the Congressional Record, for insight and meaning. Still, as Cross and other researchers suggest in exploring the decisional patterns in the Burger and Rehnquist Courts, justices select specific interpretative methods, which do not intrinsically tilt in a liberal or conservative direction, to advance their ideological goals. As Cross flatly puts it, "The justices' decisions are significantly influenced by their ideological preferences, so they may be choosing the [interpretative] method that best supports the conclusion they wish to reach for ideological purposes."[109]

While additional research must continue to investigate these possibilities and conclusions further, the justices' discretionary choices in applying clear statement rules or other process-based interpretative guides to cases surely play some role in explaining the nexus between judicial behavior and federalism policy outcomes. The interplay between rival judicial philosophies and process federalism in the context of statutory construction, therefore, is the fulcrum for understanding established precedents and judicial conflict on the Supreme Court. Long before William Rehnquist became chief justice, the judicial propensity to require plain statements from the political branches was an established part of federalism jurisprudence, affecting the scope and application of the preemption doctrine and supremacy clause, the commerce clause, congressional spending and grant administration, and state immunity under the Eleventh Amendment.[110]

In *Rice v. Santa Fe Elevator Corporation,* a "presumption against preemption" principle was created, declaring that the "historic" exercise of a state's police powers, or those commonly linked with the regulation of "traditional state functions," is not preempted unless it is "the clear and manifest purpose of Congress" to do so.[111] Two Burger Court cases, *Pennhurst State School and Hospital v. Halderman* and *Atascadero State Hospital v. Scanlon* used clear statement rules to fix Congress's responsibilities in drafting statutes that imposed grant conditions on the states through the spending power (*Pennhurst*) and to insure that the states' immunity from federal lawsuits under the Eleventh Amendment was not lost unless Congress made its intention "unmistakably clear" (*Atascadero*).[112] The *Rice, Pennhurst,* and *Atascadero* proscriptions, as well as other precedents, routinely used procedural common law justifications for imposing new and largely unanticipated constraints on congressional and agency actions in several Rehnquist Court new federalism cases.[113]

To illustrate, key precedents from the Rehnquist Court, as derived from a Westlaw search and summarized in table 3.7, show the versatility of clear statement rule application in cases purporting to defend certain federalism values as quasi-constitutional norms.[114] With *Welch v. Texas Department of Highways and Public Transportation,* a fractured Court, in a 5–4 ruling, overruled existing precedent, *Parden v. Terminal Railway of Alabama Docks Department,* to declare that a Texas employee, a seaman who was injured while working at a ferry dock, could not sue in federal court under the federal Jones Act because Congress did not convey "an unmistakably clear expression of its intention" to destroy Texas's immunity from private law-

Table 3.7. Clear Statement Rules in Rehnquist Court Federalism Cases

Case	*Language of Clear Statement Rule (in federalism issue area)*	*Federalism Interest/Value Safeguarded*
Welch v. Texas Dep't of Highways and Public Transportation (1987)	Abrogation of Eleventh Amendment immunity by Congress must be expressed in unmistakably clear language	Preservation of Role of States in Federal System
Will v. Michigan Dep't of State Police (1989)	Congress must make its intention to allow a §1983 private claim for damages against state officials unmistakably clear in a statute's language	Preservation of the Usual Constitutional Balance between the States and the Federal Government
Dep't of Revenue of Oregon v. ACF Industries, Inc. (1994)	If Congress wishes to preempt the state's decision to exempt certain classes of commercial property while taxing railroad cars in full, a decision that will disrupt the states' traditional powers over taxation, the Court will only do so if that result is the clear and manifest purpose of Congress	Federalism Principles Supporting State Sovereignty
Solid Waste Agency of Northern Cook County v. U.S. Army Corps of Engineers (2001)	Where an agency interprets a federal law invoking the outer limits of Congress's power, there must be a clear indication that Congress intended that result if it hopes to extend the federal Clean Water Act to regulate intrastate waters by requiring a permit to discharge fill material into an abandoned gravel pit with excavation trenches that have turned into seasonal ponds habituated by migratory birds	The Federal-State Framework Preventing Encroachments on Traditional State Power
City of Columbus v. Ours Garage and Wrecker Service, Inc. (2002)	Because the historic police powers of the states are not to be superseded by federal law unless that was the clear and manifest purpose of Congress, absent a clear statement to the contrary, Congress has the power to preserve, and not preempt, the state's decision to delegate its authority to localities and political subdivisions to enact safety regulations applying to tow trucks which affect interstate commerce	Protecting Traditional State Police Power and Preserving State Autonomy to Make Regulatory Choices

suits under the Eleventh Amendment. As a result, the Supreme Court's new principle established that the abrogation of Eleventh Amendment immunity by Congress "must be expressed in unmistakably clear language." Speaking for the dissent, Justice William Brennan interpreted federal law differently, observing that Congress expressly stated therein its desire to afford a federal judicial remedy and that its intent has not been changed for decades. Justice Lewis Powell's plurality opinion, which cast aside *Parden*, demonstrated that the "Court's departure from normal rules of statutory construction frustrates the will of Congress."[115]

In another 5–4 decision, Justice Byron White held for the Court that a state employee working at the Michigan Police Department could not use a civil rights statute, 42 U.S.C. § 1983 (Section 1983), to sue state officials for denying him a promotion because he was a student activist and for other political reasons. Citing *Atascadero* and analogous Eleventh Amendment rationales, in *Will v. Michigan Department of State Police* Justice White concluded that a private damages claim was not actionable since the state could not be named as a "person" subject to liability under Section 1983, reasoning Congress did not make its intention to allow a lawsuit unmistakably clear. Allowing such a claim, Justice White continued, would alter the "usual constitutional balance between the States and the Federal Government" and threaten "traditionally sensitive areas" of state regulation. Justice Brennan, again writing for the dissent, sardonically noted that "the Eleventh Amendment lurks everywhere in today's decision and, in truth, determines its outcome," even though the Court admitted that the Eleventh Amendment was irrelevant to the issue at hand. More saliently, he observed, the invocation of the clear statement wrongfully displaced the Court's responsibility to ascertain statutory intent through a review of language and other extrinsic source referents, such as Section 1983's legislative purpose, history, and general background.[116]

The balance of the examples in table 3.7 show the range with which the Supreme Court uses process federalism to decide cases protecting the states from federal incursions affecting not only the Eleventh Amendment but also tax administration, agency action involving preemption and environmental law, and local safety regulations touching upon interstate commerce. The language of the illustrations underscores the types of federalism values that are of concern to the Supreme Court, including preservation of the state's "historic police powers" and traditional functions affecting not only the federal-state balance but also broader issues of state sovereignty and autonomy. While it remains an open question whether the clear statement rules in these cases and others operate as a substitute for judicial review, the Court's imposition of clear statement rules uniformly registers the Court's "reliance on political and institutional safeguards to preserve balance in the federalism structure," a key theme in the ongoing *Usery*/

Garcia debate about the proper use of judicial power in protecting state sovereignty, autonomy, or interests against federal threats.[117]

Yet how much the Supreme Court actually relies upon the political process to enforce its conception of federalism values is often issue specific and necessarily a judicial decision that is informed by rival judicial philosophies and political considerations. While *Garcia* is best understood as a federalism principle of judicial nonaction (courts should not intervene to protect the states because states are represented well in the national political process), the Court's meticulous attention to process invites judicial supervision of federal-state legal relationships in both constitutional and statutory construction cases. Requiring Congress to speak clearly through the lens of clear statements affects how the Supreme Court construes Article I provisions (commerce, spending clauses) and the Tenth, Eleventh, and Fourteenth (Section 5) Amendments. Likewise, it affects the specificity with which Congress inserts preemption provisions into federal laws regulating goods or products circulating in interstate commerce, a focus of statutory construction cases reviewing whether state tort lawsuits remain viable as a source of legal relief for injured consumers. This latter issue, in particular, has been a recurring source of judicial and political controversy for the justices where, in a series of product liability cases, the Rehnquist Court has struggled with establishing identifiable lines of federal-state authority relative to the scope of the preemption doctrine and Congress's express or implied powers to displace private tort lawsuits invoking state legal remedies.[118]

In this light, the collective policy judgments of the Supreme Court represent the individual choices of justices who are constrained by their own preferences as well as by their own textual or nontextual understandings based in judicial philosophies. Those constraints, by definition, push and pull the justices in distinct ideological directions that often cut across ideological lines but also collide in closely decided litigation affecting citizen lives and requiring court attention. The tension is best illustrated by the Court's preemption cases. Preemption is an area of legal regulation that requires textualists, such as Justice Scalia, to interpret the law according to its plain terms and intent, presumably without the aid of external referents such as legislative history. Justice Breyer, by contrast, endorses pragmatism, a method of judicial philosophy that weighs the application of law by its consequences and purposes, a task that is inherently value driven and solicitous of using external referents.[119]

These very different viewpoints tend to polarize in statutory construction cases that require interpretation of express and implied provisions found in textual language, as in the "presumption against preemption" context. As an implied preemption issue, as dictated by *Rice*, the presumption compels the Court to protect the states from federal preemption that treads on traditional state functions (e.g., crime control, education, family law, employment matters), but in laws that the justices interpret to mean that it was Congress's "clear and manifest purpose" to allow preemption, under the supremacy clause the federal government can trump state laws regardless of their traditional quality. The meaning the justices afford to the "clear and manifest purpose" *Rice* requirement, as well as who comes out on top, the states or the federal government, depends entirely on the choices that each justice brings to an interpretative table covered with a judicial philosophy tablecloth. Also, on a deeper level, the political decision of Congress or agencies to use preemption clauses as the means to effectuate tort reform and prevent injured plaintiffs from using state law tort remedies to hold businesses and manufacturers accountable for the mistakes they make in bringing products to market remains at odds whenever the Supreme Court draws its federalism lines. At bottom, the direction that the justices take to use clear statement rules and other process-based methods of statutory (and constitutional) interpretation colors not only policy outcomes but also how the justices can agree with each other to produce coherent majority opinions and, of course, whether it is possible to generate a productive institutional dialogue between the judicial and political branches.

The nature and import of the institutional conversation between Congress, agencies, and the judiciary is also greatly shaped by the Court's discretionary application of clear statement rules. While Congress's input in the dialogue—typically manifested by the legislature's willingness to adjust statutory language *after* the Supreme Court rules that a law is ambiguous—may work to protect the states from federal overreaching, it is also plausible that the Supreme Court, in the first instance and by the judicial choices it makes, is the source and impetus for legislative action, which, in effect, sets the congressional agenda in federalism matters. While this judicial practice can be defended on institutional grounds (that the judiciary is acting in cooperation with Congress to encourage a constructive legal and political dialogue), critics can counter that the Court, and not Congress, is using its activism to bypass the constraints imposed on it through *Garcia*, thus allowing the Rehnquist Court to enforce its own substantive conception of constitutional federalism as it strives to become the true political guardian of the states.[120]

NEW FEDERALISM AND THE CONSTITUTIONAL CULTURE

By the time of Chief Justice Rehnquist's passing, the momentum behind the Supreme Court's efforts to establish a viable theory of new federalism favoring state autonomy seemed to have withered on the vine as well. While using process federalism as an alternative means to reconcile an activist judicial role with new federalism pro-state outcomes offers a certain promise in placing ongoing or more nuanced limits on federal power within the competing *Usery* and *Garcia* paradigms, the dormant commerce clause cases, especially the rulings compiled near the end of the Rehnquist Court and into the Roberts Court, reveal the polarization within the Court and the ongoing frustration the conservatives experience in trying to draw consistent judicial lines, or to rely upon each other in support of new federalism objectives, or to diminish the prospect that any of the pro-state precedents they created will remain viable in the future.

In this regard Justice Thomas's insistence, sometimes with the support of Justices Scalia and Rehnquist, that the Court revisit long-established lines of precedent that are incompatible with a textually based conception of judicial philosophy aligned with pre–New Deal constitutional doctrine warrants special notice. One could posit, as political scientists Cornell Clayton, Mitchell Pickerill, and Charles Epp, as well as legal scholar Mark Tushnet, do, that Thomas's repeated call to jettison old precedents in favor of adopting doctrine supportive of dual federalism goals will only succeed if other like-minded jurists are appointed to the Court, and, contemporaneously, external constituencies in the support structure of the legal and political environment embrace his vision of constitutional change. Although Thomas's isolated "voice [is that] of a true revolutionary" and would "indeed overturn New Deal and Great Society regulations wholesale," Thomas can only be a successful leader and show "where new justices might take the Rehnquist Court's decisions" if he has majority support on and off the bench to do it.[121]

Moreover, the lack of unity on the nation's highest court has filtered down to case law and other areas of jurisprudence that have federalism and global implications. As political scientist Thomas Keck observes, Rehnquist Court activism has conservative and progressive undertones, and the ideological direction of case outcomes remains regardless a function of "multiple jurisprudential traditions." "Legal and political influences on the Court," he argues, "are mutually constitutive" and originate from norms, ideas, and patterns of institutional behavior that are necessarily embedded in the "ongoing debates in the broader political system."[122] Linda Greenhouse makes an identical claim but explicitly ties those constitutive influences to a global constitutional culture. In referencing the increasing tendency of Rehnquist Court justices—especially but not always linked with the liberal and moderate cohort of Justices Breyer, Ginsburg, O'Connor and Kennedy—to cite to foreign law in cases involving gay rights, capital punishment, affirmative action, or even federalism cases, Greenhouse speculates the controlling majority in such cases "envisioned itself in a dialogue with the wider world beyond the country's borders and cared a fair amount about how the Court, and through it, the country, looked to that world."[123] The foreign law source and citation debate, as well as the critical point that the Supreme Court plays a unique role in promoting a certain vision of constitutional change within the constraints of a global constitutional culture, is germane to any evaluation of Rehnquist or Supreme Court new federalism.[124]

These two questions, one asking about the impact and internal or external constitutive support for Justice Thomas's brand of new federalism as expressed in religious freedom cases, and the other inquiring whether the Supreme Court's vision of new federalism is externally constrained in the context of foreign policy preemption cases and a changing international order, are the focus of case studies in the next two chapters. The concluding chapter then centers on providing insight into the unresolved issue of whether the new federalism contribution that the Rehnquist Court made in its own jurisprudence is likely to be continued in the nascent Roberts Court in light of several key new judicial appointments after 2005—namely, those of John Roberts, Samuel Alito, Sonia Sotomayor, and Elena Kagan—replacing Chief Justice Rehnquist and Justices Sandra Day O'Connor, David Souter, and John Paul Stevens.

NOTES

1. See Charles Epp, *The Rights Revolution: Lawyers, Activists and Supreme Courts in Comparative Perspective* (Chicago: University of Chicago, 1998). See also Mark Tushnet, *A Court Divided: The Rehnquist Court and the Future of Constitutional Law* (New York: W. W. Norton and Company, 2005), 13–25, and 25.

2. Tushnet, *A Court Divided,* 14–21 (suggesting Rehnquist's judicial philosophy was influenced by Justice Jackson's opposition to New Deal politics and judicial supremacy). See also Publius, "New Federalist Paper No. 1," *Publius: The Journal of Federalism* 2, no. 1 (1972): 89, 100, and 103.

3. Tushnet, *A Court Divided,* 250. A current assessment of the causes and consequences of the Rehnquist Court federalism revival is found in John Dinan, "The Rehnquist Court's Federalism Decisions," *Publius: The Journal of Federalism* 41, no. 1 (2011): 158–67.

4. See Ernest A. Young, "The Rehnquist Court's Two Federalisms," *Texas Law Review* 83, no. 1 (2004) (arguing it is important to distinguish between the Court's treatment of state sovereignty versus state autonomy). See also Cornell W. Clayton and J. Mitchell Pickerill, "Guess What Happened on the Way to Revolution? Precursors to the Supreme Court's Federalism Revolution," *Publius: The Journal of Federalism* 34, no. 3 (2004): 85–114; Kimberly Hendrickson, "Conservative Perspectives on American Federalism," *Publius: The Journal of Federalism* 34, no. 4 (2004): 1–7.

5. It is opportunistic because "where you stand depends on where you have power," dynamic because "it changes over time as values and goals shift in society," cyclical "in that changes in American federalism coincide with shifts in the society," and pro-government "in the sense that its shifting character ratchets up public-sector activism and spending over time." Richard P. Nathan, "There Will Always Be a New Federalism," *Journal of Public Administration Research and Theory* 16 (2006): 499–510, 502. See also John Dinan, "Strengthening the Political Safeguards of Federalism: The Fate of Recent Federalism Legislation in the U.S. Congress," *Publius: The Journal of Federalism* 34, no. 1 (2004): 55–83 (suggesting scholars should pay attention to the state of legislation purporting to protect the states instead of focusing just on the role and effect of Supreme Court rulings); Samuel H. Beer, "Introduction," in Timothy Conlan, *New Federalism: Intergovernmental Reform from Nixon to Reagan* (Washington, DC: Brookings Institution, 1988), xv and xxii.

6. Nathan, "There Will Always Be a New Federalism," 502–3.

7. Republican Party, "Republican Party Platform of 1968" and "Republican Party Platform of 1980," both retrieved from the American Presidency Project, University of California, Santa Barbara, www.presidency.ucsb.edu (accessed June 27, 2011). See also Timothy Conlan, *New Federalism: Intergovernmental Reform from Nixon to Reagan* (with an introduction by Samuel H. Beer) (Washington, DC: Brookings Institution, 1988); Timothy Conlan, *From New Federalism to Devolution: Twenty-Five Years of Intergovernmental Reform* (Washington, DC: Brookings Institution Press, 1998).

8. See Barack Obama, "Memorandum for the Heads of Executive Departments and Agencies," White House, May 20, 2009, www.whitehouse.gov/the-press-office/presidential-memorandum-regarding-preemption (accessed June 5, 2011); Jack Park, "Vaccines, Preemption, and Federalism Rightly Understood: Why the Supreme Court Should Find Preemption in *Bruesewitz v. Wyeth, Inc.*," Legal Memorandum No. 59, Heritage Foundation, November 12, 2010, www.heritage.org/research/reports/2010/11/vaccines-preemption-and-federalism-rightly-understood (accessed June 5, 2011).

9. George W. Bush, "Memorandum on the Interagency Working Group of Federalism (February 26, 2001)," American Presidency Project, University of California, Santa Barbara, www.presidency.ucsb.edu (accessed June 27, 2011). See also George Bush, "Memorandum on Federalism (February 16, 1999)," American Presidency Project, University of California, Santa Barbara, www.presidency.ucsb.edu (accessed June 27, 2011); Ronald Reagan, "Executive Order 12612—Federalism," American Presidency Project, University of California, Santa Barbara, October 26, 1987, www.presidency.ucsb.edu (accessed June 27, 2011).

10. Melvin I. Urofsky and Paul Finkelman, *A March of Liberty: A Constitutional History of the United States*, Vol. 2: *From 1877 to the Present*, 2nd ed. (New York: Oxford University Press, 2002), 869.

11. David B. Walker, "American Federalism from Johnson to Bush," *Publius: The Journal of Federalism* 21, no. 1 (1991): 105–19, 107. See also Conlan, *New Federalism*; Conlan, *From New Federalism to Devolution*.

12. Political scientist Kevin McMahon argues that Nixon's anti–Warren Court campaign strategy is his most enduring presidential legacy. Kevin J. McMahon,

Nixon's Court: His Challenge to Judicial Liberalism and Its Political Consequences (Chicago: University of Chicago Press, 2011).

13. Quoted in Christopher P. Banks, *Judicial Politics in the D.C. Circuit Court* (Baltimore: John Hopkins University Press, 1999), 26. See also McMahon, *Nixon's Court,* 118; Jonathan Simon, *Governing through Crime: How the War on Crime Transformed American Democracy and Created a Culture of Fear* (New York: Oxford University Press, 2007), 35, 114; David Alistair Yalof, *Pursuit of Justices: Presidential Politics and the Selection of Supreme Court Nominees* (Chicago: University of Chicago Press, 1999), 98. The complex and perhaps tenuous ideological relationship that President Nixon had with "new right" conservatives and his party in light of his conception of the presidency is identified in Keith Whittington, "Taking What They Give Us: Explaining the Court's Federalism Offensive," *Duke Law Journal* 51 (2001): 477–520, 504; Keith Whittington, *Political Foundations of Judicial Supremacy: The Presidency, the Supreme Court, and Constitutional Leadership in U.S. History* (Princeton, NJ: Princeton University Press, 2007), 189–90; and James MacGregor Burns, *Leadership* (New York: Harper and Row, 1978), 395.

14. Simon, *Governing through Crime,* 90.

15. Quoting Joseph C. Goulden, *The Benchwarmers: The Private World of the Powerful Federal Judges* (New York: Weybright and Talley, 1974), 225, in Banks, *Judicial Politics in the D.C. Circuit Court,* 23.

16. Political scientist Kevin McMahon describes the plan as "radically progressive from today's standpoint." He also observes that Nixon cast aside his "traditional Republican principles" by "institut[ing] a wage-price freeze and cost-of-living indexing for Social Security recipients" and, additionally, "helped to creat[e] the Environmental Protection Agency, the Occupational Safety and Health Administration, and other programs designed to improve the quality of air and water and to protect children and consumers against abuse." McMahon, *Nixon's Court,* 71.

17. Revenue sharing, via the consolidation of categorical grants with some block grants, was put in place, but the family aid plan, as well as many of the special revenue-sharing programs, was unsuccessful. This mixed record was colored by a sharp increase in entitlements spending and federal regulation. Conlan, *From New Federalism to Devolution,* 91–92, 97.

18. Whittington, *Political Foundations of Judicial Supremacy,* 220–25; Tushnet, *A Court Divided,* 25–27. McMahon portrays Rehnquist's appointment as "something of an accidental choice" by Nixon. McMahon, *Nixon's Court,* 251.

19. Walker, "American Federalism from Johnson to Bush," 115. See also Vincent Blasi, "The Rootless Activism of the Burger Court," in *The Burger Court: The Counter-Revolution That Wasn't* (New Haven, CT: Yale University Press, 1983), 198–217 (describing the Burger Court as one reflecting "rootless activism"); Whittington, "Taking What They Give Us," 505; Kermit L. Hall, *The Magic Mirror: Law in American History* (New York: Oxford University Press, 1989), 286–88, 329–31.

20. McMahon observes Nixon's ideal justice is something akin to strict constructionism with "flexibility" and less prone to blatant judicial activism, as illustrated by Justice Felix Frankfurter's approach to judging. McMahon, *Nixon's Court,* 117.

21. Conlan, *From New Federalism to Devolution,* 102; see also 95–101. See also Walker, "American Federalism from Johnson to Bush," 108; Richard L. Cole and Delbert A. Taebel, "The New Federalism: Promises, Programs, and Performance," *Publius* 16, no. 1 (1986): 3, 4.

22. Walker, "American Federalism from Johnson to Bush," 109. See also Advisory Commission on Intergovernmental Relations, *Regulatory Federalism: Policy, Process, Impact and Reform* (Washington, DC: Advisory Commission on Intergovernmental Relations, 1984), 2 (acknowledging a pronounced regulatory shift in the 1970s, centering on grant consolidation, grants-in-aid, and general revenue sharing, that had the effect of establishing the rationale for Reagan's new federalism as a means to lessen federal compulsion over the states); Cole and Taebel, "The New Federalism," 3 (observing a sustained trend and growing dependence of local government and cities on the federal government for aid).

23. Walker, "American Federalism from Johnson to Bush," 113; ibid., 110–12. Reagan's inaugural remarks are quoted in Irene Fraser Rothenberg and George J. Gordon, "'Out with the Old, in with the New': The New Federalism, Intergovernmental Coordination and Executive Order 12372," *Publius: The Journal of Federalism* 14, no. 3 (1983): 31–47, 35; ibid., 47. President Reagan's specific proposals and corresponding legislation in the first three years of his term are outlined in Richard S. Williamson, "A New Federalism: Proposals and Achievements of President Reagan's First Three Years," *Publius: The Journal of Federalism* 16, no. 1 (1986): 11–28.

24. Cole and Taebel, "The New Federalism," 5, citing George Peterson, "Federalism and the States: An Experiment in Decentralization," in *The Reagan Record,* ed. John L. Palmer and Isabel V. Sawhill (Cambridge, MA: Ballinger Press, 1984). See also Whittington, "Taking What They Give Us," 504 (arguing Nixon's political agenda was more pragmatic, and less ideological, than Reagan's commitment to "limited government" and federalism ideals).

25. Conlan, *From New Federalism to Devolution,* 108–9; Cole and Taebel, "The New Federalism," 10. See also McMahon, *Nixon's Court,* 252.

26. See Larry D. Kramer, "Putting the Politics Back into the Political Safeguards of Federalism," *Columbia Law Review* 100 (2000): 215–93, 290.

27. McMahon, *Nixon's Court,* 252. See also Whittington, "Taking What They Give Us," 505–6 (arguing Nixon's appointments on the Burger Court did not display sympathy for returning power back to the states and federalism cases); Yalof, *Pursuit of Justices* (outlining the differences between Nixon and Reagan judicial selection process and nominees).

28. Christopher P. Banks and David M. O'Brien, *Courts and Judicial Policymaking* (Upper Saddle River, NJ: Pearson/Prentice Hall, 2006), 132–37 (analyzing the Republican ideological selection model and others that defined the modern nomination and confirmation judicial selection process). See also Yalof, *Pursuit of Justices,* 133–34 (noting Reagan's judicial selection style, his criticism of the judiciary, and the ideological nature of the selection process); Whittington, "Taking What They Give Us," 505–6 (arguing Nixon's appointments on the Burger Court did not display sympathy for returning power back to the states and federalism cases).

29. Yalof, *Pursuit of Justices,* 135–42. See also J. Mitchell Pickerill and Cornell W. Clayton, "The Rehnquist Court and the Political Dynamics of Federalism," *Per-*

spectives on Politics 2, no. 2 (2004): 242–43 (discussing the convergence of elements of the conservative intelligentsia); Tushnet, *A Court Divided*, 38–48 (outlining the rise of strategic litigation by conservative interest groups that took as their model template similar activity by liberal activists in the 1970s).

30. Tushnet, *A Court Divided*, 35. Law scholar Mark Tushnet, in ibid, 36, is referring to the booklet from the U.S. Department of Justice, Office of Legal Policy, *Guidelines on Constitutional Litigation (February 19, 1988)* (Washington, DC: Department of Justice, 1988), which he describes as a "road map for the course constitutional conservatives hoped to take." See also Dawn E. Johnsen, "Ronald Reagan and the Rehnquist Court on Congressional Power: Presidential Influences on Constitutional Change," *Indiana Law Journal* 78 (2003): 363–412. Also, political scientist David Yalof cites Roger A. Clegg's paper, prepared while he was a special assistant to Edwin Meese, as outlining the quoted federalism criteria in the main text. Yalof, *Pursuit of Justices*, 143. See also ibid., 142–55; Whittington, "Taking What They Give Us," 504–5.

31. Richard Brust, "Reviewing Rehnquist: In What May Be the Chief Justice's Final Term, Observers Are Starting to Look at the Court's Place in History and Examine the Federalism Revolution," *American Bar Association Journal* 89 (2003): 42 (quoting law professor H. Jefferson Powell).

32. Richard H. Fallon Jr., "The 'Conservative' Paths of the Rehnquist Court's Federalism Decisions," *University of Chicago Law Review* 69 (2002): 429–94, 434–36 (arguing path dependence "functions as a capsule reference to various ways in which history and surrounding attitudes and expectations influence judicial decision-making," and it permits "the Court [to] proceed . . . along a doctrinal path . . . [as] it and the attentive public assess what the justices may properly do next in light of past experiences"). See also Johnsen, "Ronald Reagan and the Rehnquist Court on Congressional Power," 366 (arguing the roots of the Rehnquist Court's new [federalism] direction, at least in significant part, can be found in the "Reagan revolution").

33. The debate originates with Herbert Weschler, "The Political Safeguards of Federalism: The Role of the States in the Composition and Selection of the National Government," *Columbia Law Review* 54 (1954): 543–60. For two views representing opposite conclusions relative to Weschler's basic thesis, see Kramer, "Putting the Politics Back into the Political Safeguards of Federalism," 215–94; and John Yoo, "The Judicial Safeguards of Federalism," *Southern California Law Review* 70 (1997): 1311.

34. William H. Rehnquist, "The Notion of a Living Constitution," *Texas Law Review* 54 (1976): 693, 704–6.

35. See H. Jefferson Powell, "The Compleat Jeffersonian: Justice Rehnquist and Federalism," *Yale Law Journal* 91 (1982): 1317–70, 1359; and Martin H. Redish, *The Constitution as Political Structure* (New York: Oxford University Press, 1995): 44–45.

36. See T. W. Merrill, "The Making of the Second Rehnquist Court: A Preliminary Analysis," *Saint Louis University Law Journal* 47, no. 3 (2003): 569–658, 580.

37. All but eight cases (of the n = 66) are derived from the Supreme Court Dataset, 1953–2011 terms, at http://scdb.wustl.edu/analysis.php (using Data Release SCDB_2011_01). The remaining eight cases were added by the authors.

38. *Fry v. United States*, 421 U.S. 542 (1974). See Powell, "The Compleat Jeffersonian," 1320–31; Sue Davis, *Justice Rehnquist and the Constitution* (Princeton, NJ: Princeton University Press, 1989): 135–52; and Robert E. Riggs and Thomas D. Proffit, "The Judicial Philosophy of Justice Rehnquist," *Akron Law Review* 16 (1983): 555–604.

39. Rehnquist's *Fry* analysis foreshadowed other aspects of his new federalism theory. In dicta he used the Court's precedent in *Hans v. Louisiana*, 134 U.S. 1 (1890), to illustrate the framers' intent that states have "many attributes of sovereignty" that are safeguarded by the Eleventh and Tenth Amendments. Both, he wrote, register the principle that Congress cannot treat a state as if it were just another entity subject to otherwise permissible regulation. Using historical analysis and founding intent, Rehnquist endorsed *Hans*'s principle that barred a federal court from reviewing private lawsuits by state citizens against their own state. Rehnquist underscored this point by reaffirming the Supreme Court's power to say what the law is. As he explained, the *Hans* Court said, "It is not necessary that we should enter upon an examination of the reason or expediency of the rule which exempts a sovereign State from prosecution in a court of justice at the suit of individuals. This is fully discussed by writers on public law. *It is enough for us to declare its existence*." See *Fry*, 557 (quoting *Hans v. Louisiana*, 134 U.S. 1 [1890], 21; emphasis added).

40. *City of Rome v. United States*, 446 U.S. 156, 221 (1980).

41. *City of Rome v. United States*, 446 U.S. 156, 219–20 (1980), citing *The Civil Rights Cases*, 109 U.S. 3 (1883), declaring Congress's enforcement power as "remedial" only.

42. U.S. Department of Justice, Office of Legal Policy, *Guidelines on Constitutional Litigation*. See also Mark Tushnet, "William Rehnquist's Federalism," in *The Rehnquist Legacy*, ed. Craig M. Bradley (New York: Cambridge University Press, 2006), 198–202. See *City of Philadelphia v. N.J.*, 437 U.S. 617 (1978); *Hughes v. Oklahoma*, 441 U.S. 322 (1979); and *Kassel v. Consolidated Freightways*, 450 U.S. 662 (1981).

43. Legal scholar Jefferson Powell makes such a claim. Powell, "The Compleat Jeffersonian," 1362–63.

44. *National League of Cities v. Usery*, 426 U.S. 833, 842, 844–45, 849 (1976). Rehnquist uses *Coyle v. Oklahoma*, 221 U.S. 559 (1911), to illustrate the kind of attributes states possess (i.e., to make funding decisions and the like). *Usery*, 845. Much of Rehnquist's majority opinion analyzes the coercion federal law places on state officials wrestling with policy decisions concerning the delivery of governmental services. See ibid., 846–52. The level of compulsion becomes the basis to declare that the states, "in their capacities as sovereign governments," are compromised in the balance of federalism. Ibid., 852. In reaching these conclusions, Rehnquist legally diminished the precedent in *Fry v. United States*, 421 U.S. 542 (1975), as well as overruled *Maryland v. Wirtz*, 392 U.S. 183 (1968) (applying the federal Fair Labor Standards Act to state public schools and hospitals). See also Powell, "The Compleat Jeffersonian," 1325–26, and Davis, *Justice Rehnquist and the Constitution*, 143–46.

45. As Brennan put it, "Effective restraints on . . . exercise [of the commerce power] must proceed from political rather than from judicial processes." *National League of Cities v. Usery*, 426 U.S. 833, 875–76 (1976).

46. Weschler, "The Political Safeguards of Federalism." See *Garcia v. San Antonio Metropolitan Transit Authority*, 469 U.S. 528 (1985). In *Garcia*, Justice Harry Blackmun's majority opinion listed the cases registering the Court's inability to draw a clear line defining traditional state functions, or what comprised improper regulation of "states as states." See *Garcia*, 538–42. Also, the membership in *Usery* and *Garcia* was identical except for Justice Sandra Day O'Connor's 1981 confirmation. She replaced Potter Stewart and his pro-states' rights vote in *Usery* and voted similarly in *Garcia*. The *Usery* dissenters—Justices William Brennan, Thurgood Marshall, Bryon White, and John Paul Stevens—formed the majority when Blackmun switched his vote, thereby relegating the *Usery* majority (Chief Justice Warren Burger and Justices William Rehnquist, Potter Stewart, and Lewis Powell) to the dissenting bloc in *Garcia*.

47. *Edelman v. Jordan*, 415 U.S. 651 (1974), 37. See also ibid., 34, citing *Murray v. Wilson Distilling Co.*, 213 U.S. 151 (1909), 171. Rehnquist bolstered his nonwaiver argument with this language: "When we are dealing with the sovereign exemption from judicial interference in the vital field of financial administration a clear declaration of the state's intention to submit its fiscal problems to other courts than those of its own creation must be found." *Edelman*, 35 (citing *Great Northern Life Insurance Co. v. Read*, 322 U.S. 47, at 54). The judicially imposed standard of requiring clear intent was emphasized in an earlier opinion that Rehnquist joined (*Employees v. Missouri Public Health Dept.*, 411 U.S. 279 [1973]) and in the sequel to *Edelman* after remand, in *Quern v. Jordan*, 440 U.S. 332 (1979).

48. An interpretation of Rehnquist's theory of state sovereignty in Section 5 cases is found in Christopher P. Banks, "The Rehnquist Court's Theory of State Sovereignty Immunity in Federalism Cases" (unpublished paper delivered at the Southwestern Political Science Association, April 16–19, 2003, San Antonio, Texas), on file with author. For other perspectives on Rehnquist's theory of federalism, see Davis, *Justice Rehnquist and the Constitution*, chs. 7–9; Tushnet, "William Rehnquist's Federalism"; and Powell, "The Compleat Jeffersonian."

49. The Rehnquist Court's judicial behavior in protecting state autonomy and state sovereignty is analyzed in Young, "The Rehnquist Court's Two Federalisms."

50. The second Rehnquist Court thesis is asserted in Merrill, "The Making of the Second Rehnquist Court," 569–658, whereas the third is identified in Linda Greenhouse, "Foreward: The Third Rehnquist Court," in Bradley, *The Rehnquist Legacy*, xiii–xxi. See also Linda Greenhouse, "The Rehnquist Court and Its Imperiled States' Rights Legacy," *New York Times*, June 12, 2005.

51. See Dinan, "The Rehnquist Court's Federalism Decisions," 158–67; Kathleen M. Sullivan, "From States' Rights Blues to Blue States' Rights: Federalism after the Rehnquist Court," *Fordham Law Review* 75 (November 2006): 799–813; Clayton and Pickerill, "Guess What Happened on the Way to Revolution?," 85–114; Pickerill and Clayton, "The Rehnquist Court and the Political Dynamics of Federalism," 233–48; Mark V. Tushnet, *The New Constitutional Order* (Princeton, NJ: Princeton University Press, 2003), 265; and Mark Silverstein, "Conclusion: Politics and the Rehnquist Court," in *Rehnquist Justice: Understanding the Court Dynamic*, ed. Earl M. Maltz (Lawrence: University Press of Kansas, 2003), 377–291. For the view that Justices Sandra Day O'Connor and Anthony Kennedy are the true source for

understanding the Rehnquist Court legacy, see Thomas Moylan Keck, *The Most Activist Supreme Court in History: The Road to Modern Judicial Conservatism* (Chicago: University of Chicago Press, 2004), 378; and Nancy Maveety, *Queen's Court: Judicial Power in the Rehnquist Era* (Lawrence: University Press of Kansas, 2008).

52. Identifying what precisely is a federalism case for methodological purposes remains a challenge for researchers. Paul M. Collins, "Towards an Integrated Model of the U.S. Supreme Court's Federalism Decision Making," *Publius: The Journal of Federalism* 37, no. 4 (2007): 505–31. Table 3.3 adopts the coding used in the Supreme Court dataset, identifying federalism cases as those relating "to conflicts between the federal government and the states, except for those between the federal and state courts," and excludes cases involving the exercise of judicial power. See SCDB Data Codebook, 43, at http://scdb.wustl.edu/_brickFiles/2011_02/SCDB_2011_02_codebook.pdf. For federalism cases, liberal outcomes are pro-federal power, pro-executive power in executive/congressional disputes, and anti-state. Conservative outcomes are the reverse.

53. Lynn A. Baker, "Federalism and the Spending Power from *Dole* to *Birmingham Board of Education*," in Bradley, *The Rehnquist Legacy*, 205–21, 206 (suggesting *Dole* and analogous Rehnquist spending and commerce clause opinions are consistent in orienting a jurisprudence that asks if Congress can regulate an area falling within the realm of traditional state functions, a premise and rationale of *National League of Cities v. Usery*, 426 U.S. 833 [1976]). In *South Dakota v. Dole*, 483 U.S. 203, 207 (1987), the Court cited *Pennhurst State School and Hospital v. Halderman*, 451 U.S. 1 (1981), and its holding that federal law did not give substantive rights to disabled persons to sue the states under the Fourteenth Amendment enforcement or Article I spending powers, to reiterate Congress's obligation to express its intent unambiguously for the purpose of informing the states of the conditions it sets for the receipt of federal funds.

54. *South Dakota v. Dole*, 483 U.S. 203 (1987) (O'Connor, J., dissenting). See also Ann Althouse, "Variations on a Theory of Normative Federalism: A Supreme Court Dialogue," *Duke Law Journal* 42, no. 5 (1993): 979, 1001.

55. *Gregory v. Ashcroft*, 501 U.S. 452 (1991); *Coleman v. Thompson*, 501 U.S. 722 (1991).

56. *Coleman*, 501 U.S. 722 (1991); *Michigan v. Long*, 463 U.S. 1032 (1983). For an analysis of the Rehnquist-authored cases that used federalism, independent and adequate state grounds, and other deference-to-state courts' rationales before *Coleman* in death penalty habeas cases, such as *Wainright v. Sykes*, 433 U.S. 72 (1977), see Joseph L. Hoffmann, "Narrowing Habeas Corpus," in Bradley, *The Rehnquist Legacy*, 156–83.

57. Larry Yackle, "The Story of *Fay v. Noia*: Another Case about Another Federalism," in *Federal Courts Stories*, ed. Vicki C. Jackson and Judith Resnik (New York: Thomson Reuters/Foundation Press, 2010), 191, 192. See also *Coleman*, 501 U.S. 722 (1991).

58. For the liberal view, see *Coleman*, 501 U.S. 722 (1991) (Blackmun, J., dissenting) ("federalism secures to citizens the liberties that derive from the diffusion of sovereign power," and it does not "blindly protect the interests of States from any incursion by the federal courts"); and ibid., 193 (observing that *Noia*'s procedural default rule reflected the Warren Court's preference to "make *habeas corpus*

an effective mechanism for enforcing constitutional rights in criminal cases"). For the conservative view, see Althouse, "Variations on a Theory of Normative Federalism: A Supreme Court Dialogue," 979, 998, and 1009 (observing that Justice Blackmun's argument in *Coleman*, which states that federalism advances the protection of individual rights, "loses force" when "the question is the extent of congressional power as against the state, and a single individual's life or liberty is no longer the focal point" because courts, as in *Gregory*, "preserve the vigor of the state as a political entity independent of Congress, on the theory that strong states would have the ability to protect their citizens from encroachments on their rights by the national government").

59. Ernest A. Young, "The Story of *Gregory v. Ashcroft*: Clear Statement Rules and the Statutory Constitution of American Federalism," in *Statutory Interpretation Stories*, ed. William N. Eskridge Jr., Philip P. Frickey, and Elizabeth Garrett (New York: Foundation Press, 2011), 197–225, 224–25 ("Rather than overruling *Garcia* . . . the *Gregory* majority fashioned a doctrinal strategy that turned *Garcia*'s emphasis on the national political process into a meaningful safeguard for state autonomy," allowing "*Gregory v. Ashcroft* [to be a story of] using doctrinal lemons to make lemonade"). See also Althouse, "Variations on a Theory of Normative Federalism," 979–1021; and Andrzej Rapaczynski, "From Sovereignty to Process: The Jurisprudence of Federalism after *Garcia*," *Supreme Court Review* (1985): 341–419.

60. See Herman Schwartz, "The Supreme Court's Federalism: Fig Leaf for Conservatives," *Annals of the American Academy of Political and Social Science* 574 (2001): 119–31; and Steven G. Calabresi, "Federalism and the Rehnquist Court: A Normative Defense," *Annals of the American Academy of Political and Social Science* 574 (2001): 24–36. See also Merrill, "The Making of the Second Rehnquist Court," 569–658, 574 (observing that Justice White was "an old-fashioned New Deal liberal" who followed judicial restraint on social issues but also was "skeptical about claims of states' rights," thus making Justice Thomas, a conservative on social and federalism issues, the "indirect" replacement of White for purposes of understanding the reconfiguration of conservative and liberal voting blocs on the Rehnquist Court that ultimately allowed the federalist five to control case outcomes).

61. Erwin Chemerinsky, *Enhancing Government: Federalism in the 21st Century* (Stanford, CA: Stanford University Press, 2008), 32–33 (noting *Garcia* was not overruled but its premise that the Tenth Amendment was not a limitation on federal power was rejected; *New York* is only the second time since *National League of Cities* that the Tenth Amendment was used in the last fifty-five years to strike down a federal law); Tinsley E. Yarbrough, *The Rehnquist Court and the Constitution* (New York: Oxford University Press, 2000), 111 (observing relative to *New York*'s holding that "nothing in the Tenth Amendment—or any other constitutional provision, for that matter—forbids Congress to impose its delegated authority on states and localities"); and Matthew D. Adler, "State Sovereignty and the Anti-Commandeering Cases," *Annals of the American Academy of Political and Social Science* 574 (2001): 158–72. See also *Printz v. United States*, 521 U.S. 898 (1997); *New York v. United States*, 488 U.S. 1041 (1992); and *United States v. Darby*, 312 U.S. 100 (1941).

62. The vulnerable Warren Court precedents include *Katzenbach v. McClung*, 379 U.S. 294 (1964) (upholding racial antidiscrimination provisions of the Civil

Rights Act of 1964 under the commerce clause); *Katzenbach v. Morgan*, 384 U.S. 641 (1966) (upholding the voting antidiscrimination provision of the Voting Rights Act of 1965 under Section 5 of the Fourteenth Amendment); and the Burger Court ruling of *Perez v. United States*, 402 U.S. 146 (1971) (upholding the Consumer Credit Protection Act as permissible regulation of loan-sharking activities under the commerce clause). Frank Goodman, "Preface," *Annals of the American Academy of Political and Social Science* 574 (2001): 9–23, 16; and *Perez v. United States*, 402 U.S. 146 (1971). See also *United States v. Lopez*, 514 U.S. 549 (1995), and *United States v. Morrison*, 529 U.S. 598 (2000).

63. *Employment Division, Department of Human Resources of Oregon v. Smith*, 494 U.S. 872 (1990); *City of Boerne v. Flores*, 521 U.S. 507 (1997). The adoption of the general applicability of neutral laws test in *Smith* undercut a Warren Court free-exercise precedent using a balancing test under a compelling interest standard in *Sherbert v. Verner*, 374 U.S. 398 (1963) (nullifying state unemployment compensation denying benefits to a Seventh-day Adventist who refused to work on the Sabbath).

64. *City of Boerne v. Flores*, 521 U.S. 507, 515–29, 531 (1997) (Kennedy, J., Opinion of the Court).

65. See Young, "The Rehnquist Court's Two Federalisms."

66. *Seminole Tribe of Florida v. Florida*, 517 U.S. 44, 59 (1996), citing *Fitzpatrick v. Bitzer*, 427 U.S. 445 (1976), 452–56. *Fitzpatrick* is important because it adheres to the principle that Eleventh Amendment immunity can be abrogated by a federal law enacted under Section 5 authority. See also *Seminole Tribe of Florida v. Florida*, 517 U.S. 44 (1996); *Pennsylvania v. Union Gas Company*, 491 U.S. 1 (1989); *Alden v. Maine*, 527 U.S. 706 (1999); *Federal Maritime Commission v. South Carolina State Port Authority*, 535 U.S. 743 (2002).

67. Dinan, "The Rehnquist Court's Federalism Decisions," 158–67; Clayton and Pickerill, "Guess What Happened on the Way to Revolution?," 85–114.

68. *Reno v. Condon*, 528 U.S. 141 (2000); *Nevada Department of Human Resources v. Katz*, 538 U.S. 721 (2003); *Tennessee v. Lane*, 541 U.S. 509 (2004); *Gonzales v. Raich*, 545 U.S. 1 (2005); *United States v. Georgia*, 546 U.S. 151 (2006); and *Central Virginia Community College v. Katz*, 546 U.S. 356 (2006).

69. Greenhouse, "Foreword: The Third Rehnquist Court," xiii–xxi; Greenhouse, "The Rehnquist Court and Its Imperiled States' Rights Legacy"; See also Merrill, "The Making of the Second Rehnquist Court," 569–658; Tushnet, *A Court Divided*, 384.

70. Keck, *The Most Activist Supreme Court in History*, 378; Dinan, "The Rehnquist Court's Federalism Decisions," 158–67. Scholars suggesting that the Rehnquist Court made inroads in advancing new federalism goals include Sullivan, "From States' Rights Blues to Blue States' Rights," 799–813; Young, "The Story of *Gregory v. Ashcroft*," 197–225; Young, "Two Cheers for Process Federalism," *Villanova Law Review* 46 (2001): 1349.

71. Sullivan, "From States' Rights Blues to Blue States' Rights," 799–813, 809; Chemerinsky, *Enhancing Government*, 48.

72. Young, "The Story of *Gregory v. Ashcroft*," 197–225, 213, 224. See also J. F. Manning, "Clear Statement Rules and the Constitution," *Columbia Law Review* 110 (2010): 399–579; Young, "The Rehnquist Court's Two Federalisms"; William N.

Eskridge Jr. and Philip P. Frickey, "Quasi-Constitutional Law: Clear Statement Rules as Constitutional Lawmaking," *Vanderbilt Law Review* 45 (1992): 593.

73. Bradley W. Joondeph, "Federalism, the Rehnquist Court, and the Modern Republican Party," *Oregon Law Review* (2008): 117, 118–19 (observing that scholars have largely ignored those disputes involving federalism-based constraints on the states; the most significant of these constraints are the dormant commerce clause and the doctrine of preemption).

74. David M. O'Brien, "The Rehnquist Court and Federal Preemption: In Search of a Theory," *Publius: The Journal of Federalism* 23, no. 4 (1993): 21–22.

75. The law scholarship is more plentiful, and some engage in some empirical analysis specific to the Rehnquist Court, such as ibid.; David S. Day, "The 'Mature' Rehnquist Court and the Dormant Commerce Clause Doctrine: The Expanded Discrimination Tier," *South Dakota Law Review* 52 (2007): 1–51; Christopher R. Drahozal, "Preserving the American Common Market: State and Local Governments in the United States Supreme Court," *Supreme Court Economic Review* 7 (1999): 233–83. Analogous political science research includes O'Brien, "The Rehnquist Court and Federal Preemption," 15. Other law and political science analyses are found in Tushnet, "William Rehnquist's Federalism," 187–204; Jim Chen, "A Vision Softly Creeping: Congressional Acquiescence and the Dormant Commerce Clause," *Minnesota Law Review* 88 (2004): 1764–1800; Brannon P. Denning, "The Dormant Commerce Clause Doctrine: Prolegomenon to a Defense," *Minnesota Law Review* (2004): 1801–11; Mark A. Graber, "Clarence Thomas and the Perils of Amateur History," in Maltz, *Rehnquist Justice*, 70–102; Yarbrough, *The Rehnquist Court and the Constitution*; and Martin H. Redish and Shane V. Nugent, "The Dormant Commerce Clause and the Constitutional Balance of Federalism," *Duke Law Journal* (1987): 569–617.

76. Young, "The Rehnquist Court's Two Federalisms."

77. Jack M. Balkin, "Commerce," *Michigan Law Review* 109 (2010): 1–51 (analyzing different Supreme Court commerce clause interpretations in the context of rival judicial philosophies). See also *Gibbons v. Ogden*, 22 U.S. 1 (1824).

78. See Redish and Nugent, "The Dormant Commerce Clause and the Constitutional Balance of Federalism," 569–70; O'Brien, "The Rehnquist Court and Federal Preemption," 25–26. See also *Cooley v. Board of Wardens of the Port of Philadelphia*, 53 U.S. 229 (1852).

79. Chief Justice Marshall is quoted in *Willson v. Black Bird Creek Marsh Co.*, 27 U.S. (2 Pet.) 245 (1829) in Congressional Research Service, "The Constitution of the United States of America: Analysis and Interpretation (Analysis of Cases Decided by the Supreme Court of the United States to June 28, 2002)," 108th Cong., 2nd Sess. (Document No. 108-177), 224. See also Redish and Nugent, "The Dormant Commerce Clause and the Constitutional Balance of Federalism," 576–77.

80. Congressional Research Service, "The Constitution of the United States of America," 224.

81. See Redish and Nugent, "The Dormant Commerce Clause and the Constitutional Balance of Federalism."

82. Law professor Bradley Joondeph borrows the term "union-preserving" rules of federalism from Laurence Tribe's constitutional law treatise to describe the interest in preventing state economic protectionism. Joondeph, "Federalism, the Rehnquist Court, and the Modern Republican Party," 117–73, 124. Analyses

of the dormant commerce clause antidiscrimination judicial standards are found in Day, "The 'Mature' Rehnquist Court and the Dormant Commerce Clause Doctrine," 1–2; Tushnet, "William Rehnquist's Federalism," 197; Congressional Research Service, "The Constitution of the United States of America," 226.

83. Ryan D. Wheeler, "The Supreme Court Lends States a Break: Department of Revenue of *Kentucky v. Davis* and the Civic Responsibility Exception to the Negative Commerce Clause," *Pepperdine Law Review* 37 (2010): 375, 380–82; Lawrence Fogel, "Serving a 'Public Function': Why Regional Cap-and-Trade Programs Should Survive a Dormant Commerce Clause Challenge," *Wisconsin Law Review* (2010): 1313, 1330–32; see also Day, "The 'Mature' Rehnquist Court and the Dormant Commerce Clause Doctrine," 1–2; *City of Philadelphia v. N.J.*, 437 U.S. 617 (1978); *Pike v. Bruce Church*, 397 U.S. 137 (1970) (invalidating the in-state packaging requirement for cantaloupes).

84. Conceptualizing the Supreme Court's approach as tier-based should not be overstated. Many of the early Rehnquist Court dormant commerce clause cases in the state taxation area, for example, focused on a four-part test derived from *Complete Auto Transit, Inc. v. Brady*, 430 U.S. 274 (1977), a precedent that appears to use balancing analysis but also to center on determining discriminatory effect. For the view (which the present study adopts) that the Rehnquist Court has used two-tier analysis to decide these cases, see Day, "The 'Mature' Rehnquist Court and the Dormant Commerce Clause Doctrine," 1–2.

85. Joondeph, "Federalism, the Rehnquist Court, and the Modern Republican Party," 117–73, 127. See also Tushnet, "William Rehnquist's Federalism," 197.

86. Frank B. Cross and Emerson H. Tiller, "The Three Faces of Federalism: An Empirical Assessment of Supreme Court Federalism Jurisprudence," *Southern California Law Review* 73 (2000): 741, 746. Professor O'Brien makes an identical point in his study of Rehnquist Court preemption and dormant commerce clause cases. O'Brien, "The Rehnquist Court and Federal Preemption," 30–31.

87. Joondeph, "Federalism, the Rehnquist Court, and the Modern Republican Party," 117, 129–34 (appendix A identified twenty-four dormant commerce clause cases in the total of seventy-six cases, inclusive of preemption). Other studies using different time periods within the Rehnquist Court all concur that the justices ruled against state regulatory efforts in a majority of dormant commerce clause cases. See Day, "The 'Mature' Rehnquist Court and the Dormant Commerce Clause Doctrine" (state laws invalidated in ten of thirteen cases from 1992 to 2005); Drahozal, "Preserving the American Common Market," 233–83 (state laws struck down in sixteen of twenty-five cases from 1986 to 1999); and O'Brien, "The Rehnquist Court and Federal Preemption," 15 (state laws nullified in nine of fifteen cases from 1986 to 1993).

88. Joondeph, "Federalism, the Rehnquist Court, and the Modern Republican Party," 117, 129. See also Day, "The 'Mature' Rehnquist Court and the Dormant Commerce Clause Doctrine," 1–51.

89. Drahozal, "Preserving the American Common Market," 233–83.

90. Drahozal, "Preserving the American Common Market," 233–83. See also O'Brien, "The Rehnquist Court and Federal Preemption."

91. Commerce clause cases from the Supreme Court Database were located in "All Rehnquist Courts" using search identifiers narrowing the cases to interstate commerce and supremacy cases. "Dormant commerce clause" cases were identified

if the state's law regulating commerce was challenged and Congress had not passed legislation regulating the commercial area. Foreign dormant commerce clause cases were excluded. The research studies analyzing specific dormant commerce clause cases that were cross-checked against the Supreme Court Database are Joondeph, "Federalism, the Rehnquist Court, and the Modern Republican Party," 117–73; Day, "The 'Mature' Rehnquist Court and the Dormant Commerce Clause Doctrine," 1–51; Drahozal, "Preserving the American Common Market," 233–83; and David M. O'Brien, *Constitutional Law and Politics: Civil Rights and Liberties*, Vol. 2, 9th ed. (New York: W. W. Norton & Company, 2011).

92. Liberal or conservative votes were coded in the manner set forth in the Supreme Court Judicial Database, as applied to federalism cases.

93. Cross and Tiller, "The Three Faces of Federalism," 741–71; Ruth Colker and Kevin M. Scott, "Rehnquist and Federalism: An Empirical Perspective," in Bradley, *The Rehnquist Legacy*, 279, 289.

94. Six cases were excluded as indeterminate applications of tier one or two.

95. Colker and Scott, "Rehnquist and Federalism," 289.

96. O'Brien, "The Rehnquist Court and Federal Preemption," 15.

97. Frank B. Cross, *The Theory and Practice of Statutory Interpretation* (Stanford, CA: Stanford Law Books, 2009), 161, 165–66.

98. Young, "Two Cheers for Process Federalism," 16–17, 33. See also *United States v. Lopez*, 514 U.S. 549 (1995).

99. See Anita S. Krishnakumar, "Statutory Interpretation in the Roberts Court's First Era: An Empirical and Doctrinal Analysis," *Hastings Law Journal* 62 (2010): 221.

100. Young, "Two Cheers for Process Federalism," 1374 (identifying those contributions as the application of clear statement rules with the development of limits on congressional exercise of enumerated powers—that is, commerce and Section 5 of the Fourteenth Amendment, the anti-commandeering doctrine, and Eleventh Amendment state immunity precedents restricting federal judicial power); Eskridge Frickey, "Quasi-Constitutional Law: Clear Statement Rules as Constitutional Lawmaking," 593, 612–13.

101. William N. Eskridge, *Dynamic Statutory Interpretation* (Cambridge, MA: Harvard University Press, 1994), 438; and Krishnakumar, "Statutory Interpretation in the Roberts Court's First Era," 221 (analyzing statutory canons in use in the Roberts Court).

102. Young, "The Rehnquist Court's Two Federalisms," 16; Manning, "Clear Statement Rules and the Constitution," 401–3; Eskridge, *Dynamic Statutory Interpretation*, 438; and O'Brien, "The Rehnquist Court and Federal Preemption," 24–25.

103. Young, "The Rehnquist Court's Two Federalisms," 16–17.

104. Eskridge and Frickey, "Quasi-Constitutional Law," 597, 611–12.

105. James J. Brudney and Corey Ditslear, "Canons of Construction and the Elusive Quest for Neutral Reasoning," *Vanderbilt Law Review* 58 (2005): 1, 94–95.

106. Cross and Tiller, "The Three Faces of Federalism," 741, 769.

107. Cross and Tiller, "The Three Faces of Federalism," 741, 769.

108. Brudney and Ditslear, "Canons of Construction and the Elusive Quest for Neutral Reasoning," 1–116. See also Eskridge and Frickey, "Quasi-Constitutional Law," 593.

109. Cross, *The Theory and Practice of Statutory Interpretation*, 178. See also Brudney and Ditslear, "Canons of Construction and the Elusive Quest for Neutral Reasoning," 1–116; James J. Brudney and Corey Ditslear, "The Decline and Fall of Legislative History? Patterns of Supreme Court Reliance in the Burger and Rehnquist Eras," *Judicature* 89, no. 4 (January–February 2006): 220–29.

110. Young, "The Story of *Gregory v. Ashcroft*," 217.

111. *Rice v. Santa Fe Elevator Corporation*, 331 U.S. 218 (1947), 230–31. The "presumption against preemption" principle, as applied or ignored by federal judges, is highly controversial, with some legal scholars claiming that it no longer exists either in practice or by way of founding intent (based on the interpretation of the framers' view of the supremacy clause). Ernest A. Young, "Federal Preemption and State Autonomy," in Richard A. Epstein and Michael Greve, *Federal Preemption: States' Powers, National Interests* (Washington, DC: AEI Press, 2007), 264–65; Alan E. Untereiner, *The Preemption Defense in Tort Actions: Law, Strategy and Practice* (Washington, DC: U.S. Chamber Institute for Legal Reform, 2008); James T. O'Reilly, *Federal Preemption of State and Local Law: Legislation, Regulation and Litigation* (Chicago: American Bar Association, 2006), 7–8; Caleb Nelson, "Preemption," *Virginia Law Review* 86 (2000): 225.

112. *Pennhurst State School and Hospital v. Halderman*, 451 U.S. 1 (1981), and *Atascadero State Hospital v. Scanlon*, 473 U.S. 234 (1985).

113. Brudney and Ditslear, for example, find that in ten or eleven cases the "anti-preemption" canon (that in operation would not disturb state laws covering traditional or core state functions) were decided after 1984; likewise, the federalism canon requiring unmistakably clear federal language was applied in seven of the eight Eleventh Amendment immunity cases decided after 1985. Brudney and Ditslear, "Canons of Construction and the Elusive Quest for Neutral Reasoning," 43. See also Eskridge, *Dynamic Statutory Interpretation*, 438; Eskridge and Frickey, "Quasi-Constitutional Law," 593.

114. A search using Westlaw and the following search terms ("clear statement," "clear and manifest purpose," "unmistakably clear," "Congress's intent," "plain statement," "absolutely certain," "Congress's intent," "legislative intent"), as narrowed down by the search term "federalism" and the operative time period of the Rehnquist Court, yielded sixty case citations that were reviewed for analysis. The precedents discussed in the text were selected for illustrative purposes, ostensibly to provide a sense of how clear statement rules used certain language in certain types of federalism cases, as discussed in the chapter.

115. *Welch v. Texas Dep't of Highways and Public Transportation*, 483 U.S. 468 (1987), 517 (Brennan, J., dissenting). See also *Parden v. Terminal Railway of Alabama Docks Department*, 377 U.S. 184 (1964).

116. *Will v. Michigan Dep't of State Police*, 491 U.S. 58 (1989), 72 (Brennan, J., dissenting). See also ibid., 65 (White, J., Opinion for the Court).

117. Young, "Two Cheers for Process Federalism," 1386.

118. The Federalist Society, "Minutes from a Convention of the Federalist Society: The Future of Federal Preemption," *New York University Journal of Law and Liberty* 6 (2011): 184; Chemerinsky, *Enhancing Government*; Young, "Federal Preemption and State Autonomy," 249–76.

119. Antonin Scalia, *A Matter of Interpretation: Federal Courts and the Law* (Princeton, NJ: Princeton University Press, 1997); Stephen Breyer, "Our Democratic Constitution," *New York University Law Review* (2004): 245–72.

120. Brudney and Ditslear, "Canons of Construction and the Elusive Quest for Neutral Reasoning," 8–12.

121. Tushnet, *A Court Divided,* 278, 384. See also Epp, *The Rights Revolution,* 326; Pickerill and Clayton, "The Rehnquist Court and the Political Dynamics of Federalism," 233–48.

122. Keck, *The Most Activist Supreme Court in History,* 277 and 378.

123. Greenhouse, "Foreward: The Third Rehnquist Court," xiii–xxi, xviii.

124. See Donald W. Jackson, Michael C. Tolley, and Mary L. Volcansek, *Globalizing Justice: Critical Perspectives on Transnational Law and the Cross-Border Migration of Legal Norms* (Albany: State University of New York Press, 2010).

4

Federalism, Justice Clarence Thomas, and Religious Freedom in the States

As an associate justice on the Supreme Court, William Rehnquist set the "long fuse" for the new federalism revolution with his array of dissenting and concurring opinions in federalism cases in the 1970s and mid-1980s. With his promotion to chief justice by President Ronald Reagan in 1986, Rehnquist put his federalism jurisprudence into action. In contrast to Chief Justice Rehnquist's reformation of federalism as a long-term project, Justice Clarence Thomas has sought more immediate and sweeping doctrinal and constitutional change. Thomas's judicial opinions indicate a real hostility to New Deal federalism precedents and show his advocacy for an almost complete reversal of them. His off-the-bench Court speeches likewise suggest his constitutional philosophy envisions a reinvigoration of federalism as a means of checking and limiting the powers of the federal government over the states and American citizens.[1] Court watchers have labeled Thomas the "true revolutionary" on federalism matters, since his opinions in federalism cases "[show] where the new justices might take the Rehnquist Court's decisions."[2] For Thomas, recent federalism disputes on the Court's docket give him a ready platform to define some of the elements of his narrow, originalist reading of the Constitution, which sharply limits federal power in favor of the states. Not content to propound his interpretative philosophy, Thomas has also used federalism disputes to argue for the wholesale overturning of many of the classic and stable federalism precedents of the twentieth century. One notable example is *United States v. Lopez*, where, for the first time in almost sixty years, the Court overturned Congress's use of its interstate commerce clause power to regulate conduct within a state.

In *Lopez*, a divided Court split 5–4, with the majority led by Chief Justice Rehnquist, struck down the Gun Free School Zones Act in which Congress used its interstate commerce clause powers to criminalize the possession of a firearm near a public school. As the majority reasoned, sustaining Congress's power to criminalize intrastate firearm possession under the guise of regulating commerce effectively would convert the legislature's power into a "general police power of the sort retained by the states."[3] Justice Thomas's concurring opinion gives valuable insights into his views on federalism. For one commentator, Thomas's judicial line drawing makes him "a jurisprudential soul mate, apparently, of Justice [William] McReynolds and other pre-1937 laissez-faire justices" who adamantly maintained a narrow reading of Congress's interstate commerce powers so as to deny the federal government the power to enact the New Deal.[4]

For Thomas, the Court must reassess its commerce clause jurisprudence, which has "drifted far from the original understanding of the Commerce Clause." Instead, the Court must put in place an interpretation that is "more faithful to the original understanding of [the] Clause."[5] His reading of the commerce clause is originalist in scope: "At the time the original Constitution was ratified, 'commerce' consisted of selling, buying, and bartering, as well as transporting for these purposes." The original understanding of the term "commerce" sharply limited federal power to a subset of economic activities: buying, selling, and bartering, as distinct from manufacturing and other economic activities that are typically intrastate in character. Indeed, Thomas posits the Court's post–New Deal reading of the commerce clause was mistaken as a "dramatic departure in the 1930s from a century and a half of precedent."[6] His reading of the interstate commerce clause to limit federal power is buttressed by a larger interpretive point he makes in another federalism case, *U.S. Term Limits, Inc. v. Thornton*, which concerned whether a state constitution could limit the terms of service of its representatives to the federal Congress. A five-justice majority ruled that states cannot impose qualifications on Congress beyond those enumerated in the Constitution. Justice Thomas, along with Chief Justice Rehnquist and Justices Sandra Day O'Connor and Antonin Scalia, dissented. Thomas's opinion articulated a Tenth Amendment state sovereignty argument and noted an important and basic interpretative approach to the federal Constitution: judges should be reluctant "to read constitutional provisions to preclude state power by negative implication. The very structure of the Constitution counsels such hesitation."[7]

Thomas, however, was not content with redefining federalism doctrine in economic cases such as *Lopez* or qualifications for members of Congress as in *Thornton*. As the Rehnquist Court era was coming to a close, he sought to extend the Court's new federalism jurisprudence to a policy area, religious liberty and church-state relations, that is not typically associated with the federal-state relationship. In *Zelman v. Simmons-Harris*[8] and *Elk Grove Unified School District v. Newdow*,[9] Thomas argued for an interpretation of the establishment clause as a federalism provision limiting the power of the federal government over the states. For Thomas, the clause is not a rights-granting clause that protects individuals from government; rather, it is a jurisdictional clause regulating the relationship between the federal government and the states. Thus the federal government has no power to establish religion at the national level and only minimal power at best to regulate state and local religious policymaking. Moreover, the establishment clause can no longer prohibit state and local policymaking affecting religion, so more power over religious issues would devolve to states and localities. Thomas's federalism interpretation of church-state relations goes beyond the Rehnquist Court's "devolution" of power back to the states. Instead, it "insulate[s] state institutions against federal law and regulation"[10] in matters of religious policymaking.

This chapter explores the development of Justice Thomas's establishment clause federalism and how it links it to larger debates on the Court about federalism doctrine and the constitutional relationship between government and religion. Instead of assessing the historical and theoretical aspects of Thomas's thought, establishment clause federalism is measured in the context of the institutions and constituents that might be affected by changes in the law regulating church-state relations. A normative critique of Thomas's thinking is eschewed in favor of a more measured, empirical assessment that considers how other political institutions such as Congress and the presidency might logically respond to calls to treat the establishment clause as a jurisdictional aspect of the Constitution that limits national power over the states. Other constituents of religious policymaking, such as churches and religious groups, are considered too, especially in terms of how they might react to a change of church-state relations that Thomas's reinterpretation of the clause portends. Understanding Justice Thomas's federalism view of church-state relations in light of the range of constituencies it affects is salient for several reasons. First, it indicates how difficult it will be to read establishment clause federalism into the Constitution. By considering constituents ranging from the federal government and states to interest groups, churches, and even public opinion, the support structure to see this change brought to fruition probably does not exist. In contrast to many of its other federalism decisions, where political circumstances allowed the Court to "ratchet up its policing of substantive federalism without fear of a political backlash,"[11] it probably will not be able to do the same with its linkage of federalism to religious liberty and the church-state relationship. Second, by broadly defining the barriers to Thomas's proposed federalism changes to church-state relations, a more fundamental understanding of the limits to the new federalism revolution becomes more apparent.

Highlighting the barriers confronting Thomas's extension of federalism doctrine to the relationship between government and religion shows some of the real impediments to the federalism revolution itself. As scholars have noted in the context of other policy areas, the Court's revision of substantive federalism doctrine mirrors several trends in American politics, one of which is a broad-scale devolutionary thrust of power from national to state and local institutions.[12] That devolution was in part articulated by the Court, but it was enhanced and supported by federal, state, and local institutions and even public opinion.[13] Although this chapter does not explore why the Court's devolution revolution has been nominally successful, it does analyze why extending federalism to the establishment clause will most likely be unsuccessful. By identifying the reasons why Thomas's constitutional shift is likely to fail, the analysis suggests different parameters for assessing the extension of federalism to other policy areas.

Measuring Justice Thomas's attempts to recast the establishment clause also registers an important but intriguing trend in the Court's overall approach to federalism issues across the Rehnquist and Roberts Courts. Analysis of the constituents of establishment clause federalism shows that a doctrinal innovation contemplated by the Rehnquist Court will most likely not last through the Roberts Court. Thomas's reading of the establishment clause is prompted not only by his own theoretical approach to federalism in the Constitution but also by a more general trend among Rehnquist Court justices to side with state and local governments in establishment clause disputes. Thus, although Thomas proposed a doctrinal change during the Rehnquist Court, the constituencies affected by it will effectively block his interpretation, thereby nullifying its effect in the Roberts Court.

Significantly no majority on the Court has coalesced around viewing the establishment clause through a federalism lens. Justice Thomas is the only justice explicitly to endorse this interpretation. Even so, the lack of support for Thomas's reinterpretation of the clause does not render it inconsequential. Scholars point out that its federalism offensive was slow to start and only progressed in incremental stages, beginning in 1975 in then associate justice Rehnquist's lone dissent in *Fry v. United States* (discussed in chapter 3). There, he argued Congress did not have the power to apply emergency wage controls to state and local government employees.[14] His dissent "played an early role in the articulation of a strong role for federal courts in protecting federalism"[15] and "set the long fuse for the federalism revolution" that was to come once he was elevated to chief justice.[16] Rehnquist's "long fuse" approach to changing federalism doctrine was sustained by personnel changes, since "the votes supporting the federalism offensive came through replacement rather than through conversion."[17] Thus, although a critical mass of support does not exist on the Court for a federalism reading of the establishment clause, and it is unlikely that such support will materialize in the short term, the potential for change to church-state relations remains, at least as understood within the context of the Court's evolution of federalism jurisprudence.

Suffice it to say that Thomas's reading of the establishment clause is radical, if for no other reason than that it entails the reversal of the Court's incorporation of the establishment clause against the states through the Fourteenth Amendment's due process clause in *Everson v. Board of Education* in 1947.[18] Although justices have debated for over sixty years the extent to which the clause limits state and local power in discrete policy areas (from school prayer to the public display of religious symbols), before Justice Thomas's *Newdow* opinion it was never suggested that the states were immune from the clause altogether. Even though at first glance Thomas's new reading of the establishment clause entails a dramatic change to church-state law, it may not be as radical as it seems. First, and as discussed more fully below, a body of legal, historical, and political science scholarship has been developing for several decades prior to his "new" interpretation of the clause, establishing at least a foundation for his interpretation of the First Amendment.[19] Second, Thomas has consistently articulated his federalism views over time. As a result, his federalism reading of the establishment clause in *Newdow* is simply a logical extension of his views as applied to new policy areas. Third, Thomas's rethinking of church-state jurisprudence along the lines of federalism coincides with ongoing dissatisfaction within the Rehnquist Court (and prior Courts too) about religious liberty doctrine generally. By the time Thomas committed to his federalism reading of the establishment clause in 2004, clearly a majority of justices were willing to jettison the existing jurisprudential framework for judging church-state conflicts. Yet they are unable to reach agreement on what ought to replace existing doctrine, and the uncertainty continues to remain a source of political and judicial controversy.

Notably Thomas's *Newdow* opinion was already creating important linkages between the religious liberty clauses and the relationship between the federal government and the states. For example, in *Locke v. Davey*[20] the Court indicated that states often might have more leeway than the federal government does to engage in religious policymaking. The suggestion adds a different federalism dimension to how the free exercise and establishment clauses in the First Amendment affect state and local policymaking. Whereas *Locke* did not offer a federalism reading of the religious liberty clauses, it regardless asserted that the two clauses occasionally apply differently at the state level, due in large part to the interaction between federal and state constitutional guarantees of religious liberty. Scholars note that generally the Rehnquist and Roberts Court's decisions on religious liberty have a devolutionary thrust to them anyway. As political scientist Ted Jelen has argued, "The Court has appeared less willing to overturn the actions of subnational governments that appear to support or endorse religious beliefs and values. If one believes that state and local governments are likely to be responsive to the wishes of local majorities, it may be that the Court is slowly and haltingly moving in a less separationist direction . . . in its Establishment Clause jurisprudence."[21]

THE REHNQUIST COURT AND RELIGIOUS LIBERTY

Key to understanding the context of Thomas's establishment clause federalism is the broader frame relating to how the Rehnquist Court has grappled with religious liberty doctrine. In several decisions it signaled a determination to change religious liberty jurisprudence in two important ways. First, the Court's approach to the free exercise clause changed with its 1990 decision in *Employment Division, Department of Human Resources of Oregon v. Smith.* In *Smith,* a bare majority of the Court repudiated the compelling interest test as a judicial standard of review, a significant change from the approach that had guided the constitutional interpretation of free exercise doctrine for well over twenty-five years prior.[22] Although the Court narrowed its decision so that the test no longer applied to laws that were neutrally and generally applicable to all individuals (and thus not biased against a religion), *Smith* vested in state and local governments more regulatory power over religious conduct. The decision also set up a showdown with Congress, as evidenced by its response to *Smith* and the enactment of the Religious Freedom Restoration Act (RFRA), which reinstated the more stringent and religiously protective compelling interest test. Still, the Court struck RFRA down in *City of Boerne v. Flores* in 1997.[23] Thus Congress's failed attempt to reinstate the compelling interest test meant that the debate over the scope of religious freedom protected by the free exercise clause was essentially shifted to the states. Indeed, some states responded to *Boerne* by enacting their own state-level religious freedom restoration acts.[24] With the *Boerne* decision in hand, the Court's prior *Smith* opinion effectively "narrowed" the free exercise clause by abandoning the "possibility of constitutionally-required free exercise exemptions" to government policymaking.[25]

A second doctrinal issue concerned the establishment clause. Here the Court sought to change establishment clause jurisprudence dramatically by redefining the conditions under which the government can support or recognize specific religious entities and religious behavior. The main establishment clause precedent is *Lemon v. Kurtzman*, which created a tripartite methodology for judging establishment clause disputes. Under *Lemon*, government support for religion is unconstitutional if the law or policy is not secular in purpose, favors or disfavors one religion over others, or creates the conditions for excessive entanglement between government and religion.[26] While many current and former justices have penned disagreement with *Lemon* in one case or another, the Court still has been unable to overturn the forty-year precedent.[27] Thus *Lemon*'s significance as a guiding precedent is "subject to the constantly shifting coalitions on the Court."[28] Accordingly the Court's establishment clause decisions are often confusing because they fail to establish clear constitutional doctrine and, in the process, further confuse because they either ignore, modify, or gloss over existing religious liberty precedents. Although *Lemon* has the status of "the last establishment formula to command majority support,"[29] it exists mainly because a majority of justices cannot coalesce around one case to overturn it. Therefore, the justices "continue to reference *Lemon*'s analytic categories . . . as relevant to their decisionmaking, even if those categories do not determine outcomes."[30]

The commentary on the Rehnquist Court's religious liberty case law is immense and often countervailing and contradictory. Regardless, the Court's impact in this area has prominent consequences for federalism. The Court's fragmented religious liberty decisions set the conditions for an ongoing debate about the regulatory role of government—at all federal, state, and local levels—over religious liberty and religious life in the United States. Its *Smith* and *Boerne* free exercise decisions have devolved more power to state and local political processes in order to determine the extent to which government policies and law will accommodate religious conduct, thus setting up more conflict between courts and subfederal political institutions.[31] On balance, the *Smith* and *Boerne* decisions are characterized as a "decentralizing force" that "together allow states and localities to determine the degree of legislative accommodation of religious practice . . . [and] together shift the institutional locus of decisions about religious accommodations out of hierarchical, local-norm-trumping institutions—the Court and Congress—and potentially downward."[32]

The Court's attempt to revise religious liberty doctrine registers an important trend in American religious life that social scientists have long acknowledged: conflicts over religious liberty typically occur far more frequently at the state and local level. Church-state conflicts are especially acute at the local level and are "waged [as] intimate little community wars over religious practices in particular schools . . . [and as] disputes over religious services and artifacts in public parks."[33] Such tensions have their roots in the structures of American federalism, which divide political power at the national, state, and local levels and facilitate local control over certain issues. Accordingly, "the grassroots character of most church-state contests is not surprising. . . . Small-scale religious politics often involve questions of aesthetics, zoning, local taxation, or public education," and local government policymakers are often caught up in "culture war" or "morality politics" debates that are at their base disputes pertaining to the proper role of religious belief in local politics.[34] Such local disputes are regularly issues "in which the primary stakes . . . are matters of fundamental religious value or deep-seated religious belief about the propriety of behavior or activity."[35] The basic regulatory functions that form the essence of local government policymaking may also cause disruptions between religious groups and government. Thus zoning regulatory controversies between religious institutions such as churches and religious schools and local government planners are common, as are disputes over the display of religious messages on public property. As one scholar put it, "The interplay of religious and civil authority and the accommodation of each occurs locally, among neighbors, in communities."[36] Likewise, another scholar argues that the Supreme Court's approach to the establishment clause is consistent with the decentralizing trends of religious liberty in the United States. As a result, the chief justice sought to achieve a "limited reading of the Establishment Clause, one that does not substantially constrain state policymaking on matters of religion."[37]

Basic descriptive statistics show the general trend of Rehnquist Court decisions addressing First Amendment religious freedom.[38] The Court's constitutional review of federal, state, and local laws under the free exercise and establishment clauses is generally conservative in that the justices tend to support laws that accommodate religious belief in various ways. Table 4.1 illustrates the broad trends of the Rehnquist Court's review of religious liberty cases. It shows that the Rehnquist Court did not overturn government laws and regulations affecting religion. Moreover, when it did declare state and local laws unconstitutional, it only did so

Table 4.1. Rehnquist Court Review of Religious Liberty Issues, by Ideology and Constitutionality, 1986–2005

Constitutionality of the Law or Policy	*Conservative Decision*	*Liberal Decision*
No Declaration of Unconstitutionality	38	11
Federal Law Unconstitutional	2	0
State Law Unconstitutional	0	6
Local Ordinance Unconstitutional	0	2

Source: The Supreme Court Database, 1946–2011 Terms, at http://scdb.wustl.edu/analysis.php (using data release SCDB_2011_03)

in a liberal direction—that is, in a direction requiring more separation between government and religion. By implication, then, the Court sustained state and local laws as constitutional and in a conservative direction more than it overturned them. Thus the Court appears to be more supportive of subfederal religious policymaking.

Table 4.2 situates the Rehnquist Court's review of religious clause cases in the context of other Supreme Courts, from the Vinson to the Roberts Court. The larger universe of data shows the Rehnquist Court was more solicitous of state and local religious policymaking than were the others. For example, the Court under Chief Justice Warren Burger's leadership adjudicated sixty-two religious liberty disputes. Of those, it declared unconstitutional twenty-seven state laws and three local ordinances, whereas it affirmed as constitutional twenty-nine laws. In contrast, the Rehnquist Court adjudicated fifty-nine religious liberty disputes and only declared unconstitutional six state laws and two local ordinances; forty-nine laws at issue were affirmed. Accordingly, the Rehnquist Court was far more supportive of government attempts to regulate religion under the free exercise and establishment clauses. Likewise, it was also more sympathetic toward state and local government attempts to do so as compared with the Burger Court.

The broad pattern that emerges shows the Rehnquist Court is different from other Courts insofar as it rarely intervened in the government's attempt to accommodate religion. Also, it was more solicitous of state and local laws and regulations implicating First Amendment concerns. Although the Rehnquist Court did not view religious liberty in the explicit federalism terms that are defined by Justice Thomas (in that state and local government policymaking affecting religious issues should be insulated from federal interference), its behavior over time shows deep and general regard for local and state religious policymaking. The Court's general trend toward viewing at least some religious liberty disputes through a subfederal lens, when coupled with its internal dissatisfaction with the *Lemon* test and establishment clause doctrine, helped create the conditions for analytically merging federalism and religious liberty. The Court's *Locke v. Davey* ruling is instructive because it well illustrates the federalism trend.[39] *Locke*, as one of the last religion clause cases decided under Chief Justice Rehnquist's leadership, concerned Washington State's publicly funded scholarship program—which provided merit- and income-based aid to students in public and private colleges and universities within the state. Students attending religious colleges or majoring in "devotional theology" at secular institutions were ineligible for the scholarships. Although Joshua Davey received a scholarship, he was unable to apply it to his chosen college, Northwest College, due to its affiliation with the Assemblies of God denomination. Davey sued Washington,

Table 4.2. U.S. Supreme Court Review of Religious Liberty Decisions, by Case Type and Constitutionality, 1946–2010

Court	*No Declaration of Unconstitutionality*	*Federal Law Unconstitutional*	*State Law Unconstitutional*	*Local Ordinance Unconstitutional*	*Total*
Vinson (1946–1952)	11 (9.8%)	0	2 (4.8%)	0	13 (7.9%)
Warren (1953–1968)	19 (17%)	0	7 (16.7%)	0	26 (15.8%)
Burger (1969–1985)	29 (25.9%)	3 (60%)	27 (64.3%)	3 (60%)	62 (37.8%)
Rehnquist (1986–2004)	49 (43.8%)	2 (40%)	6 (14.3%)	2 (40%)	59 (36%)
Roberts (2005–)	4 (3.6%)	0	0	0	4 (2.4%)
Totals	*112*	*5*	*42*	*5*	*164*

Source: The Supreme Court Database, 1946–2011 Terms, at http://scdb.wustl.edu/analysis.php (using Data Release SCDB_2011_02)

contending that the state's restriction on where the monies could be distributed violated his rights under the free exercise clause.[40] Washington countered that its own state constitution prohibited government aid to religious institutions and courses of study in ministry education. To the surprise of many court watchers, the justices sustained Washington's program by a 7–2 vote. Chief Justice Rehnquist wrote the opinion for the Court, noting that

> [the state's] disfavor of religion (if it can be called that) is of a far milder kind. It imposes neither criminal nor civil sanctions on any type of religious service or rite. . . . It does not require students to choose between their religious beliefs and receiving a government benefit. The State has merely chosen not to fund a distinct category of instruction.[41]

Rehnquist observed that Washington's program is not hostile to religion at all but instead is representative of the important differences between states and the federal government on matters of religious policy. As he reasoned, "The subject of religion is one in which both the United States and state constitutions embody distinct views—in favor of free exercise, but opposed to establishment. . . . That a State would deal differently with religious education for the ministry than with education for other callings is a product of these views." Due to distinct constitutional traditions and provisions concerning religious liberty and the relationship between government and religion, the federal government and states do not always share the same principles. So, in Rehnquist's view, states have additional leeway for some types of religious policymaking that is foreclosed to the federal government. Linked with that view is a broader perspective about the federal Constitution's religious liberty clauses. As Rehnquist argued, the establishment and free exercise clauses are often in tension with each other. In reconciling the conflict, though, the Court has also "long said that there is room for play in the joints between them. In other words, there are some state actions permitted by the Establishment Clause but not required by the Free Exercise Clause." Washington State's scholarship program was precisely that type of state policy. As such, the state's constitution stringently prohibited state aid to religion, and therefore its prohibition of scholarships to religious schools or degree programs was justified.[42]

Rehnquist's *Locke* opinion perceived the establishment clause in more localistic terms: the establishment of religion may mean different things for different levels of government, so states and, by implication, local governments might have different relationships with religion than the federal government. For some constitutional scholars, *Locke* "does not substantially constrain state policymaking on matters affecting religion."[43] The "play in the joints" *Locke* principle may augment state policymaking, and in doing so, it implicates a wide range of religious policymaking that seeks both to exclude religion from certain public programs and also to accommodate religion. Thus *Locke* can be read broadly to favor giving more discretion to states in matters of religious policymaking. The Court's decision creates a space "that allows legislatures to express political judgments about the extent of church-state entanglement," and it shows "significant deference to legislatures."[44]

JUSTICE CLARENCE THOMAS AND ESTABLISHMENT CLAUSE FEDERALISM

In the same term in which *Locke* was decided, Justice Thomas crafted his concurrence in *Elk Grove Unified School District v. Newdow*. Thomas's opinion more directly linked federalism and religious liberty. As such, it posed an important contrast to Rehnquist's approach in *Locke*. Whereas Rehnquist noted that the "play in the joints" between the two religious liberty clauses meant that states have more leeway in certain religious policymaking areas, such as education, Thomas's approach was much more explicit: the establishment clause is a federalism provision that creates jurisdictional barriers to federal oversight of state and local religious policymaking. Rehnquist's localist reading of the First Amendment stems from the tensions created by the two religious liberty clauses. In contrast, for Thomas the establishment clause is not so much in tension with the free exercise clause; instead, it articulates a relationship between the federal government and the states that is independent of and separate from any countervailing influences of the free exercise clause. Although he does not specifically disagree with Rehnquist's "play in the joints" interpretation (being read as one, the two clauses foster more subfederal policymaking power on religious issues), Thomas insists the establishment clause has a different effect on the federal-state relationship.

The key issue in *Newdow* concerned whether the inclusion of the words "under God" in the Pledge of Allegiance violated the establishment clause when the government and the public schools required the pledge's recitation. The Supreme Court accepted the case for review only to dismiss it on prudential standing grounds since the plaintiff, Michael Newdow, had litigated on behalf of his school-age daughter even though his guardianship rights over her were concurrently in dispute. Five justices joined in the Court's decision to dismiss, and three justices concurred. Chief Justice Rehnquist, joined by Justices Sandra Day O'Connor and Thomas, concurred in the Court's judgment and offered differing arguments that the pledge does not offend the establishment clause.

Both Chief Justice Rehnquist and Justice O'Connor allowed the government more flexibility in promoting the Pledge of Allegiance because of the pledge's civil religion dimension. In their view the pledge is more of a patriotic exercise that recognizes the broad-based religious heritage of the United States. Under this view, it links to religion and the foundational principles of the Constitution, and since it makes only a ceremonial reference to a generic God and in no way refers to or endorses a specific denominational or faith-based conception of God, the reciting of the pledge in a public school is constitutional. By shifting some attention away from the notion that the establishment clause is the dividing line between religion and government and opting for an interpretation that centers on the relationship between the pledge and American political culture, Rehnquist and O'Connor thus tapped into a broader debate about the role civil religion plays in American public life.

In contrast to Rehnquist and O'Connor, Justice Thomas embraced a fundamental reconceptualization of establishment doctrine. Noting in a footnote that the Court's "jurisprudential confusion" over the clause has led to case outcomes "that can only be described as silly," Thomas viewed *Newdow* as an opportunity "to begin the process of rethinking the Establishment Clause." As he wrote, "I would acknowledge that the Establishment Clause is a federalism provision, which, for this reason, resists incorporation." Therefore, Thomas continued,

> as a textual matter, this Clause probably prohibits Congress from establishing a national religion. . . . Perhaps more importantly, the Clause made clear that Congress could not interfere with state establishments. . . . Nothing in the text of the Clause suggests that it reaches any further. The Establishment Clause does not purport to protect individual rights. . . . This textual analysis is consistent with the prevailing view that the Constitution left religion to the States. . . . History also supports this understanding: At the founding, at least six States had established religions.
>
> Quite simply, the Establishment Clause is best understood as a federalism provision—it protects state establishments from federal interference.[45]

Thomas's *Newdow* opinion is a logical extension of his concurrence in *Zelman v. Simmons-Harris*, a case featuring an issue about the constitutionality of state-sponsored school vouchers for private schools (including religious ones). There, he argued that the establishment clause "on its face . . . places no limit on the States with regard to religion. The Establishment Clause originally protected States, and by extension their citizens, from the imposition of an established religion by the Federal Government."[46] While Thomas did not detail his federalism approach in *Zelman*, he still suggested the clause allows and facilitates a different regulatory role for the states, one that is distinct from the federal government. Indeed, he argued that there might be different constitutional standards for the establishment clause depending on whether it was being applied to limit federal or state power. For Thomas, "While the Federal Government may 'make no law respecting an establishment of religion,' the States may pass laws that include or touch on religious matters so long as these laws do not impede free exercise rights or any other individual religious liberty interest."[47] After *Zelman*, Thomas used his *Newdow* concurrence to articulate more fully his federalist reading of the establishment clause, which in the process generated additional debate and perhaps a subsequent reordering of his own religious liberty jurisprudence.

While it has not yet been embraced by his colleagues on the bench, Justice Thomas's establishment clause federalism fundamentally recasts the Court's interpretative understanding of the clause and alters dramatically the boundary line between religion and government at all levels of the American federal system. By emphasizing that the Constitution "left religion to the states," Thomas's reinterpretation constrains only federal (and not state) power because, as a textual matter, the clause only prohibits national government support for a specific religion. In addition, state support for religion is unaffected, and state religious policymaking is protected from federal interference. Thus the federalism dimension for Thomas translates into an expanded role for state (and by extension local) governments over religious activity, with a sharply limited oversight role for the federal government. Thomas's reinterpretation also means that the establishment clause becomes jurisdictional in scope and application. Whereas it does not grant a specific constitutional right like the free exercise clause does, it purports instead to define the authority of different spheres of government over religious liberty in the context of American religious life. But, as a jurisdictional clause, the establishment clause does not have to be incorporated against the states. In fact, since it is not construed to be a rights-granting clause, its incorporation under the Fourteenth Amendment's due process clause is highly suspect.

HISTORICAL ROOTS AND CONTEMPORARY APPROACHES TO ESTABLISHMENT CLAUSE FEDERALISM

The ensuing discussion of federalism and religious liberty in the United States is meant to provide a cursory understanding of the foundations for Justice Thomas's current reading of the establishment clause. It is not meant to be an exhaustive treatment of a convoluted, complicated subject. Rather, it suggests that Justice Thomas's approach has historical and scholarly grounding. Indeed, as noted below, Thomas's reading of the establishment clause is supported by early commentators on the Constitution and more recent scholarship.

The idea that federalism and religious liberty (and American religious life) are intertwined with each other in fundamentally local ways can be traced to the theoretical underpinnings of federalism found in the covenantal tradition. As explored by the late Daniel Elazar and others, the propensity of early colonists to covenant with each other to frame their governments and civil societies became an "instinct" for federalism that shaped American ideas about constitutionalism in general.[48] For Elazar, there was a deliberate connection between religion, covenants, and federalism in the American context: "The people and polities comprising the United States have bound themselves together through covenants to erect the New World order, deliberately following biblical precedents." Thus, "for Americans, federalism is ultimately more than a governmental arrangement between the states. It is, rather, the basis of a way of life, or at least, a way of political life."[49] Like Elazar, others detail how early colonial settlements, "each with its own covenant or compact for local government, then became part of larger colonies . . . and then joined in a region-wide government" such as the New England Confederation. Consequently, "the federal system of 1787 was not newly devised"; rather, it had significant antecedents in the experiences of colonial governance, as political theorist Donald Lutz has noted.[50] Interpretations of early American political thought support the linkage between federalism and religious life. For example, Revolutionary War–era Americans placed a high priority on the role that local institutions played in fostering citizens' ethical lives. Accordingly, for political scientist Barry Alan Shain, "American local communalism found great support in the thought and practices of reformed Protestantism, for it demanded local autonomy to support individual salvation and godly service."[51]

While Justice Thomas does not use historical and theoretical arguments arising out of the covenantal and federalism traditions, it is important to observe that analogous traditional arguments exist. Instead, Thomas begins his discussion with one of the early commentators on the Constitution, Justice Joseph Story. In *Newdow* he maintains that Justice Story offered the "prevailing view" of the establishment clause that the Constitution "left religion to the states."[52] As Story wrote in his *Commentaries on the Constitution* in 1833, the "real object of the [First Amendment] was . . . to exclude all rivalry among Christian sects, and to prevent any national ecclesiastical establishment." Accordingly for Story,

> it was deemed advisable to exclude from the national government all power to act upon the subject. The situation, too, of the different states

> equally proclaimed the policy, as well as the necessity of such an exclusion. In some of the states, Episcopalians constituted the predominant sect; in others, Presbyterians; in others, Congregationalists; in others, Quakers; and in others again, there was a close numerical rivalry among contending sects. It was impossible, that there should not arise perpetual strife and perpetual jealousy on the subject of ecclesiastical ascendancy, if the national government were left free to create a religious establishment. . . . Thus, the whole power over the subject of religion is left exclusively to state governments, to be acted upon according to their own sense of justice, and the state constitutions.[53]

Biographers of Joseph Story argue that his view of religious liberty in the United States stemmed from "a central tenet of New England conservative ideology—that states should 'foster and encourage the Christian religion generally, as a matter of sound policy as well as of revealed truth.'"[54] Story viewed the role of state governments in somewhat activist terms, insofar as states must protect the Christian basis of the common law. As well, Story's commentary was a response to Thomas Jefferson's argument that Christianity was not part of the common law and hence not part of state legal systems. Jefferson's understanding of the common law formed the foundation for his view of the establishment clause as creating an "impregnable wall" between church and state.[55] Story's poses an alternative view of the clause, one that protects the power of states to regulate religion within their own respective jurisdictions.

A constitutional scholar, Edward S. Corwin, analyzed Story's views in the context of the Supreme Court's church-and-state decisions of the mid-twentieth century. He contended the Court "seems to have overlooked [Story's views] entirely in its researches" on what the religious liberty clauses mean.[56] Corwin criticized the Court's establishment clause cases, which in his view altered the relationship between public education and the teaching of religion. By mandating the separation of church and state in American public education, Corwin argued, the Court had codified the wrong understanding of the establishment clause. For Corwin, "States are entirely free to establish religions, provided they do not deprive anybody of religious liberty." As a result, the incorporation of the establishment clause against the states through the due process clause via the Fourteenth Amendment was counter to the purposes of that amendment. Put differently, "it is only liberty that the Fourteenth Amendment protects," Corwin argued, so "the prohibition on the establishment of religion by Congress is not convertible into a similar prohibition on the states."[57]

Another prominent commentator on religious liberty, constitutional historian Leonard W. Levy, lends credence to a federalism reading of the establishment clause too. In his highly regarded analysis of the establishment clause, Levy argues,

> As at the Constitutional Convention, a widespread understanding existed in the states during the ratification controversy that the new central government would have no power whatever to legislate on the subject of religion. This by itself does not mean that any person or state understood an establishment of religion to mean government aid to any or all religions or churches. It meant rather that religion as a subject of legislation was reserved exclusively to the states.[58]

In agreement with Levy, the late constitutional scholar James McClellan argued that one of the primary purposes of the establishment clause is "the federalism of the First Amendment and the desire of Congress in 1791 to assure the states that the new national government would have no authority over the subject of church-state relations." For McClellan, the Court has historically misinterpreted the establishment clause to allow federal intervention in church-state relations, even though "a principal underlying purpose of the First Amendment was to prevent the national government from usurping the powers of the states over the subject of church-state relations." To be sure, McClellan goes so far as to argue that states had the power to "define, without federal interference" church-state relations within their own borders.[59]

McClellan's arguments, along with contributions from other conservative legal scholars, became infused in a key establishment clause lawsuit in the early 1980s that concerned the constitutionality of Alabama's law mandating a moment of silence at the start of every public school day. Although the law's purpose was to set aside time during the school day for private meditation or prayer, in *Ishmael Jaffree v. the Board of School Commissioners of Mobile County*, federal district judge Brevard Hand ruled that the establishment clause does not prohibit Alabama's Moment of Silence Law.[60] In rejecting forty years of Supreme Court precedent clarifying the meaning of the establishment of religion, Judge Hand determined the Court had read history incorrectly. For Hand, the establishment clause protected individuals from a federal establishment of religion only and guaranteed that "the states were free to define the meaning of religious establishment under their own constitutions and laws."[61] The state of Alabama's defense centered on the premise that the First Amendment "has no application to the states," thus "the election by a state to establish a religion within its boundaries was intended by the framers of the Constitution to be a power reserved to the several states," so each state has the prerogative to establish and support religion. Relying to a large degree on McClellan's argument, Judge Hand agreed with Alabama's claims.[62]

For Hand, because the establishment clause did not apply to the states, its extension to the states through the incorporation doctrine was not constitutionally required. As he wrote, "The prohibition in the First Amendment against the establishment of religion gave the states, by implication, full authority to determine church-state relations within their respective jurisdictions."[63] For Hand, then, "the relevant legislative history surrounding the adoption of both the First Amendment and of the Fourteenth Amendment, together with the plain language of those amendments, leaves no doubt that those amendments were not intended to forbid religious prayers in the schools which the states and their political subdivisions mandate."[64] He concluded his opinion with this rejoinder to the Court: "More than any other provision of the Constitution, the interpretation by the United States Supreme Court of the establishment clause has been steeped in history. This Court's independent review of the relevant historical documents and its reading of the scholarly analysis convinces it that the United States Supreme Court has erred in its reading of history."[65]

Not surprisingly Judge Hand's decision, which overturned decades of Supreme Court precedent, was reversed on appeal by the Eleventh Circuit. Thereafter, the Supreme Court weighed in as well by affirming the circuit court's ruling in its decision in *Wallace v. Jaffree* (the litigation name changed when Governor George Wallace appealed on behalf of the local school board). The significance of the high court's repudiation of district judge Hand's opinion should not be overstated, though, as the justices remained divided over establishment clause doctrine.[66]

Regardless of the Court's decision in *Wallace*, a federalism reading of the establishment clause does have support to varying degrees from prominent constitutional thinkers and jurists across different historical eras. Thus Justice Thomas's approach cannot be dismissed outright. To do so underestimates the power of historical argumentation in constitutional decision-making. Discounting Thomas's arguments also may overlook the fact that early variants of his federalism approach have been litigated before. The failure of the *Jaffree* litigation to establish a new interpretation of the establishment clause, one that is contrary to existing Supreme Court precedent, probably will not foreclose additional attempts to change the law. Articulating historical and theoretical arguments in litigation that refute Thomas's federalism reading of church-state relations in the Constitution is not necessarily helpful in determining whether his arguments will prevail in a subsequent ruling. Nor is it helpful in providing a fuller measure of Thomas's legal rationale insofar as it pertains to the constituents with an actual stake in the debate's outcome. The next section provides a more contemporary analysis of Thomas's doctrinal shift by presenting a less historical objection to his thinking. Instead, the discussion centers more on the practical consequences of Thomas's reinterpretation for the structures inherent in American federalism.

ASSESSING ESTABLISHMENT CLAUSE FEDERALISM

A fuller assessment of establishment clause federalism situates the analysis of its importance in prior appraisals of the Supreme Court's broader federalism revolution. Relying on extant federalism commentary provides the analytical framework to determine if changing the judicial approach to understanding establishment clause doctrine is feasible. As law professor Neal Devins argues, the federalism and constitutional law scholarship has "failed to provoke the ire of lawmakers, interest groups, or the American people."[67] Devins posits several reasons for the absence of a backlash against the Court's policymaking. For instance, the Court's federalism decisions did not prevent interest groups or policymakers from pursuing their policy agendas in Congress. The usual democratic outlets in federal and state legislatures have not been foreclosed by the Court's decisions either. Also, by limiting congressional power over the states, the Court's decisions have reflected popular distrust of the federal government. Although the Court's federalism jurisprudence typically attracts minimal public attention, the public's trust in government has shifted away from the federal government and toward states and local governments. Accordingly, the public tends to be more supportive of state and local policymaking and less receptive to federal policymaking.[68] The shift in public opinion, transpiring from the 1960s to 2000, has become an important conceptual foundation to sustain the Court's new federalism jurisprudence.[69] In addition, no federalism constituency actively opposed the Court's changes to federalism doctrine. That means, for Devins, that "not only do federal lawmakers and national lobbyists gladly sacrifice federalism in order to advance other interests, but state officials also 'have systematic political interests that cause them to undermine federalism.'" Devins thus regards federalism as a "low salience issue" because "interest groups, voters, and elected officials care more about underlying policy issues that about structural protections."[70]

Similarly, law professor Robert Nagel argues that even if the Court could sustain a shift toward decentralizing power in American federalism, constituents of federalism may still finds its rulings easy to evade. Nagel observes that the "most natural constituency for states'-rights positions" consists of state and local policymakers who often find it "politically useful to shift responsibility for controversial issues to Washington."[71] Thus the levels of government with perhaps the most to gain from the Court's federalism decisions, in the form of increased policymaking power free from federal oversight or mandate, are in reality often less supportive of or ambivalent about them.

As law professor Marci Hamilton has highlighted, because state and local policymakers often let their political ambitions override their representative duties, they will also sacrifice state interests for their personal political gain while seeking to placate national lobbies that have the power to unseat them.[72] Hamilton's main argument—that Congress is not well suited to protecting the political interests of states—is highly salient because it implicitly endorses the Supreme Court's political safeguards interpretation of federalism (as discussed in chapter 3 and reflected in *Garcia v. San Antonio Metropolitan Transit Authority*). Also, her understanding of the Court's federalism decisions is important for another reason as it is premised on how the users of those decisions—namely, the political system's constituents—behave in response thereto.

In sum, scholars Devins, Nagel, Hamilton, and others suggest that an understanding of the Court's federalism revolution is incomplete without considering the responses that other institutions, groups, and policymakers have had to the Supreme Court's judicial policymaking in religious freedom cases. Especially if Devins's argument is correct that there has not been a significant backlash to the Court's decisions, gauging constituent response may aid in speculating that a doctrinal change may be forthcoming. Still, as the next section details, it is unlikely that any prospective doctrinal change will succeed because it will face significant opposition from a wide range of constituents, from Congress to interest groups and even churches, that would be affected by changes to establishment clause doctrine.

THE CONSTITUENCIES OF ESTABLISHMENT CLAUSE FEDERALISM

Congress and the Executive

There is little disagreement among federalism scholars that placing the Court's federalism decisions into a larger framework, one that accounts for how other federal institutions respond or react to the Court's decisions, is beneficial. This is especially true for Congress, as much scholarship has pointed out the various ways that it responds to and takes account of the Court's federalism policymaking, although how well Congress acts as a constituent of its changes to federalism doctrine remains controversial.[73] Nonetheless, there is little doubt that the Court's decisions affect Congress's legislative behavior. Consequently, since Congress has long played a key role in regulating religious liberty, it can be expected to respond to a federalism reading of the establishment clause too.

In considering some of the ways in which Congress may respond to such a reading, it is worth observing that Congress has maintained a long-standing (and ongoing) penchant for protecting and regulating religious liberty. As congressional historian and scholar Louis Fisher has noted, "On hundreds of occasions, Congress has decided to protect religious interests by exempting them from general laws . . . [and] the basic protection for religious interests comes from this statutory framework. . . . Legislative action not only takes the initiative in recognizing and defining religious liberties, but these statutory provisions far outstrip in number and importance the cases that have expanded religious rights."[74] Fisher's analysis primarily focuses on Congress's use of legislation to protect the free exercise rights and religious liberty of religious minorities. Thus, "the regular political process is called upon to protect religious liberty, and not merely for powerful religious groups but small ones as well." Although the bulk of federal laws regulating religious liberty exist to protect religious conduct from federal overreaching, and even though Congress does not aim to place the government's imprimatur on a specific religious belief or behavior, its long-term practice of engaging in religious policymaking may signal a latent opposition to any prospective effort to devolve more power to the states.

Another trend that Fisher and others identify is that the Congress and the states each engage in religious policymaking, but, critically, Congress has seized many policy issues for federal regulation, ostensibly by regulating activities such as school prayer or student religious conduct in school. Although states are not prohibited from enacting regulations on school prayer, trends in federal legislation and rulemaking (as discussed below) indicate that many salient federal guidelines, such as establishing when public schools must regulate or protect student religious conduct, now orient state and local policymaking around federally mandated standards.

This last point should be considered against the reality that Congress has not yet officially responded to the possibility that the establishment clause can be interpreted by the federal courts as a federalism and jurisdictional provision; as such, it may be plausible to believe that Congress would do so in the future if the prevailing law stays the same. Given the legislature's past track record of involving itself heavily in debates over drawing the line between official government action and religious activity, Congress's support for more state and local autonomy over matters of religious policymaking may be lukewarm at best. More recent examples suggest that too.

Recent Developments in Federal Law

One of the more divisive and intractable religious policies at the state and local levels relates to whether student prayer and religious activities are acceptable and protected in public schools. For over four decades the Supreme Court has tried to delineate the constitutional standards that public schools must follow in setting policies for allowing religious activities. While schools cannot establish or officially support religious conduct because doing so will result in an establishment clause violation, they nonetheless must remain solicitous of the free exercise and free speech rights of students.[75]

Although they have never been successful, many congressional legislators have long sought to use the constitutional amendment process to permit school prayer.[76] Although calls to amend the Constitution have not abated, in 1984 Congress waded into the debate over student religious expression (and indirectly school prayer) with its passage of the Equal Access Act (EAA). The EAA mandated that schools receiving federal funds cannot deny "equal access or fair opportunity" to students wishing to engage in religious, political, philosophical, or other types of speech during noninstructional school time.[77] The federal statute standardized rules to protect the rights of students to engage in speech-related conduct, such as nondisruptive prayer and other devotional activities. Supplementing the statute were administrative rules promulgated by the Federal Department of Education. Administrations on both sides of the political aisle have endorsed student religious expression by instituting broad guidelines for schools to follow. For instance, President Clinton instructed his secretary of education, Richard Riley, to issue a memorandum to all public school districts nationwide, establishing the rights of religious expression under the First Amendment's free speech and free exercise clauses. As congressional scholar Louis Fisher explains, "The memo was designed to take some of the steam out of a proposed school prayer amendment. In this memo, Clinton said nothing in the First Amendment 'converts our public schools into religion-free zones, or requires all religious expression to be left behind at the schoolhouse door.'"[78]

The executive branch sought to involve other constituencies in its policymaking on religious speech and conduct in public schools, and between 1995, when the federal guidelines were first released, and 1998, when they were released again, Secretary Riley convened three "religious-education summits" to "inform faith communities and educators about the guidelines and to encourage continued dialogue and cooperation."[79] Furthermore, in 2001 the Bush administration and Congress enacted sweeping reforms in American elementary and secondary education by implementing the No Child Left Behind Act (NCLB) of 2001, an amendment to the 1965 Elementary and Secondary Education Act (ESEA). The NCLB requires the secretary of education to issue guidelines on constitutionally protected prayer in public elementary and secondary schools. The statute also requires that, as a condition for receiving federal funds in helping to administer federal law, local educational agencies (LEAs) must certify in writing to their state educational agency (SEA) that their policies on student expression do not prevent or deny participation in constitutionally protected prayer in public schools. In accordance with the law, Secretary of Education Rod Paige issued guidelines to public schools, ostensibly to send the message that "public schools should not be hostile to the religious rights of their students and their families."[80] The rules touch upon a broad range of topics, including setting the parameters for allowing student prayer during noninstructional time at school, organized prayer groups, moments of silence, student religious expression and prayer in classroom assignments such as artwork and reports, and the selection of student religious speakers on "genuinely neutral, evenhanded criteria." Evidently the threat of losing federal monies under the ESEA is taken seriously by school districts across the country, as most of the approximately fifteen thousand that exist in the United States comply with federal school prayer guidelines.[81]

Congress's forays into legislating national standards for student religious speech and school prayer—an inherently local issue—illustrate that it may be reluctant to cede control over the policymaking area to subfederal governments. Thus school prayer legislative and administrative rulemaking from the EAA to NCLB are suggestive of a latent federal hostility to establishment clause federalism. That hostility is registered by the passage of the Religious Land Use and Institutionalized Persons Act (RLUIPA) in 2000.

Congress arguably passed RLUIPA to modify the RFRA. Whereas the RFRA reinstated the compelling interest test that was overturned by the Supreme Court in *Oregon v. Smith,* for almost all other aspects of government policymaking that address religious liberty activities the RLUIPA accomplishes the same result, with the exception of two policy areas: the religious rights of institutionalized persons and zoning and land-use controversies between religious institutions and governments. As discussed in more detail below, RLUIPA was challenged by the state of Ohio in *Cutter v. Wilkinson* under the interstate commerce and spending clauses in Article I of the Constitution, and Ohio notably argued that RLUIPA was a "blatant takeover of religious policy" from the states and, as such, remained a statute that would "aggrandize Congress's own power at the expense of States and citizens alike."[82] In affirming the law, and by holding that Congress did have the interstate commerce and spending clause powers to direct state religious policymaking, the Court affirmed implicitly Congress's ability to regulate matters of religious liberty that affect federalism. Although some states, as states, were opposed to RLUIPA, as discussed below local churches have been active consumers of the law, have used it to protect themselves from burdensome government regulations, and have challenged local land-use restrictions. Thus more than one constituent is involved in using RLUIPA's federal mandates to limit subfederal religious policymaking.

One final concern may suggest that Congress will not necessarily be receptive to a federalism reading of the establishment clause. Increasingly Congress has engaged in the practice of enacting morals legislation, something that historically has been left to the states. This is important because there are distinctions between morality and religious policymaking. Morality policymaking includes regulating abortion, pornography, gambling, capital punishment, and similar socially controversial topics of public policy. While these issues are often bound up with religion and typically expose latent religious differences among the American people, they also retain a secular dimension. But since Congress (and the Supreme Court) often addresses morality policy issues at the federal level, it may be increasingly difficult for federal and state governments to formulate a consistent policy over religious freedom that will resonate well among the citizenry in the states.[83] Moreover, routinely there are several incentives for congressional representatives to engage in morality policymaking, including the desire to garner popular support on an issue that most constituents care deeply about. As a result, the devolution of power to the local level in religious matters may or may not ultimately be perceived by members of Congress as against their own electoral self-interest, depending on whether it is linked to the pursuit of enacting morals legislation.

The Executive Branch

Federal policymaking over school prayer also displays the executive branch's influence over state and local religious policymaking. The Department of Education guidelines on student religious expression and conduct are illustrative. The executive has also been an active litigant in church-state lawsuits, even in cases to which the federal government is not a party. It is here that the executive, as a constituent of establishment clause federalism, may choose to frustrate its implementation and development.

Presidents, acting through solicitors general and other federal agencies, have historically tried to influence the development of constitutional law by participating as amicus at the Supreme Court. For example, President George H. W. Bush's solicitor general, Kenneth Starr, petitioned the Supreme Court in 1991 to overturn the *Lemon v. Kurtzman* precedent as a means to secure a legal policy that was an accommodationist (hence less separationist) reading of the establishment clause. As amicus, Starr submitted a brief for the federal government in *Lee v. Weisman*, a school prayer case, asserting that *Lemon* was wrongly decided and should be reversed. On one level Starr's legal position reflected the increasing political influence of the Christian Right in the Reagan and Bush administrations, but perhaps on another it registered the growing frustration of conservative lawyers, judges, and justices with *Lemon* as a historically flawed precedent that results in unpredictable legal doctrine when it is applied by federal courts.[84] Although Starr's efforts to overturn *Lemon* failed, Solicitor General Paul Clement in President George W. Bush's administration filed an amicus brief in *Cutter v. Wilkinson* to argue in favor of establishing RLUIPA's constitutionality. In so doing Clement specifically addressed a federalism reading of the establishment clause advocated by Ohio, as respondent, and Virginia and other states as amicus curiae.[85] The federal government's brief noted, "It is too late in the day to argue that the federal Constitution contains two different Establishment Clauses with varying levels of potency" depending on which level of policymaking—state or federal—is at issue. The Bush II administration's brief in *Cutter* made no representations about the status of the *Lemon* precedent, unlike in the Bush I era ten years earlier. However, by specifically arguing against a federalism reading of the establishment clause, it did seek to foreclose that line of reasoning as a means of doctrinal change. Thus, while it may be the case that the conservative Bush II administration would have supported changes to establishment clause precedents (and perhaps even the overturning of *Lemon*), its repudiation of Thomas's federalism approach to church-state relations signaled to the Court that it most certainly did not support that doctrinal change.

The federal government's brief argued too that the Court "rebuffed" a similar argument in *Wallace v. Jaffree* in 1985 when it overturned a federal district court judge who held the establishment clause was not incorporated against the states and thus did not constrain state policymaking. The Bush II administration's view of the *Wallace* litigation is somewhat surprising, since at the time of the case there was intense debate in the conservative Reagan administration over whether the solicitor general should support the lower federal district court's decision in *Jaffree v. Board of School Commissioners of Mobile County* that the establishment clause did not apply to the states. Several political appointees in the Reagan Justice Department wanted the solicitor general to emphasize that the district judge's interpretation of the establishment clause was correct, even though it was contrary to Supreme Court precedent. Solicitor General Rex Lee, also a Reagan appointee, adamantly refused on the grounds that supporting a lower district judge's reversal of high court precedent would effectively undermine the rule of law. On appeal to the Supreme Court, the solicitor general again chose not to ask the justices to reconsider anew establishment clause doctrine. Instead, he suggested that the issue in *Jaffree*, the constitutionality of silent student prayer, was sound under existing case law.[86] The notable point is that between the Reagan administration in the 1980s and the Bush II administration in 2000 to 2008, executive branch support for more state and local autonomy in religious policymaking waned; indeed, the executive had become more opposed to it by 2005 when RLUIPA was litigated in the *Cutter* case.

While the executive branch's hostility to a federalism reading of the establishment clause is apparent in the constitutional arguments it made in *Cutter*, still other policies suggest that the executive is supportive of national religious policymaking. One prominent example is President George W. Bush's creation of the White House Office of Faith-Based and Community Initiatives, which President Barack Obama decided to continue after the 2008 election. The White House office was created by executive order, significantly due in part to Congress's refusal to create it. Nonetheless, the office coordinated policies in the executive branch to make it easier for religious groups to compete for federal grants. Significantly, thrusting faith-based initiatives into federal administrative policymaking demonstrates that the Bush and Obama administrations prefer some level of federal oversight of state and local faith-based initiatives. This is true even though the scope of federal oversight primarily includes the activities of private charitable organizations that seek federal monies. As such, the executive's faith-based preference is extending regulatory power over state and local governments, per se. Still, the very existence of the executive policy has encouraged more religious groups to seek federal money so that they may provide faith-based services to local communities.[87]

State and Local Governments

State and local governments are important constituents of the Court's federalism and religious liberty decisions. In the wake of the Court's *Boerne* decision striking down RFRA as it applied to the states (discussed in chapter 3 and earlier in this chapter), approximately twenty-three states adopted or considered their own state-level religious freedom restoration acts to compel state and local government entities to follow a compelling interest test when regulating religious groups and institutions.[88] Conflicts between government policymaking and religion arise at the state and local level in many different contexts, ranging from prominent debates over prayer and Bible reading in public schools and the display of religious items like the Ten Commandments on public property to less noticeable yet divisive disputes over zoning and other regulations of religious property. State and local governments often clash in conflicts over church-state relations because, among other reasons, public opinion at the subfederal level is likely to be sympathetic to the government's accommodation of religion—thus it typically supports policies favoring school prayer, public religious displays, and other government observances of religion. As a consequence officials often feel enormous pressure to engage in religious policymaking that lowers the barriers between government and religion, regardless of the constitutional principles at stake.[89] Coupled with that pressure is the ominous threat of litigation: state and local governments are often direct and reluctant participants in lawsuits over church-state relations testing the boundaries of constitutional law.

Tracking litigation trends, therefore, is one way to measure how states and local governments might respond to establishment clause federalism. Since states are already prominently involved in federalism litigation, it is plausible that they will use the courts to respond to a federalism reading of the establishment clause that they may not endorse, especially considering that they are likely to have the resources to sponsor litigation and file third-party amicus curiae briefs in the U.S. Supreme Court. Filing "friend of the court" briefs are increasingly common forms of state participation in federalism debates. Not only have states become important institutional actors at the Court in their own right, but their ability to influence outcomes in federalism cases is assuming even greater significance.[90] Since state attorney generals' offices now coordinate national litigation strategies to protect state policymaking from federal intrusion, it can likewise be expected that states might use the vehicle of litigation to address and test arguments about establishment clause federalism since the interpretation, if sanctioned by the federal courts, has the potential to change dramatically the federal-state relationship.[91] Just as states are strategic litigators in federalism disputes, so too are they likely to be litigators in related religious liberty cases. Although state responses to establishment clause federalism are mixed when judged by arguments presented as direct participants or amici at the Supreme Court (and so far states have had few opportunities to present their views to the Court), how they have responded in litigation through sponsorship of cases or amici briefs can offer some preliminary insights.

Many state litigants at the Supreme Court bring with them a localistic reading of the establishment clause. Under this view, states retain the capacity to carve out a type of religious policymaking that remains free of First Amendment constraints. The states involved in *Cutter v. Wilkinson*, for example, relied on *Locke* as precedent to argue that state religious policymaking should be insulated from federal oversight. The state of Ohio argued that RLUIPA was an unconstitutional infringement of state power. Specifically, its brief asserted that the establishment clause limited congressional power over the states in two important ways. First, the clause limited federal and state power to impose religious regulations on individuals. Second, the clause's "federalist aspect," when placed in light of the structure of the Constitution, limited Congress's power to regulate state religious policymaking. As Ohio argued, when a state regulates religion within the "play in the joints" between the free exercise and establishment clauses, as established by *Locke v. Davey* in 2004, Congress may not force states to make policy choices. Furthermore, for Ohio,

> when a State exercises its *Locke* power, and selects a point between the clauses, Congress has no power to override that choice and tell the State to pick a different point in that zone. . . . The Establishment Clause's federalist aspect blocks Congress from imposing its choices on States regarding how to accommodate religion. That dooms RLUIPA.[92]

Ohio also links its federalism reading of the establishment clause to the Court's recent federalism decisions scaling back federal power over the states. Thus "the federalist aspect of the Establishment Clause is reflected in the basic constitutional framework and the system of dual sovereignty that it enacts. . . . State sovereigns, when acting within their 'respective sphere[s]'—such as in matters of religion—are not subject to federal oversight." For Ohio, RLUIPA's command that states apply the compelling interest test when regulating the religious conduct of institutionalized persons is a "direct federal intrusion on State decisionmaking about religion" that is prohibited by the federal structure of the Constitution.[93]

The Court's unanimous decision paid no heed to Ohio's federalism arguments, although Justice Thomas did write a concurring opinion in which he briefly addressed some of the points raised by the state.[94] He argued that Ohio and Virginia overstated the federalism inherent in the establishment clause:

> Ohio's vision of the range of protected state authority overreads the Clause. Ohio and its amici contend that, even though "states can no longer establish preferred churches" because the Clause has been incorporated against the States through the Fourteenth Amendment, "Congress is as unable as ever to contravene constitutionally permissible State choices regarding religious policy." That is not what the Clause says. The Clause prohibits Congress from enacting legislation "respecting an establishment of religion"; it does not prohibit Congress from enacting legislation "respecting religion" or "taking cognizance of religion."[95]

Even though Ohio lost the case, its arguments show that *Locke* is construed by at least some states to support *less* federal interference with state and local religious policymaking. In addition, Ohio sought to emphasize both the *Locke* angle to religious liberty and Thomas's concurrence in *Newdow*. Not only did *Locke* affirm that the "play in the joints" in both religious liberty clauses allowed more leeway to the states on matters of religion and public policy, but that concept also worked in tandem and inherently with federalism principles that prohibit federal "intrusion" into state religious policymaking.

The Commonwealth of Virginia filed an amicus brief in *Cutter* supporting Ohio's position. Virginia's brief, joined by several other states, emphasized a federalism reading of the establishment clause. Virginia argued that "the Federalism Purpose of the Establishment Clause mandates that the National Government may not interfere with the States' ability to make religious policy." The dual sovereignty and "double security" structured by the Constitution in part restricts the powers of the federal government so as to preserve the sovereignty of the states, and among the sovereign powers protected by this structure is "the authority to make religious policy." Prior to the ratification of the Fourteenth Amendment and the incorporation of the Bill of Rights against the states, "the States were free to do whatever they wished with respect to religion, subject only to the commands of their own State Constitutions." Yet, as Virginia argued, even though the incorporation doctrine "restricted substantially" state authority to make religious policy, "because there is 'play in the joints' between what the Establishment Clause prohibits and the Free Exercise Clause requires . . . the States retain substantial sovereign authority to make religious policy."[96]

In a subsequent case, other states tried to press a refined federalism argument to the Court. In *Hein v. Freedom from Religion Foundation* the constitutionality of President Bush's faith-based initiatives program was under contest. At issue was whether an interest group, the Freedom from Religion Foundation, had sufficient standing under Article III of the Constitution to challenge the executive branch policy. The state of Indiana, joined by eleven other states,[97] argued in an amicus brief that federalism concerns justified the reversal of the Court's precedent in *Flast v. Cohen*, which endorsed taxpayer standing in establishment clause cases, provided certain justiciability conditions are met.[98] As Indiana argued,

> Permissive treatment of state-taxpayer lawsuits undermines our federalist structure by involving federal courts in the daily functioning of state bureaucracies. The Court has repeatedly emphasized that federal courts must respect principles of federalism when cases portend judicial regulation of state programs. . . . These same concerns apply in Establishment Clause cases, which increasingly threaten to put state-government bodies under federal-court supervision.

Indiana's argument is distinct from Virginia's brief in *Cutter*. Whereas Virginia was asking for a wholesale reworking of the establishment clause through a federalism interpretation, Indiana is more limiting and seeks a less intrusive change in constitutional doctrine through reversal of the Court's earlier decisions granting taxpayer standing. Yet making it more difficult for litigants to file establishment clause lawsuits might effectively carve out more state autonomy for state religious policymaking.

As with state governments, local governments are frequently implicated in debates over religious policymaking and establishing the proper boundaries between church and state. A federalism reading of the establishment clause would delegate more power to local governments to practice religious policymaking without being tied to the same constitutional constraints that limit the federal government's policymaking ability. While many state and local governments would be constrained by their own state constitutional guarantees pertaining to the establishment and exercise of religious freedoms, the affirmation of establishment clause federalism would remove one layer of constitutional limitations on local power by removing much federal jurisdiction over states and local governments in matters of religion.

Local governments often engage in policymaking that affects religious groups and institutions through a wide variety of regulations, such as granting permits for groups to hold worship services in public parks and schools (after hours), establishing zoning variances for churches, and controlling the interactions between groups and churches in the provision of charitable services.[99] When engaged in religious policymaking, local policymakers may be pressured to respond to local public opinion that typically is more supportive of government religious accommodation, so their policymaking is likely to be influenced by the changing religious dynamics of their communities.[100]

Unlike states that make their doctrinal preferences known through litigation by filing amicus curiae briefs, local governments are not as committed to trying to develop religious liberty doctrine. In those times when they do participate in cases, local governments are usually in a defensive position; that is, they are forced to explain their accommodationist or separationist policies in order to withstand the legal challenge. As such, they typically have fewer opportunities to engage fully in the constitutional debate over how religious freedom should be interpreted. And unlike states, local governments have not specifically responded to establishment clause federalism either.

Even so, analysis of the attitudes of local officials toward religious policymaking offers guidance for assessing how this constituency may react. In one survey of city administrators in major urban areas (ranging in population size from at least one hundred thousand to over one million), political scientist Paul Schumaker asked local policymakers to respond to questions concerning morality politics issues that often involve the deeply held religious beliefs of those policymakers and others engaged in public debates on politics. Schumaker discovered a general opposition to regulating morality on the basis of religion, with many urban officials unlikely to instigate public policies linked to religious beliefs and attitudes. When local policymakers are confronted with conflicts between politics and religion, "they are generally predisposed to avoid favoring a particularly religious viewpoint through public policy."[101] This does not mean, however, that local government officials are hostile to churches and other religious groups; in fact, the opposite is probably true, as shown by the data generated by the National Congregations Study in 1998. The Congregations Study is a comprehensive survey of over twelve hundred religious congregations in the United States, and it measures how congregations respond to a wide range of political, cultural, social, and religious doctrinal issues.[102] The survey discovered that churches often have close working relationships with local governments; as a result, they rarely encounter hostility from public officials. For example, churches that apply for local permits to engage in regulated activities almost always receive those permits with little opposition from the government, with one estimate that churches encounter opposition to their permit seeking in about 1 percent of cases.[103]

There are no comparable surveys for public officials in smaller cities, towns, and rural areas, although anecdotal evidence and other survey materials suggest that they may be more supportive of more government accommodation and even sponsorship of religion. One study of how local officials deal with gay rights legislation found that the size of a community matters: the smaller a community, the less likely it will be to have an ordinance protecting gays from discrimination.[104] Similarly, in a study of support for school prayer among political activists, smaller communities tend to have higher levels of support for prayer in public schools. Since activists and officials are likely to "partake of the same subculture" and mutually reinforce those "shared values and subcultures," official support for school prayer will be stronger in smaller cities, towns, and rural areas.[105]

These findings underscore that local governments are probably the entities that will be most affected by a federalism reading of the establishment clause. As law professor Richard Schragger has noted, local governments are "central and overlooked sites for the negotiation of church-state relations." Thus a more "religion-specific theory of federalism" would lead to "increased respect for local choices."[106] Viewing church-government relations through a federalism lens would lead to more autonomy for local governments to engage in religious policymaking relatively free of federal oversight (especially judicial oversight), but it is far from clear how that newfound policymaking freedom would play out. Existing studies of public officials indicate that local governments may respond differently, depending upon a wide range of factors, from the size of a community and its urban, suburban, or rural location to the types of religious denominations present in each community and the relative growth or decline of those denominations. As constituents of establishment clause federalism, it is difficult to predict how local governments might respond, but the evidence cited above suggests that they may be significant players in federalism disputes or policymaking.

Interest Groups

Scholars have shown that legal arguments presented to the Court matter considerably and, as such, influence judicial outcomes and legal change.[107] This is very much the case in religious liberty litigation in which numerous interest groups participate and seek to influence legal outcomes from a wide range of religious and constitutional perspectives. From mainline and evangelical Protestant groups, to Catholic groups, Native American spiritualists, Jewish groups (Orthodox, Reformed, and others), and New Age spiritualists, the diversity of American religious life often coalesces around litigation. As well, groups represent the gamut of church-state perspectives, from those that argue the government should sponsor more official religious programming to those arguing for a strict separation of church and state that prohibits any official support for religion. This "pluralism of perspectives" structures the arguments to the high court in religious liberty disputes, and scholars have demonstrated that this pluralism greatly affects Supreme Court policymaking.[108]

Interest groups participating in religious liberty litigation are broadly defined as either separationist or accommodationist. Although groups will often have more nuanced views on religious liberty and church-state relations, the labels still reflect these two basic approaches to law and religion in the United States. Separationist groups generally argue that church and state must be kept apart so that neither will unduly influence or taint the other.[109] Separationist groups will be less supportive of establishment clause federalism, since it would shift more power over religious policymaking to local governments that may be more willing to accommodate religious beliefs and groups in the policymaking process. A federalism reading of the clause would also remove federal oversight of local and state policymaking, thereby making it easier for governments to support religion.

In contrast, accommodationist groups generally assert that government may use its power to aid religion. They recognize and appreciate the historical role it has played in American political culture.[110] Accommodationist groups will be somewhat favorably disposed to establishment clause federalism, ostensibly because devolving power to local and state governments allows for more government policymaking that accommodates religious belief and institutions. It also permits governments to foster more respect for the religious traditions of the United States. Similarly, some groups might extend the argument that a federalism reading of the clause would support the historical power of local and state governments to create close, mutually supportive relationships between church and state.

To date groups have had few opportunities to participate as amicus at the Court to make their preferences known. However, a trend is emerging in which some accommodationist groups are gravitating toward a federalism reading of the establishment clause, whereas separationist groups so far have been silent. In the Ten Commandments display cases of *Van Orden v. Texas* (Ten Commandments displayed on the Texas statehouse's grounds) and *McCreary Co. v. ACLU* (Ten Commandments displayed in a county courthouse), two accommodationist groups (affiliated with the Christian Right), the Eagle Forum and Focus on the Family, pressed a federalism reading of the establishment clause in their amici briefs. The Eagle Forum referenced Justice Thomas's concurrence in *Newdow* and argued that the establishment clause "reiterates the fundamental division of power embodied in the original Constitution" between the federal government and the states and should thus be read as a jurisdictional clause. The group noted that its interpretation is aligned with the Court's other federalism cases, which try to define "what is truly national from what is truly local." For the Eagle Forum, "Religion . . . is just such a uniquely local matter."[111] Focus on the Family echoed the Eagle Forum brief: "Federalism played a pivotal role in the adoption of the Establishment Clause. At the time of ratification, each state had a unique approach to dealing with the religious matters and they did not desire a uniform national standard concerning religious liberty."[112]

One prominent accommodationist group, and a very successful litigant at the Supreme Court, the American Center for Law and Justice (ACLJ), filed an amicus brief in *Van Orden* arguing that the display of the Ten Commandments on public property is constitutional because such displays are now generally secular in meaning. It is notable that the ACLJ chose strategically not to address the establishment clause federalism argument. Instead, it acted tactically to justify public religious displays using existing case law. This may indicate, as discussed shortly, an important schism among accommodationist groups as regards a federalism interpretation of religious establishment.

Separationist groups did not counter the federalism arguments presented by the Eagle Forum and Focus on the Family briefs in *Van Orden*. Nor did they address the arguments in *Cutter* or *Hein*.[113] In *Cutter*, separationist groups argued that RLUIPA was a constitutional exercise of congressional power that did not interfere with state policymaking in religious matters. In *Hein*, separationist groups argued that existing law on standing that allowed taxpayers to file establishment clause challenges to government spending should not be overturned, so a lawsuit attacking the constitutionality of the White House Office of Faith-Based and Community Initiatives should also be allowed to proceed.

One accommodationist group of significance is the American Center for Law and Justice, which is affiliated with and funded by the Christian Coalition. It is considered by many observers to be one of the primary litigation arms of the Christian Right.[114] One of its main priorities is protecting Christians' free speech rights to engage in evangelism. In the words of its lead counsel, Jay Alan Sekulow,

> We deal with problems concerning access to parks, school campuses at every level, malls, street corners and, of course, airports. . . . There were already aggressive, effective Christian organizations that specialized in litigating religious freedom issues—the National Legal Foundation and the Rutherford Institute, for example—but I saw a growing need to challenge the state's infringement upon the right of Christians to proclaim the gospel.[115]

Sekulow's comments highlight an important strategy of some Christian Right litigators: many religious liberty disputes can be recast as disputes over religious speech. ACLJ strategies involve a behavior that constitutional law scholar Steve Brown refers to as "prelitigation"—the threat to litigate a religious liberty issue gives governments a stark choice of either changing policies to protect the religious liberty interest at stake or running the risk of expensive and time-consuming litigation.[116]

The ACLJ's successful reliance on the free speech clause to force governments into accommodating religious liberty means that it is less focused on establishment clause concerns. While it does not ignore establishment clause litigation, it remains in the camp of other accommodationist groups that advocate for a "lowering" of the wall of separation between church and state, if not its eradication outright. Like similar groups, the ACLJ is also hostile to the *Lemon* precedent and its progeny. Yet it still focuses its attention on free speech. As one scholar has pointed out, "The strategic use of free speech arguments has been especially prominent in Pat Robertson's group [the ACLJ] and others to reintroduce prayer into public schools. . . . In many of these cases, Establishment Clause concerns regarding state endorsement of religion have been avoided . . . simply by treating the cases as indistinguishable from cases involving political, social, or artistic speech."[117]

The ACLJ filed or joined briefs in *Cutter* and *Van Orden*, but in neither case did it advocate a federalism reading of the establishment clause. In *Cutter* the ACLJ advocated that RLUIPA was constitutional, and in *Van Orden*, it argued that existing Court precedents allow the display of the Ten Commandments on public property since they were displayed in a secular manner that has been accepted by American culture. Additionally, in *Hein* the group argued the Court should reevaluate the flexible standing doctrines that allowed taxpayers to file establishment clause lawsuits. In none of the cases did the group touch upon establishment clause federalism. Put differently, the ACLJ's reliance on the First Amendment's free speech clause may preclude it from adopting a federalism-oriented stance toward religious liberty. This suggests that the ACLJ clearly relies on federal constitutional guarantees in litigation, especially as applied against state and local governments, so it may stand to lose an important element in its litigation strategy should states and localities be given more autonomy over religious policymaking.

There may be a real fissure between accommodationist groups and how they view establishment clause federalism. The tension relates to the competing policy objectives of different groups engaged in the religious policymaking process. One disagreement may center on the ACLJ, which may be more attached to advancing a litigation strategy that focuses on using the free speech clause and federal statutes (such as the Equal Access Act and RLUIPA) to protect the ability of churches and religious groups to engage in religious advocacy, evangelism, and church expansion. Given its strategy, the ACLJ may well find existing national constitutional and statutory law more supportive of its goals; it may therefore be unwilling to upset the current framework by allowing state and local government more autonomy over religious policymaking. Other accommodationist and Christian Right groups, such as the Eagle Forum and Focus on the Family, disagree. Their amicus briefs signal that they are more than willing to limit federal constitutional controls and oversight of state and local religious policymaking.

Churches

Like local governments and interest groups, churches and congregations are also vital constituents in religious policymaking and the law regulating religious liberty. Although a wide range of actors are affected by changes in religious liberty doctrine, from individuals engaged in religious worship to religious interest groups to government agencies, it is still true that "congregations are the core religious organizations in the United States, and they are the site of the vast majority of organized religious activity."[118] Churches are not confined to religious activity either; religion often "acts as a motivational and organizational base for political activity," especially at the local level, and "churches are part of the 'free spaces' of the public sphere that are removed from the direct control of the policy."[119] That is, churches are important organizers of political activity, yet they are often unregulated by government relative to how they generate and press their political demands on officials. Thus churches and congregations will have almost vested interests in being in a position to react to any changes in the constitutional landscape of religious liberty.

At first glance, churches may welcome the autonomy of being able to engage in the type of religious policymaking at the subfederal level that a federalism reading of the establishment clause would bring. Churches are prominent participants in local politics, they are beneficiaries of public programs and friendly zoning or tax laws, and they remain providers of government-funded services. Indeed, government grants to churches for the provision of social welfare services may greatly aid religious institutions in achieving what they perceive to be their own religious missions to their communities. As such, churches have a keen interest in seeing that local and state governments remain free from the potential restraints imposed by constitutional law. Accordingly, increasing autonomy for local and state governments may lead to a more prominent role for churches in subfederal policymaking.

However, several other important countervailing considerations indicate that churches may not necessarily welcome establishment clause federalism because it might disrupt a balance that churches have achieved, over time, with government power. For example, the National Congregations Study by sociologist Mark Chaves shows that churches that provide social services to their communities often do so in collaboration with secular groups; thus they are "deeply embedded within and even dependent on the world of secular social services and government. . . . Religiously based social services are not, in general, an alternative to secular or government-supported social service delivery. They are, rather, part of that world, likely to rise and fall with it."[120] As noted previously, the survey shows that religious groups rarely encounter hostility or rejection when petitioning the government for zoning variances, exemptions, or other policy decisions that may only benefit that specific group. Conflicts between subfederal government and churches are overstated, at least according to Chaves's survey. Changes in church-state relations brought about by establishment clause federalism may accordingly upset another balance that churches and local governments have created and maintain in order to dampen conflicts over religion and local policymaking. That churches and religious congregations rarely encounter local government hostility under the existing interpretation of the establishment clause could be affected by a federalism interpretation that gives states and local governments more autonomy and authority to engage in religious policymaking.

In addition to interaction between churches and local governments, it is also clear that religious groups like to have federal constitutional and statutory guarantees that they can use to carve out and protect their "public space," which is free from government regulation of zoning and even commercial activities. For example, churches and religious organizations can use First Amendment public forum law to gain access to government-managed spaces in order to hold religious meeting and worship services. Access to public parks and buildings for religious meetings and services is typically regulated by free speech law under the First Amendment, so the decision to grant or deny access implicates the religious policymaking of local governments, insofar as they may operate as regards concessions made to religious groups and their activities. Yet local policymaking is constrained by federal (and state) constitutional law governing freedom of expression. Under establishment clause federalism, local governments may have more power to grant or deny religious groups access to public spaces.

Just as churches use First Amendment public forum law to gain entry into government-managed property, they can now use federal law, especially RLUIPA, to limit government regulation of their own property. Legal scholars Jonathan Weiss and Randy Lowell highlight the problems that so-called megachurches sometimes pose for state and local policymaking, especially as pertains to controlling urban or suburban "sprawl."[121] Many local governments are embroiled in disputes with megachurches over growth, traffic, and land-use policies, and RLUIPA pretty much gives those churches the upper hand.

Churches may often have a disincentive to cooperate with local and state policymakers because RLUIPA effectively immunizes some of their activities, especially as relates to land use and development, from regulation.[122] The federal law not only preempts many state and local regulations, but it also requires policymakers to show a compelling government interest that outweighs a church's religious liberty interest in land use. Local governments may be hesitant to risk the costs associated with RLUIPA litigation too, which gives churches even more incentive to refuse to cooperate in zoning and other regulatory disputes.[123]

RLUIPA does not just potentially expose local governments to the increased risk of becoming tangled up in expensive litigation that will only add to the other costs of trying to settle disputes concerning regulation of churches. Some churches may view the law as one way to help them realize their mission to grow and provide religious services to the public even when government policymaking may be hostile to those concerns. Thus, as one pastor currently engaged in an RLUIPA fight (against the city of Boulder, Colorado, after the city's denial of a permit to expand his church building) put it, "When one of your core values is generosity and you are restricted from sharing what you want to share—what God has provided—we consider that to be a severe limitation."[124] The implication is that local policymakers and zoning regulations frustrate a church's ability to focus on and realize its mission to its community. The RLUIPA counters that tendency. By requiring local governments to meet the compelling interest test when regulating religious institutions, it indirectly helps those institutions follow their religiously inspired activities that run contrary to government regulations.

Another policy issue that affects churches concerns the tax exemptions and exceptions that they receive from local, state, and federal governments. All states have either statutory or constitutional provisions that exempt churches and church properties from many taxes. Historically, colonial governments tended to tax dissenting churches more than established churches. Yet, with the gradual disestablishment and the severing of official ties between state governments and churches after the American Revolution, states privatized houses of worship, thereby subjecting them to state taxation.[125] Churches have lobbied state legislatures for constitutional and statutory exemptions to a wide range of taxes for the past two hundred years.

In 1913 Congress created the modern income tax exemption for charitable, religious, and education organizations. The law has been modified continuously over the decades, but the initial federal policy of providing income tax exemptions to encourage donations to charitable and religious groups remains intact. Studies researching donation practices to churches are hard to come by, but recent estimates indicate that churches and religious organizations now receive over $100 billion per year in contributions, which accounts for approximately 35 percent of all giving to charitable organizations. One estimate posits that upward of 65 percent of adult federal taxpayers give to a church and seek the federal income tax exemption.[126] Finally, many state statutes that encourage charitable giving are based on federal tax statutes.

Federal policy on tax exemptions to encourage charitable giving to churches is an economic boon to houses of worship. It not only encourages individual taxpayer donations to churches but also and more broadly redistributes wealth to churches and charitable organizations. Federal tax policy serves as a model for states too: thus, as a policy, it affects more than just national taxation, permeating state and local revenue policymaking too.

Given the extensive reach of federal tax policy and the substantial economic subsidy to churches and other religious organizations it offers, churches may well perceive a financial disincentive to support the devolution of power over religious policymaking to state and local governments. That is, federal tax policy effectively nationalizes an incentive for taxpayers to donate to churches, and indeed taxpayers do just that. Churches reap the financial benefit from the nationalized policy, and arguably that financial benefit would be jeopardized by a federalism reading of the establishment clause. This is not to say that redefining the clause as a jurisdictional barrier to federal policymaking over states will result in federal tax law being declared unconstitutional. But shifting the balance of power to the states over many matters of religious policymaking will at minimum "muddy the waters" in terms of the relationship between federal, state, and local tax policies.

PUBLIC OPINION AND AMERICAN RELIGIOUS LIFE

Federalism scholars make much of that the fact that public opinion on issues of federalism has changed over the course of several decades. Two prominent and recent changes show more public support for state governments and less support for (and more skepticism of) the federal government. It is the case that "generalized support for sub-national governments does not necessarily translate into calls for devolution or policy responsibility," yet throughout the Court's federalism revolution, public opinion, as based on trust in levels of government, has changed.[127] The public has become less trusting of the national government and more trusting of state and local governments. Although this does not directly translate into public support for federalism and devolution, the public's increasing trust in subnational governments and its skepticism of the national government helped create a supportive environment for the Court's devolutionary federalism.[128]

The same argument cannot be made for establishment clause federalism. Although religious belief and religiosity in general correlate strongly with political beliefs, especially in "culture war" issues concerning gay rights, abortion, women's rights, and even economic and foreign policy, there is no polling data that links religious belief or religiosity to views on federalism or levels of governance. However, general trends in public opinion suggest that just as with other constituencies, the public will remain ambivalent in its support for linking federalism and church-state relations.

One indicator concerns public opinion on prayer in public schools. In general the American public tends to be accommodationist of government support for religion, as the public typically supports concrete policies such as the public display of the Ten Commandments, tuition tax vouchers, and prayer in public schools.[129] Two other trends are evident too. First, the public tends to be very hostile to Supreme Court opinions outlawing school prayer. In 1964, 80 percent of Americans disapproved of the Court's decisions. Although that measurement had declined by 2004, 60 percent of the public still disapproved of the Court's decisions.[130] Even though the polling shows the public does not approve of the Court's treatment of school prayer, another trend—that the public favors adopting a constitutional amendment to protect or permit school prayer—is perhaps more telling. Over time, the public's support for an amendment has remained relatively consistent, with support levels of 70 to 80 percent over four decades between 1964 and 2004.[131] As a result, the evidence arguably shows that the public is hostile to the intervention of one federal institution, the Court, in the debate over school prayer; conversely, the public welcomes a federal solution to the problem—a constitutional amendment to protect school prayer. To be sure, states would play a prominent role in the constitutional amendment process, but an amendment still creates a uniform, national rule that affects state and local religious policymaking.

Another trend affecting the issue of establishment clause federalism is the diversity of religious belief and nonbelief in the American religious marketplace. Measures of religious life generally show that Americans remain religiously affiliated, with upwards of 80 percent aligning with the Christian faith in some fashion. Yet the fastest-growing religious grouping comprises those who indicate that they have no religious affiliation.[132] That group now comprises 16.8 percent of Americans, and the rate has increased from approximately 8 percent of the population in the 1970s. As American religious life becomes less focused on denominational affiliation (and indeed affiliation with any specific faith at all), it is plausible that religious policymaking at the state and local levels will become less of an issue over time as policymakers respond to an increasingly diverse religious population in their communities.

Other points are germane in considering the establishment federalism clause issue. Devins posits that the Court's federalism decisions and its "anti-Congress decision-making may be in sync with public opinion."[133] Whether the public supports establishment clause federalism is unknown. There are several decades' worth of polls measuring the public's support for religious policymaking, such as school prayer and public display of the Ten Commandments, but how those polls shed light on the public's overall support for state and local religious policymaking, and the extent to which it should be relatively free from federal oversight, is still an open question that requires additional study.

Neal Devins and political scientist Keith Whittington additionally point out that larger structural arguments surrounding the Court's federalism continue to evolve. For Devins, "Social and political forces did not stand in the way of the Court's turn to federalism."[134] For Whittington, the Court's federalism jurisprudence limiting congressional power over the states is linked to a larger decentralization of policymaking authority and responsibility from the national government to the states, a shift from the "centralized positive state that was thought necessary to deal with the Great Depression and the Second World War" to a "greater appreciation for decentralized decisionmaking."[135] Thus there are important structural considerations in explaining the relative absence of hostile response by Congress and others to the Court's federalism decisions, and they largely comprise the political and social environment in which the Court operates. One conspicuous structural shift relates to the increasing inability of national institutions to deal with certain substantive policy issues and the concomitant increase in the capability of states (and local governments), coupled with "a striking deterioration in the citizenry's support for and trust in the national government relative to state and local governments."[136]

Will establishment clause federalism fit with the structure of American religious life (if indeed that structure can be defined)? American religious life is increasingly decentralized and fragmented at the organizational level, owing in part to the declining influence of national religious denominations; the rise of independent, nondenominational churches; and the tendency of religious believers to shop around to find a church or congregation that fits their needs.[137] In addition, American religious life is increasingly pluralistic with a wide range of belief systems.[138] Decentralized, consumer-driven religious institutions and religious pluralism may fit well with structuring religious policymaking so that states and local governments—those levels of government closest to religious groups, churches, and believers—have more power over church-state issues. However, religious groups and churches also compete for members,[139] and churches that are best able to compete and attract new members tend to grow. Devolving more religious policymaking power to state and local governments may increase the competition for members among local congregations, which may in turn have negative effects on the policymaking process. Put differently, evolving more authority to engage in religious policymaking at the state and local level may actually have unanticipated consequences far beyond what those who advocate establishment clause federalism intend.

RELIGIOUS FREEDOM, FEDERALISM, AND THE ROBERTS COURT

The broad-based analysis above suggests that Justice Clarence Thomas's federalism interpretation of the establishment clause most likely will not evolve to become an integrated part of the Supreme Court's purported federalism revolution. The constituencies that would be most affected by a federalism approach to church-state relations are not supportive of it; nor are Thomas's colleagues currently on the Court. Much of the analysis is premised on developments concurrent with the Rehnquist Court era.

The successor Roberts Court has yet to develop a distinctive approach to religious liberty issues, but it seems poised to continue Rehnquist Court doctrine with little if any modifications. As concerns establishment clause federalism, there are also a few indicators suggesting that even though it will refuse to gravitate toward a federalism reading of religious liberty, federalism concerns will affect how it views religious liberty disputes.

One case worth noting is *McDonald v. Chicago*, decided at the end of the Court's 2009–2010 term. *McDonald* addressed whether Chicago's ban on handguns possessed by private citizens was unconstitutional under the Second Amendment right to keep and bear arms. In a previous 2008 case, *District of Columbia v. Heller*, the Court struck down Washington, DC's handgun ban as a violation of the Second Amendment, but it left unanswered whether the same amendment is incorporated against the states. Thus *McDonald* presented to the Court that question.

In a sweeping opinion, a divided Court declared that the amendment does codify an individual constitutional right to possess firearms for the purpose of self-defense. To be sure the substance of the Court's opinion has little relevance for religious liberty, federalism, and the establishment clause except for a tangential debate between Justice Stevens's dissenting opinion and Justices Scalia and Thomas's concurring opinion. Still, their disagreement suggests that the justices may be reformulating Thomas's federalism approach in subtle ways.

First, Justice Stevens's dissent in *McDonald* relies on various constitutional theories and historical interpretations of the Second Amendment that do not always logically fit. More importantly, though, Stevens invokes Thomas's federalism argument from *Newdow* to contend that "the Second Amendment . . . 'is a federalism provision.' . . . It is directed at preserving the autonomy of the sovereign States, and its logic therefore 'resists' incorporation by a federal court against the States."[140]

In his concurring opinion (joined by Justice Thomas), Justice Scalia noted that Stevens was inconsistent. For Scalia, Stevens insists that the establishment clause is not a federalism provision, but "he does not explain why it is not, but the right to keep and bear arms is. . . . The federalism argument prevents the incorporation of only certain rights."[141] Stevens responded to Scalia's assertions in a footnote and argued that even though he does not agree with Thomas's view on the establishment, he is in agreement with the "underlying logic" of Thomas's argument that holds "if a clause in the Bill of Rights exists to safeguard federalism interests . . . it makes little sense to incorporate it."[142]

Stevens's focus on the "underlying logic" of Thomas's argument—that certain rights in the Bill of Rights are designed to safeguard broader federalism concerns—suggests that he accepts Thomas's approach to a limited extent, but not so much as to view religious liberty as a federalism interest instead of an individual right. Despite that, if Justice Stevens accepts a minimal conception of clauses in the Bill of Rights that protect federalism interests, then Justice Thomas's novel approach to the establishment clause has had at least some kind of impact. Of course, Justice Stevens retired from the Court shortly after penning his *McDonald* dissent; therefore his ability to influence current justices is minimal at best.

Another notable point about the debate between Scalia and Stevens focuses on Scalia's concurrence. In expressing his disagreement with Stevens, Scalia pays particular attention to how Stevens uses federalism as a way to protect Chicago's handgun ban from federal oversight. And although Scalia takes Stevens to task for inconsistently interpreting clauses in the Bill of Rights as federalism provisions, he offers no justification or support for establishment clause federalism. Thus Scalia relies on federalism to castigate a colleague, but he offers no indication as to his own support for that doctrine.

So far the Roberts Court has accepted few religious liberty cases for full review. Therefore the question remains open as to how the justices will view additional attempts to bring federalism into church-state constitutional law. Yet one case decided in 2011 may offer important clues about whether establishment clause federalism will make a transition from the Rehnquist Court to the Roberts Court. In *Arizona Christian School Tuition Organization v. Winn*, the Court reviewed whether an Arizona law granting tax credits for contributions to private schools, including religious schools, violated the establishment clause. Taxpayers could donate money to private school tuition organizations, which would then distribute monies collected to provide scholarships to students enrolled in private schools. A divided Court voted 5–4 that the plaintiffs, Arizona taxpayers, did not have standing to sue as taxpayers under Article III of the Constitution since their establishment clause challenge did not directly contest the constitutionality of a government expenditure.[143] The four-justice minority equated tax credits with government expenditures, so they concluded that the Arizona taxpayer plaintiffs had standing to sue.

At first glance the *Winn* decision deals with the interpretation and application of the Court's standing doctrine on when taxpayer lawsuits alleging violations of the establishment clause can be adjudicated by federal courts. However, the division among the justices shows an important and developing fissure in the nascent Roberts Court on how church-state relations might be adjudicated, with a relatively conservative five-justice majority unwilling to construe standing doctrine broadly to allow taxpayers to sue the state of Arizona and the more liberal four-justice minority advocating for an expansive view of standing to allow the lawsuit to be adjudicated.

A more detailed look at *Winn* offers clues too about whether establishment clause federalism issues will continue into the Roberts Court. The main litigants in *Winn* did not present the Court with any claims that the clause should be read as a federalism provision. The majority made no reference to federalism issues in its opinion, and even though Justices Scalia and Thomas wrote a separate concurrence, they did not make any federalism reference either; they concurred to note that *Flast v. Cohen* should be overturned. The dissenting opinion authored by Justice Elena Kagan contained no federalism arguments or references either. Even so, several amicus briefs filed in the case did reference federalism concerns, and those briefs suggest how Justice Thomas's original arguments about establishment clause federalism have changed and will perhaps be pressed upon the Court in future litigation.

One brief in *Winn* submitted by several states argued that the Court should "adhere to . . . principles of federalism . . . to limit federal courts to their proper role in Establishment Clause cases."[144] The states' brief did not refer to Justice Thomas's federalism arguments from *Newdow*; nor did it advocate for a new interpretation of the clause on the Court. Instead, relying on *Younger v. Harris*,[145] the states argued that existing federalism concerns "that counsel restraint against [federal court] injunctions against state officers administering state laws" should apply in establishment clause cases too. Thus, instead of advocating for a new federalism and jurisdictional reading of the establishment clause, the states' brief sought to extend existing case law that limits federal court interference with the administration and enforcement of state laws to disputes concerning the relationship between church and state.

The brief from the accommodationist American Center for Law and Justice omitted mentioning federalism or *Newdow*, but the brief by the Center for Constitutional Jurisprudence, also an accommodationist and politically conservative group, did endorse a federalism reading of the establishment clause. The center's brief argued, "The Establishment Clause was enacted as a measure of structural federalism to forbid the new federal government from encroaching on an area already addressed in state constitutions."[146] Other accommodationist groups reference federalism in their briefs but in different ways. The Rutherford Institute, for instance, contended that "states should be afforded greater latitude than the federal government to experiment with laws that touch upon religion—particularly when those laws concern state educational prerogatives."[147] Thus, while not endorsing a jurisdictional and federalism reading of the establishment clause, the institute relies on the traditional federalism argument that states are laboratories and should be allowed more room to experiment with religious policymaking. A similar argument is made by another accommodationist group, the Becket Fund for Religious Liberty, which argues that "sound principles of federalism" prevent federal courts from being forums for state taxpayer grievances; more importantly, federalism concerns dictate that taxpayers should seek redress from their legislature and the political process.[148]

The briefs from *Winn* suggest that some groups and states are altering their federalism arguments with regard to the establishment clause and religious liberty in general. Instead of arguing for a reinterpretation of the clause as a federalism provision, the briefs seek to affect the Court's view of state religious policymaking through more customary and established principles of federalism. That is, instead of protecting state policymaking from federal oversight through a reinterpretation of the establishment clause as a jurisdictional and federalism provision, the briefs posit that state policymaking can simply be insulated from federal oversight through the application of traditional federalism principles that safeguard the ability of states to experiment with policy outcomes and also limit federal court oversight of how state laws are administered. The briefs suggest, then, that linkages between federalism and religious liberty are still advocated by certain interest groups and states, yet the reinterpretation of the establishment clause as Justice Thomas proposed in *Newdow* is perhaps no longer considered a viable option.

To be sure, the Roberts Court did not respond to the brief writers' specific arguments. The continuing press for a federalism understanding of religious liberty and church-state relations indicates that arguments explored by Justice Thomas during the Rehnquist Court era are still around in some modified form, yet it remains unlikely that Thomas's federalism reading of the establishment clause will be adopted by the Roberts Court.

Even though the Roberts Court has not supported a federalism reading of the establishment clause and appears highly unlikely to do so in the future, its decision in *Winn* plays into the broader federalism concern of protecting states from burdensome litigation. Of note here is political scientist R. Shep Melnick's argument that the Rehnquist Court's new federalism jurisprudence protected state sovereignty in part through protecting state and local policymaking from federal oversight by developing a "variety of ways to keep private suits against subnational governments out of court altogether."[149] It is in this category of federalism decisions that the Roberts Court decision in *Winn* can properly be understood. By foreclosing in federal courts taxpayer lawsuits contesting the constitutionality of Arizona's tax credits for donations to private and religious schools, the Court in *Winn* made it more difficult to file establishment clause lawsuits against states. The Court's decision limited the power of federal courts to oversee state religious policymaking too. To be sure, this may be how the Roberts Court addresses federalism and religious liberty: instead of reinterpreting the establishment clause as Justice Thomas proposed, the

Roberts Court may simply and gradually extend the Rehnquist Court's new federalism trends to cover state religious policymaking.

NOTES

1. Justice Clarence Thomas, "Remarks," Dwight Opperman Lecture, Drake University Law School, September 24, 1999. Published in *Drake Law Review* 48 (2000): 231.

2. Mark Tushnet, *A Court Divided: The Rehnquist Court and the Future of Constitutional Law* (New York: W. W. Norton and Company, 2005), 277–78.

3. *United States v. Lopez*, 514 U.S. 549, 568 (1995).

4. Tinsley E. Yarbrough, *The Rehnquist Court and the Constitution* (Oxford: Oxford University Press, 2000), 107.

5. *United States v. Lopez*, 514 U.S. 549, 585 (1995) (Thomas, J., concurring).

6. *United States v. Lopez*, 514 U.S. 549, 600 (1995) (Thomas, J., concurring).

7. *U.S. Term Limits v. Thornton*, 514 U.S. 779, 871 (1995) (Thomas, J., dissenting).

8. 536 U.S. 639 (2002).

9. 542 U.S. 1 (2004).

10. Timothy J. Conlan and Robert L. Dudley, "Janus-Faced Federalism: State Sovereignty and Federal Preemption in the Rehnquist Court," *PS: Political Science* (July 2005): 363.

11. Neal Devins, "The Rehnquist Court: The Judicial Safeguards of Federalism," *Northwestern University Law Review* 99 (Fall 2004): 131, 139.

12. Keith Whittington, "Taking What They Give Us: Explaining the Court's Federalism Offensive," *Duke Law Journal* 51 (October 2001): 477, 498. See also Whittington, "Dismantling the Modern State? The Changing Structural Foundations of Federalism," *Hastings Constitutional Law Quarterly* 25 (Summer 1998): 483.

13. See Neal Devins, "The Majoritarian Rehnquist Court," *Law and Contemporary Problems* 67, no. 3 (Summer 2003); see also John Kincaid and Richard L. Coley, "Citizen Attitudes toward Issues of Federalism in Canada, Mexico, and the United States," *Publius: The Journal of Federalism* 41, no. 1 (2010): 53–75.

14. 421 U.S. 542 (1975).

15. Ruth Colker and Kevin M. Scott, "Rehnquist and Federalism: An Empirical Analysis," in *The Rehnquist Legacy*, ed. Craig Bradley (Cambridge: Cambridge University Press, 2006): 284.

16. Tushnet, *A Court Divided*, 255.

17. Whittington, "Taking What They Give Us," 504.

18. 330 U.S. 1 (1947).

19. Carl H. Esbeck, "The Establishment Clause as a Structural Restraint on Government Power," *Iowa Law Review* 84 (October 1998): 1; Jonathan P. Brose, "In Birmingham They Love the Governor: Why the Fourteenth Amendment Does Not Incorporate the Establishment Clause," *Ohio Northern University Law Review* 24 (1998): 1; Mark D. Rosen, "Law and Cultural Conflict: Establishment, Expressivism, and Federalism," *Chicago-Kent Law Review* 78 (2003): 669; Steven K. Green, "Reconciling the Free Exercise and Establishment Clauses: Federalism and the Establishment Clause, a Reassessment," *Creighton Law Review* 38 (June 2005): 761;

Stuart D. Poppel, "Federalism, Fundamental Fairness, and the Religion Clauses," *Cumberland Law Review* 25 (1995): 247: Richard C. Schragger, "The Role of the Local in the Doctrine and Discourse of Religious Liberty," *Harvard Law Review* 117 (April 2004): 1810; Stephen Dawson, "Agnostic Federalism: The Alabama Ten Commandments Controversy," in *A Nation of Religions: The Politics of Pluralism in Multireligious America*, ed. Stephen Prothero (Chapel Hill: University of North Carolina Press, 2006), 209–32. Arguments made by James McClellan and Robert Cord show that federalism readings of the establishment clause predate Justice Clarence Thomas. James McClellan, "The Making and the Unmaking of the Establishment Clause," in *A Blueprint for Judicial Reform*, ed. Patrick B. McGuigan and Randall R. Rader (Washington, DC: Free Congress Research and Educational Foundation, 1981); Robert L. Cord, *Separation of Church and State: Historical Fact and Current Fiction* (New York: Lambeth Press, 1982). Edward Corwin made similar arguments in discussing the Supreme Court's school prayer decisions in the 1940s. Edward S. Corwin, "The Court as a National School Board," *Law and Contemporary Problems* 14 (Winter 1949), reprinted in Alpheus T. Mason and Gerald Garvey, eds., *American Constitutional History: Essays by Edward S. Corwin* (Gloucester, MA: Peter Smith, 1970). Justice Thomas relies extensively on Philip Hamburger's *Separation of Church and State* (Cambridge, MA: Harvard University Press, 2002).

20. 540 U.S. 712 (2004).

21. Ted G. Jelen, *To Serve God and Mammon: Church-State Relations in American Politics*, 2nd ed. (Washington, DC: Georgetown University Press, 2010), 131.

22. See *Employment Division, Department of Human Resources of Oregon v. Smith*, 494 U.S. 872 (1990). The compelling interest test was introduced in *Sherbert v. Verner*, 374 U.S. 398 (1963). Although the Court did not overturn *Sherbert* at all in *Boerne*, it limited the circumstances under which the compelling interest test applied. Thus, in *Oregon v. Smith*, the compelling interest test no longer applied when a generally applicable neutral law (such as a criminal law) regulated a person or group's religiously motivated conduct. But see *Church of Lukumi Babalu Aye v. City of Hialeah*, 508 U.S. 520 (1993), which followed *Oregon v. Smith*. In *Hialeah* the Court applied the compelling interest test because the law in question was not neutral.

23. 521 U.S. 507 (1997).

24. Gary S. Gildin, "The Rise of State Law Sanctuary for Minority Religious Liberty in the Wake of the Fall of Federal Constitutional Protection for Nonmainstream Faiths," in *Democracy and Religion: Free Exercise and Diverse Visions*, ed. David Odell-Scott (Kent, OH: Kent State University Press, 2004), 89–103.

25. Kent Greenawalt, "Religion and the Rehnquist Court," *Northwestern University Law Review* 99 (Fall 2004): 145, 147.

26. 403 U.S. 602 (1971).

27. *Lemon* has been modified, though, in a series of cases. For example, in *Lynch v. Donnelly* and other cases, Justice O'Connor argued, "What is crucial is that a government practice not have the effect of communicating a message of government endorsement or disapproval of religion." *Lynch v. Donnelly*, 465 U.S. 668, 690 (1984) (O'Connor, J., concurring). O'Connor's endorsement test has been given credence by other justices. For a fuller discussion, see Frederick Mark Gedicks,

The Rhetoric of Church and State (Durham, NC: Duke University Press, 1995), 72–74; and Henry J. Abraham and Barbara A. Perry, *Freedom and the Court*, 8th ed. (Oxford: Oxford University Press, 2003), 334–35, 360.

28. Cornell Clayton, "Law, Politics, and the Rehnquist Court," in *The Supreme Court in American Politics*, ed. Howard Gillman and Cornell Clayton (Lawrence: Kansas University Press, 1999), 168.

29. Yarbrough, *The Rehnquist Court and the Constitution*, 171.

30. Herbert M. Kritzer and Mark J. Richards, "Jurisprudential Regimes and Supreme Court Decisionmaking: The *Lemon* Regime and Establishment Clause Cases," *Law and Society Review* 37, no. 4 (2003): 831.

31. See, for example, *Church of Lukumi Babalu Aye v. City of Hialeah*, 508 U.S. 520 (1993), in which the Court reviewed, and unanimously struck down, Hialeah's ordinance regulating animal sacrifices and thus a Santerian church within the community.

32. Schragger, "The Role of the Local in the Doctrine and Discourse of Religious Liberty," 1838.

33. Richard E. Morgan, *The Politics of Religious Conflict* (New York: Pegasus, 1968), 94–95.

34. Jelen, *To Serve God and Mammon*, 70–73; see also Ted G. Jelen, "Political Culture, Political Structure, and Political Conflict: The Persistence of Church-State Conflict in the United States," in *Piety, Politics, and Pluralism: Religion, the Courts, and the 2000 Election*, ed. Mary C. Segers (Lanham, MD: Rowman & Littlefield, 2002), 211.

35. Elaine B. Sharp, "Culture, Institutions, and Urban Officials' Responses to Morality Issues," *Political Research Quarterly* 55, no. 4 (December 2002): 862.

36. Schragger, "The Role of the Local in the Doctrine and Discourse of Religious Liberty," 1815.

37. Daniel O. Conkle, "Indirect Funding and the Establishment Clause: Rehnquist's Triumphant Vision of Neutrality and Private Choice," in *The Rehnquist Legacy*, ed. Craig Bradley (Cambridge: Cambridge University Press, 2006), 78.

38. The following statistics are generated from the Supreme Court Database housed at Washington University, St. Louis (www.scdb.wustl.edu). The following analyses were done using the database's website between July 10 and August 15, 2011. The broad searches focused on the Rehnquist Court era, the First Amendment issues of the free exercise clause, the establishment clause, and parochiaid; whether the law in question was declared unconstitutional; and the political direction of the decision.

39. 540 U.S. 712 (2004).

40. Davey also asserted violations of the establishment clause and his First Amendment free speech rights.

41. 540 U.S. 712, 721 (2004).

42. Importantly, Justices Scalia and Thomas argued in dissent that the state's scholarship program was a public benefit that discriminated against religion and thus violated Davey's free exercise rights.

43. Conkle, "Indirect Funding and the Establishment Clause," 78.

44. Schragger, "The Role of the Local in the Doctrine and Discourse of Religious Liberty," 1867.

45. *Elk Grove Unified School District v. Newdow*, 542 U.S. 1, 50–51 (2004) (Thomas, J., concurring).

46. *Zelman v. Simmons-Harris*, 536 U.S. 639, 671 (2002) (Thomas, J., concurring).

47. *Zelman v. Simmons-Harris*, 536 U.S. 639, 680 (2002) (Thomas, J., concurring).

48. See Daniel Elazar, "Recovenanting the American Policy," in *A Nation under God? Essays on the Future of Religion in American Life*, ed. R. Bruce Douglass and Joshua Mitchell (Lanham, MD: Rowman & Littlefield, 2000), 135–63.

49. Daniel Elazar, "The Political Theory of Covenant: Biblical Origins and Modern Developments," *Publius: The Journal of Federalism* (special issue titled "Covenant, Polity, and Constitutionalism") 10, no. 4 (Fall 1980): 22–24. See also the remaining essays in the journal and a more recent exploration of the links between federalism, religion, and covenants in William Johnson Everett, *Religion, Federalism, and the Struggle for Public Life* (Oxford: Oxford University Press, 1997).

50. Donald S. Lutz, *The Origins of American Constitutionalism* (Baton Rouge: Louisiana State University Press, 1988), 32.

51. Barry Alan Shain, *The Myth of American Individualism* (Princeton, NJ: Princeton University Press, 1994), 51–52.

52. *Elk Grove Unified School District v. Newdow*, 542 U.S. 1, 50–51 (2004) (Thomas, J., concurring).

53. Joseph Story, *Commentaries on the Constitution*, 1833 edition, section 1873, reprinted in Philip B. Kurland and Ralph Lerner, eds., *The Founders' Constitution* (Chicago: University of Chicago Press, 1987) 5: 109–10.

54. R. Kent Newmeyer, *Supreme Court Justice Joseph Story: Statesman of the Old Republic* (Chapel Hill: University of North Carolina Press, 1985), 183. Newmeyer suggests that Story's classic work *Commentaries on the Constitution* is ultimately less an academic commentary on the young Constitution; rather it is more of a manifesto in favor of constitutionalism, nationalism, and New England conservatism. Thus, Story's work is designed to counter the Jeffersonian attack on the Marshall Court, among other things.

55. James McClellan, *Joseph Story and the American Constitution* (Norman: University of Oklahoma Press, 1971), 119. Jefferson articulated his "wall of separation" approach to the establishment clause in his 1802 letter to the Danbury Connecticut Baptist Association, and Jefferson's argument has formed an important part of the modern Court's interpretation of the church-state relationship. See *Everson v. Board of Education*, 330 U.S. 1 (1947). See also Abraham and Perry, *Freedom and the Court*.

56. Corwin, "The Court as a National School Board," 205.

57. Corwin, "The Court as a National School Board," 211.

58. Leonard W. Levy, *The Establishment Clause: Religion and the First Amendment* (New York: Macmillan, 1986), 74.

59. James McClellan, "The Making and the Unmaking of the Establishment Clause," in *A Blueprint for Judicial Reform* (Washington, DC: The Free Congress Research and Educational Foundation, 1981), 316.

60. *Ishmael Jaffree v. the Board of School Commissioners of Mobile County*, 554 F. Supp. 1104 (1983).

61. *Ishmael Jaffree v. the Board of School Commissioners of Mobile County*, 554 F. Supp. 1104 (1983).

62. *Jaffree v. Board of School Commissioners of Mobile Co.*, 1114. Judge Hand wrote, "At the start the Court should acknowledge its indebtedness to several constitutional scholars. If this opinion will accomplish its intent, which is to take us back to our original historical roots, then much of the credit for the vision lies with Professor James McClellan and Professor Robert L. Cord." McClellan provided testimony during the trial to which Hand frequently refers in his opinion. Although Hand accepts Cord's argument that the establishment clause was meant to prohibit a *federal* establishment of religion, Hand states, "The Court rejects the conclusion of Professor Cord that the fourteenth amendment incorporated the establishment clause against the states. Professor Cord uncritically adopted the analysis of the United States Supreme Court in reaching his conclusion." See note 33 in the *Jaffree* opinion.

63. *Ishmael Jaffree v. the Board of School Commissioners of Mobile County*, 554 F. Supp. 1104, 1119 (1983).

64. *Ishmael Jaffree v. the Board of School Commissioners of Mobile County*, 554 F. Supp. 1104, 1129 (1983).

65. *Ishmael Jaffree v. the Board of School Commissioners of Mobile County*, 554 F. Supp. 1104, 1130 (1983).

66. When it noted probable jurisdiction, the Court limited its review solely to the question concerning whether a moment of silence per Alabama's law violates the establishment clause. It left intact the Eleventh Circuit's reversal of Judge Hand's ruling that the establishment clause does not apply to the states. See *Wallace v. Jaffree*, 466 U.S. 924 (1984). In the Court's decision on the merits, Justice Stevens wrote, "Our unanimous affirmance of the Court of Appeals' judgment . . . makes it unnecessary to comment at length on the District Court's remarkable conclusion that the Federal Constitution imposes no obstacle to Alabama's establishment of a state religion. . . . It is nevertheless appropriate to recall how firmly embedded in our constitutional jurisprudence is the proposition that the several States have no greater power to restrain the individual freedoms protected by the First Amendment than does the Congress of the United States. . . . When the Constitution was amended to prohibit any State from depriving any person of liberty without due process of law, that Amendment imposed the same substantive limitations on the States' power to legislate that the First Amendment had always imposed on the Congress' power. This Court has confirmed and endorsed this elementary proposition of law time and time again." *Wallace v. Jaffree*, 472 U.S. 38, 48–49 (1985).

67. Devins, "The Rehnquist Court," 142.

68. See Megan Mullin, "Federalism," in *Public Opinion and Constitutional Controversy*, ed. Nathaniel Persily, Jack Citrin, and Patrick J. Egan (New York: Oxford University Press, 2008), 209–34.

69. See Whittington, "Taking What They Give Us."

70. Devins, "The Rehnquist Court," 131.

71. Robert F. Nagel, "Judicial Power and the Restoration of Federalism," in *The Supreme Court's Federalism: Real or Imagined?*, ed. Frank Goodman, special issue of the *Annals of the American Academy of Political and Social Science* 574 (2001): 58.

72. Marci Hamilton, "The Elusive Safeguards of Federalism," in Goodman, *The Supreme Court's Federalism*, 99.

73. See John Dinan, "Consequences of the Rehnquist Court's Federalism Decisions for Congressional Lawmaking," *Publius: The Journal of Federalism* 34, no. 2 (Spring 2004). See also Neal Devins, "The Majoritarian Rehnquist Court," and Vicki Jackson, "Federalism and the Court: Congress as the Audience?," in Goodman, *The Supreme Court's Federalism*, 145–58.

74. Louis Fisher, *Religious Liberty in America: Political Safeguards* (Lawrence: University Press of Kansas, 2002), 231. See, generally, the whole work for a more detailed, sustained argument about the role of Congress in protecting religious liberty.

75. See the main decision banning school prayers composed and endorsed by the government, *Engel v. Vitale*, 370 U.S. 421 (1962); the decision prohibiting state-mandated moments of silence that seek to advance religious belief, *Wallace v. Jaffree*, 472 U.S. 38 (1985); and, most recently, student-initiated school prayer at high school football games, *Santa Fe Independent School Dist. v. Doe*, 530 U.S. 290 (2000).

76. See, generally, Edward Keynes (with Randall K. Miller), *The Court vs. Congress: Prayer, Busing, and Abortion* (Durham, NC: Duke University Press, 1989), 174–206.

77. The EAA came after years of congressional attempts to amend the Constitution to allow school prayer or to change federal court jurisdiction to prohibit federal judges from adjudicating school prayer cases. See Fisher, *Religious Liberty in America*, 123–46.

78. Fisher, *Religious Liberty in America*, 141.

79. See the letter from Secretary of Education Richard W. Riley to public school districts, May 1998. The letter is reprinted in the summary of the U.S. Commission on Civil Rights proceedings on schools and religion: *Schools and Religion: Executive Summary and Transcript of Proceedings Held in Washington, D.C., New York City, and Seattle Wash., Spring/Summer 1998* (December 1999), app. A.

80. Secretary of Education Rod Paige, "Secretary's Letter on Constitutionally Protected Prayer in Public Elementary and Secondary Schools," U.S. Department of Education, February 7, 2003, www.ed.gov/inits/religionandschools/letter_030207.html. For the guidelines, see "Guidance on Constitutionally Protected Prayer in Public Elementary and Secondary Schools," *Federal Register* 68, no. 40 (February 28, 2003): 9645. Also available from the federal Department of Education website at www2.ed.gov/policy/gen/guid/religionandschools/prayer_guidance.html (accessed May 25, 2011).

81. "Most Schools Complying with Prayer Guidelines," Associated Press Wire Report, May 13, 2003, www.firstamendmentcenter.org/most-schools-complying-with-prayer-guidelines (accessed May 4, 2012).

82. Brief for Respondent State of Ohio, *Cutter v. Wilkinson*, 2003 U.S. Briefs 9877; 2005 U.S. S. Ct. Briefs LEXIS 164, February 11, 2005, page 50.

83. Christopher Z. Mooney, "The Decline of Federalism and the Rise of Morality-Policy Conflict in the United States," *Publius: The Journal of Federalism* 30 (Winter/Spring 2000): 171–88.

84. See Brief for the United States as Amicus Curiae Supporting Petitioners in *Lee v. Weisman*, 1990 U.S. Briefs 1014; 1991 U.S. S. Ct. Briefs LEXIS 308, May 24, 1991, pages 11–12. As Starr noted, "The Court has not, however, invariably hewn to the *Lemon* formula. . . . Indeed, a majority of the members of this Court, recognizing the confusion that *Lemon* has spawned, has on separate occasions advocated significant revision or abandonment of the *Lemon* test." Thus, *Lee v. Weisman* offered the Court a good opportunity to replace *Lemon*.

85. Virginia submitted a brief joined by Alaska, Idaho, Iowa, Nebraska, North Dakota, Oklahoma, U.S. Virgin Islands, and West Virginia. In it the states explicitly argued that "the Establishment Clause has a Federalism Purpose that limits the power of the National Government with regard to the States. The Federalism Purpose . . . mandates that the National Government may not interfere with the States' ability to make religious policy subject only to the limitations imposed by the Constitution."

86. See Lincoln Caplan, *The Tenth Justice: The Solicitor General and the Rule of Law* (New York: Knopf, 1987), 95–106, for a detailed account of this debate.

87. Kenneth Wald and Allison Calhoun-Brown, *Religion and Politics in the United States*, 6th ed. (Lanham, MD: Rowman & Littlefield, 2011), 170.

88. Cheryl Runyon et al., "Religious Land Use—State and Federal Legislation," *NCSL State Legislative Report* 25, no. 14 (December 2000).

89. Jelen, *To Serve God and Mammon*, 57–95.

90. See, generally, Sean Nicholson-Crotty, "State Merit Amicus Participation and Federalism Outcomes in the U.S. Supreme Court," *Publius: The Journal of Federalism* 37 (2007): 599–612.

91. See, generally, Eric N. Waltenburg and Bill Swinford, *Litigating Federalism: The States before the Supreme Court* (Westport, CT: Greenwood Press, 1999).

92. Brief of Respondent State of Ohio in *Cutter v. Wilkinson*, 2003 U.S. Briefs 9877; 2005 U.S. S. Ct. Briefs LEXIS 164, pages 26–27.

93. Brief of Respondent State of Ohio, 2003, 29.

94. Justice Thomas's concurring opinion argued, in essence, that Ohio and Virginia overstated the federalism inherent in the establishment clause: "Ohio's vision of the range of protected state authority overreads the Clause. Ohio and its amici contend that, even though 'states can no longer establish preferred churches' because the Clause has been incorporated against the States through the Fourteenth Amendment, 'Congress is as unable as ever to contravene constitutionally permissible *State choices regarding religious policy.*' That is not what the Clause says. The Clause prohibits Congress from enacting legislation 'respecting an establishment of religion'; it does not prohibit Congress from enacting legislation 'respecting religion' or 'taking cognizance of religion.'" *Cutter v. Wilkinson*, 544 U.S. 1 (2005) (Thomas, J., concurring).

95. *Cutter v. Wilkinson*, 544 U.S. 1 (2005) (Thomas, J., concurring).

96. *Cutter v. Wilkinson*, 544 U.S. 1, 10 (2005) (Thomas, J., concurring). Virginia made similar arguments as a defendant in litigation in an RLUIPA case. Its feder-

alism arguments were rebuffed by a federal district judge and the Fourth Circuit Court of Appeals. See *Madison v. Riter*, 474 F. 3d 118 (4th Cir. 2006), and *Madison v. Riter*, 411 F. Supp. 2d 645 (W.D. Virginia 2006).

97. Alabama, Florida, Nevada, Oklahoma, Texas, Washington, Colorado, Michigan, North Dakota, South Carolina, and Virginia all joined in the brief.

98. *Flast v. Cohen*, 392 U.S. 83 (1968). The Court allowed taxpayer lawsuits to proceed with standing provided there is a link between the taxpayer's status as a taxpayer and the law in question, and the taxpayer must be able to show that the law exceeds constitutional limits on government spending powers.

99. The literature on interaction between local governments and religious groups and churches is voluminous. See Mark Chaves, *Congregations in America* (Cambridge, MA: Harvard University Press, 2004), 44–127; and Mark Chaves and William Tsitsos, "Are Congregations Constrained by Government? Empirical Results from the National Congregations Study," *Journal of Church and State* 42 (Spring 2000): 335–44. See also Rhys H. Williams and N. J. Demerath III, "Religion and Political Process in an American City," *American Sociological Review* 56 (August 1991): 417–31; Kenneth Wald et al., "Churches as Political Communities," *American Political Science Review* 82 (June 1988): 531–48; and John C. Blakeman, "The Religious Geography of Religious Speech," *Journal of Church and State* 48 (Spring 2006): 399–422.

100. See Jelen, "Political Culture, Political Structure, and Political Conflict," and Blakeman, "The Religious Geography of Religious Speech."

101. Paul Schumaker, "Moral Principles of Local Officials and the Resolution of Culture War Issues," in *Culture Wars and Local Politics*, ed. Elaine B. Sharp (Lawrence: University Press of Kansas, 1999), 200.

102. Chaves, *Congregations in America*.

103. See Chaves and Tsitsos, "Are Congregations Constrained by Government?"

104. See, generally, James W. Button, Kenneth D. Wald, and Barbara A. Rienzo, "The Politics of Gay Rights Legislation," in Sharpe, *Culture Wars and Local Politics*, 81–100.

105. John C. Green and James L. Guth, "The Missing Link: Political Activists and Support for School Prayer," *Public Opinion Quarterly* 53 (Spring 1989): 54.

106. See, generally, Richard Schragger, "The Role of the Local in the Doctrine and Discourse of Religious Liberty," *Harvard Law Review* 117 (Spring 2004): 1810.

107. See Lee Epstein and Joseph F. Kobylka, *The Supreme Court and Legal Change* (Chapel Hill: University of North Carolina Press, 1992), *passim*.

108. See Joseph F. Kobylka, "The Mysterious Case of Establishment Clause Litigation: How Organized Groups Foiled Legal Change," in *Contemplating Courts*, ed. Lee Epstein (Washington, DC: Congressional Quarterly Press, 1995), 93–128.

109. Kobylka, "The Mysterious Case of Establishment Clause Litigation," 94.

110. Kobylka, "The Mysterious Case of Establishment Clause Litigation," 94.

111. See Brief of Amicus Curiae, Eagle Forum Education & Legal Defense Fund in support of Respondent, *Van Orden v. Perry*, 2003 U.S. Briefs 1500, January 28, 2005.

112. Brief of Amici Curiae of Focus on the Family and Family Research Council in support of Respondent, *Van Orden v. Perry*, 2003 U.S. Briefs 1500, January 31, 2005.

113. See Brief of Amici Curiae of Americans United for the Separation of Church and State and the ACLU in support of Petitioners, *Cutter v. Wilkinson*, 2003 U.S. Briefs 9877, December 2004; and Brief of Amici Curiae, ACLU, Baptist Joint Committee for Religious Liberty, Americans United for the Separation of Church and State, People for the American Way, and the Anti-Defamation League, *Hein v. Freedom from Religion Foundation*, 2006 U.S. Briefs 157B, February 2, 2007.

114. See Ruth Murray Brown, *For a "Christian America": A History of the Religious Right* (Amherst, NY: Prometheus Books, 2002); Clyde Wilcox, *Onward Christian Soldiers: The Religious Right in American Politics*, 2nd ed. (Boulder, CO: Westview Press, 2002).

115. Quoted in Frank Guliuzza III, *Over the Wall: Protecting Religious Expression in the Public Square* (Albany: State University of New York Press, 2000), 140.

116. Steven P. Brown, *Trumping Religion: The New Christian Right, the Free Speech Clause, and the First Amendment* (Tuscaloosa: University of Alabama Press, 2002), 134.

117. Steven Gey, "When Is Religious Speech Not Free Speech?," *University of Illinois Law Review* (2000): 381.

118. Chaves and Tsitsos, "Are Congregations Constrained by Government?," 337.

119. Williams and Demerath, "Religion and Political Process in an American City," 419.

120. Chaves, *Congregations in America*, 93.

121. Jonathan Weiss and Randy Lowell, "Supersizing Religion: Megachurches, Sprawl, and Smart Growth," *Saint Louis University Public Law Review* 21 (2002): 313. Weiss and Lowell define a megachurch as a church with over two thousand congregants that provides more services outside of a traditional Sunday service. As they note, megachurches are often located in suburban areas, provide numerous religious, education, and community services, and frequently seek to establish "campuses" in order to better serve their parishioners. Such churches grow rapidly and seek to provide more services to meet increasing demand. This, in turn, can lead to an ongoing need to expand land and buildings, which leads to more conflict with local governments over such issues as increased traffic to megachurches, noise, more land devoted to marginal uses such as parking, and even conflicts over commercial and educational activities that may fall outside local and state regulation.

122. For a listing of RLUIPA litigation and the types of issues involved, see the Becket Fund's website (www.becketfund.org; accessed July 18, 2011). The Becket Fund for Religious Liberty is an interest group devoted to protecting religious expression.

123. The California city of Lake Elsinore recently paid $1.2 million to the Elsinore Christian Center to settle an RLUIPA lawsuit filed by the church after the city prohibited it from expanding by moving into a vacant grocery store. See "Elsinore Church Settles Worship Location Suit for $1.2 Million," Associated Press State & Local Wire, July 19, 2007.

124. Diana B. Henriques, "Religion Trumps Regulation as Legal Exemptions Grow," *New York Times*, October 8, 2006, Section 1, Column 5, page 1.

125. Nina J. Crimm and Laurence H. Winer, *Politics, Taxes, and the Pulpit* (Oxford: Oxford University Press, 2010), 92.

126. Crimm and Winer, *Politics, Taxes, and the Pulpit*, 59–60.

127. Mullin, "Federalism," 215.

128. See Whittington, "Taking What They Give Us."

129. Jelen, *To Serve God and Mammon*, 60–61.

130. Alison Gash and Angelo Gonzales, "School Prayer," in Persily, Citrin, and Egan, *Public Opinion and Constitutional Controversy*, 68–69.

131. Alison Gash and Angelo Gonzales, "School Prayer," 68–69.

132. Pew Forum for Religion and Public Life, Washington, DC, *U.S. Religious Landscape Survey*, 2008.

133. Devins, "The Majoritarian Rehnquist Court," 65.

134. Devins, "The Majoritarian Rehnquist Court," 71.

135. Whittington, "Taking What They Give Us," 498; see also Whittington, "Dismantling the Modern State?," 483.

136. Whittington, "Taking What They Give Us," 499–500.

137. Alan Wolfe, *The Transformation of American Religion: How We Actually Live Our Faith* (Chicago: University of Chicago Press, 2003), 37–67.

138. See Robert Wuthnow, *America and the Challenges of Religious Diversity* (Princeton, NJ: Princeton University Press, 2005).

139. See Roger Finke and Rodney Stark, *The Churching of America: Winners and Losers in Our Religious Economy* (Camden, NJ: Rutgers University Press, 1992). The Fink/Stark thesis is controversial and by no means universally accepted by church-state scholars.

140. *McDonald v. Chicago*, 130 S. Ct. 3020, 3112 (2010) (Stevens, J., dissenting).

141. *McDonald v. Chicago*, 130 S. Ct. 3020, 3057 (2010) (Stevens, J., dissenting).

142. *McDonald v. Chicago*, 130 S. Ct. 3020, 3122 (2010).

143. *Arizona Christian School Tuition Organization v. Winn*, 131 S. Ct. 1436, 1448 (2011).

The five-justice majority viewed *Flast v. Cohen*, 392 U.S. 83 (1968), as defining the conditions under which taxpayers could sue. *Flast* established that taxpayer lawsuits could proceed only if the plaintiff attacked government spending and linked that spending to a specific constitutional prohibition.

144. Amicus curiae brief in *Arizona Christian School Tuition Organization v. Winn*, submitted by Indiana, Michigan, Alabama, Colorado, Florida, Georgia, Louisiana, Mississippi, Pennsylvania, South Carolina, Texas, Utah, and Washington, 2010 U.S. S. Ct. Briefs LEXIS 1019 (August 6, 2010), 3.

145. 401 U.S. 37 (1971).

146. Amicus curiae brief in *Arizona Christian School Tuition Organization v. Winn*, submitted by the Center for Constitutional Jurisprudence, 2010 U.S. S. Ct. Briefs LEXIS 999 (August 5, 2010), 5.

147. Amicus curiae brief in *Arizona Christian School Tuition Organization v. Winn*, submitted by the Rutherford Institute, 2010 U.S. S. Ct. Briefs LEXIS 1022 (August 6, 2010), 28.

148. Amicus curiae brief in *Arizona Christian School Tuition Organization v. Winn*, submitted by the Becket Fund for Religious Liberty, 2010 U.S. S. Ct. Briefs LEXIS 1030 (August 6, 2010).

149. R. Shep Melnick, "Deregulating the States: The Political Jurisprudence of the Rehnquist Court," in *Institutions and Public Law: Comparative Approaches*, ed. Tom Ginsburg and Robert A. Kagan (New York: Peter Lang, 2005), 82.

5

Federalism and Globalization

For nearly the past two decades the U.S. Supreme Court has crafted its new federalism jurisprudence to devolve power to the states and insulate their policymaking from federal oversight. So far the Court's reassessment of federalism primarily concerns domestic policy issues. In respect to the judicial regulation of federal and state policymaking in foreign affairs, the Rehnquist and Roberts Courts have gone in a different direction by jealously protecting the federal government from state encroachments. As political scientists Timothy J. Conlan and Robert Dudley document in their study of the new federalism judicial politics, the Supreme Court has steadfastly followed a constitutional presumption that "any state activity that touches on foreign affairs" is preempted.[1] Two cases, *Crosby v. National Foreign Trade Council*[2] and *American Insurance Association v. Garamendi*[3] illustrate the principle. In *Crosby* a Massachusetts law that prohibited its state agencies from contracting with companies doing business with the Burmese government was struck down unanimously, even though the legislation was aimed at bringing economic pressure to bear on Burma to force it to respect human rights and democratic values. In *Garamendi* a California law requiring foreign insurance companies to address outstanding claims by Holocaust survivors was likewise invalidated because the legislation interfered with national prerogatives.

While the Roberts Court has not yet had the opportunity to deviate from settled doctrine, in *Medellin v. Texas* a divided Court refused to stop a Mexican national's execution on the grounds that the defendant was not given access to the Mexican consulate, a right he claimed under the Vienna Convention on Consular Relations (a multilateral treaty signed by the United States, Mexico, and many other nation-states).[4] In a similar case, *Sanchez-Llamas v. Oregon*, the Court also ruled that the Vienna Convention on Consular Relations did not explicitly require state courts to vacate criminal convictions when a defendant foreign national was not given consulate access.[5] While the cases did not involve direct state interference with national foreign policies, both implicitly raised salient federalism issues because they spoke to the constitutional issue of whether the exercise of state police powers can influence federal treaty obligations.[6] The increasing persistence in states in imposing their foreign policy directives on the federal government—and whether the Roberts Court will reverse the traditional direction of its judicial policymaking in the foreign affairs realm—remains an ongoing source of controversy in the political science and legal academies.

Accordingly, this chapter explores the issue further by evaluating whether the Court will increasingly find it difficult to apply the foreign policy preemption principle in the cases it is likely to hear as the Roberts Court matures. Just as the structural climate supporting centralization and the nationalization of policy issues morphed in the twentieth century into a structure that is more receptive to the devolution of power to the states, the onset of a rapidly changing international order suggests that the Supreme Court may be forced to reconfigure its approach to foreign policy preemption for two reasons.

First, the international system has witnessed a structural change from above, a phenomenon that has begun to transform the global order of unitary nation-states into a system that empowers subfederal units such as the American states. Many international relations scholars observe that the international order is undergoing a process of fragmentation that displaces and removes sovereign nation-states, such as the United States of America, as the sole source of international policymaking.[7] As a conceptual and historical matter, the world order has been premised on the continued existence of a global community of unitary sovereign states, with each having an independent and equal capacity to engage in international relations. In this sense, sovereign states, such as the United States, are thought to speak with one voice regardless of the contrary pressures exerted on the polity by its subfederal units. Put differently, the federal government is deemed the "sole representative of the United States in its dealings with foreign governments."[8] Nevertheless, the fragmentation of the international system into smaller units has meant that subfederal units themselves, along with other actors such as nongovernmental organizations (NGOs), are increasingly given a larger role in the conduct of international affairs than previously known. Indeed, the international system of unitary sovereign states is becoming an interrelated network of policymakers and institutions that operate independently from unitary states. For international law scholar Anne-Marie Slaughter, "A new world order is emerging. . . . The [unitary] state is not disappearing, it is disaggregating into separate, functionally distinct parts." "These parts—courts, regulatory agencies, executives, and even legislatures—are networking," she explains, "with their counterparts abroad, creating a dense web of relations that constitutes a new, transgovernmental order."[9] As a reflection of a structural shift from above, the disaggregation of the international state system greatly affects the relationship between, and policymaking of, the international community and its subfederal units.

The second factor influencing federal preemption of state foreign policy is a change from below, one initiated by subfederal states. Of their own initiative, and generally independently of national or international pressures, states are immersing themselves in new forms of policymaking that are distinguishable from past norms and practices. In the latter half of the twentieth century, state governments have become increasingly activist in foreign affairs despite the Supreme Court's traditional resistance to the states adopting a more proactive role in foreign affairs policymaking. For example, they have taken the lead in establishing their presence in directing economic policymaking initiatives that connect them to international trading partners, foreign markets for a state's exports, and more foreign direct investment (FDI).[10] By the close of the twentieth century, American states and cities pursuing these international ties had incorporated themselves as "an accepted aspect of American foreign economic policy."[11] On a different level, states have become more conspicuous in promoting morals legislation, especially as a vehicle to launch new legal policy change that advances human rights, democratization, and environmental policies, such as greenhouse gas emissions and global warming regulation. As examples, states and local governments passed ordinances and laws in the 1980s restricting government contracting with South Africa as a protest against the white apartheid government, and similar laws targeting the governments of Burma (Myanmar) and Sudan were passed in the 1990s to encourage those regimes to recognized basic human rights. Unlike the Burma sanction law declared unconstitutional in *Crosby*, the South African sanction laws were never litigated in federal courts even though the federal government questioned their constitutionality.[12] In contrast to the structural shift at the international level, where sovereign governments and international organizations develop networks that invite participation from subfederal units such as American states, the American states themselves are engaged in a structural shift of their own creation, from below the international level, that seeks a more prominent international role for the states. In contrast to the structural shift at the international level, where sovereign governments and international organizations develop networks that invite participation from subfederal units, the American states are responsible for creating another type of structural shift percolating beneath the international level—namely, one pushing for an expanded role for states in international relations.

The disaggregation of the international system and the increasing foreign policy activism of American states are two structural changes that significantly implicate federalism and foreign policy. Both factors resemble the structural shifts among political elites and institutions that undergird the rise of the Supreme Court's new federalism jurisprudence in domestic politics. The intellectual context lying beneath the Rehnquist and Roberts Courts' judicial behavior matters greatly, since new federalism legal policy is driven by justices "who regard federalism as an important priority and who are willing to exploit opportunities to advance that cause."[13]

Still, judicial ideology is not the overriding explanatory factor that dictates policy outcomes. In acknowledging the Court's turn toward favoring a state-centric brand of federalism, political scientist Neal Devins asserts that the Court's turn to federalism is linked to a shifting social and political climate that now devalues centralized governance in many policy areas and instead places more public trust in state and local institutions to solve many issues. Thus the Court's federalism cases "match popular distrust of Congress and the corresponding demise of the New Deal/Great Society nation-state."[14] For political scientist Keith Whittington, the Court's new federalism is shaped not only by the constitutional priorities of contemporary justices but also by "shifts in the underlying political structures."[15] Just as the rise of the new administrative state in the twentieth century corresponds with federalism decisions validating the progressive aims of the New Deal and Great Society, which in turn tilted the balance of federalism away from the states and toward the national government, the present movement in an opposite direction is oriented by a structural shift away from centralization. The emerging decentralization thus suggests that the states will play a prominent role setting the national policy agenda and solving social problems. Even so, the Supreme Court's new federalism is confined to the domestic realm and does not constrain the federal government's foreign affairs powers. As such, under current legal doctrine any perceived state intrusions remain presumptively unconstitutional. After a general survey of federalism principles and the degree to which they inculcate constitutional values and foreign affairs policy, the chapter presents a more nuanced analysis of the Court's foreign affairs policymaking in cases that remain in tension with the exercise of state and national powers.

FEDERALISM, THE CONSTITUTION, AND FOREIGN POLICY PREEMPTION

The attempt by states to influence foreign affairs is a long-standing tradition that is as old as the republic itself. Historically states have maintained an active presence in U.S. foreign policy; yet they play only a minimal role as direct participants in the international system.[16] Often states act in concert with the federal government to promote foreign policy change, as evidenced by the cooperative efforts of the Great Lakes states, the federal government, and Canada to regulate key natural resources through the Great Lakes Compact or, in another example, the mutual attempt to foster private and international marketplace competition through the North American Free Trade Agreement. In addition, with Congress's permission new state-federal partnerships have been created to advance compatible economic goals through treaty negotiations with foreign powers.[17]

Independent state action in foreign policy, however, is very much at odds with the conventional role states assume in American federalism. Constitutional law scholar Louis Henkin goes as far as to say that "at the end of the 20th century . . . [as] regards U.S. foreign policy[,] the states do not exist."[18] The states' invisibility in foreign policy means that their influence only extends to the point where Congress and the president acquiesce in state involvement. That the Constitution commits broad foreign policy powers to the federal government is, and to a degree always has been, in dispute. The Constitution textually reserves international commerce and treaty power to Congress, and it specifically denies several foreign policy powers to the states, including the treaty power. In contrast, the Constitution commits broad foreign policy power to the president, ranging from the signing of treaties (contingent on ratification by the Senate) to the appointment of American ambassadors (and reception of foreign ones). Consequently, by the end of the twentieth century there was little disagreement that the federal government is assigned a singularly unique constitutional place in matters of foreign policy, thereby significantly diminishing the role of states.[19]

Not surprisingly, the Supreme Court has responded in kind by creating federalism doctrines that protect against the threats states pose to the national government's constitutional authority in foreign affairs. Although the general federal judiciary is reluctant to weigh in on the substance or merits of foreign policy, the high court has actively policed the boundaries of power between states and the national government. In doing so, it has created an array of interpretive canons that presume that any state interference with national power is unconstitutional. For example, in a way that is identical to the Court's decision-making under the dormant commerce clause (discussed in chapter 3), state interference with congressional and federal power over international commerce is also generally disfavored. Furthermore, the doctrine of federal common law in foreign relations creates federal rules of decision that govern foreign relations.[20] These federalism doctrines are preemptive of state power and derive from the national government's powers over foreign affairs and constitutional federalism principles.

Foreign policy preemption doctrine also needs to be placed within the context of the Supreme Court's historical understanding of how the United States acts as a member of the international community. The classic and standard view of the international community is that it is comprised of unitary sovereign states, each with the capacity to engage in international relations with other sovereign states. This view of the world system is deeply ingrained in American political and constitutional thought. For example, one consistent theme of the Federalist Papers was that the national government must be able to successfully engage other nations in the international community in order to ensure effective government at home.[21] The Federalist Papers especially noted that one of the main weaknesses of confederations was their inability to maintain themselves in the international community. In Federalist No. 3, for example, John Jay perceived that the United States' commercial interactions with Britain, Portugal, Spain, and Prussia were of "high importance to the peace of America." Not only did Jay counsel that the United States must observe existing international law in its relations with those powerful empires; Jay also worried that the young nation's success in this regard "will be more perfectly and punctually done by one national government [as opposed to] either by thirteen separate States or by three or four distinct confederacies."[22] The assumptions that Jay made—which were premised on the key notion that the United States had to assimilate well into the international system in order to remain free from foreign threats—largely depended on the kind of government the United States turned out to be. Avoiding the appearance of being weak was equally vital. His reasoning underscored these assumptions. In his words, if foreign powers "see that our national government is efficient and well administered, our trade prudently regulated, our militia properly organized and disciplined, our resources and finances discreetly managed, our credit re-established . . . they will be much more disposed to cultivate our friendship than provoke our resentment."[23]

James Madison and Alexander Hamilton echoed Jay's arguments for a strong national government with the ability to speak for and represent the concerns of thirteen states. Writing as one in Federalist Nos. 19 and 20, they analyzed the Germanic, Swiss, and Dutch confederacies of the sixteenth and seventeenth centuries to argue that confederacies, if conceptually premised on a "sovereignty over sovereigns" framework, cannot withstand threats from outside their polities. Thus, using the Germanic confederacy to illustrate the point, Madison and Hamilton asserted that it was only able to survive in a weakened state because, in part, it was in the interests of foreign governments to keep it weak.[24] They were even more dismissive of Poland's confederacy, which "has long been at the mercy of its powerful neighbors, who have lately had the mercy to disburden it of one third of its people and territories." The Swiss confederacy was kept together partly due to "the fear of powerful neighbors," but the loose organization of cantons that "scarcely amounts to a confederacy" had resulted in divisive international relations premised on religious divisions in Swiss society: "It produced opposite alliances with foreign powers: of Berne, as the head of the Protestant association with the United Provinces [the Netherlands]; and of Luzerne, as the head of the Catholic association, with France."[25] The Federalists also examined the United Netherlands, a confederacy of republics consisting of coequal and sovereign states, to accentuate the point that its foreign affairs decisions must be based on unanimity among states. For the Federalists, the Dutch constitution is celebrated "as delineated on parchment" but working in practice toward "imbecility in the government; discord among the provinces; foreign influence and indignities; [and] a precarious existence in peace and peculiar calamities from war."[26] For Madison and Hamilton, only by ignoring their own constitution requiring unanimity of all states were the United Provinces able to conduct foreign affairs.

In Federalist Nos. 42 and 44, Madison brought his understanding of the histories of confederations to bear on the specific provisions of the 1787 Constitution. Federalist No. 42 focused on the comprehensive foreign affairs powers of the national government, as defined by the Constitution. He noted, "This class of powers forms an obvious and essential branch of the federal administration." "If we are to be one nation," he reasoned, "it clearly ought to be in respect to other nations."[27] Constitutionally vesting in the federal government broad foreign affairs authority is necessary so that the United States can speak with one voice. As illustrations he pointed to the treaty power, the power to appoint and receive ambassadors (the power over diplomacy), and the constitutional provision that removes from the states the power to define and punish piracy and felonies committed on the high seas. With his observation that a felony is "not precisely the same in any two of the States . . . and varies in each with every revision of its criminal laws,"[28] Madison inferred that the multiple state definitions of criminal felonies could only disrupt the national government's capacity to prosecute felonies committed on the high seas—a clear instance of state interference with federal policy. Furthermore, in Federalist No. 44 Madison addressed the constitutional prohibitions on state governments. In a concise discussion explaining why states are prohibited from making treaties and foreign alliances, Madison expressed his conviction that removing those powers from state control "is fully justified by the advantage of uniformity."[29] The piracy and treaties clauses, coupled with Article VI's supremacy clause, operated to "ensure that the United States, as a sovereign power, would be able and willing to take part in international transactions on a plane of equality with other sovereign powers."[30]

The Federalists make clear that the union of thirteen states will only succeed if the national government is vested with enough power to speak on behalf of all states. In one sense they appeal to the significance of cultivating "national self-respect and a sense of collective honor in dealing with outsiders,"[31] or foreign sovereign governments. Their contemporaneous analysis of European confederations demonstrates in stark terms the problems governments face when they are weak and incapable of conducting foreign relations, ostensibly because the parts of the whole undermine the collective. Put differently, the guiding presumption of the founders in designing the 1787 Constitution was that the individual states would be reduced to having only a minimal role in conducting the foreign affairs of the new United States.

Early commentators studying the American Constitution and its political history agreed with the Federalists' framing rationale regarding foreign affairs powers. The principle that the Constitution structurally empowered the federal government to speak for the nation in international affairs also meant that the states were prohibited from meddling with foreign affairs policy. U.S. Supreme Court Justice Joseph Story asserted, for instance, that the constitutional restrictions on state powers foreclosed the states from making their own treaties, for it was "utterly subversive" to national policy to otherwise "hazard the peace of the union."[32] The early Supreme Court adopted Story's reasoning and his operative assumption that the international system is comprised of unitary sovereign states in several judicial opinions. After the mid-1800s the justices shared the view that authorizing the states to conduct foreign policy ran the considerable risk of allowing selfish state interests to disadvantage national interests and create conflict with one unitary national policy.[33] In *Cohens v. Virginia,* Chief Justice John Marshall reaffirmed that the United States is constituted as a union of states that must speak with one voice. Although *Cohens* is unrelated to federal preemption because its main focus was defining the jurisdictional parameters of federal and state powers, Marshall emphasized the nature of the union in dicta when he declared,

> That the United States form, for many, and for most important purposes, a single nation, has not yet been denied. In war, we are one people. In making

> peace we are one people. In all commercial regulations, we are one and the same people . . . and the government which is alone capable of controlling and managing their interests in all these respects is the government of the Union.[34]

In other words, the great powers of foreign affairs—the power to make war and peace—were exclusively within the province of the federal government, which vicariously acted as one on behalf of the states.

Subsequently, in *Holmes v. Jennison*, Chief Justice Roger Taney announced for the Court the constitutional principle that a state cannot extradite a fugitive to a foreign government. To do so undercuts national policy because, under the Constitution, "all the powers which relate to our foreign intercourse are confided to the general government."[35] The federal government's foreign affairs policymaking, he reasoned, excludes state power because "it was one of the main objects of the Constitution to make us, so far as regarded our foreign relations, one people, and one nation; and to cut off all communications between foreign governments, and the several state authorities." As a result, he asserted that the power claimed by the states "is utterly incompatible with [the framer's] intention . . . and [it] would expose us to one of those dangers, against which the framers of the Constitution have so anxiously endeavoured to guard."[36] The Supreme Court reiterated Taney's reasoning several years later in *Chy Lung v. Freeman*, a case addressing if a state could regulate alien immigration on the grounds of public health and safety. In rebuffing the state's legislation, it extended the federal government's exclusive authority over foreign affairs by reminding the state that it could not exercise its police powers to regulate immigration. The Court reasoned, in other words, that

> the passage of laws which concern the admissions of citizens and subjects of foreign nations to our shores belongs to Congress, and not to the States. It has the power to regulate commerce with foreign nations: the responsibility for the character of those regulations, and for the manner of their execution, belongs solely to the national government. If it be otherwise, a single State can, at her pleasure, embroil us in disastrous quarrels with other nations.[37]

In another significant precedent, the *Chinese Exclusion Case* in 1889, the Supreme Court upheld a federal law that adjusted the terms of a treaty between the United States and China. Although the ruling did not directly implicate an encroachment of federal powers by the state, the Court in dicta affirmed the growing principle that "the United States, in their relation to foreign countries and their subjects or citizens are one nation." Consequently, "the government which is alone capable of controlling and managing their interests . . . is the government of the Union."[38]

That the U.S. government represents all of the states in foreign relations was the focus of the landmark precedent *United States v. Pink.* Decided during World War II, the case arose out of a conflict between the United States and the state of New York over the jurisdiction of property implicated by an executive agreement President Franklin Delano Roosevelt negotiated and signed with the Soviet Union to settle long-running property disputes arising out of the Russian Revolution. The case's outcome, which ratified the agreement and underscored the importance of letting the federal government represent the national interest in foreign affairs, declared,

> The field which affects international relations is "the one aspect of our government that from the first has been most generally conceded imperatively to demand broad national authority" and that any state power which may exist "is restricted to the narrowest of limits." . . . If state laws and policies did not yield before the exercise of the external powers of the United States, then our foreign policy might be thwarted. These are delicate matters. If state action could defeat or alter our foreign policy, serious consequences might ensue.[39]

Subsequent cases, such as *Japan Line, Ltd. v. County of Los Angeles*, adhered to *Pink*'s rationale by reiterating that "in international relations and with respect to foreign intercourse and trade the people of the United States act through a single government with unified and adequate national power."[40]

Moreover, *Zschernig v. Miller* remains a classic statement of the foreign affairs preemption presumption and its premise that foreign relations are "matters which the Constitution entrusts solely to the Federal Government." The dispute centered on Oregon's property inheritance law, which was enacted in the 1960s. It prohibited an alien from inheriting property in Oregon if that alien's home country did not have similar laws allowing the inheritance of property free from government confiscation. The state law was squarely aimed at Communist bloc countries that maintained the power to seize and confiscate private property without due process protections for the owner. As such, the Oregon legislature's alien inheritance prohibition was a political response to the Cold War and its global ideological implications. The Court's holding, which invalidated Oregon's law, is reinforced by the legal reasoning embodied in two contemporary cases, *Crosby v. National Foreign Trade Council* and *American Insurance Association v. Garamendi*.

In writing for the Court in *Zschernig*, for example, Justice William O. Douglas chose not to explore the legislative history or purpose behind Oregon's alien inheritance law, but in reviewing analogous state court precedents interpreting identical statutes, he conceded that "foreign policy attitudes—the freezing or thawing of the cold war" are the "real desiderata" of the law.[41] Justice Douglas concluded that the Oregon law impeded the federal government's exclusive control of foreign policy, even though it was only a minimal interference with federal power, writing that it "affects international relations in a persistent and subtle way" and is not a "gross intrusion" into federal power. The Court's conclusion determined that Oregon interfered with the powers of the federal government broadly defined since its law "has a direct impact upon foreign relations and may well adversely affect the power of the central government to deal with those problems."[42] Whereas Douglas's opinion for the Court did not actually stipulate that the state law specifically ran afoul of an explicit constitutional provision, the operative rationale registered a broad construction of federal foreign affairs authority. In this way the preemption principle retains the potential to cover a range of undefined activities that only tangentially address the underlying issue of whether the states could ever mount an effective challenge to federal prerogatives in this area of law and policy. In contrast, *Crosby* and *Garamendi* dealt with more direct state encroachments, thus allowing the Court to narrowly apply the constitutional principle to the exercise of specific powers, as framed by the broader purposes of the U.S. Constitution.

At issue in *Crosby v. National Foreign Trade Council* was the constitutionality of a Massachusetts law barring state agencies from doing business with corporations and individuals with economic ties with Burma. The state law linked Massachusetts's economic power as a marketplace participant to a laudable human rights goal: the furtherance of the democratization movement in Burma. Massachusetts, like Oregon, sought to influence "foreign policy attitudes," but instead of using inheritance law, it used its economic purchasing power to make a political statement and set public policy. Regardless, the Court struck the state law down as unconstitutional. Unlike *Zschernig*, in which the Court construed preemption broadly as a means to safeguard the federal government's general powers over foreign affairs, *Crosby* interpreted the Massachusetts law as a direct and continuous intrusion into federal power that interfered with explicit congressional and presidential policies toward Burma.

Using *Gibbons v. Ogden* as a controlling precedent, the Rehnquist Court reiterated that it is a "fundamental principle of the Constitution" to give Congress the license to preempt state legislation under certain conditions.[43] For example, the "entire scheme of the statute must be considered" in regard to its implied and express purposes. After acknowledging that Congress enacted a comprehensive federal statute to regulate U.S. relations with the Burmese government, the justices then weighed if the Massachusetts law was an "obstacle to the accomplishment of Congress's full objectives." In drawing the critical conclusion that it did stand as an obstacle, the Court reasoned that the state law ran afoul of federal law and the Constitution in three respects. First, Congress expressly gave the president "flexible and effective authority over economic sanctions against Burma." This created an inherent conflict between Massachusetts policy and the president's authority because it created a "state system of economic pressure against the Burmese political regime . . . [by] penaliz[ing] some private action that the federal Act (as administered by the President) may allow, [thereby] pull[ing] levers of influence that the federal Act does not reach."[44] Second, the state law operated to penalize individuals and conduct that the federal law explicitly exempted from sanctions. Third, through its articulation of a foreign policy favoring democratization and human rights in Burma, the state law remained "at odds with the President's intended authority to speak for the United States." In this fashion the public policy that Massachusetts established in foreign affairs compromises "the very capacity of the President to speak for the Nation with one voice."[45]

The Court's *Crosby* preemption decision broadly considered whether state law interfered with Congress's express delegation of power to the executive while solidifying the president's executive power to lead the nation on international issues. Whereas *Zschernig* adjudged the state law to be unconstitutional on the ground that it tangentially interfered with the foreign affairs powers of the national government, *Crosby* concluded the state law discretely impeded specific congressional and presidential powers that were exercised under the general parameters of the federal government's control over foreign relations.

Near the end of the Rehnquist Court era, *American Insurance Association v. Garamendi* was decided. There, through the passage of its Holocaust Victim Insurance Relief Act, California required insurance companies doing business in the state to disclose policyholder information about the insurance they sold to persons in Europe between 1920 and 1945. The law's purpose was to protect the interests of those deprived of insurance monies that they were owed when the Nazis rose to power. Many of the insurance policies covered Jews who were deported to concentration camps during the Holocaust. After the war, insurance companies often refused to honor the policies, even those that had not been seized, because the premiums had not remained current or the policies specified no heirs. In some instances, insurance companies denied the existence of life insurance policies outright. California's law, therefore, was a response to an ongoing debate over how best to resolve disputes over life insurance policies that were seized by the Nazi regime.

The case implicated foreign policy because President Bill Clinton signed an executive agreement with German chancellor Gerhard Schroder in 2000. Under the agreement Germany would create a multi-billion-dollar fund to compensate those who suffered under the Nazi era, so the fund retroactively covered payment of life insurance policies that were seized. In return, the U.S. federal government pledged to use its best efforts to halt litigation against German companies seeking judicial relief in American courts. The federal government's position on settling Holocaust-era insurance claims focused on mediated settlements instead of ongoing litigation to satisfy the victims' claims.

A divided Supreme Court, speaking through Justice David Souter, struck down California's law as an unconstitutional interference with the president's foreign affairs powers. As the Court reminded the state, "Although the source of the President's power to act in foreign affairs does not enjoy any textual detail, the historical gloss on the 'executive Power' vested in Article II of the Constitution has recognized the President's 'vast share of responsibility for the conduct of our foreign relations.'"[46] The majority acknowledged the California law was similar to the Massachusetts law that was reviewed in *Crosby*, observing that it applied economic pressure to achieve its legislative purpose. As applied, therefore, the California legislation "undercuts the President's diplomatic discretion" by meddling with the president's authority to use the "coercive power of the national economy as a tool of diplomacy" as he saw fit. In this sense enforcement of the California law frustrated the president's ability to use economic and diplomatic leverage and, accordingly, diminished "the very capacity of the President to speak for the Nation with one voice in dealing with other governments to resolve claims against European companies arising out of World War II."[47]

Significantly, the result is distinguishable from *Crosby*'s outcome and its underlying rationale. Whereas in *Crosby* the Supreme Court unanimously held federal law preempted the Massachusetts law directed at affecting the oppressive conditions in Burma, *Garamendi* yielded a more controversial result that divided the justices in a 5–4 vote. In addition, the dissenting justices, led by Ruth Bader Ginsburg, did not take issue with the foreign affairs preemption principle itself; rather, they objected to the majority's inference that the president clearly sought to preempt state policymaking in this instance. Specifically, the dissent reasoned that the executive agreements between the United States, Germany, and other countries established a mechanism to resolve Holocaust insurance claims, and federal law is silent about whether there should be preemption. As a consequence it was unclear at best if the executive branch intended to preempt state law, especially since the Court's majority could only vaguely refer to statements by individual members of the executive branch to support its conclusions about intent and preemption. Quite simply, using statements by the executive branch as a basis to decide the case on the critical issue of whether federal law preempts state law is not enough proof. The evidentiary bar was much higher, said Justice Ginsburg, who concluded that "the displacement of state law by preemption properly requires a considerably more formal and binding federal instrument."[48] The dissent's application of process federalism, discussed in chapter 3, led to a different outcome insofar as the dissent used it to argue that California's law did not compromise the president's ability to speak with one voice for the nation. "To the contrary," Ginsburg wrote, "by declining to invalidate [the law] . . . we would reserve foreign affairs preemption for circumstances where the President, acting under statutory or constitutional authority, has spoken clearly to the issue at hand."[49] In this light the dissenting justices insisted that the Court's interpretation of a clear statement rule could only vest in California the autonomy to regulate the settlement of Holocaust-era insurance claims, a result that was also justified because the federal government was not explicit about preempting state power under these circumstances.

One final point about *Garamendi* is worth noting. Several states joined with California in a separate amicus brief to argue that California's law is not preempted.[50] The brief emphasized the significance of Congress's regulatory power over foreign commerce by asserting that the political branches must expressly declare in federal law that state laws are to be displaced. Their position significantly relied upon two prominent Rehnquist Court new federalism precedents. In citing to *Alden v. Maine* and *Morrison v. Olsen*, the amici argued that state insurance regulations normally are protected under the Constitution's federal structure, even in circumstances that intersect with the federal government's powers over international affairs.[51] Using *Alden* as a guide, the brief reasoned that requiring Congress to explicitly and clearly preempt state regulations of commerce is "consistent with the requirements of the Tenth Amendment . . . [and] this Court has explained that 'caution should be exercised before concluding that unstated limitations on state power were intended by the Framers.'"[52] Moreover, under *Morrison*, the Court ought to recognize that California's Holocaust insurance policy falls under the general police powers reserved to the states, and a state's broad authority to protect its citizens "is deeply ingrained in our constitutional history."[53] In this fashion the states' brief linked the preemption doctrine to foreign policy, raising issues that are central to the interpretation of the Tenth Amendment, using state-friendly precedents (*Morrison* and *Alden*). In doing so, the amici sought to extend the Rehnquist Court's new federalism to an area of constitutional law that has traditionally barred state policymaking interference. Still, these arguments were not accepted by the majority and did not become a part of *Garamendi*'s controlling rationale.

This short survey of the Court's judicial interpretation of the doctrine of foreign policy preemption is not meant to be exhaustive. Rather, it is only illustrative of the consistent line of reasoning the Court has developed over time. While exceptions remain, the evidence is relatively clear that justices have elected to limit state power time and again in this area of new federalism jurisprudence. The next section begins to offer more detailed explanations of the implications of that line of judicial reasoning.

STRUCTURAL SHIFT FROM ABOVE

The Court's historical understanding of the international system as comprised of sovereign, unitary states partially justifies its legal view of foreign policy preemption. However, the Court's perspective does not match, and in many ways is out of sync with, recent disaggregation trends in the international system of states. Well-known international relations scholars concur that the world order is undergoing a critical transformation, one that had been premised on the key notion that unitary sovereign states engage with each other in bi- and multilateral rulemaking through conventions and treaties with other sovereign states. The new trend encapsulates the evolution and emergence of a new world order that is based on the existence of multiple "disaggregated" states. Under this view, national and subnational institutions develop networks of institutions and policymakers that address specific and common problems. For international relations scholars Robert Keohane and Joseph Nye, this type of globalization leads to the creation of interconnected networks that remain interdependent. Although the sovereign nation-state is not completely disappearing, and indeed remains the most important actor in global politics, it "is being supplemented by other actors—private and third sector."[54] Thus, in world politics, new agents have become active policymakers, and their identity ranges from private corporations to nongovernmental organizations that effectively operate as "subunits of government."[55] International relations scholar Anne-Marie Slaughter, whose work augments that of Keohane and Nye, concludes,

> A new world order is emerging. . . . The state is not disappearing, it is disaggregating into separate, functionally distinct parts. These parts—courts, regulatory agencies, executives, and even legislatures—are networking with their counterparts abroad, creating a dense web of relations that constitutes a new, transgovernmental order.[56]

The disaggregation of the world system does not mean that the sovereign state is vanishing from view. It means, instead, that other actors, such as nonstate organizations (multinational corporations, NGOs) and subnational or subfederal units, are gaining greater influence over the realm and practice of international politics.

For political scientist Daniel Elazar, the changing nature of the international system has significant ramifications for federalism. In his estimation, the new international system of transgovernmental networks (instead of just having sovereign states interact with each other) will cause federal states to reconfigure their political relations. As he puts it,

> The implications of this paradigm shift are enormous. Whereas before every state strove for self-sufficiency, homogeneity . . . [and] the concentration of power in a single center, under the new paradigm all states have to recognize as well their interdependence, heterogeneity, and the fact that their centers, if they ever existed, are no longer single centers but parts of a multi-centered network.[57]

Legal scholar Yishai Blank argues in this vein that subnational governments, especially localities, must be "recast as independent semi-private entities . . . [which can] no longer [be thought of as] mere state agents subsumed by their national governments."[58] Earl Fry, another eminent federalism scholar, notes too that "the growing involvement of sub-national governments in the international arena will make it progressively more difficult for national governments to speak with one voice in the foreign policy arena."[59]

The disaggregation of the global state system creates new opportunities for conventional state actors to influence the global order. In other words, domestic and international NGOs, political elites, and institutions from outside a sovereign state will seek to develop networks with units from inside that state. The emergence of networks between political institutions and elites, as well as nongovernmental groups and organizations, suggests that subnational units in a federal system will constantly face political pressure from outside their polity to become engaged in international relations. International relations scholar Ivo Duchacek observes that states within a federal system have "become targets for trans-sovereign contacts of interference" insofar as they become a focused source of attention and policymaking from a federal government.[60] That is, NGOs, multinational corporations, and even supranational institutions that are affiliated with the United Nations or regional groups (such as the European Union) will bypass national institutions that normally have power to make foreign policy. Instead, they will try to develop relationships with subnational units in an effort to influence, or even circumvent, national institutions in matters of global and domestic policy. Simply put, the groups will lobby states and localities instead of exerting political pressure on national legislatures and executives to obtain policy goals and desirable legislation.

The evidence is mounting that the disaggregation is having an effect. Not only is the sheer number of NGOs increasing, but NGOs and multinational corporations are now more focused on policy entrepreneurship than in the past.[61] The development of policymaking networks among levels of government, key groups, and political elites transforms subnational governments (and American states) into "vehicles for the advancement of policies on a global scale."[62] NGOs are now emboldened to develop connections to states and local governments within the United States, and their efforts have often been concentrated on changing policies relating to the advancement of human rights and imposing sanctions against repressive regimes abroad. For example, many international NGOs and domestic interest groups combine to pressure states and localities to enact resolutions that are designed to move the United States toward ratifying key human rights instruments and protocols, including the Convention to Eliminate All Forms of Discrimination against Women. Some localities have responded, with many cities and counties passing resolutions calling for the federal ratification of certain treaties.[63] Notably there are "few direct links between sub-national governments and international decision-making structures," such as those provided by United Nations organizations and other international institutions.[64] But this means that the fragmentation of the world order has exposed "multiple ports of entry" in which subfederal governments in the United States can inculcate international laws domestically and by which NGOs and multinational corporations can lobby state and local governments to become active participants in international policymaking.[65]

A recent study of state lawmakers shows that the participants increasingly focus their policy attention on international issues at a greater rate than two decades ago. Furthermore, they are continuously solicited to engage in international policymaking efforts by interest groups, corporations, and NGOs on a domestic and global level. To illustrate, state legislators may respond to the international concerns of immigrant groups as expressed through their constituencies, or they may react to issues raised by organized groups based outside their districts.[66] Groups, moreover, lobby states in order to pass resolutions recognizing the Armenian genocide of the early twentieth century, agricultural groups and corporations have sought state assistance to lift the embargo against Cuba, and NGOs have pressured states and municipalities to enact climate change policies that would curb greenhouse gas emissions. This latter point is buttressed by the lobbying presence of the International Council for Local Environmental Initiatives (ICLEI), an entity that works with local governments across the United States to reduce greenhouse emissions at the local level.[67] Although such environmental policymaking is essentially local and thus far has had a marginal impact on U.S. foreign policy, the local character of the interest group activity has foreign policy dimensions, as when localities and states use their influence to express disagreement with the prerogatives of national policymaking that are not doing enough to reduce greenhouse gas emissions under the Kyoto Protocol.[68]

NGOs and domestic interest groups are not the only entities developing policymaking networks with states and localities. Foreign governments have likewise lobbied state institutions on international matters. Taiwan has persuaded several states to adopt resolutions favoring its membership in the World Trade Organization (WTO), and its lobbying efforts have been manifested by the sizable staff it maintains in regional offices throughout the United States, ostensibly to "bolster its . . . political clout within the United States" (even though it is not recognized as a sovereign government by the United States).[69] Mexico has lobbied states to accept the Mexican *matrícula consular* as a valid form of identification at the state level.[70] Also, in 2006 former British prime minister Tony Blair traveled to California to sign an agreement of cooperation between the United Kingdom and the state of California to combat global warming, brokered in part by an NGO called the Climate Group.[71]

The structural change in the global system is also highlighted by the policy arguments that were at the base of understanding the legislative purpose of Massachusetts's Burma law, which was reviewed and nullified in *Crosby v. National Foreign Trade Council* (discussed above in this chapter). The 1996 Massachusetts legislation prohibited the state government from contracting and doing business with corporations having economic ties to Burma (Myanmar). Other states and municipalities were also considering similar laws, mainly due to the growing perception that the federal government was slow in developing foreign policy that would encourage Burma to democratize and protect human rights. The primary lobbying efforts were led by state-based NGOs that worked under national and global groups that were advocating for political change in Burma. Massachusetts's response in passing the law demonstrated that "NGOs, working in tandem with local governments, pose a serious challenge to the autonomy of national governments" in foreign affairs.[72] Massachusetts governor William Weld linked the Burma law to other international initiatives and initially refused to sign it unless the state legislature amended laws affecting Northern Ireland. He had previously vetoed legislation that forced state businesses to report on human rights abuses in China, but that veto was overridden. Weld eventually signed the bill, but only after intensive lobbying by the NGOs (and after being thanked by African National Congress [ANC] officials for his support for similar anti-apartheid legislation during a state trip to South Africa).[73]

Although the Massachusetts law was struck down in *Crosby*, its legislative history raises several questions. The state's policy on Burma sanctions is illustrative of how state and local governments are pressured by domestic and international groups to take up certain international causes and how they are destined to confront the demands of constituents to address proactively the types of international causes that diverse ethnic and religious constituents support as a matter of public policy.[74] Aside from conflict between the national government and state and local governments, scholars agree that the increasing involvement of NGOs in foreign policy issues at the subfederal level implicates the basic legitimacy of state (and local) policymaking processes. Legal and federalism scholar Mark Tushnet argues, in fact, that the Massachusetts Burma law "exposes some novel facets of globalization's relation to U.S. federalism, particularly in showing NGOs as new actors on the sub-national scene."[75] Because the Burma law "resulted from the local actions of a transnational movement,"[76] it inherently raises questions about the political legitimacy of state policymaking, if for no other reason than knowing that group pressure "may lead to problems of government capture by transnational NGOs," a phenomenon that would permit outside groups to manipulate policy outcomes in the lobbying process.[77] In sum, as this section has disclosed, the structural changes taking place in the international system from above have important policy consequences for federalism. The next section, in contrast, considers the impact of structural changes originating from below the established international order.

STRUCTURAL CHANGE FROM BELOW

Coinciding with changes in the international system of states are revisions occurring at the subfederal level. In general, American states and municipalities have crafted their own foreign policies by their own initiatives, and these are considered structural changes from below. Instead of responding to international groups that have turned to subfederal units—as part of the disaggregated world order—American states pursue their own foreign policies as a response to global changes, especially those concerning economic globalization.[78] Importantly, states have pursued their own foreign policies for quite some time now, although their efforts are not usually effective and generally they have little impact on national policy. But since the 1960s, states and municipalities have been increasingly aggressive about maintaining an international presence relative to the general issue of international economic development, and there has been a concomitant desire among most states to cultivate an expanded marketplace for exports and to attract more foreign direct investment. The federal government has encouraged much state economic activity.[79] By 1969 four states had opened overseas trade offices, and by 1994 there were 162 state trade offices abroad, with each representing the international trade issues of all fifty states.[80] A recent federal survey of state trade offices shows that the decline in the total number of state-maintained overseas offices (most likely due to recessionary pressures on state budgets) has not diminished the fact that, on average, states staff five overseas offices, with each superintending international trade issues and related policy concerns.

Many of those offices now use contractors instead of state employees.[81] As state and local international economic policymaking has grown, the federal government has shown little interest in attempting to control it and indeed may not even be aware of the extent of state policymaking that regularly transpires, perhaps because federal agencies, such as the Departments of State and Commerce, appear to be confused about which agency has jurisdiction over specific aspects of state economic policymaking.[82] One scholar of state trade policies speculates that state governments have become increasingly liberated to "pursue their own policy priorities [and] to meet their economic and political needs[,] while the federal government cooperates by essentially ignoring the actions of the states." Stated differently, the rapid pace of state economic policymaking growth has meant that national oversight is minimal at best, thereby making states more "accustomed to engaging in international trade more or less independently."[83]

Indicative of increased state international economic activity is the tremendous growth in state exports outside the United States. Table 5.1 shows that all states over the past twenty-five years have experienced an exponential rise in their export markets, with a few states realizing far more dramatic growth than others. Some scholars observe that "U.S. economic competitiveness begins at the grassroots level,"[84] which, if true, makes it plausible to think that states and local governments will seek more outlets and markets for their domestic products, thereby greatly influencing their capacity to engage in policymaking related to foreign affairs.

As states emerge from the Great Recession of the first decade of the twenty-first century, policymakers realize that economic recovery and growth may very well hinge on the capacity of states to build and greatly expand their export economies. For the Council of State Governments, this means that states are beginning to appreciate that tax incentives may not do much to attract new businesses or to increase jobs and wages. In their view, states are "looking for new ways to develop the economy," and some have "a strong international component for economic development" that is considered "vital" to overall economic recovery.[85] A Brookings-Rockefeller report notes as well that "growing exports is a recipe for a job-filled recovery because it takes advantage of new sources of global demand," especially from consumers in developing nations, such as Brazil, India, and China, that are seeing progress in their purchasing power.[86] In order to develop additional export markets, some states are going so

Table 5.1. State Economic Policy, 1987–1996

State	*1987, in Millions of Dollars*	*1996, in Millions of Dollars*	*% Increase 1987–1996*	*2010, in Millions of Dollars*	*% Increase 1996–2010*
Alabama	1,483	3,703	149.70%	15,500	*318.58%*
Arizona	408	1,997	389.46%	15,700	*686.18%*
Arkansas	538	850	57.99%	4,200	*394.12%*
California	32,891	98,643	199.91%	143,300	*45.27%*
Colorado	4,848	10,065	107.61%	6,700	*–33.43%*
Connecticut	4,666	13,053	179.75%	16,000	*22.58%*
Delaware	2,724	4,585	68.32%	5,000	*9.05%*
Florida	7,804	19,618	151.38%	55,200	*181.37%*
Georgia	2,432	8,618	254.36%	28,700	*233.02%*
Hawaii	160	295	84.38%	685	*132.20%*
Idaho	412	1,610	290.78%	5,200	*222.98%*
Illinois	10,230	32,225	215.00%	49,800	*54.54%*
Indiana	3,743	12,119	223.78%	28,700	*136.82%*
Iowa	1,087	2,695	147.93%	10,900	*304.45%*
Kansas	1,877	4,971	164.84%	9,900	*99.16%*
Kentucky	1,720	5,824	238.60%	19,300	*231.39%*
Louisiana	2,979	4,731	58.81%	41,300	*772.97%*
Maine	534	1,249	133.90%	3,100	*148.20%*
Maryland	1,532	3,510	129.11%	10,200	*190.60%*
Massachusetts	8,298	15,368	85.20%	26,300	*71.13%*
Michigan	19,543	38,128	95.10%	44,500	*16.71%*
Minnesota	5,556	13,889	149.98%	18,900	*36.08%*
Mississippi	448	1,222	172.77%	8,300	*579.21%*
Missouri	3,384	6,591	94.77%	12,900	*95.72%*
Montana	148	341	130.41%	1,400	*310.56%*
Nebraska	329	2,453	645.59%	5,800	*136.45%*
Nevada	269	692	157.25%	5,900	*752.60%*
New Hampshire	662	1,745	163.60%	4,400	*152.15%*
New Jersey	7,649	18,458	141.31%	32,200	*74.45%*
New Mexico	117	684	484.62%	1,600	*133.92%*
New York	29,570	44,965	52.06%	67,700	*50.56%*
North Carolina	3,472	11,587	233.73%	28,400	*145.10%*
North Dakota	163	576	253.37%	2,500	*334.03%*
Ohio	6,468	22,555	248.72%	41,400	*83.55%*
Oklahoma	967	2,538	162.46%	5,400	*112.77%*
Oregon	3,117	8,481	172.09%	17,200	*102.81%*
Pennsylvania	7,167	17,446	143.42%	34,800	*99.47%*
Rhode Island	377	955	153.32%	1,900	*98.95%*
South Carolina	1,017	4,925	384.27%	20,300	*312.18%*
South Dakota	42	397	845.24%	1,300	*227.46%*
Tennessee	2,970	9,328	214.07%	25,900	*177.66%*
Texas	18,045	48,252	167.40%	20,6600	*328.17%*

(continued)

Table 5.1. (*continued*)

State	*1987, in Millions of Dollars*	*1996, in Millions of Dollars*	*% Increase 1987–1996*	*2010, in Millions of Dollars*	*% Increase 1996–2010*
Utah	667	2,769	315.14%	13,600	*391.15%*
Vermont	266	2,611	881.58%	4,400	*68.52%*
Virginia	3,148	10,926	247.08%	17,100	*56.51%*
Washington	10,317	25,498	147.15%	53,200	*108.64%*
West Virginia	656	1,218	85.67%	6,400	*425.45%*
Wisconsin	2,940	8,410	186.05%	19,800	*135.43%*
Wyoming	60	124	106.67%	938	*656.45%*

Source: Earl Fry, *The Expanding Role of State and Local Governments in U.S. Foreign Affairs* (New York: Council on Foreign Relations, 1998), 71–72; 2010 Data, Office of Trade and Economic Analysis, International Trade Administration, U.S. Department of Commerce; State Export Data, available at http://tse.export.gov/TSE/TSEhome.aspx. Last accessed June 14, 2011. 2010 data rounded to nearest hundredth.

far as to become marketable by using their own agricultural brands.[87] If the trend holds, and even though it largely remains under the auspices of the U.S. Department of Agriculture's Foreign Agriculture Service, the states' commitment to branding their products, and concomitantly to protecting those brands in the international marketplace, will likely foster greater potential for conflicts to arise due to competing state international agricultural and federal foreign policies. States will not only seek more markets for their exports but also act to attract more foreign direct investment for their own workers. Foreign-owned businesses operating in the United States tend to pay higher wages, and although there are variations by industry, they have more stable employment patterns. Still, states are likely to seek to draw in businesses with the potential to provide better wages and benefits for their workers.

States in the pursuit of favorable outcomes in the international marketplace affect federal law in another way. The United States is the world's largest recipient of foreign direct investment (FDI), which covers a wide range of economic activity from service provision to manufacturing and enterprise creation. The federal government notes the important role that states play in attracting FDI:

> Individual states compete (often against each other) for investments on a global scale. . . . [State] agencies play an important role in investment promotion and highlight the comparative advantage of their regions and localities. . . . This decentralized system has successfully operated for decades and has yielded billions of dollars in international investment.[88]

Just as the national government acknowledges the unique and important role that states play in attracting more FDI into the country, it also must appreciate the potential for exacerbating the tension between conflicting state and federal policies that intersect on the issues of immigration, visa requirements, national security, and commercial activities that connect the United States with other countries.

Given the increased participation of states in the international marketplace, it is not surprising to think that fiscal developments will continue to impact the federal-state relationship in the United States. Political scientist Keith Whittington links the dynamic and changing nature of fiscal politics with the structural changes in American politics that are at least partly responsible for the Supreme Court's commitment in its new federalism jurisprudence to increase state sovereignty and autonomy from federal meddling. Whereas the fiscal power of the federal government expanded in kind with the rise of the administrative state for a large part of the twentieth century, the pace of federal grants to the states has slowed, causing some observers to perceive the federal government "as providing the least amount of services per taxpayer dollar" while simultaneously noticing that "state governments have increasingly been lauded for their fiscal efficacy."[89] As federal dollars flowing to the states have become scarcer, the federal government's capacity to influence state policies has diminished as well. As a result, state and local governments, as Whittington points out, focus much more attention on their own fund-raising capacities and now claim almost as large a share of gross national product as the national government. In terms of revenue generation, "states and localities . . . are now competitors with the federal government for revenue."[90]

Accordingly, the impetus that drives the states to continue to push to expand their own export markets and FDI corresponds well with the structural changes in fiscal federalism that are in progress. States now actively recruit multinational corporations with special tax incentives and the prospect of buying low-cost land, as well as offering other amenities. One key example is Alabama's efforts to recruit Mercedes, a car manufacturer with a significant global presence, to build its first North American manufacturing plant in that state. Although critics questioned the high cost to attract only one manufacturing plant that would yield only approximately four hundred jobs, supporters countered that Mercedes had the potential to create indirectly around nine thousand jobs in its supporting industries, a finding that has led other automobile manufacturers (and even high-tech industries) to express an interest in relocating their production facilities to Alabama.[91] In addition to expanding their efforts to recruit international industries to their home states, other subfederal units go to significant lengths to wrest tax monies away from multinational corporations. The state of California, for example, operates a unitary tax structure for multinational corporations, which means that the share of corporate tax owed to the state is based on a corporation's total world income. Other states do the same, and such policy decisions have caused several foreign governments, including Britain and Japan, to begin to mediate their trade disputes with the representatives of the federal and state governments through intensive, multilayered diplomacy.[92]

The presence and significance of states working to reap the economic benefits found in the international marketplace also have been felt in noncommercial areas of substantive policy. By the mid-1970s states had started to design their own foreign policies because of their opposition to federal initiatives. Texas, a mineral rich state that does not necessarily have a keen interest in the volatility of oil and gas prices, acted directly against U.S. policy by sending state "observers" to meetings of the Organization of Petroleum Exporting Countries (OPEC) to monitor OPEC's decision-making as it met to set higher petroleum prices.[93] While there is no evidence that Texas influenced OPEC pricing policies, the state's presence provides reliable indicia that it sought some level of influence in taking advantage of the new role that states see for themselves in international relations. The "Sister Cities" program at the municipal level, which advocated the enactment of state and local resolutions favoring economic sanctions against corporations doing business in South Africa, and the creation by towns, cities, and counties of "nuclear-free zones" are other examples of how subfederal entities seek to influence foreign policy directed at the Cold War, apartheid in South Africa, and American nuclear defense policy. While noneconomic policymaking initiatives in foreign affairs tend to be sporadic and arguably "exert . . . a marginal impact on U.S. foreign policy outcomes,"[94] they nonetheless remain a significant benchmark in understanding the depth of state involvement in foreign policy.

The interaction between policy entrepreneurship in international affairs and the lobbying presence of state political elites in California presents another conspicuous example of the growing role that American states are likely to play in foreign relations in the future. In 2007 then governor Arnold Schwarzenegger's state of the state address argued that California ought to use its global influence to advance the state's economic progress. Referring to the fact that if it were a nation, it "would be the sixth largest economy in the world," and in the process comparing it to "the ancient city-states of Athens and Sparta," the governor proclaimed that California has "the economic strength . . . the population and the technological force of a nation-state."[95] While his remarks are open to differing interpretations, it is plausible that Schwarzenegger at a minimum was indirectly advocating that California was in the position to adapt a more proactive global role, one in which the state could easily use its considerable economic power to sustain a formidable international presence.

Schwarzenegger's comparison of California to Athens drew off of other aspects of the governor's domestic politics. While in office Schwarzenegger signed an agreement binding California and the United Kingdom to reduce greenhouse gas emissions. While the compact is of dubious constitutionality (states are prohibited from entering into treaties and compacts without federal congressional assent), California's action is an initial, if not bold, step to assert its leadership and commitment to advancing an environmental policy that the federal government (to date) has refused to follow on the politically controversial issue of global warming. California's initiative has been compared to the type of policymaking that member states in the European Union follow, given that those member states are still considered sovereign states by the international community.[96]

Somewhat paradoxically, Congress has often encouraged state participation in foreign policy as well. With Congress's consent, states are vested with the constitutional authority to enter into compacts with foreign governments, and historically Congress has often given them permission to do so. The historical record documents that states have become parties to agreements on international border issues (the regulation of bridges, highways, and waterways), as well as on cross-border environmental issues.[97] In fact, states often enter into agreements affecting intimate local border issues (such as the site for a drainage ditch or maintenance of a bridge that spans an international boundary) and occasionally do so on the unstated assumption that congressional assent will be given.[98] Moreover, state compacts entered into with feigned congressional assent may be more the norm than the exception, perhaps evidenced by the fact that Congress or the president may not act because they simply choose not to get involved or sometimes remain unaware of what the state is doing in its foreign affairs policymaking. As legal scholar Duncan Hollis explains,

> Congress rarely has any chance to opine on what states propose to do with foreign governments. . . . States simply do not submit their arrangements with foreign powers to Congress for approval. Thus Congress frequently has no knowledge—let alone view on—what the states might be doing abroad.[99]

To illustrate, Congress has not responded to the actions of several states in 2007 that joined the International Carbon Action Partnership, an initiative that promotes greenhouse gas–reduction policies in conjunction with several European states, European Union institutions, and Canadian provinces. Additionally Congress has remained silent on agreements between select Midwestern states and Canadian provinces in 2005 relative to the intercontinental issue of resource management in the Great Lakes region, as well as on Kansas's agreement with Cuba's food trade agency in 2003 regarding the purchase of food exports.[100] In fact, most states have routinely entered into international agreements with national and subnational governments abroad, with well over four hundred agreements forged between the American states and the Canadian provinces alone.[101]

In the absence of official federal interference, it is likely that state governments will be emboldened to create and implement their own foreign policy initiatives. The distinct institutional structures that states use to advance foreign policy preferences register their increasing significance as players on the world stage. The creation of overseas trade offices is a microcosm of the growing trend, a pattern that reinforces a different kind of institutional structure for foreign policy that is not seen or evidenced by episodic travel by political elites abroad (such as when governors and legislators visit their foreign counterparts to discuss trade-related issues). The fact that states are now in the practice of institutionalizing their regional concerns in organizations such as the Mid-South Trade Council, the Western Governors' Association, or the Great Lakes Governors' Association is supplementary proof that the international order is evolving differently from how it is conventionally thought to be. The structural changes in the new world order, either from above or below, and how they are received and affect the new federalism judicial policymaking of the U.S. Supreme Court in foreign affairs are discussed next.

THE U.S. SUPREME COURT RESPONSE

Given the changing structure of the international system and the growing foreign policy activism of American states, the Supreme Court might be increasingly hampered in its ability to adhere to stare decisis and its foreign policy preemption precedents. The Court's federalism doctrine precluding states from having much of a role in foreign affairs will become (if it is not already) difficult to apply and internally divisive. In whatever the justices do in reviewing and deciding these types of cases, the Court's new federalism response will have to be measured in light of the two ongoing structural changes outlined above. In considering how it may accomplish its goals to be faithful to the law and to decide between competing claims of federal and state sovereignty in federalism cases involving foreign affairs preemption, the Court may have to play a different kind of institutional role than it is accustomed to performing, especially if it operates from the false assumption that the political international environment will remain static.

Several distinct roles in particular may define the scope and application of judicial decision-making as the new world order continues to evolve, a process that may, in turn, lead to a transformation of the Supreme Court's institutional role as an umpire of federal-state disputes. First, the justices may collectively be effectively sidelined or marginalized by structural changes from above and below. Under this scenario, other political institutions will effectively sort out the boundaries between national and state foreign policymaking, and the Court will remain at a reactive distance. Alternatively, the Court's role may become more confined, and here it will only intervene in instances when state foreign policy directly imperils national policy. A third possibility may be that the Court could create a body of common law that is more categorical but yet flexible and pragmatic in its new federalism applications—but only if it institutionally accepts the increasing prominence of states in international relations and signals through its rulings that it is willing to be flexible in its responsibility to the rule of law. Finally, the Court could be resistant to change and, as a consequence, become increasingly fractured in trying to produce majority rulings that are built upon a premise of unanimity in deciding foreign policy preemption appeals. Thus the unanimity characterizing the *Crosby* ruling could become more the exception than the rule, a pattern of judicial behavior that is identified in other types of federalism cases the Rehnquist Court heard as it neared the transition to the Roberts Court. The judicial platform for internal conflict, however, is not likely to be identified with the process federalism debate the justices have over the clarity of congressional or executive intent in laws purporting to preempt state legislative policy decisions (as in *Garamendi*). Rather, the legal and ideological lines of contention will probably be framed by the basic new federalism question of whether the states retain the autonomy ever to play a meaningful role in foreign affairs, regardless of how the political branches at the federal level respond.

At the outset it is important to acknowledge that the Supreme Court throughout its history has responded to changing conditions in the international system and accordingly altered its constitutional jurisprudence in foreign affairs. Additionally, personnel changes on the Court have brought changes to foreign affairs law, and often they conjoin with the Court's jurisprudential response to the fluidity that is a part of international affairs. To illustrate, both changes occurred contemporaneously with the New Deal in the 1930s.

Legal historian G. Edward White argues the Supreme Court's constitutional interpretation of foreign affairs law is based on almost a rudimentary view of the constitutional system. For most of the nineteenth century and up until World War I, the federal judiciary followed an orthodox view of the Constitution, one that primarily centered the federal government's foreign affairs powers in the treaty power. Under this orthodoxy, most foreign affairs issues are handled by treaties that are initiated by the president and subject to senatorial consent. Once the Senate approves, treaties become the supreme law of the land under Article VI, or the supremacy clause, of the Constitution.[102] As a working federalism principle, the Court presumed that the federal government reserved its foreign affairs powers to itself, thereby precluding states from participating in foreign affairs policymaking. Yet, as White has pointed out, "The federalism paradigm of orthodox jurisprudence was far more responsive to state concerns than might first appear."[103] In spite of the aforementioned federalism principle, the states kept some kind of international role through their interactions with foreign governments and application of policies that extended into the realm of extraditing criminal defendants to foreign governments, the promulgation of immigration regulations, and the institutional responses or retaliatory efforts that were aimed at foreign governments that dared to interfere with American corporations. As one would expect, those state policies were routinely and often challenged as violations of the federal government's exclusive foreign affairs powers.[104] In addition, the Court "intimated" that some state powers could not be infringed by the federal treaty power. In a series of cases decided between 1870 and 1900, the justices gradually strengthened the powers of the federal government and restricted state incursions into foreign affairs. In the *Chinese Exclusion Cases* (1889, 1893) and the *Insular Cases* (1901–1905), for example, the Court reiterated the basic constitutional principle that the federal government had the sole power to exclude aliens from the United States, and it possessed the sole power to acquire and govern territories.

Yet another development, set in the political context of the judicial acceptance and enforceability of executive agreements initiated by the president, demonstrates the Supreme Court's changing view of the orthodox principles of foreign affairs. Executive agreements, or international legal compacts that are negotiated by the president with foreign governments without Senate consultation or approval, were constitutionally sanctioned in *United States v. Pink* in 1942 (discussed earlier in this chapter). At issue in *Pink* was President Franklin Roosevelt's executive agreement with the Soviet Union to resolve outstanding property disputes between citizens and governments of both countries. A New York state court attempted to bypass the agreement and adjudicate the property disputes under New York law, but that ruling was struck down by the U.S. Supreme Court. A brief historical description of the events leading up to *Pink* aids in situating the constitutional and federalism salience of the legal ruling.

By World War I, the high court had recognized that there was an international dimension to the constitutional powers of the national government over foreign affairs. The international dimension was "concerned with the growing role of the United States as a sovereign nation, participating in world affairs and operating with a body of international law."[105] Several developments at the domestic and international levels prompted the Court to change constitutional doctrine in respect to foreign affairs law. By the 1920s American businesses were more aggressively seeking foreign markets, and from World War I onward, the United States often became entangled in a series of foreign policy issues that were related to its judicial attempt to secure and foster international political stability. The rise of communism and totalitarian dictatorships in Asia and Europe, in other words, "gave the Supreme Court . . . opportunities to precipitate a transformation of constitutional foreign relations jurisprudence."[106]

Intermittent but instrumental personnel changes on the federal bench also affected the Supreme Court's approach to foreign relations law. As White observes, the addition of Justice George Sutherland in 1922 led to significant change in constitutional doctrine. Prior to his appointment and confirmation, Sutherland, as a Republican senator from Utah, articulated the view that the national government's foreign affairs powers originated from its inherent powers in the Constitution. That perspective, in practice, gave federal officials almost unlimited power over external relations. Although Sutherland was not the only constitutional scholar to read the federal government's powers broadly, "he was a singularly influential force in the transformation of constitutional foreign relations jurisprudence."[107] Thus Sutherland understood what was at stake at his time in constitutional history, as White documents in his research. Sutherland, in other words, acknowledged

> the increasingly expansive and foreboding character of the emerging twentieth-century international order. Once [Sutherland] came to believe that the complex and dangerous world of twentieth-century international relations required flexible, unencumbered decision-making by foreign relations specialists, he felt it was necessary to view the foreign policy decisions of officials of the national government as primarily grounded on the inherent sovereign powers of a nation to defend itself from foreign threats.[108]

Sutherland's influence on the Court helped other justices shift their views of the foreign affairs powers too, so much so that by the 1940s "separation of powers and federalism limitations on the conduct of foreign relations by the federal executive had virtually disappeared."[109] Just as the federal government (especially the executive branch) required more flexibility to deal with mounting international concerns, including threats arising from the rise of global totalitarianism and the ideological conflict between communism and democracy as applied to American businesses operating overseas, the Court accordingly responded by changing constitutional doctrine to fit the political needs of the time.

Because the Supreme Court responded to changes in the international system in the first half of the twentieth century, it is not unreasonable to anticipate that it may have to again in light of the disaggregation of state sovereignty in the new world order that continues to grow in constitutional significance. Precisely how it will respond remains an open question. Whereas global totalitarianism and the ideological conflict between communism and democracy were perceived by national policymakers as issues of high politics in the context of an international system where sovereigns must speak with one voice, the disaggregation of the international system today creates networks among national and subnational governments and other groups that effectively bypass national policymakers and empower subnational policymakers. Thus any changes it makes to the constitutional law regulating foreign affairs may require the Court to address specific federalism concerns. The following analysis addresses the range of possibilities that may be seized upon as a judicial response.

The Sidelined Court

Throughout its history the Supreme Court has rarely chosen to intervene in constitutional foreign affairs litigation. In the times it has elected to review these cases, the justices also have generally supported the exercise of federal power by almost routinely deferring to the president and Congress whenever challenges to their authority are made. As a matter of legal doctrine, the Court assigns to the president plenary authority over international relations while simultaneously asserting that it lacks the institutional competence to resolve inherently political questions.[110] The Court's predisposition to take a narrow and constrained approach to the exercise of judicial review means that it opts to remain on the constitutional sidelines in adjudicating cases in the foreign policy realm.

The Court's self-restraint in international cases is compounded by ongoing political events and controversies relating to the pervasive relevance of state foreign policy. Just as the Court limits its own power in hearing such cases, other political institutions and social and political interests or pressures that are intimately engaged in foreign policy debates tend to restrain the Supreme Court. Two brief case studies are illustrative: the political disputes over state and local sanctions against South Africa in the 1980s and identical sanctions directed against Sudan in the early 2000s. Both examples underscore the utilization and application of state economic power to achieve foreign policy objectives. Specifically, states wielded their power as market participants in the global economy by making selective purchasing or investment decisions to leverage and lobby for legal policy change in foreign countries. In this fashion the states' market behavior is reminiscent of the Burma legal sanctions that were imposed by the Massachusetts legislature but were subsequently struck down by the Supreme Court in *Crosby* (discussed earlier in this chapter).

In the 1980s states and municipalities enacted over one hundred laws imposing restrictions on investment and business activities in South Africa as a means to pressure economically its white minority regime into ending its oppressive system of racial apartheid. State-level sanctions against South Africa ran counter to official federal policy, since under the Reagan and Bush administrations the national government focused on keeping the lines of economic and political communication open in hopes of reaching a diplomatic solution to the end of apartheid and South Africa's transition to a functioning democracy. That South Africa historically was an anti-communist ally of the United States during the Cold War significantly affected American foreign policy as well. As regards state and local sanctions, in various legal skirmishes the executive branch adopted the position that these state laws were unconstitutional on several grounds, including federalism[111]; ultimately, however, the sanctions issue was never litigated in federal courts. This is understandable, as private corporations affected by the sanctions were hesitant to engage in politically charged and expensive litigation that might have adverse economic repercussions at home, and trade associations lobbying on behalf of American corporations could not provide enough political cover to engage in litigation that might be perceived as indirect support for apartheid injustice.[112]

The absence of litigation notwithstanding, in the constitutional and policy arguments that the federal government used to justify its preference for diplomacy over economic sanctions as a means to bring about the end of apartheid in South Africa, it conceptualized foreign affairs preemption as an issue that foremost involved congressional and executive action. Federal legislation enacted by Congress and ancillary executive orders issued from the White House must clearly intend for a foreign affairs policy to supersede state policy, and as the government itself admitted, such clear directions from Congress and the president were not evident or forthcoming. Neither federal law nor executive orders unambiguously prohibited states from refusing to contract with corporations having business or investment ties to South Africa.[113]

The South African sanctions case study shows how extralegal forces can effectively sideline the Court in a constitutional debate over state foreign policy. Corporations and trade associations feared negative fallout from commencing or participating in litigation challenging the sanctions, and even though the federal government's policy was in direct opposition to state policies, it also chose not to litigate for political reasons. Congress did not seek to clarify federal policy when juxtaposed against state policy, and the executive branch opted to remain silent as well. The political branches' feigned indifference, when coupled with the fear of litigation from interested parties and other advocates, meant that federal courts had no role to play in affecting how the constitutional dispute over state foreign policy ultimately played itself out.[114] Additionally, at least some indirect evidence exists that Congress intentionally chose not to preempt state and local anti-apartheid ordinances, further complicating the phenomena of the sidelined judiciary. The legislative history of the Comprehensive Anti-Apartheid Act of 1986, the federal law that created the terms of engagement in dealing with South Africa and trying to nudge it toward democracy, included a House of Representatives resolution declaring that the bill was not intended to preempt state and local laws.[115] Congress also specifically allowed states to link contracts on federally funded highway projects to their South Africa policies, another measure of proof suggesting that Congress preferred the states to take an active political role encouraging South Africa to democratize.

The South Africa sanctions debate ended with the collapse of the apartheid system and the democratization of the country in the 1990s. Yet it is clear that the success of states in administering sanctions against South Africa lent support to levying subsequent and analogous sanctions against an assortment of foreign regimes on a variety of crosscutting international issues. By the late 1990s and early 2000s, several states had laws requiring the managers of state pension and retirement funds to monitor investments with firms doing business with foreign governments that were listed as state sponsors of terrorism by the U.S. State Department. Some states required their pension funds to divest altogether from businesses that maintained close economic ties with those governments. States also used their economic prowess and selective purchasing laws to protest the Swiss government's delay in handling insurance claims brought by Holocaust survivors; to advance democratization efforts in Nigeria, Indonesia, and Cuba; and to protest China's policies on Tibet.[116] States also followed policies to further peace efforts in Northern Ireland. In all of these areas, Congress remained silent as well, choosing also to stay metaphorically on the sidelines in deciding not to specifically preempt state foreign policies that might clash with overriding federal policy.

As with the South African sanctions, states and municipalities exerted their regulatory powers to compel the Sudanese government to stop its genocide in Darfur. In 2005 Illinois passed legislation prohibiting state and local pensions from investing in foreign governments or companies that do business with Sudan. This time, unlike in the South African experience, a trade group sued in federal court. The National Foreign Trade Council (NFTC), which successfully sued Massachusetts in *Crosby*, joined with several local pension organizations to prevent Illinois from enforcing the Illinois Sudan Act on constitutional grounds, ostensibly as an interference with the federal government's exclusive powers to regulate foreign affairs. In the case *National Foreign Trade Council v. Giannoulias,* federal district judge Matthew Kennelly, sitting in Illinois, agreed and struck down the state act on the predictable grounds that the state law interfered with Congress's plenary power to regulate foreign commerce.[117]

In late 2007 a nearly unanimous Congress passed the Sudan Accountability and Divestment Act, which authorized state and local governments to impose economic sanctions against the Sudanese government. The law's purpose was identical to those justifying similar state action—namely, to direct sanctions at an oppressive regime to cause it to reverse its genocidal policies in Darfur. While President George W. Bush signed the bill, he recognized that it had the potential to let states obstruct national policy.[118] Furthermore, even though state-generated Sudan divestment laws are similar to the South Africa divestment laws of the 1980s, it is crucial to observe that the Supreme Court did not have the opportunity to weigh in on their constitutionality. The South African sanctions were never litigated in federal court, and even in the litigation regarding the Sudan divestment sanctions that was reviewed by the federal courts in *Giannoulias,* Congress and the president wound up ratifying state and local foreign policies on the issue, thus effectively mooting the litigation for the foreseeable future.

By passing a federal law to affirm state policymaking on the Sudan/Darfur genocide issue, congressional action essentially absorbed into federal law those state foreign policies that conflicted with federal policy. In this way Congress set the minimum standards by which states could conform their regulations on Sudan so as not to interfere with the national government's ability to pursue a national policy on Sudan that was more attuned to international events. Still, whether intentionally or not, Congress effectively bypassed the Court by mooting litigation wrestling with the legal issues at hand in the federal courts. The next section analyzes a different restraint that is put on the judiciary in frustrating the possibility that it may get a chance to evaluate the constitutional issues touching upon foreign policy preemption, mainly evaluating how the Supreme Court is confined in its institutional capacity to decide such legal questions.

The Confined Court

The South Africa and Sudan sanctions case studies show how the Supreme Court's preemption of state foreign policies is contingent upon the actions of other political institutions and actors. Linked to the argument that the Court can be effectively shunted aside by other institutions in foreign policy federalism cases is another claim that the federal judiciary can be confined or limited in adjudicating only certain types of cases.

The Court's agenda space, in other words, is narrowed to the possibility of reviewing only a select number of prominent situations pertaining to state foreign policy decisions that interfere directly with national policies or only those having some type of serious impact on foreign policy.

Judging what would be a "prominent" example of state interference with national foreign policy is a subjective enterprise fraught with difficulties. In this light *Crosby* and *Garamendi*, the Burma sanctions and Holocaust insurance cases discussed earlier in the chapter, are instructive. When *Crosby* was on appeal to the federal circuit court, several state attorneys general participated as amici to advocate support for Massachusetts's law, as did several cities of various sizes. Members of Congress filed briefs both supportive and opposed to the state law too. Another litigation participant was the Commission of the European Union, which filed a brief on behalf of the EU and its member states in opposition to state law.

The EU, the Association of South East Asian Nations (ASEAN), and Japan protested to the United States, and ultimately the EU and Japan took the issue to the World Trade Organization and filed a complaint against the United States. They asserted the state law violated trade rules governing procurement. The involvement of a supranational organization in the litigation and the WTO complaint against the United States may have signaled to the Court that the anti-Burma law seriously affected the federal government's foreign policy goals. In its own amicus brief, the U.S. government pointed out that many of the United States' trading partners objected to the law and that ongoing trade discussions between the United States and the EU were being compromised by the EU's opposition to the law.[119] Similarly, the United States echoed these same concerns in its brief in *Garamendi*, arguing that the Holocaust-inspired state law created "tensions in international relations that the United States has sought to avoid, prompting protests from the governments of Germany and Switzerland."[120] By providing such information about how foreign governments perceive and respond to state policies, the federal government sought to influence the judicial policy outcome in favor of the insurance companies' interests by providing information culled from the practical operation of the international system itself.

The prospect that the Supreme Court may choose to respond to state foreign policy disputes remains judicially viable whenever certain cues or prompts are present. When foreign governments and supranational organizations (such as the EU) are involved in litigation or exert pressure on the United States in response to state foreign policies, the Court may perceive that some kind of global threshold requiring judicial input has been crossed. International opposition to state and local foreign policy in the United States might suggest that the national government's ability to speak with one voice is jeopardized by state intrusions into international relations. Thus the disputed issue in play may require a closer look in order to determine if foreign policy preemption principle should be applied to beat back the state regulation attempting to control foreign affairs policy. Opposition from foreign governments and supranational organizations may be manifested in several forms. They might file amici briefs to highlight how state policies are adversely disrupting the foreign relations of the United States and other governments, organizations, and advocacy interests. Alternatively, they might commence quasi-legal or administrative proceedings against the United States in a neutral global dispute-resolution forum, such as the World Trade Organization. The decision to start a lawsuit or an alternative dispute mechanism is a key signal that gets the attention of judicial bodies that ultimately may have to react to the formal claims that the states are interfering with the federal government's capacity to speak with one voice on vital issues of international trade and commerce.

While it remains difficult to conceive of the Court defining its role in such a way, the historical record of judicial involvement provides some indicia of the possibility becoming a reality. Since the 1950s the Court has occasionally considered the external context of global events when deciding domestic constitutional cases. When the Supreme Court was asked to rule on whether the First Amendment protects obscenity in *Roth v. United States*, the Court referred to an international consensus that was emerging on the issue. The justices acknowledged the presence of international standards regulating speech that was arguably obscene, as evidenced by several international treaties that sovereign states had joined. In more recent cases concerning the juvenile death penalty (*Roper v. Simmons*, 2005) and homosexuals' rights (*Lawrence v. Texas*, 2003), some of the justices in their decisional rationales detailed the changes in the global political and legal environment that assisted them in evaluating the constitutional question of whether it was a "cruel and unusual" punishment under the Eighth Amendment to execute minors or the developmentally challenged. The death penalty cases are replete with multiple amicus curia briefs filed by the European Union, the English and Welsh bar, and multiple international NGOs, as well as a brief joined by Nobel laureates and former heads of state, such as President Jimmy Carter and President F. W. de Klerk from South Africa. The prior discussion of Justice George Sutherland and the New Deal Court also underscores that the justices pay acute attention to global events and at least the possibility that the constitutional standards and doctrines it creates will ineluctably leave an analytical perspective that is greatly shaped by the subtle influence of transformative changes occurring in the international political and legal system.

Flexible, Pragmatic Foreign Policy Preemption

Another possible approach that the Supreme Court could take in its foreign policy preemption cases would be to jettison its foreign policy preemption principle and instead pragmatically adjudicate cases in terms of discrete policy areas. Instead of presumptively invalidating state laws that are deemed to invade the protected constitutional realm of foreign policy, the justices might opt to engage in a more categorical approach to preemption in which some state laws and policies would be sustained, depending on the specific policy area or issue concerned.

Although often portrayed as a coherent doctrinal development, the Court's new federalism jurisprudence in domestic politics is variable in scope and judicial practice. The Court has struck down federal regulation of the states in some areas but not others. In the course of devolving power to the states, the Court has contradictorily applied the preemption doctrine to nullify state laws obstructing national policy goals set by the legislature or executive. For political scientists Conlan and Dudley, one commonality among the Court's preemption decisions "is that the Court's decisions promoted the interests of business, freeing it of some state regulation or liability."[121] This hints at the prospect that the Supreme Court is more protective of mercantile interests as opposed to endorsing policy outcomes purporting to enhance state sovereignty or autonomy.

It may develop that the Court reads the same policy preference into its foreign policy preemption cases. In fact, the most recent preemption cases, *Crosby* and *Garamendi* (discussed earlier), could both be characterized as freeing businesses from state and local regulations that make the business climate in states less predictable. In order to liberate global corporations from mixed (and potentially contradictory) state and federal regulations, the Supreme Court uses its judicial discretion to preempt such regulations at the state level. *Crosby* could be interpreted in this light because it was sponsored by the National Foreign Trade Council, an interest group representing the international trade concerns of American corporations. Yet, given the outcome and lessons learned from the contemporary conflict over the constitutionality of state anti-Sudan laws, another explanation is possible. Under the principles established in *Crosby*, laws such as the Illinois Sudan law would be easy to preempt because they arguably tread on established federal foreign policy objectives. Still, because Congress elected to ratify Illinois's policy choices by subsequently enacting legislation supporting them, *Crosby*'s precedential impact is necessarily confined to the unique facts of the case. So, in the event that similar state and local sanction laws are litigated in the future, this may imply that the Court is likely to follow *Crosby* but nonetheless remain cognizant of the debate and implications of legally using state and local economic sanctions to achieve certain substantive policy results. Those controversies, by definition, implicate political practices that reflect state market participation and the attempts by states to leverage favorable business outcomes in the context of changing international competitive pressures. Even given the unconstitutionality of Massachusetts's attempt to bring about change in Burma, the Court could conclude that the implicit federal acceptance of sanctions against South Africa, when coupled with the explicit federal approval of state sanctions against Sudan, is powerful evidence that could support a policy outcome that does not favor preempting state economic regulations.

Certainly some policy areas will remain preempted. There is a high probability that the federal government's use of National Guard troops in foreign policy will be protected from the states because it is linked to the president's war powers. To illustrate, in *Perpich v. Department of Defense* a unanimous Court ruled the supremacy clause vested in the executive an exclusive and plenary federal power over military affairs, thus compelling state governors to agree to deploy their National Guard units outside the United States to engage in military training.[122] Likewise, state interference with the federal government's treaty power will most likely be judged under the supremacy clause as it has been in the past. While these exceptions speak mainly to the supremacy clause and the exclusive federal power over certain areas of foreign affairs, they are indicative of a new federalism jurisprudence favoring a categorical approach to some types of foreign relations cases. Using national security as but one example of a category that vests exclusive foreign policy powers in the federal government, at least in theory the Court could develop in other nonexclusive areas a kind of pragmatic, flexible approach to preemption based on judicial standards that distinguish one policy area from another. The difficulty in drawing categorical preemption lines is manifest, for critics will easily point out that the discretionary application of categorical or flexible standards invariably necessitates the use of personal subjectivity to decide policy outcomes—leading to the conclusion that in doing so the Court is using its judicial activism to decide foreign policy preemption cases.

Even so, it is conceivable that the Court is already adhering to some form of a categorical approach in some of its preemption cases. In disputes over the foreign commerce clause, many of which concern state taxation of foreign corporations operating from within the United States (and in specific states), the Court provided for some flexibility for state policymaking, especially in cases where the federal government has not clearly established an exclusive regulatory role. In *Container Corporation of America v. Franchise Tax Board*, the Court upheld a state tax law that departed from federal policy since it had "merely foreign resonances" that indirectly touched upon federal foreign affairs.[123] Similarly, in *Barclays Bank PLC v. Franchise Tax Board of California* the Court sustained a state corporate income tax even though it affected international trade issues that were a concern of the national government.[124] At least when a state is engaged in the traditional regulatory area of taxation, or perhaps if it can prove it is operating as a market participant in interstate commerce in a nondiscriminatory fashion, the Court is more apt to sustain state policies that touch upon foreign relations, provided Congress or the executive has not sought to preclude state policymaking.

A Divided Court?

The Rehnquist Court's devolution of power to the states partially came about through the replacement of justices who were typically opposed to a retraction of federal power. The new federalism is based not on ideological change among the justices but on personnel change over time.[125] With this in mind, ideological disagreements among current justices, coupled with the membership changes in due course, may register the development of another institutional role for the Court in deciding foreign policy preemption cases. That role is one defined by a divided Court that is unable to articulate clearly constitutional doctrine.

Ideological division among the justices is, of course, commonplace. Political scientists Conlan and Dudley posit that new federalism cases have polarized the Court along the lines of those justices who are willing to limit federal power as a means of protecting business interests and those who are more supportive of federal power that regulates business. Another type of ideological split may exist, one that affects the resolution of preemption cases in the context of structural developments in the international system and increasing state government foreign policy activism. The ideological split focuses less on a justice's own political predilections and more on how each justice views the international networks among justices and judges of different national court systems—networks that the disaggregation of the world system has fostered. Admittedly, Supreme Court decisions do not speak directly to the existence or validity of the judicial networks. Yet evidence of how justices might perceive the salience and application of such networks among foreign courts is found in their viewpoints on the use and sharing of foreign jurisprudence in American litigation.

Of recent note, many of the justices have been engaged in the debate over the appropriate use of precedents and legal sources from legal systems outside the United States. For some, like Justice Antonin Scalia, it is anathema to the American constitutional system that judges would seek guidance from constitutional sources outside a narrowly defined American constitutional tradition. Thus Scalia, in his dissent in 2005's *Roper v. Simmons* (the death penalty case discussed earlier), takes his colleagues to task for relying on foreign law to strike down state laws that allow capital punishment for juvenile offenders. As he flatly put it, "The basic premise of the Court's argument—that American law should conform to the laws of the rest of the world—ought to be rejected out of hand."[126] But for others, such as Justices Anthony Kennedy and Stephen Breyer, minimal reference at least to some non-U.S. sources is allowable. To be sure, agreeing to a role for foreign law in the United States does not directly impact federalism. But it may show a willingness on the part of some of the justices to take into account significant changes transpiring in the international order, which affect judicial policy outcomes that are filtered down to the states through federal law interpretations.

The U.S. Supreme Court's choosing to use foreign citations in its constitutional interpretation provides some evidence that the high court is cognizant of globalization trends and alterations in the international order. Progress on this front is bound to remain incremental, politically controversial, and fraught with judicial conflict. The Court's reluctance to embrace foreign law in its own jurisprudence remains a vibrant source of academic controversy and internal judicial conflict. Also, the Court's position raises an identical question about whether U.S. state courts are any different in their judicial behavior insofar as it relates to engaging in a transnational dialogue with foreign judiciaries.

While legal scholars typically claim the U.S. Supreme Court has not historically maintained a tradition of citing to foreign sources in constitutional matters,[127] some studies argue the opposite.[128] To illustrate, legal scholar David Zaring's analysis demonstrates that U.S. federal courts rarely cite to foreign decisions or courts after 1945.[129] Although there is an increasing level of citation to foreign courts, once the total number of opinions (which increased over time) is accounted for, there is little evidence that federal courts cite to foreign tribunals any more frequently than they did in years past (over a sixty-year period). Even so, Zaring concludes that seven foreign courts are cited the most (led by the Canadian Supreme Court and the French Cour de Cassation, followed by the European Court of Human Rights, the High Court of Australia, the Italian Corte di Cassazione, the Indian Supreme Court, and the Israeli Supreme Court), and, significantly, there is a higher rate and a sharp spike of citation evidence in recent decades. Through more citation activity, U.S. courts "acknowledged or recounted parallel foreign proceedings without using those proceedings to assist in the interpretation of domestic, foreign, or international law."[130] This latter finding, though, only pertains to the general way in which U.S. federal courts exhibit citation behavior.

Even so, the issue of looking abroad or adopting foreign precedents is highly relevant in political debates contesting the wisdom of using foreign law in U.S. cases involving hot-button issues of social policy, such as federalism (*Printz v. United States*, 1997), homosexual rights (*Lawrence v. Texas*, 2003), affirmative action (*Grutter v. Bollinger*, 2003; *Gratz v. Bollinger*, 2003), the death penalty (*Atkins v. Virginia*, 2002; *Roper v. Simmons*, 2005), and terrorism (*Hamdi v. Rumsfeld*, 2004).[131]

An identical controversy surrounds the proper role of U.S. state courts in citing foreign authority.[132] Scholar Mark DeLaquil presents historical evidence for the practice, observing that state courts review foreign law to interpret state constitutions or to determine how best to apply domestic law to litigation relating to the enforceability of foreign judgments and other procedural issues (service of process, discovery, or forum selection).[133] Other constitutional and legal scholars, including judges, imply state courts have a special task, and perhaps a duty, to look abroad to sharpen their legal analyses of state constitutions and local law application[134]; still others pine for state judges to gain insight in foreign cases addressing the scope of collective labor, health, education, and welfare rights.[135] Comparative law scholars Cathy Albisa and Jessica Schultz thus flatly declare, "Only state courts at this point are likely to address either positive obligations or economic and social rights. State courts have an opportunity and duty to take leadership in the development of economic and social rights jurisprudence, and are well positioned to do so with regards to both positive obligations and economic and social rights."[136]

Regardless of the political desirability of the practice, the posture U.S. courts take on the issue of foreign citation affects whether a transnational judicial dialogue is emerging in the new international order. The constitutional cross-fertilization of ideas, the use of persuasive precedential authority, and a host of cooperative endeavors transpiring between judicial associations and personal contacts arguably allow judges to become a global "community of courts."[137] The cross-fertilization of constitutional ideas is enhanced by the accessibility and use of the Internet and electronic legal databases, such as Lexis-Nexis or Westlaw.[138] Political organizations (such as the Venice Commission) or courts (like the European Court on Human Rights, the Canadian Supreme Court, or the U.S. Supreme Court) all host websites that are, in effect, public repositories of searchable sources of law. These display judicial cases (made available through court-specific search engines), off-the-bench speeches by judges, and other legal research information relating to court histories, procedures, and operations.[139]

Without a doubt, constitutional law scholars now recognize the growing influence of foreign jurisprudence on state and federal courts in the United States. Law professor Judith Resnick argues that the inflow of alien legal decisions occurs because of "multiple ports of entry" for law in the United States.[140] Accordingly, federal and state courts both use alien jurisprudence, and it is especially prevalent at the subfederal level for state courts. How Supreme Court justices perceive these multiple ports of entry for foreign law may indicate how they will view questions of federal preemption. For instance, justices who are more inclined to refer to foreign court citations and foreign sources of law in their opinions on American constitutional questions may indicate a more attentive view of the disaggregated international system. Thus, accepting that the world system is now comprised of not only unitary sovereign states but also networks comprised of regional and local governments and private transnational organizations may give rise to different applications of the Court's foreign policy preemption doctrine. Justices who view the world order less in terms of unitary states may seek to modify preemption doctrine to reflect the realities of the global system. Conversely, justices who maintain a more rigid opposition to the use of alien law will most likely accept that the Constitution acknowledges a global system in which "sovereign states are the sole source of legal authority,"[141] and global networks among subfederal governments and transnational groups are superfluous. Under this view, foreign policy preemption is determined by a larger vision of American constitutional culture that does not recognize that changes in the international system have legal or constitutional consequences.[142]

THE ROBERTS COURT AND FOREIGN POLICY COLLABORATION

The above discussion provides a basic framework for assessing how the U.S. Supreme Court may respond to the increasing foreign policy activism of American states. It has been suggested that it may be problematic for the federal judiciary to sustain its doctrinal commitment to foreign policy preemption in light of the ongoing transformation of the international system. As such, predicting the precise circumstances under which (or if) the Supreme Court under Chief Justice John Roberts will start to revisit its constitutional approach to deciding appeals centered on international relations and preemption is equally challenging. The ensuing analysis considers some of the possibilities that may orient the Roberts Court's decision-making in an issue area bound to be greatly affected by the internal and external political environment when it reviews foreign policy preemption cases in the future.

The standard account of Supreme Court policymaking in foreign affairs holds that the Court is deferential to Congress and the executive. For legal scholar David Adler, "The Court is inclined to take a narrow view of its role in foreign affairs cases . . . to grant considerable respect, latitude, and discretion to other departments when it can, and in foreign affairs cases . . . it always follows this approach."[143] As a result, the Court historically intervenes rarely in foreign affairs disputes. Perhaps because the cases infrequently appear on the docket, comparative constitutional law scholar Louis Henkin asserts that the justices do not develop any special expertise in international relations (unlike, say, tax law or administration law), and generally they do not have their own individual philosophies about foreign relations or the international system to inform their judicial decision-making perspective.[144] So it makes sense that the Court is deferential to Congress and the presidency in international relations, especially given the nature of the legal issues involved and, of course, the constraining effect of the political questions doctrine.

But perhaps more debatable is the degree and effect to which the Supreme Court is an active institutional participant in a national or international dialogue concerning federalism issues. The previous section portrays at least some of the justices as being interested in engaging foreign legal systems as a platform for understanding constitutional law within a global context. A similar observation is possible about the Supreme Court's link to its own domestic political environment. Legal scholar Mark Tushnet argues that the Supreme Court, as a constituent member of the national political order, will collaborate at times with other political institutions to sustain prevailing political ideas and policy outcomes in a specific political era. Under this paradigm, Tushnet uses the New Deal and Warren Court eras as a touchstone to comprehend the Supreme Court as fitting into the model of a collaborative judiciary—one that uses its judicial power, for example, to ratify the burgeoning regulatory state (including safeguarding the right of workers to conduct labor demonstrations). In doing so the federal judiciary has "contributed to the construction and deepening of the political coalition supporting New Deal programs in Congress and in the executive branch."[145] Likewise, just as the Supreme Court supported the New Deal as a policy idea in the federal government, so too did the Warren Court (1954–1969) cooperate with its other partners in the federal government to implement the Great Society in the 1950s and 1960s; in the process, it helped effectuate significant political change in asserting its judicial will to challenge "a sort of traditionalism associated with the 'Southern way of life' but dispersed more widely throughout the country."[146] In Tushnet's terms, the notion that the Court closely interfaces with other institutions is more than just a type of judicial deference. By supporting a particular political order during a specific political time, the Court might affirm or reject a law as a constitutional exercise of political power. In other words, what makes the

Court collaborative is that its support, over time, reflects a consistent understanding of politics that leads to a refashioning of the political order.

The Court's collaboration can be geographical and temporal in scope and application. It is geographical when it supports the national political system "that confronts resistance or indifference at the state or local level . . . [and] the Court collaborates with a national political system as that national system grapples with problems arising from the fact that the United States is a federal nation."[147] Collaboration can also be temporal, as when the Court may "collaborate with today's national political institutions against what is left over from a prior political system."[148] In Tushnet's terms geographical collaboration consists of the Court opting to sustain the federal government's regulatory authority over the states. In contrast, temporal collaboration occurs when the Court ratifies the public policies made by a prior political order, even if the current regime does not embrace or approve of those policies. For Tushnet, temporal collaboration is discernible in the Rehnquist Court's affirmation of the constitutionality of the Americans with Disabilities Act (ADA), enacted by a bipartisan Congress in 1990. But the law changed as the prevailing political coalitions transformed, and the Supreme Court reacted in kind. As Tushnet explains, "By the time the Rehnquist Court got around to interpreting the [Americans with Disabilities] Act, the national political system had changed." So, in referencing the precedent that *Board of Trustees of the University of Alabama v. Garrett*[149] established in 2001 in turning back the disability claim of a worker who allegedly was fired for missing time from work due to cancer, Tushnet suggests that the conditions underlying the ADA's enactment no longer held true for the Rehnquist Court's evaluation of its constitutionality under the structural federalism principles and political preferences a majority of the bench appeared to favor later. Thus, he concludes, "It seems quite unlikely that an act placing substantial regulatory burdens on business could be enacted today."[150]

Tushnet's model of a collaborative Court that supports a national political order is useful to further our understanding of how the Court will respond to the pressures it faces in American federalism litigation due to the disaggregation of the international order and the increasing foreign policy activism of American states. The Court's continued endorsement of the national government's exclusive powers over foreign affairs is an example of both geographical and temporal collaboration with the national government. The Court's ongoing maintenance of preemption doctrine serves as a temporal collaboration with the national government. Its rulings are supportive of official power and the prevailing political order insofar as they ratify the federal government's exclusive powers over foreign policy over different periods of American history. In cases ranging from *Cohens v. Virginia* to *United States v. Pink* and from *Zschernig v. Miller* to *Crosby v. National Foreign Trade Council,* the Court followed its historical pattern of judicial behavior by allowing the federal government to conduct international relations on behalf of the states, ostensibly so the United States is united when engaging other sovereign states in the international system. This temporal collaboration with the national government sustains its foreign affairs powers and perpetuates the view that the international system is based on sovereign, unitary states that engage each other, thus requiring (from the Court's point of view) that the United States speak with one voice in the international community.

The Court's collaboration over foreign affairs preemption is also geographical because it sustains the national government's powers over the states. This is most recently shown by the *Zschernig v. Miller, Crosby v. National Foreign Trade Council,* and *American Insurance Association v. Garamendi* cases addressing whether a state policy obstructed the national government's foreign policy authority. By validating federal power, the Court is signaling that it intends to keep cooperating with the federal government in the context of a larger understanding of federalism and the need to let federal law supersede the laws enacted in the states that assert regulatory power over foreign affairs.

An illustration of the Supreme Court's collaboration with the political branches of government in foreign affairs preemption is presented in table 5.2. The table summarizes a sample of contemporary cases and outcomes the Court has generated in this issue area. In respect to each case, the degree of collaboration is measured by policy outcomes. Case results supportive of the federal government's policy objects are deemed to be collaborative, whereas those that are not supportive are not. In addition, the legal arguments that are asserted on behalf of federal officials are important signals and indicia of interbranch collaboration as well. Thus table 5.2 includes summaries of some of the amicus curiae (friend of the Court) briefs that were filed by the executive branch to telegraph the government's wishes to the Court. Mapping patterns of collaboration or opposition to the federal government shows, to a very basic extent, the degree to which the Court continues to collaborate with the federal government by maintaining or deviating from the presumption of foreign affairs preemption.

For instance, in *Japan Line, Ltd. v. County of Los Angeles* the Court reviewed the constitutionality of a California state law that allowed local governments to levy a property tax on international shipping containers within that government's jurisdiction, even though the containers were owned by foreign corporations. The United States was not involved in the litigation as a party but participated through an amicus brief filed by the U.S. Office of the Solicitor General. The government argued the tax law conflicted with international rules on taxation and also interfered with

Table 5.2. Recent Foreign Affairs Preemption Cases from Burger, Rehnquist, and Roberts Courts, 1979–2011

Case	*Court*	*Issue*	*Executive Branch Brief*	*Does Court Agree with Executive Branch?*	*Decision*
Japan Line Ltd v. County of Los Angeles 441 U.S. 434 (1979)	Burger	Does state tax on international cargo containers violate Foreign Commerce Clause?	Yes. State tax conflicts with internationally accepted rule governing taxation of international traffic. State tax interferes with federal policy and prevents federal government from speaking with one voice on international tax issues.	Yes	8–1 State tax law is unconstitutional. It results in multiple taxations of instrumentalities of foreign commerce and prevents the United States from speaking with one voice in regulating foreign trade.
Container Corporation of America v. Franchise Tax Board 463 U.S. 159 (1983)	Burger	Does state franchise tax on multinational businesses violate Foreign Commerce Clause?	No.	N/A	5–3 State tax is constitutional. Does not violate one-voice doctrine of federal power. Tax is not fatally inconsistent with federal policy. Court notes that executive branch did not submit brief in case: "Suggests that the foreign policy of the United States—whose nuances are much more the province of the Executive Branch and Congress . . . is not seriously threatened by the law."

(*continued*)

Table 5.2. (*continued*)

Case	*Court*	*Issue*	*Executive Branch Brief*	*Does Court Agree with Executive Branch?*	*Decision*
Chicago Bridge & Iron Co. v. Caterpillar Tractor 463 U.S. 1220 (1983)	Burger	Does state income tax on multinational corporations, based on combined worldwide business income, violate Foreign Commerce Clause?	Yes. Federal government has sole power over foreign relations. State income tax impairs uniformity of federal policy.	N/A	Case dismissed for want of a federal question. Lower court decision upholding state income tax stands.
ITEL Containers v. Huddleston 507 U.S. 60 (1993)	Rehnquist	Does state tax on domestically owned shipping containers used in international commerce violate Foreign Commerce Clause?	Yes. State tax on shipping containers does not interfere with accepted international practice in a manner that impedes the nation's ability to speak with one voice.	Yes	8–1–1 Tax is constitutional. It is not prohibited by international treaty; it does not impede federal objectives, and does not infringe federal government's ability to speak with one voice.
Barclay's Bank PLC. v. Franchise Tax Board 512 U.S. 298 (1994)	Rehnquist	Does state corporate franchise tax on multinational corporations based on "worldwide combined reporting" violate the Foreign Commerce Clause?	Yes. State law impairs federal government's ability to conduct international commercial policy. Impairs uniformity in an area where uniformity is essential and prevents federal government from speaking with one voice in international trade.	No	7–2 State policy is constitutional. It does not impair federal uniformity and does not interfere with the federal government's ability to speak with one voice in international trade.

Breard v. Green 523 U.S. 371 (1998)	Rehnquist	Can a state convict and Paraguayan national use federal habeas proceedings to invoke a Vienna Convention of Consular Relations to vacate a state conviction?	Yes. The convention does not provide a judicial cause of action to have a criminal conviction vacated. Executive branch noted that it had accorded Paraguay the traditional remedy among nations for violations of the convention.	Yes	6–3 The Vienna Convention cannot be invoked in federal habeas proceedings when it has not been asserted in state proceedings, as with this case.
Crosby v. National Foreign Trade Council 530 U.S. 363 (2000)	Rehnquist	Does Massachusetts's "Burma Law" interfere with federal foreign policy?	Yes. State law discriminates against foreign commerce beyond what a state may do as a market participant. The law also departs from the carefully crafted federal policy on Burma defined by Congress and the executive branch. The law impermissibly intrudes into the national government's exclusive authority over foreign affairs.	Yes	9–0 State law is unconstitutional. It is an obstacle to congressional objectives and interferes with the delegation of power to the executive branch to develop a comprehensive, multilateral diplomatic strategy on Burma.

(*continued*)

Table 5.2. *(continued)*

Case	*Court*	*Issue*	*Executive Branch Brief*	*Does Court Agree with Executive Branch?*	*Decision*
American Insurance Association v. Garamendi 539 U.S. 396 (2003)	Rehnquist	Does state law regulating insurance companies so that outstanding life insurance claims from victims of the Holocaust are addressed interfere with federal policy, and thus is preempted?	Yes. State law intrudes into the exclusive federal power over diplomacy and commerce with foreign nations. Law threatens to impair federal government policy that favors the use of voluntary, non-adversarial mechanisms to resolve outstanding Holocaust insurance claims.	Yes	5–4 State law is preempted because it interferes with federal policy on Holocaust insurance claims embodied by executive agreements. The agreements were not expressly authorized by Congress, BUT Congress has not expressly authorized state policies or disapproved of executive policy.
Sanchez-Llamas v. Oregon 548 U.S. 331 (2006)	Roberts	Does Vienna Convention on Consular Relations create an individual right to have evidence suppressed in criminal trial or post-conviction proceedings?	Yes. Convention does not create individually enforceable right to evidence suppression.	Yes	6–3 Vienna Convention does not preempt state post-conviction procedures. Suppression of evidence is not an appropriate remedy.
Permanent Mission of India to the United Nations v. New York City 551 U.S. 193 (2007)	Roberts	Does Foreign Sovereign Immunities Act (FSIA) prohibit state taxation and liens on diplomatic properties?	Yes. FSIA and international treaties prohibit state taxation and liens on diplomatic property. State laws present adverse consequences	No	7–2 FSIA allows state tax and lien lawsuits to be litigated in U.S. federal courts.

			for the nation's foreign policy, including retaliatory measures taken against the United States.		
Medellin v. Texas 552 U.S. 491 (2008)	Roberts	Can the president direct states to implement in their criminal law the Vienna Convention on Consular Relations and an ICJ ruling?	Yes. Presidential memorandum to the states to implement the treaty is sufficient to create a binding legal rule. State criminal policy is preempted by presidential directive to apply international law.	No	6–3 Neither presidential directive nor International Court of Justice decision is directly enforceable as federal law. The Vienna Convention on Consular Relations is not self-executing, and a president cannot unilaterally execute a non-self-executing treaty.
Garcia v. Texas 131 S.Ct. 2866 (2011)	Roberts	Must a state stay an execution to determine if prisoner's rights under the Vienna Convention were violated?	Yes. Congress may pass legislation soon implementing the Vienna Convention; thus a stay of execution is warranted. Execution would cause United States to be in breach of its international obligations and will cause irreparable damage to foreign policy interests of the highest order.	No	5–4 Per Curiam opinion Court has no authority to stay a state execution pending congressional action and in light of an appeal by the president presenting "free-range assertions of foreign policy consequences." No stay of executive granted.

(*continued*)

Table 5.2. (*continued*)

Case	*Court*	*Issue*	*Executive Branch Brief*	*Does Court Agree with Executive Branch?*	*Decision*
Louisiana Safety Association of Timbermen–Self Insurers Fund v. Lloyd's of London 131 S.Ct. 3311 (2010)	Roberts	Does a "reverse preemption" state law prohibiting arbitration in insurance contracts, and allowed by federal statute, take priority over international treaties that mandate arbitration?	Yes. Court invites participation from solicitor general. State laws precluding arbitration would impact U.S. treaty obligations. Case does not warrant further review, since lower federal appellate has declared the law unconstitutional.	Yes	Certiorari denied
Goodyear Luxembourg Tires v. Brown 131 S.Ct. 64 (2010) consolidated with *McIntyre Machinery v. Nicastro*, 131 S.Ct. 2780 (2011)	Roberts	Can state courts extend jurisdiction in tort cases over international corporations, based on the stream of commerce theory?	Yes. State court jurisdiction would undermine U.S. foreign trade and foreign affairs interests. Foreign governments object to state courts expansive views of jurisdiction. Denial of state jurisdiction serves the diplomatic interests of the United States.	Yes	

the federal government's ability to create a unitary tax policy that, if in effect, could alert other foreign governments that the United States was speaking with one voice in the legal area of international taxation. The Court agreed, ruling that the state tax policy interfered with the federal government's power over foreign commerce and with its ability to speak uniformly. Importantly, the state law was not an attempt to enact a state foreign policy, like in *Zschernig*, *Crosby*, and *Garamendi*. Instead, while the tax had ramifications for U.S. interests abroad, it regardless pertained to a state tax policy covering property only situated within the state. Even so, the federal government perceived a threat to its ability to conduct international economic relations, and the Supreme Court's ruling demonstrated that the justices were sensitive to that official concern.

Japan Line does not suggest the Court always cooperates with the executive branch, as evidenced by the judicial behavior of the Rehnquist Court. In key cases, notably *Crosby* and *Garamendi* (discussed earlier), the Court agreed with the basic premise that state law frustrated the government's capacity to conduct foreign relations. The attempts of Massachusetts and California to use state policy as a vehicle to encourage democratization in Burma and to prompt international insurance companies to settle Holocaust claims were unconstitutional because they overreached. In *ITEL Containers v. Huddleston*, the Court reviewed a state law that taxed international shipping containers owned by domestic (not international) corporations.[151] In its brief, the federal government asserted there was no interference in conducting international economic relations or tax policy, so it considered the law to be constitutional. The Court agreed by sustaining the state tax law despite the implicit ramifications it had for international tax policy. In all three cases, the Supreme Court's decision aligned with the solicitor general's legal position. In this sense it collaborated with the national government for its decisions meshed with the outcome desired by the executive branch.

These findings should not be overstated, because in other cases the Rehnquist Court was not supportive of the executive branch. At issue in *Barclays Bank PLC v. Franchise Tax Board of California* was whether a state corporate franchise tax that taxed the global earnings of multinational corporations violated the foreign commerce clause. In its brief, the Office of the Solicitor General asserted the tax impaired the federal government's ability to speak with one voice on international economic policy and disrupted the uniformity of federal taxation policy relating to international businesses. The Court, however, rejected these claims by ruling that the state law did not measurably interfere with federal policy. Notably, the case outcome tracked a similar precedent established a decade earlier by the Burger Court (1969–1985). In *Chicago Bridge and Iron Co. v. Caterpillar Tractor*, the validity of a state tax that was levied on a corporation's global earnings was challenged as a foreign commerce clause violation. Through its amicus brief, the national government adhered to the traditional position that the preemption is required. Still, the Court dismissed the case because it did not present a federal question, a result that had the effect of allowing a lower state court judgment affirming the state law's constitutionality to stand. The result in *Chicago Bridge and Iron Co.* is consistent with another precedent set in the Burger Court during the same term—namely, *Container Corporation of America v. Franchise Tax Board.* There, the Supreme Court upheld a state corporate tax on the global earnings of businesses because it did not impede federal power over foreign commerce. Even though federal officials did not submit a brief outlining the U.S. government's preferences, the Supreme Court took special note that it deemed the state law to be constitutional, presumably inferring that the executive branch's silence indicated that U.S. foreign policy was "not seriously threatened by the [state] law."

The Court's decisions in *Barclays Bank, Chicago Bridge and Iron Co.,* and *Container Corporation* all deviated from the legal preferences of the federal government. Significantly, the Court did not agree with the government on two key points—namely, whether the state law interfered with the federal government's capacity to conduct foreign policy and whether the states impaired the government's ability to speak with one voice on foreign affairs. That the Court did not defer to the government's broad assertions about the dangers of state meddling with foreign policy may show that the Court is now more willing to second-guess the executive branch's claims concerning its capacity to engage in international relations and that the justices will decide for themselves when state polices reach a critical and damaging level of interference with national power. To be sure, further empirical testing is required to validate the qualitative evidence and findings suggested here.

Key cases from the Roberts Court suggest that it may be less cooperative with the national government on some foreign policy issues that implicate federalism concerns. Whether the Roberts Court will not collaborate with the government on consistently following foreign affairs preemption remains to be seen, of course, but arguably it may be the first Supreme Court in decades to devote more scrutiny to executive branch claims that state policies hinder foreign policy. In a series of cases concerning whether the Vienna Convention on Consular Relations applies to state criminal justice systems, the Roberts Court has been confronted with conflicts between U.S. foreign policy and state domestic policy. Unlike in *Zschernig, Crosby,* and *Garamendi,* where the Court was confronted with state laws that intentionally set out either to influence United States foreign policy or to establish an independent state policy, in the Vienna Convention cases (*Sanchez-Llamas v. Oregon, Medellin v. Texas*) the constitutional questions related to whether U.S. treaty obligations were preempted or otherwise affected by state criminal justice proceedings.

The U.S. ratification of the Vienna Convention meant that as a signatory state, it must grant noncitizens who have been arrested access to their diplomatic consulates. The convention does not create a form of immunity for arrestees; rather, it simply establishes a mandatory process by which they can notify their diplomats and home countries of their detention. In *Breard v. Green*, the Supreme Court considered whether a Paraguayan national, Angel Breard, who was convicted of murder and sentenced to death in Virginia, was correct in asserting that his Vienna Convention right to consular access had been violated, even though he had not raised the convention issue in state criminal proceedings. The Rehnquist Court dismissed his habeas petition, ruling that the treaty requires that its provisions be exercised in conformity with the signatory (or receiving) state. Thus, "by not asserting his Vienna Convention claim in state court, Breard failed to exercise his rights under the Vienna Convention in conformity with the laws of the United States and the Commonwealth of Virginia." The Court concluded that "having failed to do so, he cannot raise a claim of violation of those rights now on federal habeas review."[152]

Conflicts concerning the Vienna Convention and state criminal law did not abate after the *Breard* decision. The Roberts Court, for example, has confronted at least three separate cases in which such a conflict was at issue. In one, *Sanchez-Llamas v. Oregon*, the Court dealt with two prisoner appeals asserting that evidence obtained and used to convict them must be suppressed because their consulate notification rights under the treaty were violated. An amicus brief by the executive branch argued that evidence suppression is not an appropriate remedy for violations of the treaty, and the Court by a 6–3 vote agreed. It is plausible to construe the *Sanchez-Llamas* and *Breard* decisions as indicating that the Rehnquist and Roberts Courts preferred to collaborate with the executive branch on the issues raised by the legal application of the consular relations treaty. On the other hand, two other cases show the Court's interest in cooperating might be waning.

In *Medellin v. Texas*, the Court confronted a direct (and rare) conflict between the states and the executive branch over the implementation of an international treaty stemming from litigation between the United States and Paraguay in the International Court of Justice (ICJ). Paraguay sued the United States over violations of the Vienna Convention (Angel Breard was a Paraguayan national) and won a judgment from the ICJ ordering the United States to comply.[153] In response, President George W. Bush issued an executive memorandum to the states instructing them to comply with the ICJ's decision and the consular relations treaty in criminal prosecutions. Relying on the president's memorandum and the ICJ decision,

Jose Medellin filed a Texas state habeas corpus petition contesting his death sentence for murder. In its amicus brief, the United States argued the president's order sufficiently created a binding legal rule that states must follow; consequently, the United States has a compelling obligation to follow the ICJ decision and treaty for several reasons, including to ensure reciprocal observance by foreign governments, promote better foreign relations, and reaffirm the United States' commitment to the rule of law. In short, the United States asserted that the president's directive to the states was a valid exercise of his foreign affairs powers.

The Roberts Court, by a vote of 6–3, rejected Medellin's appeal. It stated that "while the ICJ's judgment in *Avena* creates an international law obligation on the part of the United States, it does not of its own force constitute binding federal law that pre-empts state restrictions."[154] Regarding the president's memorandum, the majority observed that the Vienna Convention is a non-self-executing treaty whose implementation on U.S. soil requires further congressional input. Even though the president "has an array of political and diplomatic means available to enforce international obligations . . . unilaterally converting a non-self-executing treaty into a self-executing one is not among them."[155] In addition, the Court rejected the government's argument that the president's broad foreign affairs powers allow him to direct the states to follow an ICJ decision and international treaty. The Court could find very few sources or long-standing international practices to justify such presidential power.

Although Medellin's initial habeas petition was unsuccessful, he filed another request for a stay of execution, alleging that Congress or Texas might determine that the Vienna Convention should be followed and accordingly pass statutes to that effect. The Court denied the stay. In so doing, it emphasized that the executive branch "is well aware of the proceedings and has not chosen to seek our intervention." In fact, the Court offered, "Its silence is no surprise [because] the United States has not wavered in its position that petitioner was not prejudiced by his lack of consular access."[156]

A follow-up case to *Medellin, Garcia v. Texas*,[157] presented the Roberts Court with similar issues during the 2010–2011 term. A prisoner on Texas's death row sought a stay of execution. This time the executive branch, now under the control of President Barack Obama's administration, filed an amicus brief asking to grant the stay because a bill to enact the terms of the Vienna Convention was pending in Congress. This meant that the execution would place the United States in violation of its treaty obligations and, from the administration's point of view, harm the country's foreign policy interests, which are "of the highest order."[158] The Court, divided 5–4, in a per curiam (unsigned) opinion, denied the stay because Congress has not enacted any legislation implementing the convention or ICJ

Avena decision, also known as *Case Concerning Avena and Other Mexican Nationals* (*Mex. vs. U.S.*). As a result, the Court chose not to intervene in the criminal state proceedings only on the prospect that Congress will legislate on the policy issues at hand. Moreover, the Court, in an exasperated tone directed at the administration, instructed that it has no authority to stay an execution in light of an executive branch argument "presenting free-range assertions of foreign policy consequences."[159]

The cases addressing the legal effect of the Vienna Convention on Consular Relations underscore that two different dynamics are at work that may affect the degree of collaboration that the federal judiciary will have with the national government on foreign policy issues. The first dynamic comes from *Breard* and *Sanchez-Llamas.* They indicate the Court will support the executive branch in consular relations issues (and perhaps other treaty disputes) when the administration does not try to extend treaty obligations too deeply into state policymaking affecting traditional areas of state criminal justice policy. The solicitor general in both cases—and across Democratic and Republican presidencies—argued the Vienna Convention does not create rights directly enforceable at the state level. The second dynamic comes in the *Medellin* and *Garcia* cases. Each was decided after the International Court of Justice's decision in 2004, which held that the United States had violated the consular treaty. Thereafter the Bush administration took the position that states must follow a presidential memorandum implementing the terms of the treaty, but the Court fundamentally disagreed. The Court refused to intercede in state executive politics as well, even though, as in *Garcia,* the federal executive branch argued that not halting a foreign national execution in a situation raising the possibility that consular rights were compromised would jeopardize the federal government's foreign policy. For the Roberts Court, the Vienna Convention required additional congressional deliberation and statutory action in order to make it enforceable at the state level. Thus the Court did not allow federal action to impair the traditional operation of state criminal justice policies.

The Vienna Convention cases are different from *Crosby, Garamendi,* and *Zschernig,* all of which concerned policies in which states sought to advance their own foreign policy agendas and impaired the government's ability to conduct foreign policy on a national basis—its power to "speak with one voice" in the international system. The Court's decisions can be interpreted as collaborative: on constitutional grounds it struck down the state laws and, in doing so, took seriously the arguments of the federal government that the states were interfering with basic foreign affairs powers that the Constitution does not delegate to the states. As collaborative decisions, they were geographical (federal law trumped state law) and temporal (an established line of precedents protecting the federal foreign affairs powers was followed, dating back to the Marshall Court in the early 1800s). In contrast, the Vienna Convention cases indicate the Roberts Court places a real limit on the level of cooperation it wishes to have with the political branches on foreign policy concerns. When the federal government (especially the executive branch) raises foreign policy issues by disrupting core state functions, such as prosecuting defendants and administering criminal justice, the Court is inclined to veto preemption. The *Medellin* series of cases shows the Roberts Court will not accept the foreign policy concerns of the nation as enough justification to interfere with state criminal justice. The Roberts Court has shown that it will collaborate with the federal government against the states in that area of federalism if the federal government elects to stay silent on the issue.

Other cases from the Roberts Court are instructive as well. *Permanent Mission of India to the United Nations v. New York City* presented the Court with a complicated question of state tax law, federal statutory interpretation, and foreign policy.[160] New York City levied property taxes on parts of the Indian Mission to the United Nations that housed nondiplomatic personnel. When India refused to pay the taxes, the city placed liens on the property and sued to enforce them against India in a New York state court. After the case was removed to federal court, the Indian Mission claimed diplomatic immunity under a federal statute, the Foreign Sovereign Immunities Act (FSIA), arguing that its mission was diplomatic property and therefore the state taxes and liens did not have to be paid. In its brief the executive branch adopted India's position by asserting that FSIA and international treaties prohibited state taxation and liens, but also adding that not proving immunity would have adverse consequences for the nation's foreign policy—including the possibility of retaliatory measures being taken against the United States. The Roberts Court disagreed by interpreting the FSIA differently and contrary to the government's wishes.[161] *Permanent Mission of India* points in a direction that infers that the Roberts Court might be reluctant to collaborate with the federal government if foreign policy concerns are bound up with state and local tax administration—just as in *Medellin*, when foreign policy concerns are implicated in state criminal justice procedures.

The rules for preemption cases may be different, though, in state civil litigation cases heard in the Roberts Court. In *Louisiana Safety Association of Timberme–Self Insurers Fund v. Lloyd's of London*, at issue was a rare example of "reverse preemption"—a litigation scenario involving congressional legislation permitting states to prohibit arbitration clauses in insurance contracts, even if the state laws are contrary to international treaty obligations the United States accepts.[162] In an amicus brief filed by the solicitor general at the Supreme Court's request before the case was accepted for full review, the United States claimed that state laws prohibiting arbitration would force the United States to violate certain treaty obligations.

Moreover, since lower appellate courts had declared the state law unconstitutional, the brief suggested that no further review was warranted. The Court presumably agreed and denied certiorari, allowing the lower appellate decision against the state to stand. In *Goodyear Luxembourg Tires v. Brown*, at issue was whether a state could claim tort jurisdiction over international corporations based on the "stream of commerce" theory and based upon the corporation's economic activities that had an effect in the state, even though the corporation had very few, if any, direct economic ties to that state.[163] In its brief the executive branch indicated that allowing state court jurisdiction would undermine U.S. foreign trade and foreign affairs interests. Moreover, foreign governments have objected to an expansion of state jurisdiction over international corporations, and the diplomatic interests of the United States are best served by denying states the power to adjudicate similar tort cases. A divided Court agreed with the government—although only four justices joined in the per curiam opinion, with three other justices concurring and two dissenting. The Court's opinion observed that the international corporation being sued had never engaged in any state activities that revealed intent to invoke or benefit from state law. As a result, allowing state jurisdiction violated the due process clause of the Fourteenth Amendment. Even though the case outcome aligned with the federal government's preferences, the Court decided the case on Fourteenth Amendment instead of federalism grounds.

CONCLUSION

The analysis above suggests that the Roberts Court will be confronted with federalism conflicts caused by the interrelationship between the international system, the foreign policy powers of the national government, and the increasing foreign policy activism of the American states. Pressures to change the structures of American federalism and the balance of power between the national government and the states will be caused by globalization and the disaggregation of the international system and by states seeking a more prominent international role for themselves. Supreme Court precedents historically support the exclusive powers of the national government over foreign affairs and conversely minimize the role of the states, yet the structural changes highlighted above are likely to make it difficult for the Court to continue to apply settled doctrine consistently and coherently. The Court may be encouraged by structural forces beyond its control to change constitutional doctrine to better fit the changing realities of international politics.

To understand how the Court will resolve such disputes, analysis must go beyond mere judicial ideology and instead account for a far wider range of political economic factors and the changing structure of the international system. The new federalism cases decided by the Rehnquist and Roberts Courts affect domestic politics and are measured according to whether the outcome protects state sovereignty and autonomy or validates the federal government's power to regulate in a certain policy area. In general, justices divide ideologically over whether they are more oriented toward protecting states' rights or the regulatory powers of Congress and the national government. This typology among the justices does not lend itself to a complete understanding of the Court's policymaking in foreign affairs disputes that implicate the federal-state relationship, however. As this chapter indicates, a far more nuanced understanding of the Court's role in foreign affairs and of the international and domestic political environment in which it operates is key to explaining its policymaking.

For example, as the political and legal disputes over state and local policies on South Africa and Sudan made clear, the Court's ability to decide foreign affairs disputes is affected by litigant choices, interest group strategies, and the actions of Congress and the president. By the same token, the dispute over sanctions against Burma (Myanmar) and the clash over the resolution of Holocaust insurance claims suggest not only that Congress and the presidency are relevant to the Court's policymaking but that international organizations such as the European Union are seeking to exert more influence over the Court's decisions. Therefore, the lines the Court draws in conflicts concerning foreign affairs and federalism will be dependent on the actions of other political branches, states, and even foreign governments and international organizations. Those lines are likely to be affected also by changes in the Court's personnel and a changing international political order.

Although judicial ideology will perhaps be less important in foreign affairs cases than in domestic new federalism cases, it will still be relevant for analysis in a modified form. The review of the Court's policymaking above implicitly acknowledges that how justices view the international system will matter in deciding cases. Whether justices recognize the changing structure of the international system and the attendant development of networks among subfederal governments and institutions (and even among judges and justices in different countries) or conclude that such structural changes can have no impact on American constitutional development will be highly significant for how the Court draws the line in the future. This is not to suggest there are only two approaches that the Court can take. It does propose, though, that the standard accounts of judicial ideology in domestic federalism cases are simply inadequate to the task of understanding the Court's policymaking in foreign affairs cases concerning conflicts between states and the national government. More important than whether a justice is conservative or liberal will be how that justice views the relationship between the changing international system and the Constitution.

Finally, it is the case that the Court has historically supported the national government's claim of plenary power over foreign affairs. Indeed, the Court has written that claim into constitutional law, and it has for the most part followed that interpretation consistently through its preemption of state policies that affect foreign affairs. However, there is some evidence from the Rehnquist and Roberts Courts that the Court may be a less reliable partner in its support for the national government. Although more empirical study is needed, case analysis from both Courts shows some early trends in policymaking and indicates that the Roberts Court may not be as deferential and supportive of the federal government as the Rehnquist Court was. Whether this is an enduring change—and if it is, why—are questions that require further study.

NOTES

1. Timothy J. Conlan and Robert L. Dudley, "Janus-Faced Federalism: State Sovereignty and Federal Preemption in the Rehnquist Court," *PS: Political Science* (July 2005): 364.

2. 530 U.S. 363 (2000).

3. 539 U.S. 396 (2003).

4. 544 U.S. 660 (2005). President George W. Bush issued a directive that the American states and state courts should comply with the Vienna Convention on Consular Relations and an International Court of Justice (ICJ) decision to that effect, since the United States had signed the treaty and remains a party to ICJ jurisdiction under limited circumstances. The Court dismissed Medellin's appeal in 2005 to give Texas courts time to comply with the president's directive. The Court accepted a second appeal from Medellin and determined in a short per curiam opinion that it was too remote to argue that the Vienna Convention and ICJ decision had bearing on Medellin's substantive claims seeking a stay of execution. The Court did not address federalism arguments directly.

5. 548 U.S. 331 (2006).

6. Note, though, that the Court has made it clear that under the supremacy clause, states must follow international treaties ratified by the United States that are self-executing and thus automatically apply to the states, as well as ratified treaties that have been specifically implemented by congressional action. See *Hauenstein v. Lynham*, 100 U.S. 483 (1880).

7. Robert Keohane and Joseph Nye, "Governance in a Globalizing World," in *Power and Governance in a Partially Globalized World*, ed. Robert Keohane (New York: Routledge, 2002), 193–219; Jessica T. Mathews, "Power Shift," *Foreign Affairs* 76 (1997): 50–66; Anne-Marie Slaughter, *A New World Order* (Princeton, NJ: Princeton University Press, 2004); and Anne-Marie Slaughter, "The Real New World Order," *Foreign Affairs* 76 (1997): 183–97.

8. Richard B. Bilder, "The Role of States and Cities in Foreign Relations," *American Journal of International Law* 83 (1989): 823.

9. Slaughter, "The Real New World Order," 184.

10. Earl H. Fry, *The Expanding Role of State and Local Governments in U.S. Foreign Affairs* (New York: Council on Foreign Relations, 1998); John M. Kline, "Continuing Controversies over State and Local Foreign Policy Sanctions in the United States," *Publius: The Journal of Federalism* 29 (1999): 111–34.

11. Daniel J. Elazar, *Constitutionalizing Globalization: The Postmodern Revival of Confederal Arrangements* (New York: Rowman & Littlefield, 1998): 29.

12. See Constitutionality of South African Divestment Statutes Enacted by State and Local Governments (April 9, 1986) in *Opinions of the Office of the Legal Counsel of the United States Department of Justice*, Vol. 10 (1986). Anti-apartheid sanctions were litigated in state courts. See *Board of Trustees of Employees' Retirement System v. Mayor of Baltimore*, 317 Md. 72 (1989).

13. Keith Whittington, "Taking What They Give Us: Explaining the Court's Federalism Offensive," *Duke Law Journal* 51 (2003): 509.

14. Neal Devins, "The Majoritarian Rehnquist Court?," *Law and Contemporary Problems* 67, no. 3 (2004): 63.

15. Keith Whittington, "Dismantling the Modern State? The Changing Structural Foundations of Federalism," *Hastings Constitutional Law Quarterly* 25 (1998): 488.

16. See, generally, Fry, *The Expanding Role of State and Local Governments*; Brian Hocking, *Localizing Foreign Policy: Non-Central Governments and Multilayered Diplomacy* (New York: St. Martin's Press, 1993); Julian G. Ku, "Gubernatorial Foreign Policy," *Yale Law Journal* 115 (2006): 2380–2415.

17. Louis Henkin, *Foreign Affairs and the Constitution*, 2nd ed. (Oxford: Oxford University Press, 1996): 151–53.

18. Henkin, *Foreign Affairs and the Constitution*, 150.

19. See, generally, Bilder, "The Role of States and Cities in Foreign Relations."

20. Jack Goldsmith, "Statutory Foreign Affairs Preemption," *Supreme Court Review* (2001): 202–4.

21. Jeremy Rabkin, *Law without Nations: Why Constitutional Governance Requires Sovereign States* (Princeton, NJ: Princeton University Press, 2005), 65.

22. *The Federalist Papers* (with an introduction by Clinton Rossiter) (New York: New American Library, 1961), 43.

23. *The Federalist Papers*, Federalist #3, 49.

24. *The Federalist Papers*, Federalist #19, 132.

25. *The Federalist Papers*, Federalist #19, 133–34.

26. *The Federalist Papers*, Federalist #20, 134–35.

27. *The Federalist Papers*, Federalist #42, 264.

28. *The Federalist Papers*, Federalist #42, 266.

29. *The Federalist Papers*, Federalist #44, 281.

30. Rabkin, *Law without Nations*, 90.

31. Rabkin, *Law without Nations*, 65.

32. Justice Joseph Story, *A Familiar Exposition of the Constitution of the United States* (New York: Harper, 1883), 146.

33. David Halberstam, "The Foreign Affairs of Federal Systems: A National Perspective on the Benefits of State Participation," *Villanova Law Review* 46 (2001): 1022–25.

34. *Cohens v. Virginia*, 19 U.S. 264, 413–14 (1821).

35. 39 U.S. 540, 571 (1840).

36. *Holmes v. Jennison*, 39 U.S. 540, 576–77 (1840).

37. 92 U.S. 275 (1875).

38. 130 U.S. 581, 604–5 (1889).

39. *United States v. Pink*, 315 U.S. 203, 232–33 (1942).

40. *Japan Line, Ltd. v. County of Los Angeles*, 441 U.S. 434, 448 (1979).

41. *Zschernig v. Miller*, 389 U.S. 429, 438 (1968).

42. *Zschernig v. Miller*, 389 U.S. 429, 442 (1968).

43. *Crosby v. National Foreign Trade Council*, 530 U.S. 363 (2000), citing *Gibbons v. Ogden*, 22 U.S. 1 (1824).

44. *Crosby v. National Foreign Trade Council*, 530 U.S. 363, 376–77 (2000).

45. *Crosby v. National Foreign Trade Council*, 530 U.S. 363, 381 (2000).

46. *American Insurance Association v. Garamendi*, 539 U.S. 396, 415 (2003) (quoting *Youngstown Sheet and Tube v. Sawyer*, 343 U.S. 579 [1952]).

47. *American Insurance Association v. Garamendi*, 539 U.S. 396, 424–25 (2003).

48. *American Insurance Association v. Garamendi*, 539 U.S. 396, 443 (2003) (Ginsburg, J., dissenting).

49. *American Insurance Association v. Garamendi*, 539 U.S. 396, 443 (2003) (Ginsburg, J., dissenting).

50. The states were California, Alabama, Maine, Maryland, Massachusetts, Minnesota, Nevada, New Jersey, New York, Ohio, Texas, and Washington, along with the Commonwealth of Puerto Rico. The commissioner of insurance of the state of California defended the law, but California also chose to join with other states in a separate brief.

51. *Alden v. Maine*, 527 U.S. 706 (1999); *United States v. Morrison*, 529 U.S. 598 (2002).

52. "Brief of the States of California et al., as Amici Curiae Supporting Respondent in *American Insurance Association v. Garamendi*," 2002 U.S. Briefs 711, March 26, 2003, 17 (quoting *Alden v. Maine*, 527 U.S. 706, 739 [1999]).

53. "Brief of the States of California et al.," 21 (quoting *United States v. Morrison*, 529 U.S. 598, 619 [2002]).

54. Keohane and Nye, "Governance in a Globalizing World," 202.

55. Keohane and Nye, "Governance in a Globalizing World," 210.

56. Slaughter, "The Real New World Order," 184; see also Slaughter, *A New World Order*.

57. Elazar, *Constitutionalizing Globalization*, 19.

58. Yishai Blank, "Localism in the New Global Legal World Order," *Harvard International Law Journal* 47 (2007): 263–81, 264.

59. Fry, *The Expanding Role of State and Local Governments*, 16.

60. Ivo Duchacek, "Perforated Sovereignties: Towards a Typology of New Actors in International Relations," in *Federalism and International Relations: The Role of Subnational Units*, ed. Hans J. Michelmann and Panayotis Soldatos (Oxford: Oxford University Press, 1990), 14.

61. See Maryann Cusimano Love, "Nongovernmental Organizations: Politics beyond Sovereignty," in *Beyond Sovereignty: Issues for a Global Agenda*, ed. Maryann Cusimano Love (Belmont, CA: Thompson, 2003): 71–95. See also Jack H. McCall and Brandon P. Denning, "States Rights and Foreign Policy: Some Things Should Be Left to Washington," *Foreign Affairs* 79 (2000): 9–15.

62. Blank, "Localism in the New Global Legal World Order," 263.

63. Judith Resnick, "Foreign and Domestic Affairs: Rethinking Horizontal Federalism and Foreign Affairs Preemption in Light of Translocal Internationalism," *Emory Law Journal* 57 (2007): 31–92.

64. Peter J. Spiro, "New Players on the International Stage," *Hofstra Law and Policy Symposium* 2 (1997): 19–37.

65. Judith Resnick, "Law's Migration: American Exceptionalism, Silent Dialogues, and Federalism's Multiple Ports of Entry," *Yale Law Journal* 115 (2006): 1564–1670.

66. Timothy J. Conlan, Robert L. Dudley, and Joel F. Clark, "Taking on the World: The International Activities of State Legislatures," *Publius: The Journal of Federalism* 34 (2004): 195.

67. Miranda A. Schreurs, "From the Bottom Up: Local and Subnational Climate Change," *Journal of Environment and Development* 17 (2008): 343–55.

68. Resnick, "Foreign and Domestic Affairs," 294.

69. Fry, *The Expanding Role of State and Local Governments*, 96.

70. Conlan, Dudley, and Clark, "Taking on the World," 196.

71. "United Kingdom and California Conclude Agreement on Global Warming," *American Journal of International Law* 100 (2006): 933. Officials from the Bush administration had scheduling conflicts and were unable to attend the 2006 meeting between Prime Minister Blair and Governor Arnold Schwarzenegger. The official White House response was that the agreement was simply an extension of the climate agreement between Bush and Blair at the 2005 G-8 Summit. See Edwin Garcia and Paul Rogers, "Unusual State-Nation Pact Puts Distance Between Leaders, Bush," *San Jose Mercury News* (California), August 1, 2006, A1.

72. Terrance Guay, "Local Government and Global Politics: the Implication of Massachusetts' Burma Law," *Political Science Quarterly* 115 (2000): 363–64.

73. Guay, "Local Government and Global Politics," 356.

74. Hocking, *Localizing Foreign Policy*, 8–31; John Kline, "Managing Intergovernmental Tensions: Shaping a State and Local Role in US Foreign Relations," in *Foreign Relations and Federal States*, ed. Brian Hocking (London: Leicester University Press, 1993), 105–22.

75. Mark Tushnet, "Globalization and Federalism in a Post-*Prinz* World," *Tulsa Law Journal* 36 (2000): 41.

76. Mark Tushnet, *The New Constitutional Order* (Princeton, NJ: Princeton University Press, 2003), 145.

77. See Tushnet, "Globalization and Federalism in a Post-*Prinz* World."

78. We realize that there is a "chicken-egg" argument here about which comes first in terms of causality. That is, did states become active in foreign policy prior to the disaggregation of the world system, or did changes in the world system at the top cause states to become more activist in influencing foreign policy?

79. Thomas J. Price, "State Development Agencies as International Actors and the Decentralization of United States Foreign Economic Policy," *Publius: The Journal of Federalism* 11 (1981): 37–48, 37.

80. Timothy J. Conlan and Michelle A. Sager, "The Growing International Activities of the American States," *Policy Studies Review: Symposium, Globalization's Impact on State and Local Economic Development Policy* 18, no. 3 (2001): 16.

81. See, generally, U.S. Government Accountability Office, Report to the Chairman, Committee on Finance, U.S. Senate, *Export Promotion: Commerce Needs Better Information to Evaluate Its Fee-Based Programs and Customers*, March 2009, GAO-09-144.

82. Price, "State Development Agencies as International Actors," 47.

83. Michelle Sager, *One Voice or Many? Federalism and International Trade* (New York: LFB Scholarly Publishing, 2002), 35, 120.

84. Fry, *The Expanding Role of State and Local Governments*, 120.

85. Mary Branham, "Business Incentives Not a Stimulus for State Economies," Council for State Governments, April 21, 2011, http://knowledgecenter.csg.org/drupal/content/business-incentives-not-stimulus-state-economies (accessed June 15, 2011).

86. Bruce Katz and Emilia Istrate, "Boosting Exports, Delivering Jobs and Economic Growth," Brookings-Rockefeller Project on State and Metropolitan Innovation, Washington, DC, January 2011, 1.

87. See the Council for State Governments, "States Creating Their Own Agricultural Brands," Capitol Research, April 2011.

88. "Assessing Trends and Policies of Foreign Direct Investment in the United States," U.S. Department of Commerce, International Trade Administration, July 2008, 7–8.

89. Whittington, "Dismantling the Modern State?," 503.

90. Whittington, "Dismantling the Modern State?," 504.

91. See Edwin I. Gardner Jr., Robert S. Montjoy, and Douglas J. Watson, "Moving into Global Competition: A Case Study of Alabama's Recruitment of Mercedes Benz," *Policy Studies Review* 18, no. 3 (2001): 80–91.

92. See Hocking, *Localizing Foreign Policy*, 130–50.

93. Fry, *The Expanding Role of State and Local Governments*, 45.

94. Kline, "Continuing Controversies over State and Local Foreign Policy Sanctions in the United States," 111–34.

95. Governor Arnold Schwarzenegger, California State of the State Address, January 9, 2007.

96. See Schreurs, "From the Bottom Up," 343–55.

97. Henkin, *Foreign Affairs and the Constitution*, 153.

98. Henkin, *Foreign Affairs and the Constitution*, 155.

99. Duncan Hollis, "Why State Consent Still Matters: Non-State Actors, Treaties, and the Changing Sources of International Law," *Berkeley Journal of International Law* 23 (2008): 1079–80.

100. Hollis, "Why State Consent Still Matters," 1083.

101. Fry, *The Expanding Role of State and Local Governments*, 73.

102. G. Edward White, *History and the Constitution: Collected Essays* (Durham, NC: Carolina Academic Press, 2007), 213–20.

103. White, *History and the Constitution*, 220.
104. White, *History and the Constitution*, 221.
105. White, *History and the Constitution*, 224.
106. White, *History and the Constitution*, 248.
107. White, *History and the Constitution*, 228. Constitutional law scholars are well familiar with Sutherland's Supreme Court decisions that view the national government's foreign affairs powers broadly and especially give the executive branch very flexible powers to make international policies. See *United States v. Curtiss-Wright Export Co.*, 299 U.S. 304 (1936), and *U.S. v. Belmont*, 301 U.S. 324 (1937).
108. White, *History and the Constitution*, 284–85.
109. White, *History and the Constitution*, 281.
110. David Gray Adler, "Court, Constitution, and Foreign Affairs," in *The Constitution and the Conduct of American Foreign Policy*, ed. David Gray Adler and Larry George (Lawrence: Kansas University Press, 1996), 44–45. See also Henkin, *Foreign Affairs and the Constitution*, 147.
111. U.S. Department of Justice, *Constitutionality of South African Divestment Statutes Enacted by State and Local Governments*, 10 U.S. Op. Off. Legal Counsel 49 (April 6, 1986), www.law.georgetown.edu/clinics/hi/99-474.pdf (accessed April 22, 2012).
112. David D. Caron, "The Structure and Pathologies of Local Selective Procurement Ordinances: A Study of the Apartheid-Era South Africa Ordinances," *Berkeley Journal of International Law* 21 (2003): 159–84, 183–84.
113. U.S. Department of Justice, *Constitutionality of South African Divestment Statutes*, 23–24. It is important to note here that the Burma sanction laws struck down in *Crosby* are very similar to anti-apartheid sanctions from the 1980s. Yet the Court based its constitutional decision on the fact that state laws interfered with the framework created by Congress for addressing democratization in Burma and that framework gave the president significant leeway in choosing appropriate policies for Burma. Thus the Court did not look to whether Congress or the executive had clearly preempted state laws; instead, its main inquiry was the extent to which state laws impinged upon a foreign policy framework created by those two branches.
114. To be sure, the sidelining of the Court, and federal judges in general, is probably a result that most judges would agree with. Judges would most likely prefer that the political branches resolve such disputes.
115. Robert Stumberg and Mathew C. Porterfield, "Who Preempted the Massachusetts Burma Law? Federalism and Political Accountability under Global Trade Rules," *Publius: The Journal of Federalism* 31 (Summer 2001): 191–92.
116. Congressional Research Service, "State and Local Economic Sanctions," Washington, DC, 2007.
117. *National Foreign Trade Council v. Giannoulias*, U.S. District Court for the Northern District of Illinois, Eastern Division, 2007 U.S. Dist. LEXIS 13341, February 23, 2007, Decided.
118. Amy Gardner, "Bush Signs Bill to Pressure Sudan, Letting States and Localities Curtail Investments," *Washington Post*, January 1, 2008, A7.
119. U.S. Brief in *Crosby v. National Foreign Trade Council*, 1999 U.S. Briefs 474, 2000 U.S. S. Ct. Briefs LEXIS 96, February 14, 2000, 17.

120. Brief for the United States as Amicus Curiae Supporting Petitioners in *American Insurance Association v. Garamendi*, 2002 U.S. Briefs 722, 19.

121. Conlan and Dudley, "Janus-Faced Federalism," 365.

122. 496 U.S. 334 (1990).

123. 463 U.S. 159 (1983).

124. 512 U.S. 298 (1994).

125. See Whittington, "Taking What They Give Us."

126. 543 U.S. 551, 624 (2005).

127. Mark Tushnet, "The United States: Eclecticism in the Service of Pragmatism," in *Interpreting Constitutions: A Comparative Study*, ed. Jeffrey Goldsworthy (New York: Oxford University Press, 2006), 45–47.

128. Steven G. Calabresi and Stephanie Dotson Zamdahl, "The Supreme Court and Foreign Sources of Law: Two Hundred Years of Practice and the Juvenile Death Penalty Decision," *William & Mary Law Review* 47 (2005): 743–909.

129. David Zaring, "The Use of Foreign Citations by Federal Courts: An Empirical Analysis," *Journal of Empirical Legal Studies* 3 (2006): 297–331.

130. Zaring, "The Use of Foreign Citations by Federal Courts," 307, 320.

131. Aharon Barack, *The Judge in a Democracy* (Princeton, NJ: Princeton University Press, 2006), 203. See also Frank Michelman, "Integrity-Anziet?," in *American Exceptionalism and Human Rights*, ed. Michael Ignatieff (Princeton, NJ: Princeton University Press, 2005), 245; and Justice Ruth Bader Ginsburg, "'A Decent Respect to the Opinions of [Human]kind': The Value of a Comparative Perspective on Constitutional Adjudication," Supreme Court of the United States, July 30, 2010, www.supremecourt.gov/publicinfo/speeches/viewspeeches.aspx?Filename=sp_07_30_10.html (accessed April 22, 2012).

132. Mark Wendell DeLaquil, "'Outsourcing Authority?' Citation to Foreign Court Precedent in Domestic Jurisprudence: Foreign Law and Opinion in State Courts," *Albany Law Review* 69 (2006): 697–707. See also Shirley S. Abrahamson and Michael J. Fischer, "All the World's a Courtroom: Judging in the New Millennium," *Hofstra Law Review* 26 (Winter 1997): 273–92.

133. DeLaquil, "Outsourcing Authority?," 698, 704.

134. Helen Hershkoff, "Transforming Legal Theory in the Light of Practice: The Judicial Application of Social and Economic Rights to Private Orderings," in Varun Gauri and Daniel M. Brinks, eds., *Courting Social Justice: Judicial Enforcement of Social and Economic Rights in the Developing World* (New York: Cambridge University Press, 2008).

135. Martha F. Davis, "The Spirit of Our Times: State Constitutions and International Human Rights," *New York University Review of Law and Social Change* 30 (2006): 359–409.

136. Cathy Albisa and Jessica Schultz, "The United States: A Ragged Patchwork," in *Social Rights Jurisprudence: Emerging Trends in International and Comparative Law*, ed. Malcolm Langford (Cambridge: Cambridge University Press, 2008), 248.

137. Slaughter, *A New World Order*, 68–69.

138. Slaughter, *A New World Order*, 72.

139. Slaughter, *A New World Order*, 72.

140. Judith Resnick, "Law's Migration: American Exceptionalism, Silent Dialogues, and Federalism's Multiple Ports of Entry," *Emory Law Journal* 57 (2006): 31–92.

141. Rabkin, *Law without Nations*, 269.

142. To be sure, a conservative justice like Justice Scalia may well recognize the disaggregation of the international community and may indeed see some utility to international judicial networks. Yet a conservative jurist might also argue that such changes do not alter America's constitutional structure of federalism, even though those changes have profound political ramifications.

143. Adler, "Court, Constitution, and Foreign Affairs," 46.

144. Henkin, *Foreign Affairs and the Constitution*, 1996.

145. Mark Tushnet, "The Supreme Court and the National Political Order: Collaboration and Confrontation," in *The Supreme Court and American Political Development*, ed. Ronald Kahn and Ken I. Kersch (Lawrence: University Press of Kansas, 2006), 120.

146. Tushnet, "The Supreme Court and the National Political Order," 121.

147. Tushnet, "The Supreme Court and the National Political Order," 125.

148. Tushnet, "The Supreme Court and the National Political Order," 126.

149. 531 U.S. 356 (2001).

150. Tushnet, "The Supreme Court and the National Political Order," 127.

151. 507 U.S. 60 (1993).

152. *Breard v. Green*, 523 U.S. 371, 376–77 (1998).

153. The ICJ decision is known at the *Avena* decision; *Case Concerning Avena and Other Mexican Nationals* (*Mex. v. U.S.*), 2004 I. C. J. 12.

154. *Medellin v. Texas*, 552 U.S. 491, 522–23 (2008).

155. *Medellin v. Texas*, 552 U.S. 491, 525–26 (2008).

156. *Medellin v. Texas*, 554 U.S. 491, 759, 761 (2008).

157. 131 S. Ct. 2866 (2011).

158. United States Brief, *Garcia v. Texas*, 131 S. Ct. 2866 (2011).

159. *Garcia v. Texas*, 131 S. Ct. 2866 (2011).

160. 551 U.S. 193 (2007).

161. The Court remanded the case to a lower federal district court, which found that India was liable for the property taxes under state, federal, and international law. On remand the district court ruled for the City of New York that the property liens were lawful. *City of New York v. Permanent Mission of India to the UN*, 538 F. Supp. 2d 701, 2008 U.S. Dist. LEXIS 20550 (S.D.N.Y., 2008). India appealed to the Second Circuit Court of Appeals, which overturned the lower district court because the U.S. State Department intervened and issued a notice under the Foreign Missions Act (a federal statute) that under federal law a "benefit" enjoyed by foreign states for their diplomatic properties is an exemption from all local and state property taxes. New York City appealed that ruling to the U.S. Supreme Court, which denied certiorari in 2011. See *City of New York v. Permanent Mission of India to the UN*, 131 S. Ct. 1553, 179 L. Ed. 2d 297, 2011 U.S. LEXIS 1454 (U.S., 2011); *New York v. Permanent Mission of India*, 2011 U.S. LEXIS 4951 (U.S., June 27, 2011).

162. 131 S. Ct. 3311 (2010).

163. *Goodyear Luxembourg Tires v. Brown*, 131 S. Ct. 64 (2010), consolidated with *McIntyre Machinery v. Nicastro*, 131 S. Ct. 2780 (2011).

6

The Roberts Court and New Federalism

When President Barack Obama released his 2013 budget proposal during his reelection campaign, it was sharply criticized as an illegitimate attempt to bring the country out of the lingering effects of the Great Recession. Although it was defended by the White House as a way to jump-start the economy by strengthening the nation's infrastructure and its manufacturing base, its underlying political message was to tax the rich and spend billions of dollars on the administration's domestic priorities. Its fanciful nature was ridiculed by liberal pundit Dana Milbank, who colorfully described it as a form of political dodge ball because it "begins with a broken promise, adds some phony policy assumptions, throws in a few rosy forecasts and omits all kinds of painful decisions." For his part, conservative Senate minority leader Mitch McConnell (R-KY) seemed more offended than surprised by the proposal because he dismissed it as "merely a campaign document," implying that it could only be viewed as an ideological ploy that was not fooling anyone.[1]

In spite of their political differences, both Milbank and McConnell were united in taking aim at the legitimacy of the president's progressive policy agenda and its attendant lawmaking priorities. In his op-ed, Milbank observed that the president's earlier budget projections were grossly understated: legislatively enacting the proposal would force the federal government to carry a $600 billion annual deficit for the next ten years, thus adding $1 trillion to the national debt with new spending. For Senator McConnell, Milbank was repeating the same conservative mantra that was once voiced by President Ronald Reagan but now is championed by Tea Party enthusiasts, which calls for an end to all rampant spending so that the federal government can become fiscally responsible to the American public, a necessity during times of budget uncertainty.[2] Viewed in this ideological light, Obama's controversial budget proposal reflects the basic constitutional objection to health-care reform—a legal issue that weighs the scope and implications of federal overreaching and one that will be settled by the U.S. Supreme Court by the end of its 2011–2012 term.[3]

In the context of the 2012 presidential election, the debate over the federal government and President Obama's political agenda registers the old and new progressive trends that have become touchstones for understanding new federalism policy as it is interpreted and put into action by the White House, Capitol Hill, the U.S. Supreme Court, and state governments. The enactment of sweeping federal legislation in pursuit of a liberal mandate, such as the Patient Protection and Affordable Care Act (PPACA), the Dodd-Frank Wall Street Reform and Consumer Protection Act (Dodd-Frank), and the financial stimulus under the American Recovery and Reinvestment Act (Recovery Act), raises fresh questions about whether the private sector and state governments are being appropriately regulated in the national economy by federal law. For example, while the health-care reform package ignited a firestorm for imposing a governmental mandate on individuals to buy health insurance, whether any or all of the complex legislation beyond the mandate will survive judicial review remains an open question. Several insurance companies have balked at complying with regulations that dictate how they provide coverage or set insurance rates, and although state actors played an instrumental part in protecting their own universal and particularistic interests in safeguarding the role that states play in controlling and minimizing the costs of delivering health-care services, clearly not all state legislatures have responded well to the PPACA and the policy decisions to expand Medicaid benefit coverage and to create American Health Benefit Exchanges (which states must run in order to make the legislation work at the ground level).[4] In different ways, two other federal laws, Dodd-Frank (which sharply increases federal regulatory oversight over the financial services and insurance industries) and the Recovery Act (a law supplying $840 billion in fiscal relief and grant aid to the states), additionally expand the profile and presence of the federal government as it wades into areas of insular corporate practice and a realm of public policy that traditionally has been the province of state governments. These areas include mortgage and insurance underwriting, debt-collection and credit-reporting practices, educational policy, health-care reform, environmental protection, and transportation services.[5]

While its precise parameters remain uncertain, legal and political scholars agree that the ideological shape and direction of new federalism policy is intrinsically tied to President Obama's election and its political aftermath. In other words, "federalism under Obama is federalism in service of progressive policy, not a general devolution of power and resources to the states."[6] That a distinct type of intergovernmental cooperation is emerging, which could be referred to as a "hybrid model of federal policy innovation and leadership" under Obama's style of federalism, remains plausible.[7] Under this view the political synergy of federalism is intertwined with the aspirations, successes, and failures of liberal and conservative presidential administrations alike.[8] Moreover, other constitutive forces will influence the scope of the federal and state relationship because any explanation of the modern state of federalism must account for innovations or changes in state law that do not always accord with, or even rebut, federal omnipotence, such as in the contentious policy areas of greenhouse gases and energy regulation, gay rights, immigration control, and medicinal marijuana.[9]

Consequently, the underlying political dynamics of progressive government—which encompass the response to it by state governments and Obama's political opponents in the aftermath of the 2010 midterm election and in light of the presidential reelection campaign—assume special relevance as they manifest themselves in the types of fundamental questions of new federalism policy that the Roberts Court is likely to resolve when challenged in courts.[10] The precise role the Court will play in light of its predecessor's contributions to advancing states' rights and sovereignty remains highly ambiguous yet potentially quite significant. While scholars have analyzed the Rehnquist Court's federalist revival mostly in terms of the justices' constitutional rulings that scaled back federal governmental power, it is also important to consider if new restraints are put on state autonomy with analogous interpretations of the dormant commerce clause or perhaps by statutory construction, as in process federalism cases (see chapter 3). Questions of administrative federalism and whether the executive branch aggressively or narrowly enforces the federal preemption of state law through regulations are especially germane. Ostensibly through the release of his May 2009 preemption memo (see chapter 1) and his administration's strategic decision to adopt partial preemption and concurrent regulatory policies, President Obama has begun to reverse the Bush administration's preemption policies that previously tilted strongly in favor of centralizing government. For some scholars, Obama's reversal has cast new light on the impact of state governance because it has had the effect of "unleashing states to use their energies and political incentives to act on behalf of consumers."[11] Furthermore, as the earlier chapters remind us, the legal precedents that lie at the base of federalism ideas are routinely shaped by a myriad of ideological forces operating within the domestic and global political environments, which in time become authoritative principles that comprise the substantive content of new federalism policies. In this regard, social scientists observe that the Obama administration's federalism response to the recession has "provided a new if temporary window for an expansive counter cyclical financial partnership with the states," thereby allowing at least some states to become "progressive allies in regulatory areas ranging from climate change, financial market reform and mortgage relief."[12]

For all of these reasons President Obama's first term in office constitutively represents some of the challenges that the Roberts Court will face as it forges its own institutional identity in the wake of the Rehnquist Court and the pro-state legacy it may have left behind. One area of exploration concerns whether the Roberts Court is handling the same type of constitutional or statutory issues that the Rehnquist Court did in federalism cases, and with what result. This topic is worth scrutinizing in light of the judicial appointments that Presidents George W. Bush (Roberts and Alito) and Obama (Sotomayor and Kagan) made at a pivotal time when the Rehnquist Court ended and the Roberts Court began. In considering the new appointments' impact, a related inquiry asks if the early assessments of the Roberts Court, which tend to portray the justices as a business-friendly and activist bench, have any merit in light of the federalism outcomes that the justices produced in the Roberts Court's first six terms.[13] One academic report, for example, which was commissioned to analyze the issue, found that the Roberts Court held in favor of business interests 61 percent of the time, a rate that surpassed rulings issued from the Rehnquist Court (over a five-term period) and, as compared to prior periods, a percentage that exceeds the average rate of 42 percent for all Courts since 1953.[14] Another closely related subject is whether the justices are still committed to interpreting the U.S. Constitution in structural terms, a facet of judicial behavior that is usually linked with the Rehnquist Court's solicitude for state dignity and sovereignty, as framed by a dual federalism model. These topics, which generally focus on whether the nature and scope of new federalism has changed with the arrival of the Roberts Court, are especially relevant in light of the perception among scholars that "the Roberts Court has been relatively quiet" in this area of federalism law and policy.[15]

This chapter first explores the nature of the Court's new appointments (Roberts, Alito, Sotomayor, and Kagan) to discover what their general approach to judging is and, to the extent they can be uncovered, what their federalism viewpoints were before they joined the high court. Such revelations may help to identify their positions on the maturing Roberts Court. Next, the chapter surveys the Roberts Court federalism docket and situates it against predecessor Courts. Aggregate decisional trends, such as the frequency of federalism cases, their ideological direction, and whether the justices aggressively pursued federalism goals by reversing congressional statutes or existing precedent, are briefly outlined. Key Roberts Court cases, which span the realm of statutory construction and constitutional interpretation, are highlighted to reveal decisional patterns that might suggest whether any linkages can be drawn to Rehnquist Court new federalism or if the Roberts Court is establishing new jurisprudential pathways. The last section provides an overall assessment of the Roberts Court's new federalism in light of some of the difficulties the justices will face in future litigation that will only come to define the political landscape of the new federalism paradigm as it continues to grow through the ongoing legal interpretation of key precedents and statutory text.

FEDERALISM AND THE NEW ROBERTS COURT APPOINTMENTS

By 2003 the Rehnquist Court's new federalism jurisprudence was largely entrenched in Supreme Court policymaking, and the justices followed it consistently, arguably with a few exceptions. With Chief Justice William Rehnquist's departure in 2005; the retirements of Justices Sandra Day O'Connor, David Souter, and John Paul Stevens in subsequent years; and their replacements by Justices Samuel Alito, Sonia Sotomayor, and Elena Kagan, conditions exist for the Court to be on the verge of shifting federalism either to the right, toward a more protectionist view of state power as advocated by long-serving justices Antonin Scalia and Clarence Thomas, or toward a more moderate approach favored by veteran justice Anthony Kennedy, who most often was one of the swing votes in closely decided federalism decisions. That many of the new federalism decisions were closely decided suggests too that they may be easy to change or modify by new personnel on the Court and shifting coalitions among the justices.

A preliminary assessment of how Chief Justice Roberts and Justices Alito, Sotomayor, and Kagan might affect the Court's federalism policymaking is gleaned from studying their respective nomination hearings in front of the Senate Judiciary Committee. To be sure, other materials such as prior judicial decisions offer insight too, and three of the four recent nominees to the Court served on lower federal circuit courts of appeals prior to their elevation to the Supreme Court. Chief Justice John Roberts was promoted from the U.S. Court of Appeals for the District of Columbia, and Justices Samuel Alito and Sonia Sotomayor were elevated from the Third and Second Circuits, respectively. Justice Elena Kagan had no prior judicial experience and was serving as President Obama's U.S. solicitor general when nominated to the Court. Chief Justice Roberts and Justice Alito decided a few federalism cases as lower circuit judges, and their decisions prior to their nominations suggest that they would follow the Rehnquist Court's federalism jurisprudence.[16] Justice Sotomayor decided only a few federalism disputes on the Second Circuit, and as with Roberts and Alito, her decisions generally indicate an acceptance of new federalism doctrine. Of course, Justice Kagan has no prior federalism judicial record; thus, her nomination record does not offer the same set of materials for analysis as do the others. Reviewing the Senate Judiciary Committee hearings provides a data set common to all four recent nominees, and it also perhaps overcomes the fact that circuit court judges such as Roberts, Alito, and Sotomayor may, in many instances, be reluctant to depart from established Supreme Court precedent anyway.

Recent analyses of the Supreme Court confirmation process suggest a dual approach to understanding how confirmation hearings proceed based on the respective goals and influences of the Judiciary Committee members and the nominees themselves. The process is more than just a set of public hearings in which senators ask questions of nominees. There are far more subtle (and not so subtle) attempts by both sides to influence not only the outcome of the hearings and nomination but also public opinion, constitutional interpretation, and the prospective judicial policymaking of the Court as an institution, as eminent scholar of the confirmation process Professor Henry J. Abraham has shown.[17]

Scholars studying the confirmation process have noted the multifaceted role of the Senate Judiciary Committee. For example, in a study of Supreme Court confirmation hearings, political scientist Stephen J. Wermiel reviewed the communication between senators and nominees. He pointed out that especially in the aftermath of Robert Bork's confirmation hearings in the 1980s, senators on the Judiciary Committee used the hearings to emphasize to nominees that they must be willing "to profess a belief in some threshold constitutional value" in order to get confirmed. Committee members go beyond the historical imperative to determine if a nominee has the intellect and temperament for the job and now proceed to influence the nominee's constitutional interpretation by identifying points of constitutional concern to which the nominee should respond.[18] Other scholars, such as Michael J. Gerhardt, confirm Wermiel's analysis that senators use hearings to influence a nominee's constitutional interpretation and, by doing so, exercise a gatekeeping function in which they try to keep certain constitutional viewpoints away from the courts altogether. Keith Whittington has researched the content of congressional committee hearings as well, and his analysis of the rhetoric by Judiciary Committee members validates the argument that senators use nomination hearings to influence the direction of Supreme Court constitutional doctrine. Somewhat surprisingly, Whittington's research also shows that the Judiciary Committee was not interested in discussing the new federalism: the Rehnquist Court's federalism policymaking "does not appear to have led to more constitutional deliberation in congressional committees."[19]

Recent scholarship on the confirmation process has shifted the focus away from what senators say during hearings to a more nuanced look at the interactions between nominees and committee members. Political scientists Dion Farganis and Justin Wedeking use a data set of thousands of individual level exchanges premised on questions and answers between senators and Court nominees during confirmation hearings. They suggest, broadly speaking, that confirmation hearings are more than just instances of constitutional grandstanding by senators. Rather, they are examples of evasiveness by nominees eager to get to the Court by avoiding the pitfalls that led to Judge Robert Bork's failure to get confirmed in the 1980s. Based on the give-and-take between individual senators and nominees, Farganis and Wedeking conclude that nominees have become more elusive in answering senators' questions. However, this is primarily due to the type of increasingly complex and multifaceted questions that senators now ask, many of them on controversial issues, such as abortion or the right to privacy, as well as issues that continually appear on the Court's docket. When asked such questions, nominees have a tendency to invoke the Ginsburg Rule and refuse to provide specific answers to constitutional questions that will require their decisions should they be confirmed. The so-called rule is derived from Judge Ruth Bader Ginsburg's Supreme Court nomination hearing in the 1990s, when she refused to provide detailed answers to constitutional issues likely to be on the Court's docket in the future. However, even though nominees have a greater tendency to give evasive answers to complex constitutional questioning by senators, Farganis and Wedeking conclude that nominees still provide candid answers to questions most of the time.[20]

The Senate Judiciary Committee's emphasis on fostering constitutional dialogue with Supreme Court nominees, with individual senators using hearings to press for specific constitutional interpretative approaches and to influence the Court's policymaking, coupled with the relatively high level of candor from nominees themselves, underscores the fact that confirmation hearings are more than just staged political events designed to influence public opinion more than constitutional interpretation. Also, content analysis of Senate hearings is a valuable approach for measuring the degree to which senators emphasize specific doctrinal developments originating from within the Court itself, with the goal of influencing the development of constitutional law. To that end, table 6.1 uses a simple content analysis of the confirmation hearings of Chief Justice Roberts and Justices Alito, Sotomayor, and Kagan to compare and contrast the specific concerns addressed by senators and nominees alike. Using specific terms and Court cases and measuring how often each was

Table 6.1. Frequencies of Key Language in Confirmation Hearings (Roberts, Alito, Sotomayor, and Kagan)

Word, Phrase, or Case	*Roberts*	*Alito*	*Sotomayor*	*Kagan*
Federalism-Related Terms				
Commerce Clause	97	32	12	44
Interstate Commerce	23	29	4	14
Sovereign Immunity	15	1	4	2
States' Rights	6	2	0	3
Federalism	4	18	0	8
Tenth Amendment	2	0	4	4
Eleventh Amendment	1	0	0	0
Preemption	1	0	0	2
Political Safeguards	0	0	0	0
Clear Statements	0	3	0	0
Wickard v. Filburn	26	1	0	0
National League of Cities v. Usery	0	5	0	0
Garcia v. SAMTA	0	4	0	0
U.S. v. Lopez	23	44	3	19
Morrison v. U.S.	25	48	0	17
Seminole Tribe v. Florida	1	0	0	5
Gonzales v. Raich	2	14	1	0
Non-Federalism Related Terms				
Foreign Law	13	22	87	41
Takings	6	2	19	6
Abortion	71	152	68	69
Roe v. Wade	124	219	41	16
Boerne v. Flores	3	5	1	0
Kelo v. City of New London	13	10	42	10

Source: Senate Judiciary Committee Hearings

mentioned by a senator or nominee, the content analysis shows some interesting trends across the four nomination hearings.[21]

First, the issue that seemed to appear most consistently across the four hearings is abortion. This is not surprising, given how abortion and the right to privacy (and *Roe v. Wade*) have consumed American political and constitutional debate for the past four decades. Of note too, but with no real bearing on federalism as of yet, is the growing interest in "foreign law" during the Sotomayor and Kagan hearings, which is likely a result of increasing references to foreign jurisprudence by individual justices on the Court and the growing political backlash, especially among conservative senators and legal scholars, against that practice. There is also some discussion of the Fifth Amendment's takings clause, especially during

Sotomayor's hearing, which is most likely due to the Court's decision in *Kelo v. City of New London*.

Second, searches of various federalism-related terms and Court cases indicate a curious trend. During the Roberts and Alito hearings, federalism seemed to be of some concern, with much discussion devoted to the interstate commerce clause and the foundational new federalism cases of *United States v. Lopez* and *United States v. Morrison*. As discussed in more detail below, these dialogues between senators and nominees were to elicit responses from Roberts and Alito as to their views of the Court's more restrictive view of federal power. Interestingly, these references are generally absent from the confirmation hearings of Sonia Sotomayor, but they return during Elena Kagan's hearings, again with the goal of divining Kagan's views on the Court's federalism decisions.

Importantly, the nomination hearings of Chief Justice Roberts and Justices Alito, Sotomayor, and Kagan reveal a common thread of support among all four for the new federalism jurisprudence. This is not to say that all four retain the same level of support for current federalism doctrine and states' rights. But when senators inquired among the respective nominees as to their views on specific federalism cases such as *United States v. Lopez, United States v. Morrison*, or *Seminole Tribe of Florida v. Florida*, all four responded that those cases were settled law. To be sure, it is highly unlikely that a potential justice would repudiate a Supreme Court precedent, since to do so would certainly jeopardize his or her confirmation. Yet just because a nominee might be self-interested does not mean his or her answers are any less candid.

At their separate confirmation hearings, the first two replacements on the Court after the advent of new federalism, Chief Justice John Roberts and Justice Samuel Alito, addressed the scope of congressional commerce regulation, but each expressed different levels of support for it. Although liberal critics argue that Roberts's DC Circuit dissent in *Rancho Viejo, LLC v. Norton* reflected a narrow conception of commerce authority in environment cases, other evidence showed a healthy respect for limiting state sovereignty.[22] Thus, in discussing Congress's use of its commerce clause powers at issue in *Gonzales v. Raich*, he acknowledged the nearly conclusive weight of New Deal precedents under the commerce clause and declared that *United States v. Lopez* and *United States v. Morrison* "did not junk all the cases that came before." In contrast, when asked about *Raich* at his own hearings, Judge Alito interpreted *Lopez* differently by implying that it did not necessarily preserve the Court's post–New Deal commerce clause precedents, perhaps because of his dissent as a Third Circuit judge in *United States v. Rybar*.[23] In *Rybar*, Judge Alito dissented from the ruling that Congress could regulate intrastate possession of machine guns under the commerce clause. In disagreeing, Alito dismissed his colleagues' ringing endorsement of federal power over intrastate conduct because it reduced the *Lopez* precedent to being "a constitutional freak."[24]

The Judiciary Committee hearings show that essential to Roberts's and Alito's commerce clause analysis is the sufficiency of congressional findings, and their respective testimonies both show a tendency to defer to Congress on interstate commerce, spending, and sovereign immunity issues. Hence, Roberts indicated that he sees few constraints on congressional commerce power so long as there is proof that the activity under review is adequately connected to interstate commerce. As he explained to the committee, if judges get to the "point of reweighing congressional findings, that starts to look more like a legislative function," and courts must "make sure that they're interpreting the law and not making it."[25] Similarly, Alito testified that judges must have "great respect" for congressional fact-finding, and he most likely would not have dissented from the Third Circuit's *Rybar* decision sustaining federal regulation of machine guns had Congress compiled findings linking the intrastate possession of machine guns to interstate commerce.[26]

Such commentary reveals that each justice gives great weight to empirical proof, but doing so can cut both ways and either advance or hinder state interests. Whereas heightened scrutiny of congressional fact-finding arguably protects individual rights in the states by imposing limits on legislative influence, it also may become the basis for trumping state claims to Eleventh Amendment sovereignty immunity or, alternatively, for increasing federal enforcement against individual rights based on Section 5 of the Fourteenth Amendment. In legal terms, if Congress expresses a clear and unequivocal intent to waive state immunity or, in Section 5 cases, can establish a congruence and proportionality between the exercise of federal power and the target of the regulation, the testimonies suggest that each jurist is likely to give preference to federal prerogatives.

The affinity to look for empirical facts is illustrated by Judge Roberts's confirmation discussion of Section 5 abrogation of state immunity in cases alleging discrimination under the federal American with Disabilities Act (ADA), an issue in *Board of Trustees of the University of Alabama v. Garrett* (2001) and *Tennessee v. Lane*. In *Garrett*, the Court insulated Alabama from a federal lawsuit by a discharged state employee and cancer victim alleging discrimination under the ADA's Title I. In *Lane*, federal power was extended to let a paraplegic plaintiff who was denied physical access to a court sue Tennessee under the public accommodations provision, or ADA's Title II. In spite of the different outcomes, Roberts asserted that in both cases the Court did not substitute its policy judgment for that of Congress. Instead, it engaged in principled decision-making by focusing on whether Congress established unequivocal factual findings that state governments transgressed federal disability law, which therefore justified a waiver of state sovereign immunity.[27] Thus, for Roberts, Congress may remedy antidiscrimination practices in the states under Section 5 in appropriate factual circumstances.

The justices' confirmation hearings also disclose their general support for Congress's authority under the spending clause to compel states to waive their Eleventh Amendment immunity if they receive federal monies, provided there is a clear nexus between the federal law's purpose and state spending. Roberts and Alito supported Congress's exercise of its spending power under *South Dakota v. Dole* in requiring states to fulfill conditions before they receive federal monies if the federal law is built upon a firm foundation of congressional fact-finding.[28] Indeed, as a DC Circuit judge Roberts endorsed *Barbour v. Washington Metropolitan Area Transit Authority*, which held that a state entity could be sued in federal court because Congress statutorily declared its intent to condition the receipt of federal monies upon a waiver of state immunity. Although Alito's views of congressional spending power were not detailed in any prior cases, he acknowledged *Dole*'s precedential value as giving Congress "very broad authority" over federal spending. Congress could therefore "attach all sorts of conditions to receipt of federal aid," provided they are clear and relevant to the purposes of funding.[29]

Roberts's and Alito's confirmation hearings provide fewer clues as to their positions on federal preemption of state law, and as table 6.1 shows, there was very little discussion of preemption issues in any of the four hearings anyway. For Judge Alito, his Third Circuit decision in *New Jersey Payphone Association v. Town of West New York* provides hints as to his views on federal preemption. At issue was whether a municipality's grant of an exclusive pay phone franchise on public rights of way is preempted by the 1996 Telecommunications Act. Although the court held that the local ordinance was preempted, Judge Alito declined to reach the preemption question by reasoning that it was unnecessary to do so. As he explained,

> The rationales behind the doctrine of avoiding constitutional questions except as a last resort are grounded in fundamental constitutional principles—the "great gravity and delicacy" of judicial review . . . and principles of federalism. . . . Moreover, the federalism rationale is pertinent here because we have the option of avoiding invocation of federal supremacy over local laws. Therefore, resolving this case on state-law grounds does less violence to principles of federalism and dual sovereignty.[30]

Thus Judge Alito viewed preemption prudentially and perhaps as a last resort when overarching federalism principles are at stake.

Whereas some of Alito's views on preemption were disclosed, Roberts's position is hard to discern. Yet some of his off-the-bench writings have federalism overtones that are sensitive to states' rights, and they suggest he respects justiciability requirements. Of the eleven publications Judge Roberts listed in the Senate Judiciary Committee questionnaire, two law reviews speak to the protection of individual property rights in the states in the takings and contract clause context: he advocates against strict judicial construction of constitutional text because it would diminish those rights.[31]

The pre–Supreme Court portraits of each jurist, moreover, may address ideological differences that they have with the justices they are replacing and with whom they are serving on the bench. For instance, Roberts has publicly distanced himself from endorsing an originalist or strict understanding of constitutional text, and his declaration sets him apart from Justices Scalia and Thomas.[32] Similarly, but only if one overlooks the antinationalist position he took in *Rybar* in light of *Lopez*, Judge Alito's later acknowledgment of Congress's broad and evolutionary commerce power at his Supreme Court confirmation hearing tends to set him apart from Justice Thomas's originalist reading of the interstate commerce clause (which makes a distinction between commerce and other forms of economic activity).[33] Also, whereas Justice Alito's posture on the scope of Congress's spending authority is less clear, Chief Justice Roberts's inclination to defer to Congress in federal conditional spending cases may distinguish him from Justice Sandra Day O'Connor, who dissented in *Dole*. Finally, on the question of whether the national political process can effectively safeguard the states' interests in structural terms, it is noteworthy that Justice Alito implied in *Rybar* that normative limits on federal power exist outside the political process. As a result, Justice Alito arguably does not agree with the political safeguards argument; accordingly, he may be closer to Justice O'Connor's federalism jurisprudence.

The next Supreme Court nominee, Judge Sonia Sotomayor, was promoted from the U.S. Court of Appeals for the Second Circuit by President Barack Obama. She faced much less questioning about federalism, congressional power, and states' rights than Chief Justice Roberts and Justice Alito. When senators did raise federalism and related issues in their questioning, they did not seem so interested in prompting an extended discussion on those topics. For instance, in a relatively short exchange with Sotomayor, Democratic senator Diane Feinstein from California inquired as to her views on Congress's commerce clause powers and the extent to which justices should defer to congressional authority. Judge Sotomayor invoked the Ginsburg Rule and responded that she could only talk about congressional power in broad strokes, given that cases concerning that very issue would likely come before her as a Second Circuit judge or even a Supreme Court justice if she were confirmed. However, Sotomayor specifically mentioned the *Lopez* and *Raich* decisions as establishing "broad principles" in commerce clause cases, and although the Court pays careful attention to congressional findings, in *Raich* the Court also showed that "each situation will provide a unique factual setting that the court will apply those principles to."[34] Senator Feinstein expressed an additional concern that the Court's decisions would allow federal judges to interpret restrictively federal environmental laws such as the Clean Air and Clean Water Acts and noted that she hoped Judge Sotomayor would go to the Supreme Court "with the sensitivity that this body has to be able to legislate in those areas. They involve all of the states and they are very important questions involving people's well being, control of the environment, the air, the water, et cetera."[35]

There were few other mentions of federalism, states' rights, or the commerce clause powers of Congress. Even conservative Republican senator John Cornyn from Texas made no reference to federalism, even though he did so during the subsequent nomination for Elena Kagan. In Sotomayor's case, Cornyn raised concerns that she might use foreign law and invent new constitutional rights in her decision-making, and he generally focused his questioning on the issues of abortion and affirmative action. Another conservative senator, Republican Tom Coburn from Oklahoma, did raise specific concerns about federalism even though the main gist of his questioning of Sotomayor mirrored Cornyn's with a similar focus on her views on abortion and the use of foreign law by federal judges. Senator Coburn asked Sotomayor if she considered the Court a check on Congress's use of its commerce clause powers, as the framers intended it to be, and whether she would follow the "plain meaning" of the Constitution. Specifically, he asked if she believed that "our Federal courts enable the Federal Government to exceed its intended boundaries by interpreting Article I's commerce clause and necessary and proper clause to delegate virtual unlimited authority to the Federal Government?" Judge Sotomayor replied simply that "the question for the court in any particular situation is to determine whether whatever branch of government or state is acting within the limits of the Constitution."[36] Coburn further asked Sotomayor if she had any concerns about the expansive use of congressional power over commerce, especially given the increasing national debt, to which Sotomayor replied that the Constitution gives primary authority for settling that question to the Senate and the House of Representatives. Sotomayor also refused to answer Coburn's question about whether courts have abandoned the "plain meaning" of the Constitution, thereby rescinding their power to limit the power of Congress. To answer that question, as she noted, would prejudge cases that might come before her in the future.

Judge Sotomayor's confirmation hearing sheds some light on her approach to the new federalism. While her answers to the Judiciary Committee indicate a fidelity to the Court's federalism precedents, only two—*United States v. Lopez* and *Gonzales v. Raich*—were discussed in detail during her testimony. In her view, though, the Court's precedents point to a case-by-case analysis heavily dependent on the facts of each specific dispute. To be sure, the federalism questions that senators asked were generally abstract and not well designed to elicit whether she supported the Court's federalism jurisprudence or not.

The most recent Judiciary Committee hearings for a Supreme Court nominee showed some senators returning to a focus on federalism. President Obama nominated his solicitor general, Elena Kagan, to replace Justice John Paul Stevens, who retired after serving on the Court for over three decades. Kagan had no prior judicial service, unlike the recent nominees to the Court. For Republican senator John Kyl from Arizona, her "thin body of work" raised significant concerns about "federalism, free speech, and national security," a point that was echoed in part by Texas senator Cornyn, who argued that federalism was an area of "obvious inquiry" during Kagan's confirmation hearing. Senator Jeff Sessions, Republican from Alabama, inquired as to whether Kagan considered herself a "legal progressive" and noted that the progressive movement has a negative influence in Supreme Court cases on federalism, economic liberties, and property rights.[37]

Cornyn asked pointed questions of Kagan concerning her views on federalism. For example, he inquired whether "cases in recent decades largely eliminated the important role of the Supreme Court in checking the size and scope of the federal government." She responded, "Senator Cornyn, I guess I actually think that in recent decades the Court has suggested that there are some limits on the scope of the Federal Government," and she contrasted the Court's placing limits on national power with Chief Justice John Marshall's Court, which viewed power in expansive terms. Cornyn responded with an inquiry about her views on the Tenth Amendment: "The Tenth Amendment, which I think most people sort of popularly view as an expression of our Federal system and the fact that the States and individuals retain power that's not been delegated to the Federal Government, has largely, in my opinion, been rendered a dead letter by Supreme Court decisions." With a vague reference to the individual mandate provisions for health insurance passed in the Patient Protection and Affordable Care Act, he continued, "If Congress can force people who are sitting on their couch at home to purchase a product and penalize them if they don't purchase the government-approved product, it seems to me there is no limit to the Federal Government's authority, and we've come a long, long way from what our Founders intended. Do you agree?" She responded that the Court has given "broad discretion" to Congress when it regulates the channels, instrumentalities, and objects that substantially impede interstate commerce, with the main limits on congressional power coming through the Court's *Lopez* and *Morrison* decisions, which protect activities traditionally regulated by the states. In follow-up questioning on a subsequent day of the hearings, Senator Cornyn asked if she agreed with the Court's decisions in *Lopez* and *Morrison,* to which she replied, "I've refrained from agreeing or disagreeing, but I do believe that *Lopez* and *Morrison* are settled law and entitled to the precedential weight" accorded to other Supreme Court opinions. Cornyn noted a memo she wrote during her time with the Clinton administration in which she characterized the *Seminole Tribe of Florida v. Florida* case as an effort by a bare majority on the Court to recalibrate the balance of power between the states and the national government, to which Kagan again responded that *Lopez, Morrison,* and now *Seminole Tribe* were settled law and that she had "no plan, no agenda, no anything to mess with them." Finally, Cornyn asked her to name an economic activity that is outside Congress's regulatory powers under the interstate commerce clause; Kagan responded that she would not even try to do that, since the Court's existing jurisprudence (again in *Lopez* and *Morrison*) makes a distinction between economic and noneconomic activity when determining the limits of federal power.[38]

In questions similar to Cornyn's, conservative Republican senators Coburn from Oklahoma and Sessions from Alabama asked Kagan about her views of the commerce clause powers of Congress, to which she responded, again, that the Rehnquist Court's decisions in *Lopez* and *Morrison* are settled law and establish that the clause only allows Congress to regulate economic activity.[39] Coburn articulated his view of the role of the high court in checking and limiting the commerce clause powers of Congress and argued that the Court has ignored this fundamental role, with disastrous results: "What we found ourselves today on the Commerce Clause is that, through a period of precedent-setting decisions, we have allowed the Federal Government to become something that it was never entitled to become." Kagan responded yet again that "there are limits on the Commerce Clause . . . articulated by the court in *Morrison* and in *Lopez,* which are primarily about non-economic activity," and she noted that those precedents establish that Congress cannot regulate noneconomic activity under the clause.[40]

In contrast to Cornyn, Coburn, and Sessions, Democratic senator Benjamin Cardin from Maryland asked Kagan to discuss her views on when the Court should defer to congressional policymaking, with specific attention to environmental policy: "Do you agree that the Federal Government working with the states has a unique role in protecting our environment and that the government must hold public lands and waters in trust for future generations? And will you give deference to Congress as we attempt to carry out that mandate?" Kagan responded that "Congress certainly has broad authority under the Constitution to enact legislation involving protection of the environment. And I think that when Congress enacts such legislation the job of the Courts is to construe it consistent with Congressional intent."[41] Thus, although she reads current Court precedent as limiting Congress's power over interstate commerce to economic issues only, Kagan also shows some support for a broad congressional power of environmental regulation. Perhaps more importantly, her emphasis on respecting congressional intent places her in some opposition to the new federalism. By showing judicial deference to Congress, she adheres to the model of judging that so alarmed Senator Coburn in that she might mitigate the role of the Court as an external check on the powers of Congress and become complicit in helping to expand the powers of Congress. In terms of federalism, by showing such deference to Congress, Kagan might not prioritize the independent constitutional limits on federal power that the new federalism cases tend to require.

Somewhat telling in this regard are her responses to written questions submitted by senators prior to her confirmation hearing. Senator Cornyn asked an intriguing question concerning the treaty power of the national government and whether Congress and the president could use an international treaty to enact the PPACA's individual mandate provision if it was struck down by the Court. Kagan invoked the Ginsburg Rule, as she noted that his question concerned a "hypothetical statute arising from a particular set of hypothetical circumstances," and if such a case came to the Court, she would "consider all the briefs and arguments presented."[42] When asked whether the Tenth Amendment gives "textual protections to federalism, apart from the broader structure set up by the Constitution," Kagan relied on the Court's precedents in *United States v. Darby* and *New York v. United States* and the writings of Justice Joseph Story and wrote that the amendment is an "affirmation" of a "necessary rule of interpreting the Constitution."[43] While Kagan's response seemed to acknowledge that the Tenth Amendment is only a "truism" as announced by the Court in *Darby*, by stating that it is a rule of interpretation instead of a textual protection for federalism, she may be closer to judicial liberals who do not generally interpret the amendment as an affirmative barrier to federal power in favor of the states.

In sum, the confirmation hearings of the most recent chief justice and justices—Roberts, Alito, Sotomayor, and Kagan—suggest that none of the personnel changes will dramatically disrupt the new federalism jurisprudence. It is unlikely that some of the four justices will significantly add their voices in support of Justice Clarence Thomas's radical federalism that confines congressional power to its eighteenth-century understanding, and it is also unlikely that some will add their support to overturning the new federalism to reinstate the twentieth-century understanding of federalism premised in the New Deal. While it is likely that Chief Justice Roberts and Justice Alito may be more inclined to adhere to the limiting principles of federalism derived from the *Lopez* and *Morrison* line of cases, and Sotomayor and Kagan may be more willing to sustain congressional power vis-à-vis the states, none of the four appointments will disrupt the new federalism in the short term.

The Judiciary Committee hearings for all four justices also show some important differences in how senators view the new federalism. To be sure, federalism as an issue at the confirmation hearings for Roberts, Alito, Sotomayor, and Kagan took a backseat to abortion, the right to privacy, and questions about each candidate's own judicial philosophy. The relative lack of interest among senators shows that perhaps the new federalism is now ingrained in the policymaking process and is more accepted by lawmakers. When federalism was discussed, it was often in the context of a senator pressing his or her own constitutional interpretation on the nominee. Thus Senator Cornyn, no doubt prompted and alarmed by Congress's use of its interstate commerce clause powers to pass the individual mandate provision in the PPACA, communicated his view of federalism to Elena Kagan and solicited her support for the Court's decisions that limit federal power vis-à-vis the states and her views on the limits of Congress's power over interstate commerce. In contrast, Senator Cardin asked Kagan the extent to which she would defer to Congress to support its mandate to protect the environment. Senator Feinstein's questioning of Sonia Sotomayor was in a similar vein, in which she prompted Sotomayor to support Congress's power to legislate on questions concerning the "people's well being [and] control of the environment." As illustrations, the questions by Cornyn, Cardin, and Feinstein are instances of senators pressing their approach to federalism and constitutional interpretation on the nominees; they are also, for Cornyn, forms of encouragement to adhere to existing federalism precedents as a means to limit congressional power and, for Cardin and Feinstein, suggestions to the nominees to find the exceptions to current federalism doctrine that justify more deference to and support for congressional power, especially in policy areas supported by congressional liberals.

One final point needs to be made concerning the absence of discussion of preemption at all four hearings. Preemption is a complex constitutional doctrine that the Court applies to determine when federal law trumps, or preempts, a conflicting state law. As discussed in more detail below, preemption has been a vital aspect of the new federalism from the Rehnquist through the current Roberts Courts; thus, that it was not a topic of questioning and discussion at the last four Court confirmation hearings is somewhat of a mystery worthy of further investigation. However, as the discussion of preemption later in this chapter makes clear, the ideological conflicts between the justices most recently confirmed to the Court are revealing themselves in this area of federalism policymaking, especially with regard to the extent to which the Court gives deference to Congress on federal law. Yet deference in preemption cases does not seem to be the main dividing line between Roberts, Alito, Sotomayor, and Kagan. What does emerge as the main point of division, as the discussion below explains in more detail, concerns whether a federalism case outcome is pro- or anti-business. Here, Roberts and Alito tend to decide federalism disputes in a more pro-business manner than Sotomayor and Kagan. To be sure, the pro-business outlook of each of the nominees was not considered by the Senate Judiciary Committee but may indeed emerge in future hearings.

NEW DIRECTIONS OF FEDERALISM IN THE ROBERTS COURT

An initial perspective into Roberts Court federalism is supplied by table 6.2. The table collects and ideologically codes only "federalism" cases, as defined by the Supreme Court Judicial Database, across the Rehnquist, Warren, and Burger Courts. The data from the Roberts Court (n = 25) represents only a fraction of the time relative to the other Court eras; thus the data is inherently constrained, and any inferences drawn from it can only be speculative.[44] Still, some decisional patterns are discernible, on a tentative basis. The table records that the Roberts Court is more on pace to support liberal, or pro–federal government, outcomes at a slightly higher level (64 percent) than the Rehnquist (54 percent) and Burger (59 percent) Courts, but slightly less than the Warren Court (71 percent). Also, the trend favoring centralization is proportionately matched by a lower percentage of conservative, or pro-state, outcomes (36 percent), a rate analogous to the Burger Court (38 percent) and perhaps even the Warren Court (27 percent), but less than the Rehnquist Court (46 percent). Furthermore, the table suggests that the Roberts Court is not yet as assertive in striking down federal (4 percent) or state (0 percent) laws as the other Courts are. With a 100 percent adherence to stare decisis, it has not yet shown a willingness to overturn precedent to reach federalism outcomes, as the Rehnquist Court did in a similar period of time when it struck down "24 federal laws and 25 state or local laws, an average of three federal laws and three state or local laws each term," between the 1994 and 2000 terms.[45]

Table 6.2. Federalism Decisional Trends, U.S. Supreme Court, 1953–2010

	Warren Court (1953–1968)	*Burger Court (1969–1985)*	*Rehnquist Court (1986–2004)*	*Roberts Court (2005–2010)*
Number of Federalism Rulings	94	108	124	25
Decision Direction				
Liberal	71%	59%	54%	64%
Conservative	27%	38%	46%	36%
Declaration of Unconstitutionality				
None	88%	93%	88%	96%
State Law, Regulation, Constitution	11%	6%	6%	0%
Municipal/Local Ordinance	1%	1%	0%	0%
Congressional Act	0%	0%	6%	4%
Precedent Alteration				
None	98%	97%	96%	100%
Formal Alteration	2%	3%	4%	0%

Source: The Supreme Court Dataset, 1953–2011 Terms at http://scdb.wustl.edu/analysis.php (using Data Release SCDB_2011_01, SCDB_2011_03)

The implications of alleged Roberts Court activism has been detailed in a study commissioned by the *New York Times* to investigate the Roberts Court's overall (and not just federalism) docket. The research is significant insofar as it was done by leading political science and legal scholars in the field. In analyzing five terms, it reports the Roberts Court is slightly more conservative in its decision-making than the Rehnquist or Burger Courts (although the finding is not statistically significant). Moreover, it finds that the Roberts Court is significantly more likely to produce conservative decisions in antitrust, merger, bankruptcy, public utility regulation, federal/state consumer protection, labor arbitration, and employment discrimination cases. More cautiously, it adds that "it might be reasonable to conclude that the [Roberts] Court is distinctly favorable toward business interests" because it is inclined to grant certiorari to a larger fraction of liberal lower court decisions than the Rehnquist Court did (68 percent as opposed to 60 percent). As a result, under this view, the Roberts Court is more business friendly, at least if the pattern of reversing a higher fraction of those appeals from lower courts continues.[46] As noted in chapter 1, however, these findings must be balanced against other research challenging the notion that the Roberts Court is a business-friendly bench.[47]

The Roberts Court docket and the possibility that it favors business are investigated further by exploring a sample of forty-six federalism cases from the Supreme Court Judicial Database and other sources, spanning the Roberts Court's first six terms.[48] The sample shows 62 percent of federalism rulings are decided in a liberal (pro-federal) direction, whereas 38 percent are conservative (pro-state) (figure 6.1).[49] The bulk of cases are statutory construction (59 percent) instead of constitutional law (30 percent) decisions; a smaller percent (11 percent) are mixed statutory and constitutional cases (figure 6.2).[50] The docket's composition is consistent

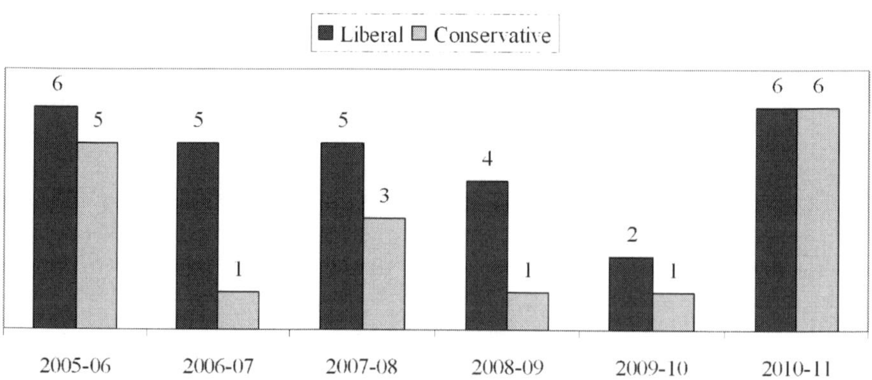

Figure 6.1. Federalism Cases in Roberts Court, 2005–2011

with findings revealing the Roberts Court is especially interested in resolving business and commercial regulation preemption (statutory construction) appeals that often are decided liberally, in favor of the federal government, as well as with related arguments saying the Roberts and Rehnquist Courts are not that protective of states' rights or sovereignty in certain instances, such as in deciding preemption and the constitutionality of state regulation under the dormant commerce clause (see chapter 3).[51] This latter point is significant because the sample is top-heavy with statutory preemption appeals and, to a lesser degree, constitutional cases consisting of Eleventh Amendment, commerce clause, and miscellaneous subject matter. As a result, it appears that "preemption has emerged as the contemporary federalism battleground" in the Roberts Court.[52]

While the subset does not capture all the different facets of federalism,[53] it suggests the Roberts Court is setting an agenda that is more attentive to statutory instead of constitutional claims. If so, that distinguishes its judicial decision-making from Rehnquist Court new federalism since it is commonly argued that the "federalism five" pro–states' right bloc is prone to using constitutional interpretation as the preferred vehicle to create favorable state-oriented precedents.[54] With this in mind, the ensuing analysis surveys the doctrinal rationales, voting alignments, and outcomes of cases in order to detect if additional comparisons can be made between the two Courts. The focus is on the decisions comprising the bulk of Roberts Court judicial decision-making—namely, preemption, Eleventh Amendment, and commerce clause appeals. After considering key Roberts Court preemption cases, the discussion addresses constitutional cases resolving the scope and application of Eleventh Amendment and commerce clause appeals. The last part of the case discussion briefly

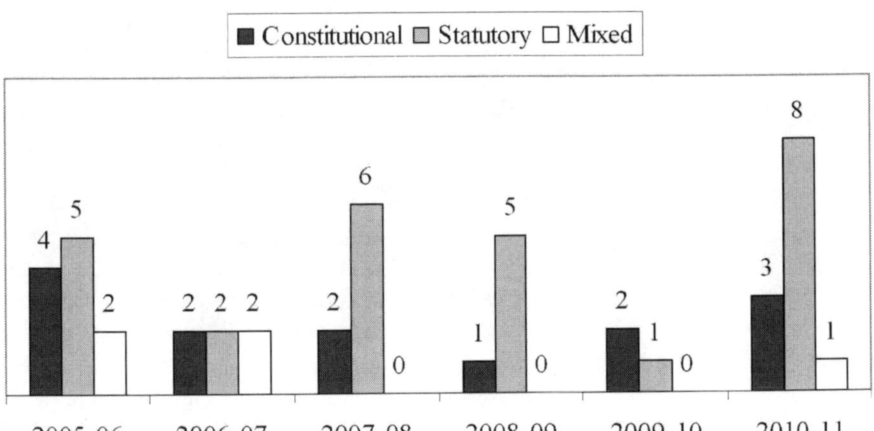

Figure 6.2. Type of Federalism Cases in Roberts Court, 2005–2011

assesses other significant rulings that afford insight into relevant new federalism decisional behavior.

Statutory Construction Cases: Preemption

So long as Congress properly acts within the scope of its enumerated powers, it enjoys authority under the U.S. Constitution's supremacy clause to override state laws that conflict with federal legislation.[55] The challenge courts face is deciding whether Congress expressly or by implication intended to preempt state regulation, a determination requiring judges to engage in statutory construction. In express preemption cases, courts apply canons of statutory interpretation (discussed in chapter 3) to give meaning to the terminology Congress uses in the legislation to supersede state laws, whereas in implied preemption cases, courts may infer congressional intent in the absence of express language signifying what it meant.[56]

Searching for congressional intent is complicated by the innate ambiguity of statutory text or, sometimes inexplicably, plain language appearing in savings clauses that purport to clarify a federal statute's preemptive scope. Savings clauses, designed to give states the flexibility to set regulatory conditions not covered by the statute, are commonly found in environmental or consumer protection laws. In this context, their existence is a reaction to the centralizing effects of regulation that threatens to undermine in states the exercise of traditional police powers that safeguard citizen health, safety, and welfare. In this light, they reflect Congress's desire to protect some spheres of state regulatory authority in areas increasingly dominated by overarching federal interests; arguably, they also provide courts with incentives to respect state law by insisting that regulated entities demonstrate that Congress clearly expressed its intent in the statute to foreclose state common law remedies.[57] Yet some laws, such as the federal Clean Air Act, are more problematic to construe because they have multiple express or savings clause provisions in the same statute. The multiplicity of provisions favoring and rejecting preemption only serves to make the task of judicial interpretation more difficult.[58]

Still, standing alone savings clauses are analogous to a canon of statutory construction, the "presumption against preemption," which courts routinely use in the search for congressional intent during statutory interpretation.[59] Its operative force, which leans toward the recognition of state powers, comes from *Rice v. Santa Fe Elevator Corporation*. In *Rice* the Supreme Court held that courts should hesitate to give preemptive effect to federal laws regulating state police powers unless Congress indicates a clear and manifest purpose to do so. The majority ruling supplies several examples signifying a clear and manifest purpose: (1) when the "scheme of federal regulation" is "so pervasive as to make reasonable the inference that Congress left no room for the states to supplement it," (2) when federal law may "touch a field in which the federal interest is so dominant that the federal system will be assumed to preclude enforcement of state laws on the same subject," or (3) when "state policy may produce a result inconsistent with the objective of the federal statute."[60] Notably, what constitutes a "clear and manifest purpose" according to *Rice* closely tracks issues of implied preemption (e.g., where a preemptive intent is inferred because Congress occupies the field or, instead, when there is a conflict between federal and state law; conflict preemption may encompass the subcategories of obstacle and impossibility preemption).[61]

In theory, the presumption is arguably a state-friendly legal provision that works in tandem with savings clauses, which also explicitly reserve power to the states in predefined areas of regulation, and perhaps the presumption's operation is similar to the judicial recognition of the longstanding *Erie* doctrine's having a pro-state effect (*Erie* obliges federal courts to apply state law in commercial or tort lawsuits unless Congress has specifically preempted common law in regulation).[62] Under this view, the sum of these provisions gives justices solicitous of state-centric federalism values ample opportunities to make them into judicial policy in Supreme Court appeals. In making that connection to the Rehnquist Court, law professor Jamelle Sharpe hypothesizes that "there are clear parallels between the Court's approach to preemption cases and its approach to the 'new federalism' cases" linked with the Rehnquist Court because "both immerse the Court in questions of federalism, statutory interpretation, and the relationship between them." In regard to the presumption against preemption, she intuits that its judicial application is "consistent with the largely state-favoring work of the Court's new federalism cases . . . [since they] indicate that the default rule of 'Our Federalism' is that states hold regulatory sway absent overt and specific indications by Congress to the contrary."[63]

Yet academic studies of Rehnquist Court preemption observe that the type of new federalism theory described above does not match new federalism reality.[64] Most scholars generally assert what Professors Michael Greve and Jonathan Klick do in their empirical assessment of 105 Rehnquist Court preemption cases decided from 1986 to the 2003–2004 term. They note preemption cases register about 8 percent of the Court's civil docket (averaging roughly seven per term in the first and second Courts), and within the sample there is a fairly robust contingent of state common law tort cases (39 percent). Relative to outcomes, about 50 percent are unanimously decided, and in 25 percent of "contested" cases (with more than two dissents), the chance of preemption increases. Yet they doubt there is a clear link between pro-preemption and pro-business outcomes suggesting, in fact, that an "anti-business story" can be told about the results.[65] Perhaps most importantly, conservative justices conventionally associated with pro-state sympathies vote most consistently for preemption, whereas liberals stereotypically thought to be inclined toward centralization side most regularly with the states. While on balance the exact configuration and strength of the voting blocs remains fluid, the most cohesive conservative pro-preemption bloc is Chief Justice William Rehnquist and Justices Antonin Scalia, Sandra Day O'Connor, and Anthony Kennedy; the most reliable liberal anti-preemption group includes Justices John Paul Stevens, Ruth Bader Ginsburg, David Souter, and Stephen Breyer. At first blush, and notably in contrast to the pivotal role they often play in federalism cases, Justices O'Connor and Kennedy are not the swing votes in preemption cases because Justice Thomas appears to replace them, but whether that is true or not becomes less clear in contested cases because the composition of the blocs themselves, as well as the presence of any identifiable pivot justice, is fluid and unpredictable, especially in the Court's latter years. Still, a key finding is that there is a "massive discontinuity" or a "judicial flip-flop" relative to the stereotypical view that conservative justices are more state friendly, and liberals are less so, in federalism outcomes. In preemption cases, Greve and Klick argue, the opposite is true.[66]

The proposition the Roberts Court is following an identical decisional trajectory is tested by examining a subset of cases (n = 27) decided after 2005 in the preemption area. The rulings are drawn from the sample (n = 46) of all federalism cases being considered in this chapter.[67] So that decisional trends and voting behavior address the possibility that the Roberts Court is state centric and business friendly, two sets of tables are constructed. Whereas both tables record preemption decisions having a discernible pro- or anti-business effect, they are distinguishable because table 6.3 displays anti-preemption (conservative) results favoring state governments, whereas table 6.4 outlines (liberal) decisions sustaining the federal government. Each table also exhibits decisional federalism implications relative to the business effects the cases express as a matter of legal doctrine or public policy. In addition, a sense of the unanimity or conflict that the outcomes generate is suggested by each table, which segregates the justices' votes into blocs.

Although the case subset is small, some preliminary observations are worth mentioning. As figures 6.1 and 6.2 suggest, most Roberts Court federalism cases consist of statutory construction adjudications (twenty-seven) moving in a liberal (pro–federal government) direction. Of the statutory construction cases addressing preemption, twenty-two of twenty-six (85 percent) of the rulings have a discernable business effect—that is, the case holding is supportive of the general business interest at issue in the

Table 6.3. Anti-Preemption Decisions Favoring State Government in Roberts Court, 2005–2011

Case/Term	*Decisional Outcome/Implications*	*Majority*	*Dissent*
Pro-Business Effect			
2007–2008			
Fla. Dep't of Revenue v. Picadilly Cafeterias (2008)	Corporate debtor can claim state tax exemption in bankruptcy	**Th**, Sc, K, So, RG, Ro, Al	**Br**, St
Anti-Business Effect			
2008–2009			
Altria Group v. Good (2008)	Cigarette makers are liable under state tort law	**St**, K, So, RG, Br	**Th**, Sc, Ro, Al
Wyeth v. Levine (2009)	Drug makers are liable under state tort law	**St**, K, So, RG, ***Br***, ***<u>Th</u>***	**Al**, Sc, Ro
Vaden v. Discover Bank (2009)	Creditor lost in debt collection litigation	**RG**, Sc, K, So, Th	***<u>Ro</u>***, St, Br, Al
Cuomo v. Clearing House (2009)	State prosecutors can investigate racial discrimination in national bank practices	**Sc**, St, RG, So, Br	***<u>Th</u>***, Ro, K, Al
2010–2011			
Chamber of Commerce v. Whiting (2011)	Businesses restricting employment of illegal aliens are subject to legal sanctions	**Ro**, Sc, K, Al, Th	**Br**, RG, **Soto**
Williamson v. Mazda Motor (2011)	Carmakers are liable under state tort law	**Br**, Sc, K, RG, Ro, Al, ***Soto***, ***<u>Th</u>***	N/A
Smith v. Bayer Corp. (2011)	Federal court in class action cannot use federal law to stop similar class action pending in state court	**Ka**, Br, K, RG, Th, Ro, Al, Sc, Soto	N/A

Note: Chief Justice Roberts (Ro); Justices Stevens (St), Scalia (Sc), Kennedy (K), Souter (So), Ruth Bader Ginsburg (RG), Thomas (Th), Breyer (Br), Alito (Al), Sotomayor (Soto), Kagan (Ka). Justices authoring opinions are in bold type. Concurrences are italicized; Special Concurrences and Concurring/Dissenting Opinions are italicized and underlined. Justice Kagan did not participate in *Williamson v. Mazda Motor of America* (2011) or *Chamber of Commerce v. Whiting* (2011).

Source: The Supreme Court Dataset, 1953–2011 Terms, at http://scdb.wustl.edu/analysis.php (using Data Release Id: SCDB_2011_03); SCOTUSblog Case Stat Pack, at www.scotusblog.com/reference/stat-pack.

Table 6.4. Preemption Decisions Favoring Federal Government in Roberts Court, 2005–2011

Case/Term	*Decisional Outcome/Implications*	*Majority*	*Dissent*
Pro-Business Effect			
Buckeye Check v. Cardegna (2006)	Contract dispute arbitrated under federal law	**Sc,** St, K, So, RG, Br, Ro	**Th**
Merrill Lynch v. Dabit (2006)	Federal law bars securities fraud class action	**St,** Sc, K, So, RG, Th, Br, Ro	None
Norfolk So. Railway v. Sorrell (2007)	Federal law bars state tort liability standard	**Ro,** St, Sc, K, ***So***, Th, Br, Al, ***<u>RG</u>***	None
Watters v. Wachovia Bank (2007)	Federal law bars state licensing compliance for banks	**RG,** K, So, Br, Al	**St,** Sc, Ro
CSX v. Ga. State Bd. (2007)	Railroad can challenge tax liability under federal law	**Ro,** St, Sc, K, So, Th, RG, Br, Al	None
Riegel v. Medtronic (2008)	Federal law bars state tort lawsuit against medical device manufacturer	**Sc,** K, So, Br, Th, Ro, Al, ***<u>St</u>***	**RG**
Preston v. Ferrer (2008)	Contract dispute must be arbitrated under federal law	**RG,** St, Sc, K, So, Br, Ro, Al	**Th**
Rowe v. NH Motor Transport (2008)	Federal law bars state regulation of tobacco products	**Br,** St, K, So, Th, Ro, Al, ***Sc***, ***RG***	None
Chamber of Comm. v. Brown (2008)	Federal law bars use of state funds for unionization	**St,** Sc, K, So, Th, Ro, Al	**Br**, RG
CSX v. Ala. Dep't of Revenue (2011)	Railroad can challenge state tax discrimination	**Ka,** Ro, Sc, K, Br, Al, Soto	**Th,** RG
Brueswitz v. Wyeth (2011)	Federal law bars state tort lawsuit against vaccine manufacturer	**Sc,** K, Th, Ro, Al, ***Br***	**Soto,** RG
AT&T Mobility v. Concepcion (2011)	Availability of class action arbitration in state law barred under federal law	**Sc,** Ro, K, Al, ***Th***	**Br,** RG, Soto, Ka
Pliva v. Mensing (2011)	Federal law bars state tort lawsuit against drug manufacturers	**Th**, Sc, Ro, Al, K	**Soto,** RG, Br, Ka
Anti-Business Effect			
Shady Grove v. Allstate (2010)	Federal class action rules preempt state law	**Sc**, Ro, Th, Soto, ***<u>St</u>***	**RG**, K, Br, Al

Note: Chief Justice Roberts (Ro); Justices Stevens (St), Scalia (Sc), Kennedy (K), Souter (So), Ruth Bader Ginsburg (RG), Thomas (Th), Breyer (Br), Alito (Al), Sotomayor (Soto), Kagan (Ka). Justices authoring opinions are in bold type. Concurrences are italicized; Special Concurrences and Concurring/Dissenting Opinions are italicized and underlined. Justice Alito did not participate in *Buckeye Check Cashing v. Cardegna* (2006) or *Merrill Lynch v. Dabit* (2006). Justice Thomas did not participate in *Watters v. Wachovia Bank* (2007). Justice Kagan did not participate in *Brueswitz v. Wyeth* (2011).

Source: The Supreme Court Dataset, 1953–2011 Terms, at http://scdb.wustl.edu/analysis.php (using Data Release Id: SCDB_2011_03); SCOTUSblog Case Stat Pack, at www.scotusblog.com/reference/stat-pack.

case.[68] Of those cases, 36 percent are conservative anti-preemption outcomes favoring state governments, but only one case (13 percent) has a pro-business effect while the remainder (87 percent) are anti-business (table 6.3). In contrast, less than two-thirds (64 percent) of preemption rulings are liberally decided for the federal government, and all but one outcome (93 percent) favor business (table 6.4). Furthermore, seven cases that have a business effect (32 percent) consider whether state common law tort remedies are preempted, and of those cases, three (43 percent) have an anti-business effect in anti-preemption cases, while four (57 percent) preemptively supplant state law with a pro-business effect (tables 6.3 and 6.4).

While the significance of outcomes and voting alignments in the anti-preemption table must not be overstated due to the small subset sample size in table 6.3, the information is meaningful if used only to paint a rough portrait of early Roberts Court decisional trends and patterns. The contested cases especially open a window into the operative judicial philosophies that orient the justices' resolution of cases. In this light, it is reasonable to assert that anti-preemption outcomes are some evidence that the justices favoring state interests do so by casting votes in that direction. With these limitations and perspectives in mind, the data captures the ideological flip-flop Professors Greve and Klick record in their preliminary assessment of Rehnquist Court preemption cases. Restated, members of the liberal group typically perceived to be supportive of presumption (and who stand in contrast to their colleagues, who are thought to be solicitous of states' rights) are, by and large, not. As Professors Greve and Klick surmise, four liberal justices—Stevens, Ginsburg, Souter, and Breyer—coalesce in at least three of the most contested (two dissents or more) cases (*Altria Group v. Good, Wyeth v. Levine,* and *Cuomo v. Clearing House*). In contrast, Chief Justice John Roberts (a proxy for Rehnquist), Scalia, Alito (a proxy for O'Connor), and Kennedy represent the dissenting four-member conservative group.[69]

The ideological division is sharpest in two cases, *Altria* (5–4) and *Wyeth* (6–3), involving preemption of state tort law remedies, while *Cuomo* (5–4) tangentially has a racial discrimination backstory in the context of a state prosecution involving allegedly corrupt federal banking practices. Tipping the balance toward anti-preemption and joining the four-justice liberal bloc are Kennedy (*Altria*), Kennedy and Thomas (*Wyeth*), and Scalia (*Cuomo*). Notably, in the last of the five most contested cases, *Chamber of Commerce v. Whiting* (pertaining to the preemptive scope of federal immigration law), the 5–4 split is ideologically inverted by situating conservative justices in the anti-preemption majority, with liberals occupying the preemption space in dissent.[70] Issues of express and implied preemption, as well as their interpretative relationship to savings clauses and the *Rice* presumption against preemption, predominately appear in the contested anti-preemption cases (table 6.3). Accordingly, because critics of the Rehnquist Court accuse it of not using otherwise arguably straightforward methods of statutory construction in preemption cases that favor the states,[71] two state common law cases (*Altria* and *Wyeth*), plus one state immigration case (*Whiting*), are briefly considered next to see if the same is true of the Roberts Court.

At issue in *Altria Group v. Good* is whether an injured smoker's claim that *Altria*'s cigarette labeling fraudulently concealed hidden health risks allegedly linked to ingesting "light" cigarettes is based on a state law "requirement" or "prohibition" that federal law expressly preempts. The issue forced the justices to revisit a landmark but highly controversial Rehnquist Court decision, *Cipollone v. Liggett Group, Inc.*, which interpreted the Federal Cigarette Labeling and Advertising Act (FCLAA) and its amendments to preempt state-based requirements or prohibitions imposed in products liability and other tort actions. As the nation became more politically conservative in the 1980s and 1990s after the Reagan presidency, *Cipollone* and its fractured plurality opinion (authored by Justice Stevens) helped fuel the onset of "preemption wars" fought between Congress, agencies, and the courts over the issue of tort reform and the extent to which corporate defendants could assert *Cipollone* as a successful preemptive defense against state products liability claimants in actions involving the tobacco, pharmaceutical, medical device, and automobile industries.[72] Of critical importance in *Altria*, and what divided the justices in *Cipollone*, is whether the plaintiff's claim is a "failure-to-warn" or "warning neutralization" state-based requirement that *Cipollone* held is preempted under federal law or, conversely, a permissible, nonpreempted fraud claim relating to misrepresentation of a product's harmfulness.[73]

In writing for the anti-preemption bloc (plus Justice Kennedy) in a 5–4 decision, Justice Stevens held the state-based claim must be construed as a nonpreempted fraud action. He stressed the search for congressional intent is framed by the federal law's purposes and objectives underlying its express preemption provisions, which he in turn interpreted narrowly by citing to the *Rice* presumption against preemption. He reasoned federal law did not intend to displace a state's authority to bar deceptive statements in cigarette advertisements, a principle fully consistent with *Cipollone* and other precedents.[74] Nor did he see the plausibility of implied preemption, indicating that the possibility of winning on a state-based fraud claim is not an obstacle to agency (Federal Trade Commission) policies allowing warnings to be communicated in a specific fashion endorsed by regulations. In dissent, Justice Thomas took issue mainly with Stevens's invocation of a "purposes and objectives" methodology to discover congressional intent, preferring instead to construe the statute strictly without resorting to a vague and ill-defined *Rice* presumption that is wrongly being used to defeat a clear expression of preemption. Thomas's arguments are shared by Justice Scalia, who joined the dissent, and both conveyed a similar position in Scalia's *Cipollone* opinion (then joined by Thomas).

Altria is notable for the lines drawn by the Roberts Court justices in express preemption cases. Whereas Justice Kennedy cast an anti-preemption vote by aligning with Stevens's purposes and objectives position, Chief Justice Roberts and Justice Alito took a more rigid textual approach that disfavors using the *Rice* presumption against preemption; in doing so, Roberts and Alito sided with Thomas and Scalia while distancing themselves from the votes cast by the justices they replaced—namely, Chief Justice Rehnquist and Justice O'Connor, both of whom signed on to Justice Stevens's plurality opinion in its entirety in *Cipollone*.[75] Identical ideological fault lines are drawn by the justices in *Wyeth v. Levine*, but this time the differences manifest themselves in an implied preemption context.

In *Wyeth*, discussed briefly in chapter 1, the Court refused to accept the drug manufacturer's defense that an injured plaintiff's state-based failure-to-warn claim is preempted by federal law. The tort victim argued that the company's drug labeling should have been changed to tell patients of the higher risks of using an IV-push, instead of a lower-risk IV-drip, to administer an anti-nausea drug. Wyeth's defense countered that the labeling could not be changed, due to implied impossibility and obstacle preemption: the federal Food and Drug Administration (FDA) had to approve the change in order to for it comply with the law, and changing the label would obstruct the purposes of federal drug regulation. Neither rationale convinced the state jury, which awarded the tort victim compensation for the loss of her arm, which was amputated after it became gangrenous when the high-risk IV-push method was administered by clinicians.

Using his understanding of the federal law's purposes and objectives, in a 6–3 majority opinion Justice Stevens rejected each defense as well, reasoning the *Rice* presumption against preemption and the existence of a savings clause in the law's legislative history showed Congress was sensitive to giving consumers the option to seek state tort remedies if they are injured by harmful products. Congress's silence in not providing for an independent legal remedy beyond state law is additional evidence of its intent to safeguard consumer safety. Furthermore, Stevens dismissed the company's claim that the FDA expressly preempted in its regulations state common law, ostensibly through its interpretation of congressional intent through the agency's "preemption by preamble." For Stevens, the absence of an express preemption provision did not give exclusive oversight to the

FDA to handle drug regulation, and what Congress said in the law, not what the FDA interpreted the law to be through its regulatory preamble statement, controls the judicial analysis and therefore the case upholding the state-based tort claim.[76]

While Justice Alito's dissent (joined by Roberts and Scalia) acknowledged the FDA's authority to preempt state law, Justice Thomas wrote a special concurrence assenting to the result but not the majority's rationale. Using a structural federalist view of constitutional authority oriented from the principles of dual sovereignty, Thomas restated his objections to the Court adopting a congressional purposes and objectives approach to construing federal law, preferring instead to use a strict textual analysis. Even more significant is Thomas's declaration that he could not, in future cases, endorse implied obstacle preemption doctrine because it encourages judicial activism in an often futile quest to identify congressional intent. As he stated, the Court's "pre-emption jurisprudence facilitates freewheeling, extratextual, and broad evaluations of the 'purposes and objectives' embodied within federal law," leading "to decisions giving improperly broad pre-emptive effect to judicially manufactured policies, rather than to the statutory text enacted by Congress pursuant to the Constitution and the agency actions authorized thereby."[77] Neither Justice Scalia nor any other justice agreed with Thomas's disavowal of obstacle preemption analysis, a clue that he continues to be an outlier in the Court's new federalism jurisprudence.[78]

The ideological conflict is even more on display in *Chamber of Commerce v. Whiting* (2011), a 5–3 ruling by Chief Justice Roberts supporting Arizona's right to control the illegal immigrant workforce against the federal government's attempt to preempt state licensing laws that penalize businesses that hire illegal aliens. Like many of the cases reaffirming state power in table 6.3, *Whiting* is a closely decided ruling having an anti-business effect, but unlike in the state tort cases, the conservatives—Roberts, Scalia, Kennedy, Alito, and Thomas—are in the majority, with the liberals—Breyer, Ginsburg, and Sotomayor—in dissent. Of primary importance to Roberts is the federal immigration statute's savings clause, a provision that irrefutably authorizes the state to use the licensing provisions of the Legal Arizona's Workers Act to stop Arizona employers from hiring unauthorized aliens. In addition to condoning the federalism principle that Arizona has a right to control the immigrant workforce under its police powers, Roberts declares, but not with the support of Justice Thomas, that there is no implied preemption either since the Arizona legal requirement to use the federal E-Verify system to confirm employment eligibility does not conflict with or present an obstacle to achieving the aims of federal immigration laws.[79] Notably, Roberts's opinion has become a signal to the states since at least a dozen have used *Whiting* to rewrite their own laws seeking to blunt the impact of unauthorized aliens entering the labor market.[80]

In *Whiting*, however, Roberts's anti-preemption rationale, which relies heavily on textualism in construing the federal immigration statutes, is not accepted by either of the separate dissents registered by Justices Breyer (with whom Ginsburg joined) and Sotomayor. Both dissents take a Justice Stevens–like approach to statutory construction. Each argues the statutory context of federal immigration law—namely, its legislative history, purpose, and express language—clearly demonstrates Congress's intent to preempt contrary state laws. Each justice also thought Roberts misinterpreted the federal law's savings clause, since Congress only meant for states to use their licensing police powers to recruit or refer workers for employment, not to regulate all facets of in-state business activity touching upon immigration control. Expanding the reach of the savings clause thus undercuts the purposes of federal immigration regulation, which sought to protect lawful workers from being discriminated against and, concomitantly, to insulate lawful employers from wrongful prosecutions or sanctions.[81]

One possible explanation of the results in contested anti-preemption cases like *Altria*, *Wyeth*, and *Cuomo* (and by implication *Whiting*) is offered by Professor Gillian Metzger, who concludes, "To a significant degree, the Justices' differing stances on preemption [track] the division between liberals and conservatives on the Court, suggesting that a major driver behind the decisions may be different ideological stances on tort reform and the benefits of regulation."[82] Partisan differences on the bench erupt over even more arcane regulatory subjects, such as measuring the scope of judicial deference to agency interpretations of congressional preemption statutes (as the disagreement between a conservative justice like Alito, who was willing to defer to FDA authority in *Wyeth*, and a liberal justice like Stevens, who was not so willing, attests). In the tort-preemption context, then, ideologically motivated judicial behavior centers on whether it is better to accept the regulatory judgment of agency experts, as opposed to questioning it through the wisdom of state common law juries.[83] Political scientists using descriptive and empirical methods likewise agree that the underlying politics of regulatory reform, as well as the choices made by conservative justices in favor of states' rights, are key ideological dimensions of Supreme Court decision-making in federalism cases.[84] As Thomas McGarity observes in his study of preemption wars on the national and state level, the political dynamics of tort reform in the 1980s and 1990s are manifested by efforts to scale back government at the national level. Heavily regulated businesses, such as the tobacco, pharmaceutical, medical device, and automobile industries, extensively lobbied their conservative allies in Congress and the White House to limit the scope of their tort liability due to claims that their products were unsafe. Their efforts were countered by trial bar and consumer groups, which exerted their own pressure on liberal representatives to reaffirm the notion that injured plaintiffs have the right to sue and receive compensation, especially in state lawsuits.[85]

Apart from the anti-preemption rulings just discussed, the degree to which preemption friction will continue to play itself out in the Obama presidency—which has taken a narrow stance on preemption in contrast to the expansive posture expressed by the George W. Bush presidency—is an open question that is also addressed in Roberts Court pro-preemption cases decided after 2005.[86] In contrast to anti-preemption outcomes that mainly indicate an anti-business effect, the cases detailed in table 6.4 are predominately business friendly. They also cover a wider range of business activity in litigation: whereas the anti-preemption subset addresses tort reform, tax law, immigration, banking practices, and debt collection, the preemption subset features some of the same issues, plus those centering on arbitration and class action lawsuits in different factual settings. These impressions, however, must be gauged against empirical research, which reaches divergent conclusions about whether there is a pro- or anti-business effect in Rehnquist or Roberts Court cases.[87]

While the cases are few, and it is easy to overstate their collective significance, examining the cases indicates there is more unanimity and less contestation in preemption disputes favoring centralization.[88] Within that dynamic the disharmony between the conservatives and liberals is somewhat muted, but there appears to be more cohesion among the conservative bloc of justices, with the exception of Justice Thomas, who writes dissenting opinions in three of the fourteen cases (*Buckeye Check Cashing v. Cardegna*, *Preston v. Ferrer*, and *CSX v. Alabama Department of Revenue*).[89] The most acute disagreements appear in two contested cases, one addressing state tort law (*Pliva v. Mensing*) and the other weighing the availability of class arbitrations in state law (*AT&T Mobility v. Concepcion*). Ideology is more crosscutting in *Shady Grove Orthopedic Associates v. Allstate Insurance*. Each case is briefly discussed next.

In sharp contrast to the defeat suffered by the pharmaceutical company in *Wyeth*, manufacturers of generic drugs earned a victory when the 5–4 ruling in *Pliva v. Mensing*, written by Justice Thomas, was announced in an identical failure-to-warn case.[90] The injured consumers were prescribed Reglan, a brand-name drug put on the market with a strong FDA warning to use carefully, as those taking it over an extended time risked getting tardive dyskinesia, an often irreversible movement disorder. The pharmacists, however, gave the plaintiffs Metoclopramide, a generic with a weaker warning that said very little about the high risks involved. So they argued the generic drug company should have changed its label to reflect the stronger warning of the brand name. Yet, in holding the plaintiff's state common law claim was impliedly preempted under federal law, the Court reversed course by accepting the Food and Drug Administration's view that Pliva could not legally strengthen its product labeling for the generic without prior FDA approval. The difference in this case, said Thomas, is that it was impossible for the generic drug manufacturer to comply with federal and state law simultaneously: federal law requires that the generic label match the brand-name label, but state law commands that a safer label be attached to the generic, and under federal regulations, the FDA first had to approve any drug labeling change.[91]

Although the Supreme Court based its judgment on the doctrine of implied impossibility preemption, Justice Kennedy did not join the part of the Thomas opinion that interpreted the supremacy clause as a non obstante provision.[92] But Chief Justice Roberts and Justices Scalia and Alito did—a sign, perhaps, that the strict textualism of the Court's most conservative justices is gaining traction on the bench in the Roberts Court in a fashion that differs from the Rehnquist Court, at least in statutory construction cases. Under that view, only the plain words of the federal statute are given effect, which in turn, through non obstante principles, eliminates the need for judges to strain to reconcile the disparate meanings of federal and state law. For Thomas, "When the 'ordinary meaning' of federal law blocks a private party from independently accomplishing what state law requires, that party has established preemption."[93] In addition, Thomas did not see the *Wyeth* precedent as making any difference in the result because the manufacturer, which was a brand-name competitor in that case, had the unilateral power to strengthen its own drug label without first getting FDA approval, thus meeting its state common law duty.

While the *Wyeth* precedent may not have affected *Pliva*'s textual analysis, the Court's composition in all likelihood did, especially in erecting a new supremacy clause non obstante principle that enjoys the support of at least four conservative justices. Even though Justice Kennedy did not go along with Thomas's non obstante supremacy clause interpretation, with Stevens and Souter off the bench, by switching his position and casting the deciding vote in *Pliva*, he opted to join forces with the *Wyeth* dissenters, who then consisted of Alito, Scalia, and Roberts (and vicariously Thomas, who concurred only in the result in *Wyeth*). The remaining liberal justices in the *Wyeth* majority—namely, Ginsburg and Breyer—became the *Pliva* dissenters who aligned themselves with Sotomayor and Kagan as the replacements for Souter and Stevens. In opting to join the conservatives, Justice Kennedy again illustrated that he remains a pivotal swing justice in many of the Court's cases.[94] Even so, given the inversion of the prevailing and dissenting ideological coalitions in *Pliva*, it is not surprising that Sotomayor's dissent echoes the same principles Stevens repeated in *Wyeth* in arguing against preemption, mainly by using a purposes and objectives approach to statutory interpretation and strongly disavowing non obstante.[95]

With congressional purpose as the touchstone for her preemption analysis, Sotomayor invoked the *Rice* presumption against preemption in reasoning Congress afforded to states the authority to regulate health and safety matters through the traditional exercise of police powers. As such, Congress chose not to preempt state law tort actions against generic or brand-name drug companies. It follows that Congress's silence did not give the FDA plenary power to regulate drug law safety—a point Justice Stevens makes in *Wyeth*. In this light, rebutting the *Rice* presumption in the context of impossibility preemption is difficult to do. In other words, showing a "mere possibility of impossibility is not enough"—especially since Pliva conceded it could have asked the FDA for a label change, which in turn would likely oblige the agency to pressure the brand-name manufacturer to relabel and ultimately compel the generic to do the same. In this sense the high burden of satisfying impossibility has been reduced to meeting it with a hypothetical possibility that Pliva was powerless to change the label without FDA approval.[96]

Moreover, with a type of rhetorical flourish that resonates with a Rehnquist-like structurally based view of the U.S. Constitution, Sotomayor's dissent finds the blind deference the majority gives to the FDA offensive because it undermines respect to the states "as independent sovereigns" in the "federal system," a principle that undermines the plurality's "novel" reinterpretation of the supremacy clause under a non obstante theory. Accordingly, Sotomayor concludes the Court has it backward in giving less credence to state authority (under the *Rice* presumption) while encouraging courts to turn a blind eye and reflexively eliminating state tort remedies, all with the help of an artificially constructed textually based version of preemption doctrine that infers a congressional intent that simply does not exist.[97]

The next two cases, *AT&T Mobility v. Concepcion* and *Shady Grove Orthopedic Associates v. Allstate Insurance*, highlight the justices' ideological differences in arbitration and class action litigation; however, they go in different public policy directions as a result of the latter ruling.[98] In *Concepcion*, consumers disputed the validity of a two-year cell phone contract after they were charged $30 in sales tax after purchasing the phones, which they thought were going to be free. The contract they signed was a boilerplate agreement with a mandatory binding arbitration clause, plus another that waived their right to sue in a class action. On appeal the Supreme Court had to decide whether a lower state court rule, expressed in *Discover Bank v. Superior Court*, was preempted by the Federal Arbitration Act (FAA) because state law dictated that class action waivers in contracts with arbitration clauses are unenforceable if they are unconscionable. Notably, the FAA had a savings clause permitting contract defenses to be raised under state law as well.[99]

But in holding there was implied obstacle preemption, in a 5–4 decision Justice Scalia reasoned litigant consumers must challenge such contracts in an individual capacity, which meant that they could not use a class action to press their claims collectively against the corporate defendant. Allowing them to use a class action or the FAA's savings clause to sue under a state law (via the *Discover Bank* rule) disfavoring arbitration, Scalia asserted, would create an obstacle that got in the way of achieving Congress's intent to enact a uniform body of law designed to enforce private contract arbitration agreements.[100] In a dissent by Justice Breyer and joined by Justices Ginsburg, Sotomayor, and Kagan, the majority's obstacle reasoning is challenged by invoking the FAA's savings clause and the presumption that Congress does not lightly preempt common law actions. For the dissenters, the FAA is fully consistent with, and not an obstacle to, the legislature's intent to let the judiciary enforce contract arbitration agreements that may be illicit. Under this view, the Court mistakenly undermines "the legitimacy of a State's action," which in turn violates "the federalist ideal, embodied in specific language in [the FAA], [that] should lead us to uphold the California law, not to strike it down."[101]

The significance of *Concepcion* is reflected in the ongoing efforts by Congress to reverse forced arbitration agreements that favor big corporations with remedial legislation.[102] For critics, in *Concepcion* and identical cases, including *Buckeye Check Cashing v. Cardegna* (enforcing an arbitration clause in a payday loan contract even though the contract may violate state law), *Preston v. Ferrer* (holding that federal arbitration law preempts review of an agreement by a state agency even though the parties agreed to arbitrate), *Wal-Mart v. Dukes* (restricting the availability of class action lawsuits in an employment discrimination case), and *Citizens United v. Federal Election Commission* (affirming the First Amendment right of corporations to spend freely in political campaigns), the Roberts Court is abusing its discretion by strengthening corporate interests while discouraging access to courts by those suffering civil rights violations or other inequities. Highly publicized depictions of the justices as disinterested in oral argument in permitting human rights groups to sue corporations in U.S. courts for human rights violations does little to abate the view of liberals that the Supreme Court under Chief Justice John Roberts is more aptly known as the "Corporate Court."[103]

Still, there is some evidence that the pro-business criticism is arguably misplaced. Rulings from the case subset record outcomes in which the Supreme Court restricts corporate interests (tables 6.3 and 6.4). In *Shady*

Grove Orthopedic Associates v. Allstate Insurance, the defendant insurance company was sued in district court for not paying out its claims on a timely basis, thereby subjecting it an additional liability of having to pay statutory interest on accrued debts if they lost the underlying action. When the plaintiffs sought to certify the lawsuit as a class action from the trial court, Allstate countered by stating New York law banned class actions in cases seeking statutory penalties. On appeal to the Supreme Court, the justices had to decide if state law, which is expressed in a procedural rule banning class actions, is preempted by Rule 23 of the Federal Rules of Civil Procedure, which authorizes them. In a 5–4 ruling in which Justice Stevens provided the swing vote, in *Shady Grove* Justice Scalia held that Rule 23 took precedence over a conflicting state law, therefore preempting it. While the justices disagreed among themselves as to the scope of the Court's holding under the facts at hand and the *Erie* doctrine (referred to earlier in this chapter), the essential principle coming out of *Shady Grove* is that federal procedural rules governing class actions take precedence over contrary state rules trying to limit their scope.[104] Moreover, in *Smith v. Bayer Corporation*, in a unanimous decision written by Justice Elena Kagan, the Supreme Court ruled a federal court could not use the federal Anti-Injunction Act to preempt a state court's decision to certify a class action that was similar to one that terminated in federal court (on the grounds it was the same claim but involving different parties) (see table 6.3). In doing so the corporate defendant did not succeed in stopping state court certification of the class action.

As a result of these two cases, it is not surprising that Public Citizen, a consumer interest group that often lines up against corporations in litigation, characterizes *Shady Grove* as "enhanc[ing] the ability of consumers (particularly New York consumers) to access the federal courts to pursue class remedies in cases where individual litigation may not be practical or affordable." With respect to *Bayer Corporation*, the consumer organization likewise hailed it as one of the few victories it achieved in the 2010–2011 term, declaring, "The ruling prevents corporations from relying on procedural games to deny injured consumers their day in court."[105]

From all indications, preemption issues will continue to garner the attention of the justices. At roughly the halfway point in the 2011–2012 term, the Court had accepted for review or scheduled oral argument for several petitions involving express and implied preemption.[106] In the final analysis, the debate and disagreements revolving around judicial decisions to preempt (or not) are invariably framed, and sometimes dictated, by the vagaries of judicial philosophy, conceptions of the judicial role in the democratic process, and the nuances of statutory construction, which are all directed at answering the core question of what Congress intended when it tried to override state laws. As such, they remain critical to understanding new federalism principles, as construed by the Roberts Court, for several reasons.

Deciding the scope and application of federal statutes that explicitly reserve authority for the states in savings clauses will continue to raise judicial conflict along ideological lines. Similarly, whether the justices interpreting statutes will be amenable to giving the states more regulatory powers by applying the *Rice* presumption against preemption will remain significant as a contested issue as well. Moreover, preemption decisions have a political safeguards and process federalism dimension that affects any evaluation of the Supreme Court's federalism impact. In other words, judicial decisions regularly register a belief that court action may be necessary to protect the different legal doctrines or federalism values deemed to be at stake. Often that may translate into a judicial choice about whether traditional state functions are being respected by the political system. Process-based federalism arguments and clear statement rules (discussed in chapter 3) are likely to remain a significant part of those judicial choices because they may do the following: (1) aid the court to expand the power of the federal government; (2) return power back to the states; (3) provide legitimacy for pursuing underlying public policies that lurk beneath judicial outcomes, such as basic disagreements over tort reform and contentious social issues like same-sex marriage, environmental protection, commercial regulation, and consumer safety; or (4) underscore the degree of judicial deference a court will give to agencies as they strive to define the regulatory issues of our time within congressional mandates.[107] As this chapter has shown, rival theories of judicial philosophy and statutory construction, such as Justice Stevens's purposes and objectives approach or, conversely, Justice Thomas's or Justice Scalia's commitment to textualism, underscore the salience of ideology as it is applied to judicial attempts to discern congressional intent and the scope of preemption. Identical issues of constitutional interpretation remain a part of the Roberts Court's new federalism docket as well, and those cases are briefly considered next, mostly in the Eleventh Amendment and dormant commerce clause context.[108]

Constitutional Cases: The Eleventh Amendment and Commerce Clause

While the foregoing infers the Roberts Court has shifted much of its new federalism agenda toward statutory construction cases involving preemption, 30 percent of the cases in the sample under review are decided on constitutional grounds, and a smaller percentage (11 percent) consists of mixed statutory and constitutional cases (figure 6.2). Thus it remains important to consider if the Roberts Court is pushing the new federalism envelope in the same manner as its predecessor was thought to do in its federalist revival. As set against the Roberts Court's earlier ruling in *United States v. Comstock*, a controversial decision greatly expanding Congress's necessary and proper clause powers in federalism cases, court watchers initially speculated before they were decided that two cases, *Bond v. United States* and *Sossamon v. Texas*, might supply some evidence that the Roberts Court might be moving away from an analogous federalist revival if they ultimately reaffirmed federal and not state powers. In other words, if either or both failed to limit centralization, then it "would be a strong signal that the new federalism project of the Rehnquist Court has been derailed."[109] Yet both cases did precisely the opposite in relative terms, so at least at some analytical level, it is defensible to analogize them with old-style Rehnquist Court new federalism jurisprudence. In the first case (*Bond*), at least rhetorically, the Tenth Amendment retains some analytical force as a structural restraint on federal powers. In the second (*Sossamon*), the Eleventh Amendment is applied by the Court to limit federal judiciary authority to entertain private actions for money damages against state prison systems, even if they accept federal subsidies.

In *Bond v. United States* federal officials indicted defendant Bond for violating part of an anti–chemical weapon treaty the United States ratified in 1997, reasoning the chemicals used to harm a victim fell within the scope of a federal prohibition and an international treaty ban. The defense argued Congress was powerless to create a law that displaced criminal law enforcement decisions that were traditionally reserved to the states under the Tenth Amendment. Through Justice Anthony Kennedy the Supreme Court unanimously declared that the federal system protects not only the integrity of the states in their own right but also citizen or individual liberty flowing from the diffusion of governmental authority. Because "individual liberty secured by federalism is not simply derivative of the rights of the States," Bond was deemed to have legal standing to raise her challenge against the federal government so long as the case-and-controversy requirements of Article III jurisdiction were satisfied. As Kennedy concluded,

> In this case . . . where the litigant is a party to an otherwise justifiable case or controversy, she is not forbidden to object that her injury results from disregard of the federal structure of our Government. Whether the Tenth Amendment is regarded as simply a "truism" . . . or whether it has independent force of its own, the result here is the same.[110]

Accordingly, under the principles of federalism and the Tenth Amendment, as precedent *Bond* may signal to litigants that they may have legal rights to bring private federal lawsuits based on arguments that federally enacted laws violate the sovereign prerogatives of states, a principle that can only encourage the strategic use of the Tenth Amendment as an instrument to curb national encroachments in constitutional litigation purporting to tread on states' rights.

Identical judicial language, framed in new federalism rhetoric and structural interpretations of the U.S. Constitution, is found in *Sossamon v. Texas*, an Eleventh Amendment case. *Sossamon* is one of five Eleventh Amendment rulings issued from the Roberts Court in its first six terms (table 6.5), suggesting that the justices are remaining attentive to an important area of law into which the Rehnquist Court made significant inroads during some portion of its federalist revival (see chapter 3). In *Sossamon*, a Texas prisoner sued Texas in federal court for money damages, claiming that his rights to religious worship in prison were compromised under the federal Religious Land Use and Institutionalized Persons Act (RLUIPA) of 2000. RLUIPA represents Congress's second attempt to expand religious freedom in light of the Supreme Court's decision in *City of Boerne v. Flores* (discussed in chapter 3), a ruling that invalidated the 1993 Religious Freedom Restoration Act (RFRA) because Congress lacked Section 5 (of the Fourteenth Amendment) power to change the status of constitutional religious expression rights. But unlike the RFRA, which was grounded on Section 5 (of the Fourteenth Amendment) authority, the RLUIPA used Congress's Article I spending and commerce powers as a basis to prevent states and localities from using their own laws to chill or impede religious freedom.[111]

In asserting his claims, Sossamon argued that Texas voluntarily accepted federal funds as a subsidy to help run its prison system, which inferred that he had the right as a prisoner to sue Texas in federal court; Texas, however, claimed an Eleventh Amendment sovereign immunity defense, arguing that Texas did not consent to be sued and the receipt of federal monies did not operate as a waiver that took its immunity away. The judicial resolution of these competing arguments thus turned on issues of statutory construction and process federalism (discussed in chapter 3). Put simply, did the congressional statute (RLUIPA) supply clear notice to the states that they could be sued in federal court for committing religious discrimination if they accepted federal subsidies? Speaking through Justice Clarence Thomas in a 6–2 decision joined by Chief Justice John Roberts and Justices Anthony Kennedy, Antonin Scalia, Ruth Bader Ginsburg, and Samuel Alito, the Supreme Court sided with Texas in *Sossamon*. It decreed Congress lacked the authority to let Texas be sued in a private action for money damages.[112]

Working from the premise that "dual sovereignty is a defining feature of our Nation's constitutional blueprint," and asserting that granting "immunity from private suits has long been considered 'central to sovereign

Table 6.5. Eleventh Amendment and Commerce Clause Decisions in Roberts Court, 2005–2011

Case/Term	*Federalism Dimension*	*Ideological Direction*	*Vote*
Eleventh Amendment			
2005–2006			
U.S. v. Georgia (2006)	American with Disabilities Act/prison conditions	Liberal	9–0
Central Virginia Community College v. Katz (2006)	Article I (Bankruptcy Clause)/debt collection	Liberal	5–4
Northern Insurance Co. v. Chatham (2006)	County Insurance Liability/property damage	Liberal	9–0
2010–2011			
Sossamon v. Texas (2011)	Religious Land Use and Institutionalized Persons Act/prisoner right to religious freedom	Conservative	6–2
Virginia Office for Protection v. Stewart (2011)	Developmental Disabilities Assistance and Bill of Rights Act/Protection and Advocacy for Individuals with Mental Illness Act/disability rights	Liberal	6–2
Commerce Clause			
2005–2006			
**Rapanos v. U.S. Army Corps of Engineers* (2006)	Clean Water Act/regulation of private property	Conservative	4–1–4
2006–2007			
United Haulers v. Oneida-Herkimer (2007)	Dormant Commerce Clause/solid waste regulation	Conservative	6–3
2007–2008			
Dep't of Revenue of Kentucky v. Davis (2008)	Dorman Commerce Clause/tax discrimination	Conservative	7–2

*Statutory Construction Case (mostly addressing preemption; plurality opinion and concurrence address commerce power)

Source: The Supreme Court Dataset, 1953–1022 Terms, at http://scdb.wustl.edu/analysis/php (using Data Release Id: SCDB_2011_03); SCOTUSblog Case Stat Pack, at http:www.scotusblog.com/reference/stat-pack.

dignity,'" Thomas reasoned Congress and the RLUIPA did not "unequivocally express" in a "clear declaration" that Texas was amenable to suit. The statutory ambiguity meant that Texas's sovereign immunity remained intact, even if Texas chose to accept federal monies. The RLUIPA's text, detailing that "a person may assert a violation . . . as a claim or defense in a judicial proceeding and obtain appropriate relief against a government," did not adequately convey to the states that the federal government authorized private lawsuits under its spending powers. As Thomas flatly concluded, "Without such a clear statement from Congress and notice to the States, federal courts may not step in and abrogate state sovereign immunity." Justice Sotomayor, joined by Justice Breyer, saw things differently in dissent: the phrase "appropriate relief" is commonly understood to mean money damages in lawsuits, so Congress gave plenty of notice to Texas that it was subject to civil liability if it accepted monies under federal law.[113]

Of the five Eleventh Amendment cases identified in table 6.5, *Sossamon* is the only one limiting Congress's power to abrogate state immunities. Two rulings, *United States v. Georgia* (allowing a disabled prisoner to sue the state prison for constitutional violations pertaining to his confinement) and *Central Virginia Community College v. Katz* (holding that the bankruptcy clause abrogates state immunity), were decided early in the Roberts Court but without Justice Samuel Alito's participation; a third, *Northern Insurance Co. v. Chatham County* (holding the county could not assert immunity because it is not an "arm" of the state), is one of the two unanimous rulings pertaining to the trio, whereas the justices sparred considerably more in *Central Virginia*, producing a 5–4 decision largely split along ideological lines (with Justice O'Connor as the swing vote, joining the liberal bloc of Stevens, Souter, Ginsburg, and Breyer) over the issue of the proper meaning of the bankruptcy clause as a structural element of the constitutional framework.

These decisions, while significant, are relatively inconclusive as doctrinal statements or signals about the judicial lines the Roberts Court is drawing in state-immunity cases, especially since the membership has appreciably changed with the loss and addition of four new justices after 2005. In that light, the invocation of Rehnquist-like structural principles in the constitutional analysis in *Sossamon* arguably may be some indication that some justices are cognizant of the need to exert their authority to protect state sovereignty in certain circumstances. Additional evidence pointing in that direction is found in *Virginia Office for Protection and Advocacy v. Stewart*, a 6–2 ruling concerning the effect that *Ex Parte Young* doctrine has in permitting state officials to be sued in Eleventh Amendment challenges.[114]

The critical point of contention in *Virginia Office for Protection and Advocacy* relates the scope of the *Ex Parte Young* doctrine. For the majority of the justices—namely, Scalia, Kennedy, Thomas, Ginsburg, Breyer, and Sotomayor—*Ex Parte Young* is given a rather expansive reading (as an "exception" to state immunity) to permit an independent state agency that is investigating the deaths of mentally disabled patients to sue a state official in federal court to obtain patient records that are being withheld in violation of federal law. In rejecting the immunity defense of the state administrator, the Supreme Court interpreted the scope of the *Ex Parte Young* doctrine to mean that federal courts are empowered to grant injunctions for prospective relief against state officials if there is a violation of federal law. The *Young* exception to state immunity, Justice Scalia explains in the controlling opinion, only extends to situations in which a state official, who is not technically acting as a "state" for immunity purposes, cannot abide by the federal court's directive not to violate federal law, which in this case the administrator could not do, triggering the exception and allowing the state official to be sued in spite of the immunity that the Eleventh Amendment ordinarily offers. That sort of "straightforward" *Young* analysis dictates the result here, and it did not matter much that the entity suing was not a citizen, but rather an independent state agency.[115]

Yet for Chief Justice Roberts, it mattered considerably, for it changed how the *Young* exception is supposed to work as a narrow exception to state immunity. In a dissent joined by Justice Alito, Roberts complained that the state suffers an indignity to its sovereignty in a federal lawsuit whenever adversarial litigation pits a component of the state, an independent agency, against another part of the state, a state official. *Ex Parte Young*, in other words, should not be doctrinally expanded to let a state sue itself in federal court. Notably, to reach this conclusion, Roberts relied heavily on two Rehnquist Court precedents, *Seminole Tribe of Florida v. Florida* and *Idaho v. Coeur d'Alene Tribe of Idah*, both of which are regularly cited by scholars as proof positive of a federalist revival as an aggressive extension of Eleventh Amendment state-immunity principles.[116]

Perhaps more so than in *Sossamon*, the positions the justices take in *Virginia Office for Protection and Advocacy* underscore the different levels of commitment that each justice has to advancing dual federalism ideals. The willingness of Scalia to join with the liberal cohort of Ginsburg, Breyer, and Sotomayor (Justice Kagan did not participate) may be an indication of how far Scalia is willing to go *not* to lend a voice to protecting state sovereignty interests in a dual federalism framework. Equally insightful is Justices Kennedy and Thomas's assent in a concurrence to the line Scalia drew in extending the reach of *Young* as an exception to state-immunity principles, but with the caveat that they would adopt more of a balancing test, or a careful weighing of the competing interests involved—namely, the federal interest against the sovereign or dignitary interests of a state—to decide the issue on a case-by-case basis. At the far end of the conservative spectrum, and occupying that ideological space in new federalism jurisprudence that is reminiscent of taking a moderately aggressive judicial safeguards approach in narrowly applying the *Young* exception to Eleventh Amendment cases, lies the chief justice and Samuel Alito, who both seem to draw a more rigid line in exercising their discretion in an effort to protect the special federalism interests of states.

As discussed in chapter 3, the Rehnquist Court took assertive positions during part of its existence to erect substantial, if not contradictory, limitations on the federal government through its interpretation of the commerce clause. Among its most important contributions to advancing a federalist revolution and limiting congressional commerce authority are the *United States v. Lopez* and *United States v. Morrison* precedents, but their precedential effect has been muted by other key cases, such as *Gonzales v. Raich*.[117] Unquestionably, the Roberts Court will revisit its commerce clause jurisprudence to decide the constitutional fate of the Obama administration's health-care legislation, and the precedents just cited will play a key role in that analysis. Thus, in evaluating the Roberts Court's contribution in regard to the scope of the commerce power, chapter 3 also reminds us that the Supreme Court's dormant commerce clause jurisprudence may be relevant as well.

The latest, and perhaps most significant, opportunity for the Roberts Court to make its mark in the area is Justice Souter's opinion for the Court in *Department of Revenue of Kentucky v. Davis*. As discussed in chapter 3, the Supreme Court has approached regulating state authority under the negative component of the commerce clause by first determining if there is facial discrimination (i.e., state laws that smack of economic protectionism, which prevent out-of-state competitors from taking advantage of local markets). Thereafter, the justices typically apply *Pike v. Bruce Church*'s undue-burden balancing test (i.e., judicially determining if the benefits of the challenged state regulation to local economies outweigh the burden it places on interstate commerce). The Rehnquist Court proved that it was not especially deferential to state regulation in these cases. Most justices remained divided about which test ought to control the analysis, with Justices Thomas and Scalia often repeating their call for a complete repudiation of the doctrine's use in future cases.[118]

In *Department of Revenue of Kentucky*, the Roberts Court signaled that it might be taking a different approach to deciding negative commerce clause cases. There, the Court ruled that the dormant commerce clause does not prohibit a state from exempting its state and local bonds from state taxation while taxing government bonds issued outside its borders. The Court's decision ratified the common practice in the states, which have long exempted their own bonds from taxation (while taxing bonds from other states), thereby preserving their sovereign interests in regulating finance and debt service. Perhaps more significantly, it did so by going beyond the conventional tools of analysis described above and instead exploring other rationales. Souter, for example, looked to *United Haulers Association v. Oneida-Herkimer Solid Waste Management Authority*, which upheld a "flow-control" ordinance requiring trash haulers to deliver solid waste to a processing company operated by a state public authority. In relying on that precedent, the Court will ask itself if the state law is performing a "government function" that benefits its citizens—that is, if the function "benefit[s] a clearly public facility, while treating all private companies exactly the same," then the state law is likely to withstand dormant commerce clause scrutiny and be upheld.[119] As some court watchers suggest, the recognition of a government function test, and perhaps to a lesser degree the possibility that the Court is considering a "market-participant" exception to dormant commerce clause analysis, may allow the Roberts Court to establish a more protective sphere for state economic regulatory activities that are grounded in traditional federalism values.[120]

CONCLUSION

The above analysis of Roberts Court policymaking in federalism cases suggests some important comparisons with its predecessor Rehnquist Court. Just as the prior Court devoted attention to preemption, and many justices did so mainly to continue working toward a more comprehensive vision of federalism in the constitutional order, so too will the Roberts Court continue to address preemption disputes with a view toward refining the principles of preemption doctrine within the larger context of federal-state relations. Preemption disputes will be settled by the Roberts Court with an eye toward articulating workable principles on statutory construction, and it is here that the justices will demonstrate the widest range of disagreement. However, that range of disagreement seems to be affected less by the amount of deference a specific justice accords to Congress and more according to the rival theories among the justices about the appropriate role the states should play in regulation, especially in the context of pro-business or pro-consumer litigation. There is no doubt that the justices will continue to disagree over textualist approaches to statutory interpretation in preemption cases, but the Roberts Court's decision-making shows that a relatively new ideological divide has crept into its preemption decisions, and that divide has as much to do with the rival economic philosophies within the Court (in terms of how much or how little the government should regulate businesses and corporate interests) as it does with traditional judicial conflicts over statutory interpretation and the proper role of the federal government.

Along these lines, a fair argument can be made that the Roberts Court will chip away at the political safeguards approach to federalism defined in the divisive *Garcia* decision. By approving of process-based approaches to federalism and clear statement rules, the Roberts Court is, to a degree, mirroring the Rehnquist Court. Thus, even though the political safeguards approach asserts that states are generally protected from federal encroachment through their participation and representation in the national political system, especially given their prominent role in the Senate, the Rehnquist and Roberts Courts have both demonstrated tendencies to show less regard for the strength of those safeguards and more solicitude for making sure that Congress itself respects those safeguards, especially by making its intent to regulate state functions clear and unmistakable. Linked with this is the Roberts Court's focus on justiciability issues and its handling of justiciability doctrines to make it more difficult for plaintiffs to use federal courts to litigate claims against state governments. In this sense, its manipulation of justiciability doctrines can be considered a kind of inverse political safeguard—that is, by removing the federal judicial process from questioning state power through litigation in a select group of cases, the Court effectively protects states from federal intrusions.

With Tenth and Eleventh Amendment cases, the Roberts Court continues to act much like its predecessor. It employs the same general rhetoric about the Tenth Amendment and state sovereignty. Recent decisions have shown the Court's regard for maintaining the Tenth Amendment as a protective barrier for states against federal power, and likewise its Eleventh Amendment decisions, although they are few, limit federal power too. While the Roberts Court has continued to adjudicate state-immunity cases, it seems that it is more interested in refining the existing precedent from the Rehnquist Court rather than making wholesale changes to it, as the *Virginia Office for Protection and Advocacy* case illustrates in the context of the *Ex Parte Young* doctrine.

Finally, as with the Rehnquist Court, the Roberts Court remains internally divided over federalism. Similar judicial conflicts that affected outcomes in federalism decisions in the Rehnquist Court are evident in the Roberts Court too, and in close cases the typical voting dynamic is 4–4 with one justice serving as a swing vote. Justice Sandra Day O'Connor was often the swing vote through the Rehnquist Court era, and more recently (and since her retirement), Justice Kennedy has emerged as the swing vote in cases involving a wide range of policy areas, including federalism. Justice Thomas remains the ideological outlier, a position he carved out for himself during the formative phase of the new federalism jurisprudence. It is not surprising that there is continuity in the judicial conflict over federalism within the Supreme Court. To be sure, given the increasing partisan polarization within Congress and the entrenched conflicts between the states and the federal government over regulatory issues concerning policy areas such as public education, health care, and federal preemption of state contract and tort laws, ideological wrangling among the Court's justices is to be expected. The extent to which exigencies external to the Court, such as the brutish polarization in Congress, affect the disagreements among the justices is unknown but cannot be discounted. While ideological blocs within the Court are visible, most cases are decided without ideology being the driving factor. It is the case that the constitutive political environment has a lot to do with the cases coming to the Court, who hears them, and what the outcomes will be. Just as surrounding political events in the 1980s and 1990s affected the kinds of conflicts that came to the Court and perhaps encouraged Chief Justice Rehnquist and like-minded justices to take a serious and far-reaching look at federalism as a limiting principle of national government power, so too will the political climate external to the Court still affect its federalism decision-making. Some of the catalytic issues of the last three decades affecting federalism remain too, in that the political system and political elites often employ the means and rhetoric of decentralization in policymaking, states continue to professionalize their bureaucracies and enjoy much more trust among the public than ever before, and the ever present fiscal problems of the national government impair its ability to effectively engage and regulate many policy areas.

In sum, the foregoing analysis shows new federalism is inherently a political principle. It is constitutively shaped by constitutional, ideological, and institutional structures that traditionally lie at the base of U.S. Supreme Court policymaking in domestic and global federalism milieus across time. While its contemporary manifestation originates in the presidential politics of the Nixon and Reagan administrations, the judicial formation of new federalism postulates began in earnest with the Rehnquist Court's federalist revival that sought to put new limitations on the exercise of official federal power by the Congress and executive agencies. While the post–New Deal gravitation toward centralization and the force of constitutional directives or text favoring national supremacy are consistently strong in select areas of federalism jurisprudence, the internal and exogenous constraints the justices confront on and off the bench—the intractability of 5–4 decisions, the lack of unanimity among conservative justices in the pursuit of federalism ideals and preferences, the reluctance of relevant constituencies to accept or comply with Supreme Court rulings, and the instability of a changing international order—have all made it increasingly difficult for the Supreme Court to speak with one collective voice on matters of discrete areas of new federalism judicial policy that the justices themselves have had a hand in creating. The old, new, and progressive elements of federalism or legal policy change, and the Supreme Court's role in producing it, particularly after the 1990s, remains in flux, as it has been from the founding to today.

In this light, the future direction of new federalism judicial policymaking is likely to be shaped by the issues raised in this chapter and throughout the book. Since the Roberts Court is still a relatively young bench, with only six full terms under its belt, the justices will continue to weigh in on issues that the Rehnquist Court has already debated but that the justices in control of the bench deem need further adjustment. Such issues include the weight the Roberts Court gives to existing precedents that expand or limit federal authority in spending clause, preemption, commerce clause, Section 5 (of the Fourteenth Amendment), Eleventh Amendment, or Tenth Amendment cases; where the Roberts Court stands in regard to the aggressive exercise of judicial review and as a participant in the political or judicial safeguards debate; the extent to which the Roberts Court uses process federalism principles, or clear statement rules, as checks on national authority and statements of substantive quasi-constitutional doctrine; the scope and application of Roberts Court's policymaking in response to a changing international order and globalization trends; and whether the Roberts Court has the resilience to overcome internal divisions and speak as a unified bench on the new federalism precedents it creates.[121] Perhaps more so than was the case with its predecessor, any contribution that the Roberts Court makes in its new federalism jurisprudence is likely to be judged against the criticism that the Supreme Court is politically biased in its decisionmaking toward business interests, a common theme of academic studies and punditry, and on how it ultimately weighs in on the poignant legal challenges made to President Barack Obama's health-care litigation, perhaps the most significant new federalism issue to be decided by the U.S. Supreme Court in the past generation.

NOTES

1. Dana Milbank, "Obama's Budget Games," *Washington Post*, February 14, 2012; Carol E. Lee and Damian Paletta, "Obama Seeks New Taxes on Rich," *Wall Street Journal*, February 14, 2012; and Jeff Zients, "The 2013 Budget," The White House Blog, February 13, 2012, www.whitehouse.gov/blog/2012/02/13/2013-budget-0 (accessed April 22, 2012).

2. Shama Gamkhar and J. M. Pickerill, "The State of American Federalism 2010–2011: The Economy, Healthcare Reform and Midterm Elections Shape the Intergovernmental Agenda," *Publius: The Journal of Federalism* 41, no. 3 (2011): 361–94.

3. Bradley W. Joondeph, "Federalism and Health Care Reform: Understanding the States' Challenges to the Patient Protection and Affordable Care Act," *Publius: The Journal of Federalism* 41, no. 3 (2011): 447–70 (surveying the major issues presented by health-care litigation that require Supreme Court resolution).

4. Gamkhar and Pickerill, "The State of American Federalism 2010–2011," 361–94, 368. See also John Dinan, "Shaping Health Reform: State Government Influence in the Patient Protection and Affordable Care Act," *Publius: The Journal of Federalism* 41, no. 3 (2011): 395–420.

5. Gillian E. Metzger, "Federalism under Obama," *William & Mary Law Review* 53 (2011): 567, 571–97 (surveying Obama federalism legislative and executive initiatives); Ben Protess, "Collection and Credit Firms Facing Broad New Oversight," *New York Times*, February 16, 2012; and Paul Manna and Laura L. Ryan, "Competitive Grants and Educational Federalism: President Obama's Race to the Top Program in Theory and Practice," *Publius: The Journal of Federalism* 41, no. 3 (2011): 522–46.

6. Metzger, "Federalism under Obama," 567, 569–70.

7. Timothy J. Conlan and Paul L. Posner, "Inflection Point? Federalism and the Obama Administration," *Publius: The Journal of Federalism* 41, no. 3 (2011): 421, 443.

8. Conlan and Posner, "Inflection Point?," 421–46.

9. Gamkhar and Pickerill, "The State of American Federalism 2010–2011," 361, 376–77.

10. Gamkhar and Pickerill, "The State of American Federalism 2010–2011," 361, 379.

11. Conlan and Posner, "Inflection Point?," 422, 442. See also Metzger, "Federalism under Obama," 567–619; Gillian E. Metzger, "Administrative Law as the New Federalism," *Duke Law Journal* 57 (2008): 2023.

12. Conlan and Posner, "Inflection Point?," 422.

13. Adam Liptak, "Court under Roberts Is Most Conservative in Decades," *New York Times*, July 24, 2010; Adam Liptak, "Justices Offer Receptive Ear to Business Interests," *New York Times*, December 18, 2010.

14. Lee Epstein, William M. Landes, and Richard A. Posner, *Is the Roberts Court Pro-Business?*, Lee Epstein, University of Southern California, December 17, 2010, http://epstein.usc.edu/research/RobertsBusiness.pdf (accessed April 22, 2012).

15. Gamkhar and Pickerill, "The State of American Federalism 2010–2011," 379.

16. Christopher P. Banks and John C. Blakeman, "Chief Justice Roberts, Justice Alito, and the New Federalism Jurisprudence," *Publius: The Journal of Federalism* 38, no. 3 (Summer 2008): 576–600.

17. See, generally, Henry J. Abraham, *Justices, Presidents, and Senators* (Lanham, MD: Rowman & Littlefield, 2008).

18. Stephen J. Wermiel, "Confirming the Constitution: The Role of the Senate Judiciary Committee," *Law and Contemporary Problems* 56, no. 4 (1993): 121–44. See also a report by the Congressional Research Service by Denis Steven Rutkus, "Questioning Supreme Court Nominees about Their Views on Legal or Constitutional Issues: A Recurring Issue," CRS Report 7-5700, R41300 (June 23, 2010).

19. Michael J. Gerhardt, "The Federal Appointment Process as Constitutional Interpretation," in *Congress and the Constitution*, ed. Neal Devins and Keith Whit-

tington (Durham, NC: Duke University Press, 2005), 122; and Keith Whittington, "Hearing about the Constitution in Congressional Committees," in Devins and Whittington, *Congress and the Constitution*, 95, 103. See also Bruce Peabody's review of survey data on the 86th and 106th Congresses, which shows an interesting trend. In 1959, 38 percent of members of the 86th Congress reported that Congress should pay special attention to federal-state relations. By 1999, only 29 percent of members of the 106th Congress agreed with that statement. Thus, it is very likely that the interest in federalism issues among congressional members has declined just as the Court has increased its focus on federalism and states' rights. See Bruce Peabody, "Congressional Attitudes Towards Constitutional Interpretation," in Devins and Whittington, *Congress and the Constitution*, 49.

20. Dion Farganis and Justin Wedeking, "No Hits, No Forecasts, No Previews: An Empirical Analysis of Supreme Court Nominee Candor from Harlan to Kagan," *Law and Society Review* 45, no. 3 (2011): 525, 554–55. See also Margaret Williams and Lawrence Baum, "Questioning Judges about Their Decisions," *Judicature* 90, no. 2 (September–October 2006), 73–80.

21. To be clear, this analysis does not measure agenda space in that it does not indicate how much time was devoted to discussion of a specific issue, nor does it indicate the tenor of the exchange between committee members and nominees.

22. Paul Alexander Fortenberry and Daniel Canton Beck, "Constitutional Interpretations of Article III and the Commerce Clause: Will the 'Hapless Toad' and 'John Q. Public' Have Any Protection in the Roberts Court?," *University of Baltimore Journal of Environmental Law* 13 (2005): 55–94, 81–84.

23. Simon Lazarus, "Federalism R.I.P.? Did the Roberts Hearing Junk the Rehnquist Court's Federalism Revolution?," *DePaul Law Review* 56 (2006): 1, 29.

24. *United States v. Rybar*, 103 F.3d 273, 287 (1996).

25. Committee on the Judiciary, U.S. Senate, *Confirmation Hearing on the Nomination of John G. Roberts Jr. to Be Chief Justice of the United States*, S. Hrg. 109-158, 109th Cong., 1st Sess. (Washington, DC: U.S. Government Printing Office, 2005), 219.

26. Committee on the Judiciary, U.S. Senate, *Confirmation Hearing on the Nomination of Samuel A. Alito Jr. to Be an Associate Justice of the United States*, S. Hrg. 109–277, 109th Cong., 2nd Sess. (Washington, DC: U.S. Government Printing Office, 2006), 389.

27. Committee on the Judiciary, U.S. Senate, *Confirmation Hearing on the Nomination of John G. Roberts Jr. to Be Chief Justice of the United States*, 420–21.

28. *Confirmation Hearings on Federal Appointments: Hearing, Part 1*, S. Hrg. 108-135 (Part 1), 108th Cong., 1st Sess. (Washington, DC: U.S. Government Printing Office 2003), 267.

29. Committee on the Judiciary, U.S. Senate, *Confirmation Hearing on the Nomination of Samuel A. Alito Jr. to Be an Associate Justice of the United States*, 621.

30. *New Jersey Payphone Association v. Town of West New York*, 299 F.3d 235 (3rd Cir). (2002), 249–50.

31. See John G. Roberts Jr., "Contract Clause—Legislative Alteration of Private Pension Agreements," *Harvard Law Review* 92 (1978): 86–99 (unsigned student note), and "The Takings Clause," *Harvard Law Review* 91 (1978): 1462–1501 (unsigned student note).

32. Committee on the Judiciary, U.S. Senate, *Confirmation Hearing on the Nomination of John G. Roberts Jr. to Be Chief Justice of the United States*, 298–99; see also *Confirmation Hearings on Federal Appointments: Hearing, Part 3*, S. Hrg. 108-135 (Part 3), 108th Cong., 1st Sess. (Washington, DC: U.S. Government Printing Office, 2003), 57.

33. Committee on the Judiciary, U.S. Senate, *Confirmation Hearing on the Nomination of Samuel A. Alito Jr. to Be an Associate Justice of the United States*, 628.

34. Committee on the Judiciary, U.S. Senate, *Confirmation Hearing on the Nomination of Sonia Sotomayor to Be Associate Justice of the United States Supreme Court*, 111th Cong., 1st Sess., July 13–16, 2009, serial no. J-111-34, 100.

35. Committee on the Judiciary, U.S. Senate, *Confirmation Hearing on the Nomination of Sonia Sotomayor to Be Associate Justice of the United States Supreme Court*.

36. Committee on the Judiciary, U.S. Senate, *Confirmation Hearing on the Nomination of Sonia Sotomayor to Be Associate Justice of the United States Supreme Court*, 466.

37. See individual statements by Senators Kyl, Cornyn, and Sessions: *Hearings before the Senate Judiciary Committee, the Nomination of Elena Kagan to Be an Associate Justice of the Supreme Court of the United States*, U.S. Senate, 111th Cong., 2nd sess., June 28–30 and July 1, 2012, serial no. J-111-98, 20, 31, 69.

38. *Hearings before the Senate Judiciary Committee*, 160–62.

39. *Hearings before the Senate Judiciary Committee*, 230.

40. *Hearings before the Senate Judiciary Committee*, 182.

41. *Hearings before the Senate Judiciary Committee*, 188.

42. *Hearings before the Senate Judiciary Committee*, 462.

43. *Hearings before the Senate Judiciary Committee*, 511.

44. The Supreme Court dataset identifies federalism cases as those relating "to conflicts between the federal government and the states, except for those between the federal and state courts," and excludes cases involving the exercise of judicial power. See SCDB Data Codebook, 43, at http://scdb.wustl.edu/_brickFiles/2011_02/SCDB_2011_02_codebook.pdf. For federalism cases, liberal outcomes are pro-federal power, pro-executive power in executive/congressional disputes, and anti-state. Conservative outcomes are the reverse.

45. Mitchell J. Pickerill and Cornell W. Clayton, "The Rehnquist Court and the Political Dynamics of Federalism," *Perspectives on Politics* 2 (2004): 233–48. This data can be juxtaposed against comparable statistics from the Judicial Database (thirty-two and twenty-four federal laws struck down in Rehnquist and Warren Courts, respectively, and the Roberts Court nullifying six in five years, although none involving federalism cases). Erwin Chemerinsky et al., "The Supreme Court 2009 Term Overview and 2010 Term Preview," *Touro Law Review* 27, no. 1 (2011): 33, 48–49. The Roberts Court reversals are in the Supreme Court Database, http://scdb.wustl.edu/analysisCaseListing.php?sid=1002-HOTSPOT-1374 (accessed February 25, 2012); reversals from the earlier periods are in the Supreme Court Database, for the Rehnquist Court, at http://scdb.wustl.edu/analysisCaseListing.php?sid=1002-SLIPKNOT-8165 (accessed February 25, 2012) and, for the Warren Court, at http://scdb.wustl.edu/analysisCaseListing.php?sid=1002-LONGJOHN-9681 (accessed February 25, 2012).

46. Using the Judicial Database for cases decided after 1953, the *New York Times*–commissioned study used a regression that controlled for the direction of the lower court decision in relation to the type of business cases it studied. For each case, the study adopted the database's coding decisions relative to whether the Court reached a liberal or conservative decision (liberal decisions are anti-business, anti-employer, pro-liability, pro-competition, pro-consumer, and the like). See Epstein, Landes, and Posner, *Is the Roberts Court Pro-Business?*; see also Liptak, "Justices Offer Receptive Ear to Business Interests."

47. See Jonathan H. Adler, "Business, the Environment, and the Roberts Court: A Preliminary Assessment," *Santa Clara Law Review* 49 (2009): 101; Robin H. Conrad, "The Roberts Court and the Myth of a Pro-Business Bias," *Santa Clara Law Review* 49 (2009): 997–1017.

48. The Supreme Court Dataset, 1953–2011 terms, at http://scdb.wustl.edu/analysis.php (using Data Release ID SCDB 2011-03); SCOTUSblog Case Stat Pack, at www.scotusblog.com/reference/stat-pack. Federalism cases apart from the dataset were added if they adjudicated basic issues of federal supremacy and state sovereignty (e.g., challenges to state laws that are allegedly contrary to federal or constitutional law or challenges to federal laws that are allegedly against state sovereignty). Christopher M. Parker, "Ideological Voting in Supreme Court Federalism Cases, 1953–2007," *Justice System Journal* 32, no. 2 (2011): 206, 213; Paul M. Collins, "Towards an Integrated Model of the U.S. Supreme Court's Federalism Decision Making," *Publius: The Journal of Federalism* 37, no. 4 (2007): 505–31. The forty-six cases selected for analysis are in appendix A.

49. *Massachusetts v. EPA*, 127 S. Ct. 1428 (2007) is excluded from the forty-six total cases because it had both a liberal (pro-government) and a conservative (pro-state) outcome.

50. The percentage of statutory and constitutional cases is derived in light of the coding decisions made relative to the forty-six-case sample. At least two cases (*Rapanos* and *Watters*) involved statutory construction issues, and three (*Arlington*, *Massachusetts*, and *Brown*) have constitutional issues. For simplicity they are put into the mixed category. Thus, twenty-seven statutory cases included all of the forty-six in the sample under review except constitutional and mixed cases; fourteen constitutional cases did not include statutory and mixed cases but included all foreign policy preemption cases (*Sanchez-Llamas v. Oregon*, 548 U.S. 331 [2006]; *Medellin v. Texas*, 552 U.S. 491 [2008]; and *Permanent Mission of India to the U.N. v. New York City*, 551 U.S. 193 [2007]), and one comity case (*Levin v. Commerce Energy, Inc.*, 130 S. Ct. 2323 [2010]). The mixed five cases are *Rapanos v. U.S. Army Corps of Engineers*, 126 S. Ct. 2208 (2006); *Arlington Central School Dist. Bd. v. Murphy*, 126 S. Ct. 2455 (2006); *Massachusetts v. EPA*, 127 S. Ct. 1428 (2007); *Watters v. Wachovia Bank*, 127 S. Ct. 1559 (2007); and *Brown v. Plata*, 131 S. Ct. 1910 (2011) because they decided constitutional and statutory construction issues.

51. William H. Pryor Jr. et al., "Minutes from a Convention of the Federalist Society (Litigation: The Future of Federal Preemption)," *New York University Journal of Law and Liberty* 6 (2011): 184–230. Timothy J. Conlan and Robert L. Dudley, "Janus-Faced Federalism: State Sovereignty and Federal Preemption in the Rehnquist Court," *PS: Political Science and Politics* 38, no. 3 (2005): 363–66;

Banks and Blakeman, "Chief Justice Roberts, Justice Alito, and New Federalism Jurisprudence," 576–600.

52. Gillian E. Metzger, "Federalism and Federal Agency Reform," *Columbia Law Review* 111 (2011): 1, 2.

53. Joseph F. Zimmerman, *Horizontal Federalism: Interstate Relations* (Albany: State University of New York Press, 2011).

54. See Pickerill and Clayton, "The Rehnquist Court and the Political Dynamics of Federalism," 233, 240 (stating, "In general, the Court has launched its federalism offensive on two broad fronts: reviving the idea of state sovereignty under the Tenth and Eleventh Amendments; and limiting congressional regulatory power under the Interstate Commerce Clause and under Section Five of the Fourteenth Amendment").

55. Under Article VI's supremacy clause, validly enacted laws and treaties of the United States "shall be the supreme law of the land . . . anything in the Constitution or Laws of any State to the contrary notwithstanding."

56. Jamelle C. Sharpe, "Legislating Preemption," *William & Mary Law Review* 53, no. 1 (2011): 163, 175–76.

57. Sandi Zellmer, "When Congress Goes Unheard: Savings Clauses' Rocky Judicial Reception," in *Preemption Choice: The Theory, Law, and Reality of Federalism's Core Question*, ed. William W. Buzbee (Cambridge: Cambridge University Press, 2009), 144, 146.

58. Christopher H. Schroeder, "Supreme Court Preemption Doctrine," in Buzbee, *Preemption Choice*, 119, 121.

59. Schroeder, "Supreme Court Preemption Doctrine," 121, 123.

60. *Rice v. Santa Fe Elevator Corporation*, 331 U.S. 218, 230 (1947).

61. Schroeder, "Supreme Court Preemption Doctrine," 119, 125.

62. *Erie Railroad v. Tomkins*, 304 U.S. 64 (1938). For a discussion of *Erie*'s vertical preemptive effects on state law, see Michael Steven Green, "Horizontal *Erie* and the Presumption of Forum Law," *Michigan Law Review* 109, no. 7 (2011): 1237, 1240; and Andrew J. Kazakes, "Relatively Unguided: Examining the Precedential Value of the Plurality Decision in *Shady Grove Orthopedic Associates v. Allstate Insurance Co.*, and Its Effects on Class Action Litigation," *Loyola of Los Angeles Law Review* 44, no. 3 (2011): 1049, 1052–53.

63. Sharpe, "Legislating Preemption," 163, 213–14.

64. See Bradley W. Joondeph, "Federalism, the Rehnquist Court, and the Modern Republican Party," *Oregon Law Review* 87, no. 1 (2008): 117, 129; Michael S. Greve and Jonathan Klick, "Preemption in the Rehnquist Court: A Preliminary Empirical Assessment," *Supreme Court Economic Review* (2006): 49–50, 57; Conlan and Dudley, "Janus-Faced Federalism," 363–66, 364; and Richard H. Fallon Jr., "The 'Conservative' Paths of the Rehnquist Court's Federalism Decisions," *University of Chicago Law Review* 69, no. 2 (2002): 429, 462–63.

65. Greve and Klick, "Preemption in the Rehnquist Court," 43, 68.

66. Greve and Klick, "Preemption in the Rehnquist Court," 80, 82–85.

67. See the appendix for a listing of the twenty-seven preemption cases.

68. *Winkleman v. Parma City School District*, 550 U.S. 515 (2007), is excluded from the twenty-seven statutory construction cases because it did not involve preemption.

69. It is reasonable to assume Roberts and Alito share the same general conservative judicial philosophy. See Banks and Blakeman, "Chief Justice Roberts, Justice Alito, and New Federalism Jurisprudence," 576–600.

70. This presumes Chief Justice John Roberts and Justice Samuel Alito are ideologically consistent with the justices they replaced (Rehnquist and O'Connor), and the same could be said relative to Justice Sonja Sotomayor replacing Souter. Justice Elena Kagan did not participate in *Whiting*. The five most contested cases (with three dissents or more) are *Altria, Wyeth, Cuomo, Whiting,* and *Vaden v. Discover Bank* (2009). In *Vaden,* however, ideology is crosscutting because a mix of liberals and conservatives coalesces in the majority and dissenting opinions.

71. See Mary J. Davis, "The 'New' Presumption against Preemption," *Hastings Law Journal* (2010): 1217; Zellmer, "When Congress Goes Unheard," 144–66; and Conlan and Dudley, "Janus-Faced Federalism," 363–66.

72. Thomas O. McGarity, *The Preemption War: When Federal Bureaucracies Trump Local Juries* (New Haven, CT: Yale University Press, 2008). See also Alan E. Untereiner, *The Preemption Defense in Tort Actions: Law, Strategy and Practice* (Washington, DC: U.S. Chamber Institute for Legal Reform, 2008), 86–100.

73. *Cipollone v. Liggett Group, Inc.*, 505 U.S. 504, 530–31 (1992) (holding state law damages claims and claims based on express warranty, intentional fraud, or conspiracy not preempted, whereas failure-to-warn and so-called neutralization of federally mandated warnings to the extent those claims rely on omissions or inclusions in manufacturer's advertising or promotions are preempted).

74. Most notably, *Lorillard Tobacco Co. v. Reilly*, 533 U.S. 525 (2001); *Cipollone v. Liggett Group, Inc.*, 505 U.S. 504 (1992).

75. Rehnquist and O'Connor joined all seven parts of Stevens's plurality opinion. *Cipollone v. Liggett Group, Inc.*, 505 U.S. 504 (1992).

76. *Wyeth v. Levine*, 555 U.S. 555 (2009).

77. *Wyeth v. Levine*, 555 U.S. 555 (2009) (Thomas, J., concurring in result).

78. C. M. Sharkey, "Against Freewheeling, Extratextual Obstacle Preemption: Is Justice Clarence Thomas the Lone Principled Federalist?," *New York University Journal of Law and Liberty* 5 (2010): 63–208. See also T. Sandefur, "Clarence Thomas's Jurisprudence Unexplained," *New York University Journal of Law and Liberty* 4 (2009): 535–658; Mark A. Graber, "Clarence Thomas and the Perils of Amateur History," in *Rehnquist Justice: Understanding the Court Dynamic*, ed. Earl M. Maltz (Lawrence: University Press of Kansas, 2003), 70–102.

79. *Chamber of Commerce v. Whiting*, 131 S. Ct. 1968 (2011). Justice Thomas did not join the conservative bloc on the issue of federal E-Verify's implied preemption of state laws in Parts II-B and III-B of Roberts's opinion.

80. Continuing statewide efforts to enact immigration reform have stopped in anticipation of the Supreme Court's grant of certiorari in *Arizona v. United States* (Docket 11-182), which will review the constitutionality of an even harsher version of immigration reform, as expressed in SB 1070, to be decided after oral argument, which the Court has set for April 25, 2012. Pamela M. Prah, "States Eye Arizona-Like Immigration Measures," Stateline, January 28, 2011, www.stateline.org/live/details/story?contentId=545698 (accessed April 22, 2012).

81. In regard to the state licensing (savings clause) exception in the federal immigration law, Justice Breyer "read the words 'licensing and similar laws' as

covering state licensing systems applicable primarily to the licensing of firms in the business of recruiting or referring workers for employment, such as the state agricultural labor contractor licensing schemes in existence when the federal Act was created." For him, "this reading is consistent with the provision's history and language, and it minimizes the risk of harm to lawful workers and employers trying to comply with immigration law." *Chamber of Commerce v. Whiting*, 131 S. Ct. 1968 (2011) (Breyer, J., dissenting). Justice Sotomayor expresses a similar view: *Chamber of Commerce v. Whiting*, 131 S. Ct. 1968 (2011) (Sotomayor, J., dissenting).

82. Gillian E. Metzger, "Article: Federalism and Federal Agency Reform," *Columbia Law Review* 111 (2011): 1, 5.

83. Mary J. Davis, "The Association of American Law Schools 2011 Annual Meeting: Section on Torts and Compensation Schemes Symposium: The Case against Preemption: Vaccines & Uncertainty," *Indiana Health Law Review* 8 (2011): 291, 293.

84. McGarity, *The Preemption War*; Parker, "Ideological Voting in Supreme Court Federalism Cases, 1953–2007," 206–34.

85. McGarity, *The Preemption War*.

86. Preemption by federal administrative agencies has been limited by President Obama's Preemption Memorandum, which directs agencies to use preemption "only with full consideration of the legitimate prerogatives of the States and with a sufficient legal basis for preemption." Barack Obama, "Memorandum for the Heads of Executive Departments and Agencies," White House, May 20, 2009, www.whitehouse.gov/the-press-office/presidential-memorandum-regarding-preemption (accessed June 5, 2011). See also Metzger, "Federalism under Obama," 567–619; Lawrence S. Ebner, *President Obama's "Preemption Memo": Much to Do about Very Little* (Washington, DC: Washington Legal Foundation, 2009). But Metzger acknowledges that the Obama administration's position in the courts has been more equivocal, sometimes favoring it and sometimes not. Metzger, "Federalism under Obama," 567, 596.

87. Contrast Epstein, Landes, and Posner, *Is the Roberts Court Pro-Business?*, with Adler, "Business, the Environment, and the Roberts Court"; Conrad, "The Roberts Court and the Myth of a Pro-Business Bias"; and Greve and Klick, "Preemption in the Rehnquist Court," 43–94.

88. Three or more dissents are cast in only four of the fourteen cases, or less than a third.

89. In contrast, Scalia votes with the majority in all fourteen cases; Roberts and Kennedy, in thirteen; and Alito, in ten (with one nonparticipation).

90. In *Pliva*, the injured consumers developed digestive disorders (tardive dyskinesia) after taking a generic form of the drug Reglan, used to treat digestive tract illness.

91. *Pliva v. Mensing*, 131 S. Ct. 2567 (2011) (Thomas, J., opinion for the Court).

92. See Caleb Nelson, "Preemption," *Virginia Law Review* 86 (2000): 225, which Thomas cited to in *Pliva* in support of that interpretation. *Pliva v. Mensing*, 131 S. Ct. 2567 (2011).

93. *Pliva v. Mensing*, 131 S. Ct. 2567 (2011).

94. Chemerinsky et al., "The Supreme Court 2009 Term Overview and 2010 Term Preview," 33, 35 (referring to the John Roberts Court as the Anthony Kennedy Court over the first five terms).

95. *Pliva v. Mensing*, 131 S. Ct. 2567 (2011) (Sotomayor, J., dissenting).

96. *Pliva v. Mensing*, 131 S. Ct. 2567 (2011) (Sotomayor, J., dissenting).

97. *Pliva v. Mensing*, 131 S. Ct. 2567 (2011) (Sotomayor, J., dissenting). Significantly, Justice Sotomayor's analysis closely tracks the dissent (joined by Justice Ginsburg) she filed against Justice Scalia's preemption analysis in *Bruesewitz v. Wyeth*, 131 S. Ct. 1068 (2011), an express preemption case involving the preclusion of a failure-to-warn state tort case against a vaccine manufacturer that was delivered earlier in the term (discussed in chapter 1). As she did in *Pliva*, Sotomayor looked beyond the words of the National Childhood Vaccine Act to conclude that the statutory context, and the congressional purpose, is not to preempt all design defect vaccine state tort actions. For some commentators, the Supreme Court's increasing reliance on "hyptertextual analysis" in preemption cases is casting doubt on whether the *Rice* presumption against preemption is destined to any role in future Roberts Court cases. Davis, "The Association of American Law Schools 2011 Annual Meeting," 291, 307–13.

98. *Shady Grove Orthopedic Associates v. Allstate Insurance*, 130 S. Ct. 1431 (2010); *AT&T Mobility v. Concepcion*, 131 S. Ct. 1740 (2011).

99. *AT&T Mobility v. Concepcion*, 131 S. Ct. 1740 (2011). See also *Discover Bank v. Superior Court*, 113 P.3d 1110 (2005).

100. *AT&T Mobility v. Concepcion*, 131 S. Ct. 1740 (2011) (Scalia, J., opinion for the Court).

101. *AT&T Mobility v. Concepcion*, 131 S. Ct. 1740 (2011) (Breyer, J., dissenting).

102. Such legislative proposals are the Arbitration Fairness Act, as well as the Consumer Mobile Fairness Act. These are discussed in the context of the issue, and *Concepcion*, in Senate Judiciary Committee, "Arbitration: Is It Fair When It Is Forced?," U.S. Senate, Committee on the Judiciary, October 13, 2011, www.judiciary.senate.gov/hearings/hearing.cfm?id=8bbe59e76fc0b6747b22c32c9e0a33f6 (accessed April 22, 2012). See also Alliance for Justice, "Arbitration Activism: How the Corporate Court Helps Business Evade Our Civil Justice System," Alliance for Justice, 2011, www.afj.org/connect-with-the-issues/the-corporate-court/arbitration-activism-how-the-corporate-court-helps-business-evade-our-civil-justice-system.pdf (accessed April 22, 2012).

103. Roberts Barnes, "Court Skeptical about Overseas Corporate Abuse Suits," *Washington Post*, February 29, 2012 (referring to *Kiobel v. Royal Dutch Petroleum* and *Mohamad v. Palestinian Authority*, both raising the issue of corporate liability under the Alien Tort Statute and Torture Victim Protection Act). For the criticism of the "Corporate Court," see Alliance for Justice, "Arbitration Activism." The Supreme Court's rulings in this vein are also criticized for limiting access to courts. Judith Resnick, "Fairness in Numbers: A Comment on *AT&T v. Concepcion, Wal-Mart v. Dukes*, and *Turner v. Rogers*," *Harvard Law Review* 125 (November 2011): 78–170. See also *Buckeye Check v. Cardegna*, 546 U.S. 440 (2006); *Preston v. Ferrer*, 552 U.S. 346 (2008); *Citizens United v. Federal Election Commission*, 130 S. Ct. 876 (2010); and *Wal-Mart v. Dukes*, 131 S. Ct. 795 (2010).

104. *Shady Grove Orthopedic Associates v. Allstate Insurance,* 130 S. Ct. 1431 (2010). The case result produced odd coalitions of ideologically mismatched justices in the plurality opinion. See "Analysis: Sorting Out an *Erie* Sequel," SCOTUSblog, March 31, 2010, www.scotusblog.com/2010/03/analysis-sorting-out-an-erie-sequel.

105. "Public Citizen Successes in the U.S. Supreme Court—2010 Term," Public Citizen, www.citizen.org/Page.aspx?pid=484 (accessed April 22, 2012); "*Shady Grove Orthopedic Assocs., PA v. Allstate Ins. Co,*" Public Citizen, www.citizen.org/litigation/forms/cases/getlinkforcase.cfm?cID=531 (accessed April 22, 2012). See *Smith v. Bayer Corporation,* 131 S. Ct. 2368 (2011).

106. See *National Meat Association v. Harris* (federal law expressly preempts state regulation of swine at slaughterhouses under federal inspection); *Douglas v. In Living Center* (scheduled for oral argument October 3, 2011); *Kurns v. Railroad Friction Products* (scheduled for oral argument on November 9, 2011); and *Arizona v. United States* (scheduled for oral argument on April 25, 2012).

107. Metzger, "Administrative Law as the New Federalism," 2023.

108. Bradford R. Clark, "Process-Based Preemption," in Buzbee, *Preemption Choice,* 192–213.

109. Gamkhar and Pickerill, "The State of American Federalism 2010–2011," 384.

110. *Bond v. United States,* 131 S. Ct. 2355 (2011) (Kennedy, J., opinion for the Court).

111. *Sossamon v. Texas,* 131 S. Ct. 1651 (2011). See also *City of Boerne v. Flores,* 521 U.S. 507 (1997).

112. *Sossamon v. Texas,* 131 S. Ct. 1651 (2011).

113. *Sossamon v. Texas,* 131 S. Ct. 1651 (2011) (Thomas, J., opinion for the Court). See also ibid. (Sotomayor, J., dissenting).

114. *Virginia Office for Protection and Advocacy v. Stewart,* 131 S. Ct. 1632 (2011).

115. *Virginia Office for Protection and Advocacy v. Stewart,* 131 S. Ct. 1632 (2011) (Scalia, J., opinion for the Court).

116. *Virginia Office for Protection and Advocacy v. Stewart,* 131 S. Ct. 1632 (2011) (Roberts, J., dissenting). See *Seminole Tribe of Florida v. Florida,* 517 U.S. 44 (1996), and *Idaho v. Coeur d'Alene Tribe of Idaho,* 521 U.S. 261 (1997). See also Mark Tushnet, "William Rehnquist's Federalism," in *The Rehnquist Legacy,* ed. Craig Bradley (Cambridge: Cambridge University Press, 2006), 187–204.

117. *United States v. Lopez,* 514 U.S. 549 (1995); *United States v. Morrison,* 529 U.S. 598 (2000); and *Gonzales v. Raich,* 545 U.S. 1 (2005).

118. Joondeph, "Federalism, the Rehnquist Court, and the Modern Republican Party," 117–73. See also *Pike v. Bruce Church,* 397 U.S. 137 (1970).

119. *United Haulers Association v. Oneida-Herkimer Solid Waste Management Authority,* 550 U.S. 330, 342 (2007).

120. Lisa M. Slepnikoff, "A Bigger and Better Market-Participant Exception? Examining Justice Souter's Revision of the Market-Participant Exception to the Dormant Commerce Clause in *Department of Revenue of Kentucky v. Davis,*" *South Dakota Law Review* 55 (2010): 356. See also "Analysis: When Does 'Public Purpose' Justify Protectionism?," SCOTUSblog, May 19, 2008, www.scotusblog.com/?p=7188 (accessed April 22, 2012).

121. See, generally, Ernest A. Young, "The Story of *Gregory v. Ashcroft*: Clear Statement Rules and the Statutory Constitution of American Federalism," in *Statutory Interpretation Stories*, ed. William N. Eskridge Jr., Philip P. Frickey, and Elizabeth Garrett (New York: Foundation Press, 2011), 197–225; E. A. Young, "The Rehnquist Court's Two Federalisms," *Texas Law Review* 83, no. 1 (2004); E. A. Young, "Two Cheers for Process Federalism," *Villanova Law Review* 46 (2001): 1349; and Gamkhar and Pickerill, "The State of American Federalism 2010–2011," 361–94.

Postscript

The Supreme Court of the United States decided two key rulings as it closed out the 2011–2012 term. Whereas *Arizona v. United States* upheld the federal preemption of three of four provisions of an immigration state law (S.B. 1070), *National Federation of Independent Business v. Sebelius* upheld the individual mandate (to buy health insurance) as a tax while limiting the power of Congress to require state compliance with Medicaid expansion under Article I's spending and welfare clause relative to President Barack Obama's health-care reform, the Patient Protection and Affordable Care Act (PPACA). While each case is politically significant, *National Federation of Independent Business* may help distinguish the Roberts Court from its predecessor and arguably reinforce the Supreme Court's political legitimacy in years to come. A brief analysis of each case explores these possibilities in light of the major themes of this book.

Without Justice Elena Kagan's participation, *Arizona v. United States* yielded a 5–3 vote and four separate opinions written by Justices Anthony Kennedy (opinion for the Court), Antonin Scalia (concurring and dissenting), Samuel Alito (concurring and dissenting), and Clarence Thomas (concurring and dissenting). The controlling opinion, joined by conservative Chief Justice Roberts and liberal Justices Ruth Bader Ginsburg, Stephen Breyer, and Sonia Sotomayor, reasons that Congress expressly preempts Section 3 of S.B.1070 on the grounds that federal immigration law completely displaces Arizona's authority to make it a state crime for aliens to be in the country without proper registration documentation. Two other provisions—one imposing criminal penalties on undocumented aliens for seeking or procuring employment in Arizona (Section

5(C)) and the other giving Arizona police authority to arrest, without a warrant, any individuals who are otherwise legally in the country but suspected of committing deportable offenses (Section 6)—are invalid because the plurality determined that they impliedly conflicted with federal law. By creating new criminal sanctions against aliens in the workplace and by interfering with the arrest procedures used by federal officials to enforce immigration laws, Kennedy's opinion ruled that the employment ban and the warrantless arrest provision are obstacles to achieving the full purposes and objectives of the congressional intent underlying federal immigration law.

Yet the plurality did not strike down perhaps the most controversial aspect of Arizona law. Section 2(B) gave the police the power to check the immigration status of those who are lawfully stopped and detain them until their status to remain in the country is determined. As Section 2(B) had not yet gone into effect, it was impossible for the justices to know if its operation presented a federal and state law conflict. Although Justices Scalia, Alito, and Thomas differed on the reasons why Section 2(B) is not preempted, the Court was of one mind in declaring Arizona could legally ascertain the immigration status of those who are lawfully stopped on other grounds. This aspect of the ruling, which Arizona Governor Jan Brewer hailed as a victory for states' rights, will give other state legislatures interested in controlling the immigrant population incentive to devise similar laws. Still, it will generate additional litigation in state and federal courts that will have to answer the constitutional question the Roberts Court sidestepped this term.

Arizona v. United States significantly highlights the ideological differences of the justices on the preemption issue. Generally, *Arizona* is consistent with studies finding that the chances of preemption increase in contested cases, and in ratifying the tendency of allegedly state-friendly and conservative justices, such as Kennedy and Roberts, to preempt Arizona law regulating alien registration and employment, as well as allowing warrantless searches by police. In contrast, the preemption votes by Kennedy and Roberts (joining the liberal bloc of Ginsburg, Breyer, and Sotomayor) cuts against traditional ideological lines and stands in contrast to their anti-preemption analysis in *Chamber of Commerce v. Whiting* (discussed in chapter 6) by their endorsement, in implied conflict fact patterns, of discovering congressional intent by looking at the federal law's purposes and objectives in the statutory framework governing immigration, notably a facet of nontextualist judicial philosophy.

In *Arizona* the most strident advocates of new federalist philosophy favoring state sovereignty are Justices Scalia, Alito, and Thomas. Justice Kennedy's majority opinion, it should be recalled, emphasized that the national government enjoys broad powers over immigration, in part because of its foreign policy ramifications. Under this view the executive branch has the duty to ensure that its immigration enforcement policies are in sync with foreign policy choices in light of dynamic nature of the international system. Thus Kennedy's preemption is grounded in a classic understanding of the international system comprised of sovereign governments, as the United States government must speak on behalf of the fifty states. This classic view tends to disregard the disaggregation of the international system into many different actors, from sovereign national governments to subnational government and other political institutions that affect international relations. Still, in countering the suggestion that preemption is appropriate in curbing state law governing alien registration and warrantless searches because it is inconsistent with foreign policy principles, Justice Scalia responds that every sovereign, even those in the international realm, is fully vested with authority to exclude from its borders unwanted aliens as a traditional exercise of their regulatory powers over immigration matters. Using an originalist judicial philosophy, he interprets the U.S. Constitution in structural terms, arguing that historically American states have long held the basic prerogative to control their territories as a core and inherent attribute of sovereignty. While Scalia does not explicitly recognize the disaggregation of the international system, he assigns great weight to recognizing a state power to exclude aliens that is based on inherent state sovereignty. In doing so, he implicitly affirms a more activist role for American states in the international system, at least if Arizona's law does not plainly conflict with federal law. Scalia's views reflect a divide among the justices over issues of state sovereignty in the Constitution, with concomitant results for how states engage the international system.

Justice Thomas likewise narrows federal preemption by concluding that nothing in the statutory text of federal immigration law conflicts with Arizona's regulations. In *Arizona* he insists that the purposes and objectives approach to divining an implied congressional intent only encourages freewheeling judicial activism. Thomas's position can also be linked to Justice Scalia's views. As noted in chapter 4, Justice Thomas argued that the establishment clause must be reinterpreted as a federalism provision protecting state religious policymaking from federal intrusion. Yet Thomas's attempt to gather support for that principle most likely will fail because there was a lack of a support structure for his interpretation. Thus, even though some state governments agreed with his position in some establishment clause litigation, most others did not, including his colleagues and other political and social institutions. In contrast, Scalia's state sovereignty interpretation in immigration policy may have a more enduring impact on federal-state relations because Scalia argues that states retain sovereign prerogatives over immigration. As such, Scalia's argument may influence state litigation strategies, which, in turn, may lead to a growing state activism in foreign affairs issues since there is an underlying support structure in state politics that encourages it (as noted in chapter 5). In general, the disaggregation of the international system only encourages the further development of constitutional theories that states retain sovereignty over functions that touch upon foreign affairs. Whereas Justice Thomas's attempt to redefine the establishment clause is likely to fail, Justice Scalia's invocation of state sovereignty may gain more traction since the support structure for it is external to the Court and the ideology of the justices.

Justice Alito, in contrast, signals he is more receptive to preemption in some aspects of the immigration context by agreeing with the plurality to allow police checks of immigration status, and to nullify Arizona law pertaining to alien registration on express preemption grounds. Yet on the remaining issues of implied conflict preemption he alone applies process federalism principles to support Arizona's prerogatives as a sovereign state. Citing Court precedents and the express language of federal immigration law, Justice Alito reasons that Arizona has authority to control the alien employment, a traditional role and function of state government under its police powers, and to give police officers the discretion to make warrantless arrests of aliens, unless Congress has manifested a clear intent to do so—a process-based restraint that is found in the *Rice* presumption against preemption (discussed in chapters 3 and 6). Resorting to the presumption against preemption in the *implied* context is noteworthy because Justice Alito (and Chief Justice Roberts) refused to apply it in dissent in other *express* preemption factual settings supporting state law (such as *Altria Group v. Good*, the cigarette labeling discussed in chapter 6, in which Alito, and Roberts, joined Thomas's dissent in arguing *in favor* of federal preemption). The line Alito draws in *Arizona* thus suggests that the text of the law (or at least the type of preemption case at issue in conjunction with legal standards), and not ideological conceptions of states' rights *per se*, may be a better predictor of judicial outcomes, at least in some contested instances of social policy.

National Federation of Independent Business v. Sebelius produced two basic holdings: (1) by a 5–4 vote, the individual mandate was construed as a tax for constitutional purposes, and thus upheld as a valid exercise of congressional spending powers for the general welfare; and (2) by a 7–2 vote, the part of the PPACA that expands Medicaid coverage was an unconstitutional exercise of congressional spending authority insofar as it conditioned the receipt of federal dollars upon the threat of losing preexisting federal Medicaid subsidies if the states did not wish to be a part of implementing the expansion. In order to reach these conclusions, the Court gave itself the power to address the case's merits by interpreting the monetary sanction for not purchasing insurance under the PPACA as a penalty and not a tax, which meant that the federal Anti-Injunction Act was not a bar to exercising jurisdiction until the penalty provision became effective in 2014. By upholding the individual mandate, the Court did not have to nullify the rest of the PPACA, which has the effect of validating the whole statute and its various provisions (e.g., preventing insurance companies from denying coverage based on preexisting conditions, insuring minors under their parent's health insurance until the age of twenty-six, and so forth).

The ruling is unique for several reasons. First, it features the choice by Chief Justice Roberts, a conservative, to cast the deciding fifth vote by joining his four liberal colleagues, Justices Ginsburg, Breyer, Sotomayor, and Kagan, in the part of the opinion for the Court (written by Roberts) that upheld the individual mandate as a tax under congressional spending power. Second, on the individual mandate issue, Chief Justice Roberts only spoke for himself in that part of the controlling opinion in limiting Congress's authority under the commerce clause to impose the mandate. Yet, in a rare joint-authored dissent, written collectively by Justices Scalia, Kennedy, Thomas, and Alito, there was general agreement that the individual mandate and the rest of the PPACA could not be sustained under the commerce clause (or under any other reason). Third, as revealed by Justice Ginsburg's concurring and dissenting opinion, only Justice Sotomayor (and Ginsburg) concluded that the Medicaid expansion was valid under congressional conditional spending powers. That meant that two liberal justices, Breyer and Kagan, joined the five conservatives on the Court in holding that Congress overreached when it forced the states to go along with expanding Medicaid coverage or else lose all federal Medicaid dollars, thus setting new limits on congressional spending for the general welfare.

Not only do the three separate opinions (by Roberts, Ginsburg, and the four-justice dissent) reveal a Court divided among itself along ideological grounds on key issues of constitutional doctrine and new federalism politics, but this case also underscores crucial themes in this book. Although most scholars thought that *National Federation of Independent Business* and the individual mandate issue would be decided on commerce clause grounds, five justices (Roberts, Ginsburg, Breyer, Sotomayor, and Kagan) judged the PPACA's "shared responsibility payment" as a tax (and not a penalty) for constitutional purposes, mostly because it operates to raise tax revenues if a citizen refuses to buy an insurance product by 2014. It did not it matter that the payment was designed to regulate with a social purpose in mind—in this case, to give incentives to buy and expand health insurance coverage—and, contrary to the dissent, it was not a prohibited direct tax. Writing alone but with the implicit support of the dissent, the chief justice's opinion for the Court uses a structural interpretation of the Constitution to declare that there was a formalistic distinction between "activity" and "inactivity" under commerce clause precedent. Only economic *activities* are legitimately regulated. In this instance, Congress overreached by trying to regulate an *inactivity*—that is, the failure to buy health insurance in accordance with the PPACA's directives and sanctions. In making this distinction, Roberts's logic harkens back to an earlier but long discarded constitutional jurisprudence that sought to limit national powers and enhance state powers by construing permissible regulatory activities in terms of whether they were "production" or "manufacturing," or if they were "direct" and "indirect." In addition to drawing a line in saying that the commerce clause cannot vest in Congress the power to regulate what citizens will not do, Roberts cited state-friendly new federalist cases, such as *Printz v. United States* and *New York v. United States*, to state that the individual mandate could not be sustained as part of the whole health-care package under Article I's elastic ("necessary and proper") clause, as Congress lacked the enumerated authority to enact it in the first place.

All but Justices Ginsburg and Sotomayor joined that part of Roberts opinion for the Court which held that Congress could not use its Article I spending powers to take away existing Medicaid funds from the states if the federal government forces states to participate in expanding Medicaid coverage to certain classes of needy enrollees. Using process-based federalism cases that underscore the need for Congress to make clear statements about its statutory intent in enacting the PPACA, the majority of justices declared that state officials must have a clear choice to accept the conditions imposed by the federal government in exchange for receiving federal monies under the cooperative Medicaid grant program. In euphemistically describing the choice given to the states to expand coverage or risk losing those monies as a "gun to the head," states were not put on clear notice when they signed on to the original version of Medicaid that the coverage would expand in the way it did under the PPACA many years later. As the pressure Congress put on the states turned into compulsion, the Court ruled, Congress went too far in asserting its spending authority, but since that threat (of the loss of existing funds) is removed, the PPACA is still viable as law because states will have the choice to expand coverage or not, in accordance with their sovereign prerogatives.

For her part, Justice Ginsburg (joined by Sotomayor) did not agree with the majority's suggestion that the conditional withholding Medicaid funds to the states is a violation of Congress's spending powers, reasoning that the states were fully aware that Congress may change or amend the terms of the Medicaid agreement in the future. Citing clear statement rules and process-based federalism principles, she argues the states were unambiguously given notice of the consequences of what would happen if there is no compliance with the conditions Congress sets for receipt of the monies. Moreover, using a non-interpretivist (living constitution) and pragmatic approach to constitutional interpretation, she gathered the support of the three other liberals (Breyer, Sotomayor, and Kagan) on the commerce clause issue. As applied to the mandate, Ginsburg states that Congress reasonably concluded that insuring the uninsured under the PPACA substantially affects interstate commerce and, accordingly, the Court had to show great deference to that legislative determination. She dismisses the notion by the chief justice that there is a meaningful constitutional difference between regulating activity or inactivity, and unlike Roberts, she maintains that Congress enjoys implied powers under the necessary and proper clause to exact a penalty from citizens who do not choose to buy health insurance, citing the example that states could not enact health-care reform without having a mandate in place (as in the case of Massachusetts).

For the four-justice-authored dissent by Scalia, Kennedy, Thomas, and Alito, the Constitution's structure—and the new federalist principle that Congress can only act pursuant to its enumerated and delegated authority—determines that Congress could not impose the mandate on citizens, as it violates their freedom not to buy health insurance if they choose not to have it. Under this view, shared by Roberts, only economic activities are capable of being regulated under the commerce clause, even if supplemented by the implied authority of the necessary and proper clause. If the congressional power extends to regulating economic inactivity, the dissent argues, there are no effective limits and Congress could, if it wishes, regulate the simple act of breathing in and out. Unlike Roberts, though, the dissent argues the Court rewrites the PPACA by interpreting the mandate as a tax, especially when the statute defines the sanction of not complying with it as a penalty. The PPACA's Medicaid expansion likewise is unconstitutional since it improperly allows Congress to coerce the states into compliance under the spending authority—a conclusion that is supported by the lack of clear notice Congress gave in the statutory scheme about what the conditions for receiving grant monies are under the Court's process-based federalism precedents, and in light of the states' traditional role over managing the health and welfare of its citizens. The last point the dissent makes, which may have influenced the chief justice's vote, is that the whole PPACA must fall because the PPACA cannot survive in its entirety without the individual mandate, which is constitutionally invalid under the commerce, spending, or necessary and proper clauses.

The Court's opinions in the Arizona immigration and health-care cases show that the justices remain at odds over the contours of new federalism politics. Although the justices have voiced support for new federalism precedents in their confirmation hearings or decision-making, how those principles apply in cases in certain areas of social policy remains uncertain. While the individual ideological predispositions of the justices affect the Court's policymaking, the responses by state governments to judicial decisions have an ideological dimension as well. Many Republican governors, state attorneys general, and legislators support Arizona's immigration law while Democratic state politicians are generally opposed to it. The partisan ramifications of the Court's health-care ruling have prompted many Republican governors to pledge not to implement the law until after the 2012 presidential election, a policy position that will have significant consequences if the Republicans win control of the presidency and Congress so that they can repeal the law outright. The Court's division over the individual mandate does little to ease the simmering tensions among state politicians.

The states' responses to the immigration and health-care laws reveal that the Court's policymaking in federalism disputes is also influenced by political institutions and forces external to the Court itself. Just like the Rehnquist Court, the Roberts Court must contend with activist states that use federalism doctrine to protect their interests. The new federalism will also be affected by political blocs within states, such as the right-wing Tea Party movement, that seeks to curtail severely the powers of the federal government in favor of the states. The ongoing conflicts between the states and the national government over health care and immigration may well shift the balance of power within some states to Tea Party politicians, who will be most inclined to gravitate to the federalism ideologies espoused by Justices Thomas and Scalia.

In sum, these two landmark cases illustrate that new federalism is here to stay in the Roberts Court. The Court's 7–2 decision in the health-care case, invalidating the expansion of Medicaid, shows that the liberal and conservative justices can agree on when Congress crosses the line between encouraging and coercing the states to make policy choices, perhaps positioning the Court to limit congressional spending powers in subsequent cases. It also suggests that the Roberts Court will continue to develop the jurisprudence of antifederal coercion, most likely in a way that protects the states and limits federal power, and that process federalism principles are likely to be a vibrant source of judicial conflict, as well as the difference, in defining specific policy outcomes in highly contentious cases. Moreover, the fact that five justices determined that Congress could not use its commerce clause powers to force individuals to purchase health insurance is significant since now the Court's majority appears committed to revisiting the scope and application of Congress's commerce powers in a way that differs from earlier Court eras. Given that Congress historically and presently relies on its commerce and spending authority to pass sweeping social and political reforms, it is all the more relevant that a majority on the Roberts Court is interested in narrowing their application. Much of the post–World War II progressive legislative agenda, ranging from the Civil Rights Acts and the Great Society legislation of the 1960s to education reform in the early 2000s, is premised on an expansive reading of Congress's interstate commerce clause powers. Furthermore, since the individual mandate and its progressive ideals underlying the Obama administration and health-care reform were validated but only made possible by the crucial decision of Chief Justice Roberts to join the liberal bloc on the Court, *National Federalism of Independent Business* may herald the beginnings of a different sort of federalism revolution in the Roberts Court that continues to set it apart from the Rehnquist Court.

Appendix

Federalism Cases Decided in the Roberts Court, 2004–2011

Case/Citation	*Case Type*	*Federalism Issue*
U.S. v. Georgia 546 U.S. 151 (2006)	Constitutional	Eleventh Amendment; Fourteenth Amendment, §5
Gonzales v. Oregon 546 U.S. 243 (2006)	Statutory	Preemption
Central Va. Comm. College v. Katz 546 U.S. 356 (2006)	Constitutional	Eleventh Amendment
Buckeye Check Cashing v. Cardegna 546 U.S. 440 (2006)	Statutory	Preemption
Merrill Lynch v. Dabit 547 U.S. 71 (2006)	Statutory	Preemption
Northern Ins. Co. v. Chatham 547 U.S. 189 (2006)	Constitutional	Eleventh Amendment
Arkansas Dep't of HHS v. Ahlborn 547 U.S. 268 (2006)	Statutory	Preemption
S. D. Warren Co. v. Maine Board of Environmental Protection 547 U.S. 370 (2006)	Statutory	Preemption
Rapanos v. U.S. Army Corps of Engineers 547 U.S. 715 (2006)	Mixed	Constitutional (Commerce Clause) Statutory (Preemption)
Arlington Central School Dist Bd. v. Murphy 548 U.S. 291 (2006)	Mixed	Constitutional (Spending Clause) Statutory (Individual Disabilities Education Act)
Sanchez-Llamas v. Oregon 548 U.S. 331 (2006)	Constitutional	Foreign Policy Preemption

Norfolk Southern Railway Company v. Sorrell 549 U.S. 158 (2007)	Statutory	Preemption
Massachusetts v. EPA 549 U.S. 497 (2007)	Mixed	Constitutional (Justiciability) Statutory (Clean Air Act)
Watters v. Wachovia Bank 550 U.S. 1 (2007)	Mixed	Constitutional (Commerce Clause, Tenth Amendment) Preemption
United Haulers Association v. Oneida-Herkimer Solid Waste Mangmt. Auth. 550 U.S. 330 (2007)	Constitutional	Dormant Commerce Clause
Winkelman v. Parma City School Dist. 550 U.S. 516 (2007)	Statutory	Justiciability
Permanent Mission of India to the U.N. v. New York City 551 U.S. 9 (2007)	Constitutional	Foreign Policy Preemption
CSX Transportation, Inc. v. Georgia State Board of Equalization 552 U.S. 9 (2007)	Statutory	Preemption
Riegel v. Medtronic, Inc. 552 U.S. 312 (2008)	Statutory	Preemption
Preston v. Ferrer 552 U.S. 346 (2008)	Statutory	Preemption
Rowe v. New Hampshire Motor Transport Ass'n 552 U.S. 364 (2008)	Statutory	Preemption
Medellin v. Texas 552 U.S. 491 (2008)	Constitutional	Foreign Policy Preemption
Department of Revenue of Kentucky v. Davis 553 U.S. 328 (2008)	Constitutional	Dormant Commerce Clause

(*continued*)

Case/Citation	*Case Type*	*Federalism Issue*
Fla. Department of Revenue v. Piccadilly Cafeterias 554 U.S. 33 (2008)	Statutory	Preemption
Chamber of Commerce of the U.S. v. Brown 554 U.S. 60 (2008)	Statutory	Preemption
Altria Group, Inc. v. Good 555 U.S. 70 (2008)	Statutory	Preemption
Wyeth v. Levine 555 U.S. 555 (2009)	Statutory	Preemption
Vaden v. Discover Bank 556 U.S. 49 (2009)	Statutory	Preemption
Harbison v. Bell 556 U.S. 180 (2009)	Statutory	Preemption
Polar Tanker, Inc. v. City of Valdez 129 S. Ct. 2710 (2009)	Constitutional	Tonnage Clause
Cuomo v. Clearing House Ass'n 129 S. Ct. 2710 (2009)	Statutory	Preemption
Shady Grove Orthopedic Associates v. Allstate Insurance 130 S. Ct. 1431 (2010)	Statutory	Preemption
United States v. Comstock 131 S. Ct. 3026 (2010)	Constitutional	Article 1 § 8 (Necessary and Proper Clause; Tenth Amendment)
Levin v. Commerce Energy, Inc. 130 S. Ct. 2323 (2010)	Constitutional	Comity

Bruesewitz v. Wyeth 131 S. Ct. 1068 (2011)	Statutory	Preemption
CSX Transportation v. Ala. Dep't of Revenue 131 S. Ct. 1101 (2011)	Statutory	Preemption
Walker v. Martin 131 S. Ct. 1120 (2011)	Statutory	Preemption
Williamson v. Mazda Motor of America 131 S. Ct. 1131 (2011)	Statutory	Preemption
Va. Office for Protection and Advocacy v. Stewart 131 S. Ct. 1632 (2011)	Constitutional	Eleventh Amendment
Sossamon v. Texas 131 S. Ct. 1651 (2011)	Constitutional	Eleventh Amendment
AT&T Mobility v. Concepcion 131 S. Ct. 1740 (2011)	Statutory	Preemption
Brown v. Plata 131 S. Ct. 1910 (2011)	Mixed	Constitutional (Eighth Amendment) Statutory (Federal Court Jurisdiction)
Chamber of Commerce v. Whiting 131 S .Ct. 1968 (2011)	Statutory	Preemption
Smith v. Bayer Corporation 131 S. Ct. 2368 (2011)	Statutory	Preemption
Bond v. United States 131 S. Ct. 2355 (2011)	Constitutional	Justiciability; Tenth Amendment
Pliva, Inc. v. Mensing 131 S. Ct. 2567 (2011)	Statutory	Preemption

Source: The Supreme Court Dataset, 1953–2011 terms, at http://scdb.wustl.edu/analysis.php (using Data Release ID SCDB_2011_03); SCOTUSblog Case Stat Pack, at www.scotusblog.com/reference/stat-pack.

Index

Note to Index: An *f* denotes a figure; an *n* denotes a note; a *t* denotes a table.